THE SPLENDOU..
THAT WAS 'IND

A SURVEY OF INDIAN CULTURE AND CIVILISATION

(FROM THE EARLIEST TIMES TO THE DEATH OF EMPEROR AURANGZEB)

BY

K. T. SHAH, B.A., B.SC. (LOND.)

Barrister-at-Law.

Professor of Economics, University of Bombay.

FOREWORD

BY

THE MARQUESS OF ZETLAND, G.C.S.I., G.C.I.E.

(formerly Earl of Ronaldshay) Author of
"The Heart o. Aryavarta," "The Life of Lord Curzon," Etc.

———

With 11 Illustrations in Colour,
329 Half-tone Illustrations and 5 Maps.

———

BOMBAY:

D. B. TARAPOREVALA SONS & Co.

"Kitab Mahal": Hornby Road

1930

जगद्धात्रीं देवीमुखस्मरामि वन्दे भगवतीम् HAIL, USHAS! VIRGIN GODDESS OF THE DAWN

RESURGAM

स्वप्नो नु माया नु मतिभ्रमो नु ।
क्लिष्टं नु तावत्फलमेव पुण्यम् ॥
असंनिवृत्त्यै किमतीतमेतत् ? —
मनोरथानैव तटप्रपाताः ॥

(adapted from *Shakuntalam*.)

FOREWORD

BY

The Marquess of Zetland, G. C. S. I., G. C. I. E.

(formerly Earl of Ronaldshay)

It may well be thought that in undertaking to give, within the compass of a single volume, a picture of India through the ages—for that in effect is what he here sets out to do—Professor Shah is embarking upon a task of no ordinary difficulty. The canvas is so vast, the span of time so great, the material under view so varied, that a mind of unusual grasp is required to wield the brush, which shall prove capable of painting a picture in true perspective without at the same time unduly sacrificing detail. It seems to me that Professor Shah has faced this difficulty courageously and with success. He has realised the fact that a survey within these limits must be descriptive rather than disputatious; popular rather than learned—learned, that is to say, in the more technical meaning of that word, for of the learning and scholarship of the author there is ample evidence on almost every page. And since it is with the permanent rather than with the ephemeral in the life story of the Continent that the author is concerned, he has brought his tale to a close with the decline and fall of the Mughal Empire, two centuries and more ago. Hence it is that the political controversies which hum so persistently and so jarringly round modern India are very properly ignored.

In his opening chapters Professor Shah sets the scene, so to speak, amid which the story of India has been enacted. With a few rapid strokes of the brush he paints in the physical characteristics of the land; and from the handiwork of Nature he passes on to the craftsmanship of man. We see great cities rising before our eyes—Ayodhya, the Capital of the Raghus; Pataliputra, the seat of Government of the famous Mauryan line; and—speeding down the centuries—Vijayanagar, a Hindu capital whose beauty was such as to surprise Abdur Razaak the Persian into declaring, that neither the pupil of the eye had ever seen a place like it, nor the ear of intelligence been informed that there existed anything to equal it in the world. And in a later chapter devoted to architecture, he examines in greater detail the claims of the Indian peoples to distinction in this particular field of human achievement. Here the relationship between Hindu and Indo-Muhammadan architecture is traced, and the characteristic features of each discussed. Outstanding examples of different types of building—temples and palaces, tombs and mosques—are depicted for purposes of illustration. And better still, the reader is provided with data, which enable him to grasp not merely the outward appearance of a building, but the origin and significance of its component parts. Whence, for example, comes what Professor Shah speaks of as "the most peculiar feature of temple architecture throughout India," namely, the Shikhara or curvilinear spire? To this, as to many similar questions, he provides the answer: "The spire or Shikhara was, in its earliest form . . . a kind of chimney over the temporary tabernacle of the Vedic cult, to permit the smoke from the sacred fire to escape." It is scarcely necessary to point out that the religious buildings of India, striking as they undoubtedly are even to the uninstructed gaze, acquire in the eyes of the visitor, furnished with information on points such as these, a new interest and a more impressive beauty.

And what of the peoples to whose aptitudes and genius has been due the Splendour that was Hind? From its earliest days India has been a land of Saints and Heroes, and from the capacious wallet at his disposal, the author selects with a nice discrimination figures from the long procession of Gods and demi-Gods which pass imposingly across the epic literature of the Continent. Yet it must not be supposed that modern research has not furnished material for accounts scarcely less picturesque, perhaps, and certainly more accurate than those contained in folk tales and the epics; and from story we pass to history, from Divinities and Super-men to Kings, great, indeed, judged by all human standards, but lacking the aura of mystery which crowns the half-mythical heroes of tradition. Professor Shah lays stress on the curiously regular rhythm with which the greatness of India as an Empire has ebbed and flowed. From the decline of the Mauryas we have to wait a hundred and fifty years for Kanishka before India rises once more on a wave of Imperial greatness; and from the death of Kanishka a further two centuries before the coming of the Guptas ushered in a golden age in the story of Indian statecraft, literature and art. And so the tale unfolds in alternating periods of flowering and decay, until a new turn is given to Indian history with the advent, 1,000 years after Christ, of the militant vanguard of Islam. It is to the author's credit that he pays generous tribute to the contributions made in many directions by these invaders to the Splendour that was Hind.

But the greatness of India is not to be found solely—nor even mainly—in the achievements of her warriors and kings. The genius of the Indian peoples has found its happiest, and perhaps its highest, expression in literature, philosophy and art; and in Professor Shah's pages the reader will find spread before him the gradual evolution of Indian culture from its earliest ascertained beginnings in the archaic Sanskrit of the Vedic hymns. In a chapter devoted to poetry and the drama the relationship is traced between the epics in their earliest forms sung in the vernacular by village bards, and the polished Sanskrit poetry of Kalidasa; while the place of the drama in Indian literature provides the author with a subject for suggestive and instructive discussion. To names familiar to all who claim any acquaintance with the better known masterpieces of Indian literature, are added many others less generally known, but with equal claims to fame in one or other of the different branches of the Indian literary tree.

From Poetry and Drama Professor Shah passes on to Philosophy and Religion; and here the difficulty of compression must have been great indeed. So many and so fine-spun are the webs woven by the speculative minds of India round the great central doctrine of the Hindu peoples— that of Karma and Rebirth—that a less skilful writer might well have lost the thread of his own narrative in a maze of intricate and bewildering detail. That he has not done so is greatly to his credit. The place of Buddhism and Jainism in Indian metaphysics is deftly shown, and a brief sketch is then given of the main tenets of the six orthodox systems, proper but not undue stress being laid on the idealistic monism of the Vedanta as expounded by the most famous of the Commentators Shankaracharya, and the dualistic realism of the Sankhya system associated with the name of Kapila. But congenial though speculation in the sphere of metaphysics always was to the meditative Indian mind, other mental sciences were not neglected; and Professor Shah next indulges in a rapid but highly informative survey of some of these, notably those of language and of political economy. In this section of his work attention is rightly drawn to that mine of information on social and political organisation of the times, the Artha-Shastra of Kautilya.

Perhaps the aspect of Indian civilisation on which the average Westerner is least instructed is the extent and richness of its culture. The man who reads Professor Shah's pages will thereafter have no excuse for pleading ignorance on this score. And herein lies the special value of his book.

No one who knows anything of India at all is unaware of her achievements in such arts as architecture and sculpture. Proof of her proficiency in these respects meets the eye of the visitor at every turn. Professor Shah, as must be clear from what I have already written, ignores neither the greatness of her master-builders nor the genius of her artists; but he places her achievements along these lines in proper perspective by displaying the many other arts and sciences in which from time to time her peoples have excelled. Tradition, he tells us, speaks of 72 arts for gentlemen claiming to have enjoyed a liberal education. And these arts ranged from proficiency in the lore of love to a mastery of mathematics, and from skill in music and dancing to a capacity of horse judging and chariot driving. In the case of women, a supreme dancer, he declares, could trace the pattern of a peacock blindfold on the dancing floor, simply by the rhythmic placing of her toe marks; and if packets of colour were placed on the floor with appropriate tints at the required distances she could give all the variegated hues of this brilliant bird. There is a delightful dissertation on Indian music which may be commended to those whose knowledge of the subject is based on the casual hearing of a tom-tom; and there is an equally interesting treatise on Indian painting. And when Professor Shah comes to consider the standard attained to by Indians in by-gone days in the sphere of industry and commerce, he is able to call in as witnesses to their skill in metal working, those remarkable iron pillars of Delhi and of Dhar, which prove conclusively that centuries ago iron was wrought and welded in India on a scale which has become possible only in very recent times in the largest foundries of the West.

In his chapter on the Social System of the Hindus, Professor Shah has naturally a good deal to say on the subject of Caste. Unlike the more extreme social reformers, he holds the view that this ancient institution if shorn of undue rigidity, " with its catholic welcome to all—old as well as new—races and creeds to be absorbed into a common though complex unity," is an essential condition of the welding of the polygenous and polyglot peoples of the continent into an Indian nation. Here he is doubtless treading on delicate and controversial ground. But he states his view temperately, and in support of it he appeals to the teaching of history: " Rebels, of course, there always will be, as well as protestants. Saints and seers have in the past, from Mahavira and Buddha to Nanak, Kabir and Keshub Chunder Sen, more than once attempted to eradicate the very principle of caste; but like some pliant bamboo grove in one of her primeval forests, the caste-system of India has bent before the blast and has reasserted itself the moment the fury of reform has spent itself." Similarly, the Western reader will listen with interest and respect to all that Professor Shah has to say on the frequently misunderstood question of the position of Woman in Indian society, and upon the Indian ideal of Marriage.

In the space appropriate to a Foreword it has been possible to touch upon a few only of the many subjects dealt with by Professor Shah. But enough has, perhaps, been said to make it clear that the Indian reader will find much in the ensuing pages to add to the feelings of legitimate pride with which he contemplates the goodly heritage that is his; while for the Western reader the book will provide a key to much that ordinarily remains hidden from him, and will furnish him with the means of viewing, with added interest and a more sympathetic understanding, the varied achievements of many centuries of human endeavours, which have gone to the making of the Splendour that was Hind.

Zetland.

PREFACE

This work has developed out of a series of Lectures on the *Outlines of Indian Civilisation*, planned for the second term of 1927-8, and delivered in the first term of 1928-29, at St. Xavier's College, Bombay. The scope of the work has been considerably increased since the first plan was made; but even so, it is necessarily a bare survey only of the several directions in which the spirit of the Indian Civilisation manifests itself. The model ultimately kept before my mind was Mr. J. C. Stoddart on the *Glory That Was Greece*, and the *Grandeur That Was Rome*. But to any one familiar with the relative size, either of Greece, or of Rome in the Republican times on the one hand, and of India on the other; to any one bearing in mind the more extensive scope in time adopted in this work, it will not at all be surprising that the sketch here attempted to be made of the *Splendour That Was 'Ind* gives only glimpses of the arts and graces, the beauty and culture, of the several races and provinces that make up the India of history. Each of the great natural divisions of India has enough in the story of its civilisation to provide material for a work similar to this; each of the epochs into which our history naturally divides itself could furnish substance enough for such a purpose; each of the topics here considered has already inspired more than one remarkable monograph, and further researches may afford still more material for similar enrichment.

Naturally, then, the present work is in the form of a mere outline, a kind of general introduction to the manifold beauties and glories of Ancient, Medieval, and Muhammadan India. In the models on Greece and Rome already named, the treatment is more definitely chronological than it seemed suitable to the present writer to adopt for purposes of this work. A purely historical treatment for such a vast and complex entity as India through the ages is all but impossible, if one desires to have anything like a complete outline of the picture under each head. Besides, a chronological account may give the position without showing clearly the importance of a given topic, especially on such a canvas. The plan has, therefore, been followed in this work, as in the Lectures on which it is based, of viewing the progress of the several subjects herein selected as evidencing *The Splendour That Was 'Ind*, each in its own setting, through successive centuries, until we come to the decline of the last great Empire on the Indian soil. The survey stops, in most chapters, with the end of the Great Mughals, (1707 A.C.); contemporary history being avoided, not only as likely to crowd the picture unduly, but also as not unlikely to introduce a discordant note in the general harmony of the theme.

The work being, thus, only an attempt to popularise the knowledge about many an unseen beauty and splendour of India, it would be out of place in this Series of University Extension Lectures to look for any original research, or special contribution to the sum total of our knowledge about India. Marks of scholarship have, therefore, been studiously avoided,—even such as the careful transliteration in Roman characters of Sanskrit or other Indian words. Names of places and persons already standardised in their English garb (like *Delhi* for *Dehli*); and words of Indian origin already assimilated in the Anglo-Indian glossary, have been used in the familiar form, without the scholarly index of a dash or a stress or a point on any particular letter. Besides, the scholarly writers do not seem themselves to be quite agreed upon the canons of transliteration; and so, if a meticulous reader discovers the same word spelt differently in the same section,—e.g. Sanchi spelt also *Sanci* by certain of the more modern writers, he will lay the blame, it is to be hoped, at the door of the right party. The style and scope of this work, just as much as my purpose, also forbade any needless display of borrowed scholarship or special research; though the ingrained vanity of a writer cannot but be tickled, if some painstaking reader flatters him by the discovery of any original contribution to the lore about India in the following pages. Even the Bibliography is select, rather than sufficient, or exhaustive. It is for the reader to judge how far the attempt has succeeded.

A Preface is not the place for inserting a special pleader for the success of the work. But it may well be taken advantage of to mention my debt of gratitude to those who have helped me in the work. Special mention and acknowledgment have been made in each instance, throughout the body of the work, of each standard author and his work, wherever the same has been relied upon, or borrowed from, for statements made in the text. In consonance with the ideal held in view throughout the work of making it popular rather than learned, quotations from such writers have been kept within a reasonable margin; while references to them have been minimised to the utmost possible. That does not mean, however, that I am unaware of my debt to other workers in this vast field, or unwilling to make ample acknowledgment of the same. A short, but, it is hoped, a select Bibliography appended will indicate the nature and extent of my obligation in this behalf.

Of more direct personal assistance, four or five cases at least must be specifically mentioned. The Rev. Fr. Heras, S. J., Professor of History, St. Xavier's College, Bombay, is too devoted a worker in the field of Indian historical research to demand a special expression of gratitude for himself. I, however, cannot, for that reason, pass in silence over the invaluable assistance received from this passionate student of Indian history, not only in organising the Lectures on which the work is based, but also in discussing many points dealt with in these pages, in supplying rare or little known sources of information and in providing Illustrations for the Lectures which accounted in no small degree for their success. The Rev. Fr. Zimmermann, S. J., Professor of Sanskrit in the same College, is another friend, whose willing consent to read over parts of this work,—particularly those concerning the Literature and Philosophy of this country,—has been of immense help to me, as also the similar contribution of Prof. Radhakrishnan of Calcutta. Captain Gladstone Solomon, Principal of the Bombay School of Art, was kind enough, at the instance of another friend, to look over and make useful suggestions regarding the Section on Painting in India. He has also glanced through the Sections dealing with the Sculpture and Architecture in India. Dr. Ghurye, my colleague in the University School of Economics and Sociology, has helped very considerably to make the Chapter dealing with India's Social System as exact as was possible under the circumstances.

Sir T. W. Arnold was obliging enough to read through the entire MS., and make many detailed as well as general suggestions, for the full benefit of which I cannot but be immensely grateful to that old friend and kindly scholar. In fact, his warm appreciation of the work in MS., went a long way in restoring confidence, which at first was somewhat shaken because of the comparative unfamiliarity with the field to be surveyed; and hence the obligation to Sir Thomas is doubly due.

X

The appreciation of the Marquess of Zetland, implicit in the Foreword, demands another expression of gratitude, which I am deterred from a more ample recognition by a fear lest the reader should suspect us,—the writer of the Foreword and of the work proper,—of having formed a Mutual Admiration Society.

Other friends, too numerous to be particularised, have also contributed to the enrichment of this work by discussion or suggestion, to all of whom I am grateful.

I am indebted to my son Sharatchandra for helping to compile the Index and the Bibliography.

Messrs. D. B. Taraporevala Sons & Co., the Publishers of this work are really the originators of the idea embodied in this work. They have spared no pains in securing appropriate illustrations wherever suggested by me and in ensuring a fitting get-up for the work. If the work meets with the success hoped for, it will in no slight degree be due to them.

There is one friend and helper, however, whose contribution is so considerable to this work, that a separate, specific, mention is impossible to avoid. Miss G. J. Bahadurji, M. A., L. T., C. L., Principal, Alexandra High School for Girls, has, from the very inception of this project, helped materially in every part of it, and through every phase of it. She has carefully read through every line of the work, and made in almost every instance the most invaluable suggestions for improvement, which I must gratefully acknowledge. The Chapters and Sections relating to the Fine Arts in India are virtually her creations. Herself a painter of note, her criticism and suggestion in connection with that portion of the work were reinforced by the opinion of Capt. W. E. Gladstone Solomon, obtained at her instance. A master of the technique and theory of Music, her advice and comment in that Section have also proved most materially useful. Even if I were to regard it as a contribution, the debt of gratitude would be unspeakable. As a matter of fact, however, the work is practically as much hers as mine and only an inveterate sense of native modesty has prohibited the addition of her name as a joint author. Under the circumstances, it would be meaningless to express my debt of gratitude in mere words to such a selfless collaborator.

K. T. SHAH.

School of Economics and Sociology,
Bombay, 1st October, 1929.

PUBLISHERS' NOTE

With the increasing interest in India, so widely felt at the present time, there is a distinct need for illustrated works to provide a vivid presentment of India's glorious achievements in Art, Architecture, History, Science, Literature, Philosophy, Religion, etc. Several very finely illustrated works, on one or more of these subjects, are now available; but their high prices place them out of the reach of the majority of the readers. The publishers have, therefore, felt that there is room for such a work as the present one, of moderate price, and so accessible to the majority of readers. They have been fortunate in securing the pen of Prof. K. T. Shah whose qualifications for this comprehensive presentment of India's manifold achievements may best be expressed in the words of Sir T. W. Arnold, who was kind enough to go through the whole of the typescript. Says he :—

> "I can unhesitatingly recommend you to undertake the publication of this finely conceived and admirably carried out volume. The comprehensiveness of the subject-matter leaves out no aspect of the subject-matter deserving of mention and its pages contain something to appeal to every class of reader. It would be impertinent on my part to praise the learning and scholarship of Professor Shah and (so far as my knowledge of the history and literature of India extends) his text appears to me to be historically correct. The enthusiasm of the author for his subject reveals itself in the elevation of style and the choice of his diction; the interest of the reader is sustained throughout, and the arrangement of the text is clear and logical."

As regards the illustrations reproduced in this work, the publishers have been advised by the author of the work; but they alone are responsible for the actual selection for reproduction. They are greatly indebted to all those who have supplied them with photographs and paintings. They have also selected several illustrations from various publications. Every care has been taken to make appropriate acknowledgment to the owners of all copyrighted pictures; but if any necessary acknowledgments have been omitted, the publishers trust that the copyright-holders will accept this, their acknowledgment and apologies.

CONTENTS

BIBLIOGRAPHY

I. GEOGRAPHICAL AND DESCRIPTIVE

	Cambridge History of India Vols. I and III.
	Records of Geological Survey of India, (Vol. XXIX), *Ancient Geography of Gondwana Land,* by W. S. Blanford.
	Murray's Handbook for India, Burma and Ceylon.
HOLDICH, SIR T. H.	*India,* (Regions of the World Series, Ed. Mackinder).
MACKINDER, H. J.	*Eight Lectures on India.*
FORREST, G. W.	*Cities of India, Past and Present.*
CUNNINGHAM, A.	*The Ancient Geography of India, Buddhist Period.*
ABBOT, G. F.	*Through India with the Prince.*
MENPES AND STEEL	*India.*
WHISTLER, HUGH	*In the High Himalayas.*
THURSTON, E.	*Madras.*
DOUIE, SIR J.	*The Punjab.*
O'MALLEY, L. S. S.	*Bengal, Bihar, Orissa and Sikkim.*
VILLIERS STEWART, C.M.	*Gardens of the Great Mughals.*
MOLYNEUX AND YOUNG-	
HUSBAND	*Kashmir.*
FANSHAW	*Delhi — Past and Present.*
MOIN-UD-DIN AHMED	*The Taj and its Environments.*
HUNTER, W. W.	*Indian Empire.*
,,	*Imperial Gazetteer.* (26 Vols. and 27th of Atlas).

II. ARCHAEOLOGICAL AND DEMOGRAPHICAL

	Memoirs of the Archaeological Survey of India.
	Journals of the Royal Asiatic Society.
	Cambridge History of India.
	Census Reports (1871-1921).
	Epigraphia Indica.
CODRINGTON,	
K. de B.	*Ancient India.*
LASSEN	*Indische Alterthumskunde.*
DUTT, R. C.	*History of Civilisation in Ancient India.*
STEEL, F. A.	*India Through the Ages.*
BARNETT, L. D.	*Antiquities of India.*
RAPSON E. J.	*Ancient India.*
ANDERSON, J. D.	*The Peoples of India.*
HOLDERNESS, T. W.	*Peoples and Problems of India.*
RISLEY, H. H.	*The Peoples of India* (2nd Ed.)
GRIERSON, G. A.	*The Linguistic Survey of India.*
BEAL, S.	*Buddhist Records of the Western World.*
TILAK, B. G.	*Vedic Chronology and Vedanga Jyotisha.*
CHILDE, V. G.	*The Aryans.*

BIBLIOGRAPHY
III. and IV. HISTORICAL AND BIOGRAPHICAL

DUTT, R. C.	*Ramayana and Mahabharata.*
SMITH, V. A.	*Early History of India.*
,. ,,	*Cambridge History of India Vols. I and III.*
,, ,,	*Asoka.*
,, ,,	*Akbar, the Great Mogul.*
,, ,,	*The Oxford History of India.*
ELPHINSTONE, M.	*History of India.*
ELLIOTT	*History of India as Told by its own Historians.*
SARKAR, J. N.	*India of Aurangzeb.*
,, ,, ,,	*History of Aurangzeb 5 Vols.*
,, ,, ,,	*Anecdotes of Aurangzeb.*
,, ,, ,,	*Mughal Administration.*
,, ,, ,,	*Shivaji.*
RANADE, M. G.	*The Rise of the Maratha Power.*
GRANT DUFF, J. C.	*A History of the Marathas.*
SEWELL, R.	*A Forgotten Empire: (Vijayanagara).*
IRVINE, W.	*The Later Mughals.*
TOD	*Annals of Rajasthan.*
MONRO, W. D.	*Stories of Indian Gods and Heroes.*
MANNUCCI	*Storia di Mogor 4 Vols.?*
SACHAU, E. C.	*Alberuni's India.*
BERNIER, F.	*Travels in India of European Travellers.*
DOWSON, J.	*Hindu Classical Dictionary.*
NIVEDITA (SISTER) AND	
COOMARASWAMY, A. K.	*Myths of the Hindus and Buddhists.*
MUKERJI, R.	*Shri Harsha* (Rulers of India Series).
BANA-BHATT	*Harsha-Charita.*
KALHAN (ED. A. M. STEIN)	*Rajatarangini.*
KINCAID, C. A.	*Folktales of Sindh and Gujerat.*
MC. CRINDLE, J. W.	*Ancient India as described by Megasthenes and Arrian.*
ABUL FAZL	*Ain-i-Akbari,* or Institutes of Akbar Blochmann's as well as Gladwin's Translations.
IRVINE, W.	*The Army of the Indian Mughals.*

V. LITERARY

(N. B. Works on Indian classical and Vernacular Literature named in the text are separately listed).

MAX-MÜLLER, F.	*History of Ancient Sanskrit Literature.*
FRAZER, R. W.	*Literary History of India.*
MACDONELL, A. A.	*Sanskrit Literature.*
,, ,, ,,	*India's Past.*
KEITH, A. B.	*A History of Sanskrit Literature.*
,, ,, ,,	*Sanskrit Drama.*
CALDWELL, R.	*A Comparative Grammar of the Dravidian Languages.*
P. GRIFFITHS, R. T. H.	*The Hymns of the Rig Veda.*
PADHYE, K. A.	*Beauties from Kalidas.*
POPE	*History of Manikka Vachagar (also Naladiyar).*
SUNDARAM PILLAI, P.	*Some Milestone in the History of Tamil Literature.*

VI. SCIENTIFIC WORKS (Indian Classical Works in this Section listed separately).

BARTH, A.	*The Religions of India.*
SHAMASHASTRY, R.	*Kautilya's Arthashastra.*
DEUSSEN, P.	*The System of Vedanta.*
OLDENBERG, H.	*The Life of Buddha.*
ARNOLD, E.	*The Light of Asia.*
DASGUPTA, S.	*Yoga as Philosophy and Religion.*
MAX-MÜLLER, F.	*The Six Systems of Indian Philosophy.*
RADHAKRISHNAN, S.	*Indian Philosophy*, 2 Vols.
,,	*Hindu View of Life.*
BOULTING	*Four Pilgrims.*
WOODROFFE, SIR J.	*The Serpent Power.*
RONALDSHAY, EARL OF.	*The Heart of Aryavarta.*
COWELL AND GOUGH	*Sarva-Darshana-Sangraha.*

VII. FINE ARTS

SMITH, V. A.	*History of Fine Art in India and Ceylon.*
FOUCHER, A.	*The Beginnings of Buddhist Art.* (Ed. L. A. and F. W. Thomas).
CLEMENTS, E.	*Introduction to the Study of Indian Music.*
FOX-STRANGWAYS, A. H.	*The Music of Hindustan.*
MARSHALL, J. A.	*Guide to Sanchi.*
COOMARASWAMY, A. K.	*History of Indian and Indonesian Art.*
,, ,, ,,	*Mirror of Gesture.*
,, ,, ,,	*Dance of Siva.*
,, ,, ,,	*Rajput Painting.*
,, ,, ,,	*Portfolio of Indian Art.*
MEHTA, N. C.	*Studies in Indian Painting.*
GRIFFITHS	*Paintings in the Buddhist Caves at Ajunta.*
SOLOMON, GLADSTONE, W. E.	*The Women of the Ajunta.*
BROWN, PERCY	*Indian Painting under the Mughals.*
KÜHNEL AND GOETZ	*Indian Book Painting.*
HURLIMANN, M.	*Picturesque India.*
BHATTACHARYA, B. C.	*Indian Images.*
HAVELL, E. B.	*The Ideals of Indian Art.*
,, ,,	*Indian Architecture.*
,, ,,	*A Hand-book of Indian Art.*
,, ,,	*Indian Sculpture and Painting.*
,, ,,	*The Himalayas in Indian Art.*
,, ,,	*Artistic and Industrial Revival in India.*
KRISHNA SHASTRY, H.	*South Indian Images of Gods and Goddesses.*
JAGADISHA IYER, P. V.	*South Indian Shrines.*
BINYON, L.	*Court Painters of the Great Mughals.*
DEY, M. C.	*My Pilgrimage to Ajunta and Bagh.*
BOULTING	*Four Pilgrims.*
	Dancing Ancient and Modern.
	Indian Art at the British Empire Exhibition.
	Examples of Indian Sculpture at the British Museum.

VIII. ARCHITECTURAL AND MONUMENTAL

FERGUSSON, J.	*Indian and Eastern Architecture. 2 Vols.*
HAVELL, E. B.	*Indian Architecture.*
,, ,,	*Cambridge History of India.*
,, ,,	*Guide to Ellora and Ajunta.*

IX. INDUSTRIAL AND COMMERCIAL

SMITH, V. A.	*Akbar, the Great Mogol.*
MORELAND, W. H.	*India at the Death of Akbar.*
,, ,,	*From Akbar to Aurangzeb.*
KENNEDY, J.	*The Early Commerce of Babylone with India* (1898) (Journal of the Royal Asiatic Society).
RHYS DAVIDS, T. W.	*Buddhist India.*
RHYS, DAVIDS, T. W.	*Economic Condition in Ancient India* (Economic Journal).
McCRINDLE, J. W.	*Ancient India as Described by Megasthenes and Arrian.*
SACHAU, E. C.	*Alberuni's India.*
SEWELL, R.	*A Forgotten Empire.*
MUKERJI, R. K.	*A History of Indian Shipping.*
ABUL FAZL	*Ain-i-Akbari.*

X. SOCIAL—MANNERS AND CUSTOMS

BÜHLER	*Digest of Hindu Law.*
JOLLY	*Law and Custom in India.*
G. D. BANNERJI	*Hindu Law of Marriage and Stridhan.*
B. K. SARKAR	*Positive Background of Hindu Sociology.*
P. N. BANNERJI	*Public Administration in Ancient India.*
ABUL FAZL	*Ain-i-Akbari.*
NIVEDITA, SISTER	*Web of Indian Life.*
DE LAET	*The Empire of the Great Mogol.* Translated by J. S. Hoyland, Ed. by S. N. Bannergee, 1928.
LANMAN	*Jatakmala (Harvard Oriental Series (Vol. I).*
	Imperial Gazetteer of India.
	Annual Reports of Moral and Material Progress.
	Census Reports, 1871-1921.

LIST OF CLASSIC SANSKRIT, PRAKRIT, OR INDIAN VERNACULAR WORKS AND AUTHORS MENTIONED IN THE TEXT

AUTHOR	WORK
	Rig-Veda, Sama Veda, Yajur Veda, Atharva Veda
TISSA	Katha-Vattu (Prakrit)
KASHYAPA	Abhidhamma-Pitaka (Buddhist Metaphysics)
UPALI	Vinaya-Pitaka (,, Rule of Ecclesiastical Life)
ANANDA	Sutta-Pitaka (,, Aphorisms or Parables of Buddha)
	Questions of King Milinda (System of Dogmatism)
BUDDHA-GHOSHA	Visuddhimagga (Compendium of the *Hinayana* ideal of Arhat)
,,	Atthashalini (being commentary on Dhammasamghani)
	Chronicles :—Dipavamsa and Mahavamsa
VALMIKI	Ramayana (Sanskrit Epic)
VYAS	Mahabharata ,, ,,
ASHWAGHOSHA	Buddha-Charitra (Sanskrit Epic of Buddha's Life)
,,	Sundarananda (Sanskrit Poem)
,,	Gandistotra (Sanskrit Lyric)
,,	Sari-Putra-Prakarna (Sanskrit Drama—Life of Sari-Putra)
KALIDASA	Kumrara-Sambhava (Sanskrit Epic on the Birth of the War God)
,,	Raghu-Vamsa (Chronicles of the House of Raghu—S. Epic)
,,	Megha-Duta (Sanskrit Lyric—Cloud Messenger)
,,	Ritu-Samhara (,, ,, —The Seasons)
,,	Abhignana-Shakuntalam (Sanskrit Drama)
,,	Malavika-Agnimitram (,,)
,,	Vikramorvashiyam (,,)
VATSABHATTI	Prashasti (Panegyric of Sun in the Temple at Mandasor)
BHARAVI	Kiratarjuniyam (Sanskrit Epic—Fight of Arjuna with Shiva)
,,	Bhattikavyam (Sanskrit Epic)
BHARTRIHARI	Niti-Shatakam (Ethical Centaine)
,,	Shringara-Shatakam (Erotic Centaine)
,,	Vairagya-Shatakam (Renunciation Centaine)
MAGHA	Shishupala-Vadha (Sanskrit Epic)
KUMARADAS	Janaki-Harana (Sanskrit Epic)
KAVIRAJA	Raghava-Pandaviyam (Sanskrit Epic)
	Nalodaya (Sanskrit Poem on a Mahabharata Episode)
AMARU	Amaru-Shatakam (Sanskrit Lyric Erotic)
JAYADEVA	Gita-Govindam (,, ,, ,,)
SHUDRAKA	Mrichha-Katikam (Sanskrit Drama—The Little Clay-Cart)
BHASHA	Plays (Sanskrit Drama)
BHAVABHUTI	Uttara-Ramacharitram (Sanskrit Drama—Later Phase of Rama's Life
,,	Malati Madhava (,, ,,)
SHRI HARSHA	Ratnavali (Sanskrit Drama)
,,	Priya-Darshika (Sanskrit Drama)
,,	Nagananda (Sanskrit Drama)
VISHAKHADATTA	Mudra-Rakshasa (Sanskrit Drama)
BHATTA-NARAYANA	Veni-Samhara (Sanskrit Drama—Binding of the Braid)

BIBLIOGRAPHY

AUTHOR	WORK
RAJA-SEKHARA	Bal-Ramayana (Sanskrit Drama for Juveniles)
,,	Bal-Bharata (Sanskrit Drama for Juveniles)
,,	Karpura-Manjari (Prakrit Poem)
KRISHNA-MISHRA	Prabodha-Chandrodaya (Sanskrit Drama)
DANDIN	Dasha-Kumara-Charita (Sanskrit Romance—Prose—Story of 10 Princes)
,,	Kavyadarsha (Sanskrit Treatise on Poetics)
SUBANDHU	Vasavadatta (Sanskrit Romance—Prose)
BANA BHATTA	Kadambari (,, ,, ,,)
,, ,,	Harsha-Charita (Sanskrit Biography—Prose)
DHANAPALA	Tilaka-Manjari (Sanskrit Romance)
KSHEMENDRA	Brihat-Katha (Sanskrit Stories)
SOMADEVA	,, ,, (Original by Gunadhya in Prakrit—Paishachi)
,,	Yasastilaka
JAIN MONKS	Naladiyar (Tamil Poem)
TIRUVALLUVAR	Kurral (,, ,,)
MANIKKA-VACHAGAR	Tamil Poems
TIRU-GNANA-SAMBANDHA	,, ,,
TULSIDAS	Ramayana (Hindi Epic Poem)
SUR DAS	Sur-Sagar (Hindi Poem)
CHANDA	Prithwi-Raj Rasa (Hindi Epic)
KABIR	Hindi Poems—Shabdavali; Sukha-Nidhan
NARSIMHA MEHTA	Gujarati Poems
MIRABAI	Gujarati (Hindi) Poems
RAMANANDA	Hindi Poems
CHANDIDAS	Bengali Poems
BIDYAPATI THAKUR	Bihari (Hindi) Poems
TUKA-RAM	Marathi Abhangs (Poems)
	Ghata-Karpana
	Chaura-Panchashika
	Pancha-Tantra (Sanskrit Prose (?)—Collection of Fables)
	Katha-Sarit-Sagara (Collection of Stories—Prose)

LIST OF PHILOSOPHIC OR SCIENTIFIC WORKS, MENTIONED IN THE TEXT, FROM CLASSIC SANSKRIT OR PRAKRIT

AUTHOR	WORK
HINDU CANONICS	The Vedas and Commentaries thereon
	Brahmanas
	Aranyakas—Forest Treatises
	Upanishads
JAIN CANONICS	Sutras, Angas, Upangas, Mul Sutras, Chheda Granthas
BUDDHIST CANONICS	The Three Pitakas
MADHAVACHARYA	Sarva-Darshana-Samgraha (Compendium of Indian Philosophy)
SHANKARACHARYA	Commentaries on the Upanishads
,,	Moha-Mudgara
JAIMINI	Purva-Mimamsa-Sutra (Commentators: Shabara, Kumaril, Madhava)
BADARAYAN	Vedanta-Sutra (Commentator—Shankaracharya)
ISHWAR-KRISHNA	Sankhya-Karika (Treatise on Sankhya, system of Kapila)
KRISHNA (?)	Bhagvad-Gita (Commentator Shankaracharya)
PATANJALI	Yoga-Sutra
GAUTAMA	Nyaya-Sutra (Indian Logic)
YASKA	Nirukta (Grammatical Work on Vedic Sanskrit)
PANINI	Shabdanushasana (Standard Sanskrit Grammar)
KATYAYANA AND PATANJALI	Sanskrit Grammarians
VAMANA AND JAYADITYA	Kashika-Vritti (Sanskrit Grammatical Treatise)
BHATTOJI DIKSHIT	Siddhanta-Kaumudi (Sanskrit Grammatical Treatise)
HEMACHANDRA-ACHARYA	Works on Grammar and Philology (Jain)
VARARUCHI	Grammar of Prakrit Languages
AMAR SINH	Amar-Kosha (Sanskrit Lexicography)
HALAYUDHA, YADAV-PRAKASHA	Lexicographers (Sanskrit)
DHANANJAYA AND HEMA-CHANDRA-ACHARYA	Lexicographers—Jain
	Apastambiya-Dharmashastra (Sociologic Treatise)
MANU	Manava-Dharma-Shastra (Sanskrit Sociologic Treatise)
YAGNAVALKYA	Smriti (Sanskrit Sociologic Treatise)
VIGNANESHWARA	Mitakshara—Commentary on Yagnavalkya's Treatise
JIMUTAVAHANA	Dayabhaga—Commentary on the Hindu Law of Inheritance
KAUTILYA	Arthashastra (Compendium of Economics, and Politics)
VATSAYANA	Kamasutra (Treatise on the Science of Love)
VARAHA-MIHIRA	Pancha-Siddhantika (Treatise on Astronomy)
ARYABHATTA	Astronomer anterior to Varaha-mihira, holding Heliocentric Theory
BRAHMA-GUPTA	Astronomer of the VII Century A. C.
BHASKARA-ACHARYA	,, ,, XII ,, ,,
BHASKARA-ACHARYA	Lilavati (Treatise on Arithmetic)
,,	Bija-Ganita (Treatise on Algebra)
BHARATA	Natyashastra (Science of Dramaturgy)
SHUSHRUTA AND CHARAKA	Indian Medicine and Surgery

BIBLIOGRAPHY

AUTHOR

WORK

Abhinaya-Darpana—Mirror of Gesture

Sangita-Ratnakara—Treatise on Music

Vishnudharmottara—Treatise on Indian Painting and Image-making

Jyotish-Vedanga ⎫

Garga-Samhita ⎪

Surya-Pannati ⎬ Works on Astrology or Astronomy

Surya-Siddhanta ⎭

Shilpa-Shastras—Science of Mensuration

Manasara—Compendium of Measurement for Architects, etc.

LIST OF ILLUSTRATIONS

Hail, Ushas! Virgin Goddess of the Dawn (reproduced in colour) . . . . . . *Frontispiece.*

CHAPTER I. INDIA: A PANORAMIC VIEW

CHAPTER IV. MAKERS OF HISTORY AND BUILDERS OF EMPIRE

CHAPTER VII. MUSIC AND DANCING; PAINTING AND SCULPTURE

LII. SOME INDIAN INSTRUMENTS

CHAPTER VIII. TEMPLES AND TOMBS: PALACES
AND PLEASANCES

XXXII

THE SPLENDOUR THAT WAS 'IND

CHAPTER I

INDIA: A PANORAMIC VIEW

"No one who travels through the length and breadth of the continent of India," says the Imperial Gazetteer, "can fail to be struck with the extraordinary varieties of its physical aspects. In the North rise magnificent mountain altitudes, bound by snowfield and glacier in eternal solitude. At their feet lie smooth wide spaces of depressed river basins; either sandy, dry, and sun-scorched, or cultivated and water-logged under a stormy moisture-laden atmosphere. To the South spreads a great central plateau, where the indigenous forest still hides the scattered clans of aboriginal tribes; flanked on the west by the broken crags and castellated outlines of the ridges overlooking the Indian Ocean, and on the south by gentle, smooth, rounded slopes of green upland. Something at least of the throes and convulsions of nature which accompanied the birth of this changeful land is recorded in the physical aspect of the mountains and valleys which traverse it; and an appeal to the evidence of the rocks is answered by the story of its evolution."

India is an ancient land,—even as age goes in geology. The records of her people are lost in mist still hanging thick on the origins of modern civilisation. Without speculating upon earlier civilisations, now vanished from the ken of mankind except for fossil remains, offering more a challenge to the imagination than a conviction to the intellect as to the morals and manners of the races that peopled the continents now buried underneath the stormy billows of the Indian Ocean; without straining unbearably the suggestion of the Vedic hymns, or stressing impossibly the evidence of geologic strata in and around the first Aryan home in India; the remark may still be ventured that the forefathers of the modern Indian in the Indo-Gangetic plain came to this country 4000 or 5000 years ago; and that when they left the defiles of the Hindu Kush debouching on the Kabul and the Indus Valley, they were faced by peoples as respectable as any that the adventurous vanguard of the Indo-European family found in any part of Europe or Asia. The Dravids of the South, beyond the all but impenetrable barrier of the Vindhya and the Satpura Ranges, were a mighty race, boasting their own independent culture and civilisation of an antiquity before which the Aryans invading India from Iran and Turan were veritably moderns; and though the North was North, and the South was South, and never the twain did meet for countless centuries; though even after centuries of impact and close interaction, each race retained its own individuality in speech, in skin, in features, the Indian people of to-day throughout the vast peninsula from Kashmir to Cape Comorin and from Karachi to Calcutta have erected, by ages of contact and mutual influence and intermixture, a common heritage, which might well suggest to a modern student a sacred thread of fundamental unity binding the people of the peninsula into an indivisible whole.

1

This is true only of India proper. That which now makes up the political entity known as the British Empire of India contains units—both geographic and ethnological,—which are by no means one with the India of classic tradition or modern ambitions. The frontiers of India have been well defined by Nature herself; and though her handiwork has more than once been sought to be improved upon by the ambition of man, the only unity of the Indian continent and the Indian people is to be found within the limits set by Nature herself. The foam-flecked waves of the Indian Ocean, dashing upon her age-old shores, define a boundary along a coastline of 2000 miles on the west and the east, which no ingenuity of man can set back. The steep escarpment of the Western Ghats coming sharply down almost to the thin white line of the sandy-shore only serves to throw in bold relief this natural boundary, giving at the same time a warning to the ambitious visitor from over the Seas that the home of the chosen people, walled in by mountains and girt round by oceans, is safe, at least on that side, from his designs. On the east, the rise of the land from the coast westward is gentle and gradual, but unmistakable. But even there the defence of the people is amply provided for, if not by an impenetrable wall of mountains, by the absence of any safe harbourage or steady anchorage on that long open coast. The broad, fair bosom of the Daughter of the Creator—Brahmaputra—marks, with her collateral, the Meghna, the natural frontier of India on the East; and though the political boundary on the East stretches far beyond Brahmaputra through dense forest and impenetrable jungle up to the confines of China, that region and its people have no greater affinity with India proper than Burma and the Burmese. From the south-westward bend of the Brahmaputra to the turn of the Indus on the north, are the giant Himalayas, guarding eternally the home of the Aryans. Like sleepless sentinels they stand, armed in all their panoply of unpioneered forests, and unscaled summits, each with its dazzling helm of flashing snow, for a serried length of 1500 miles. Passage for the seasoned mountaineer and his hardy beast might be found at infrequent intervals through this stupendous wall of nature. But the cost in time and energy would be so immense, that no considerable wave of human invasion has ever worked its way to the fertile plains of the Gangetic Delta.

The natural boundary of India in this region almost coincides with the actual. On the north-west, however, the vicissitudes of history have moved the frontier back and forth, like the tide-line on an open coast. The Indus is the River of India *par excellence.* It gives the land its name and forms its natural boundary. And yet, for countless centuries, the ebb and flow of the might of India has traversed its mighty stream far into the basin of its western tributaries, and receded to the banks of the eastern and southernmost of its Punjab confluents. The Land of the Seven Rivers as known to the ancient Aryan of the Vedic Age, or of the Five Rivers as familiarised in the classic style of the Persian, Punjab, has ever been held to be Indian soil. But the land beyond the Indus on the west had always been equally debatable ground. The mountains in this region are a limb of the sprawling giant Himalayas stretching from the confines of China to the borders of Iran and

PLATE I

THE GATEWAY OF INDIA, BOMBAY

ENTRANCE TO PRINCE'S DOCK, BOMBAY

PLATE II

3   BALLARD PIER FROM THE HARBOUR, BOMBAY

4   A PANORAMIC VIEW OF MT. ABU

Turkestan. But the trans-Indus mountains are not impenetrable, as the serried phalanx of the Himalayas. The passes across the towering Hindu Kush are few and perilous, but well-defined and richly frequented. Through them have rushed wave upon wave of foreign invasion and conquest in the countless centuries of our recorded history. The search for a "scientific frontier" has pushed the debatable margin in recent times many a broad league to the west of the Indus; but it may be questioned if the mighty classic stream does not itself provide a sufficient and efficient frontier, even as the Rhine does between the warring Franks and Teutons. Certainly, with the exception of the people of Sind on both banks of this ocean-like stream, the tribes and races to the northward and westward of the Indus hold no affinity in race or culture to the people of this country. And so we may complete the outline of nature's boundary for India by these two mighty rivers on the West, and the East, the Indus and the Brahmaputra, both having their origin in the snow-fed lakes of the Himalayas, but each ultimately flowing into the sea that bathes and refreshes the feet and the flanks of the Mother 2000 miles from the other.

Let us, now, cast a glance at the sub-continent thus defined. In everything but mere area, India rivals the most considerable countries of the world. By itself it is larger than all Europe minus the Russia of the Tsars; and though Russia, the United States, and China excel her in point of size, China alone could surpass her in point of man-power. Taken collectively, her history and traditions are more ancient; her peoples more varied and numerous; her civilisation more rich, more gripping, and more lasting, than those perhaps of any other single country of the modern world. A rapid survey of the principal features of this wonderful mother of the arts and graces, of the religions and philosophies, of civilised humanity would amply repay the trouble of a careful study.

India may be studied from innumerable starting points. A modern painter has pictured the map of India as a *grande dame* of to-day, with her head in the heights of the Himalayas to the north, her hair streaming in the shape of mighty forests along the foot of this, with one arm curved kimbo to represent Kathiawar, and her feet dipping into the waves of the southern ocean. Her classic laureate, unfamiliar with the modern aeroplane, has nevertheless described her as seen by the Cloud-Messenger flying in the sky from the summit of the South-Western mountains, where the rain-charged clouds even now seem to have their port of entry, from the ocean to Mount Kailasa, the abode of the Gods, the source of the Holy Ganges and of the Mighty Indus. But his idiom is inaccessible, his diction inimitable, his imagery unfamiliar, his sonorous strains, his deft and delicate touches of a master-hand, impossible to a mere modern, even though he may be familiar with the pilot's view of the land from the cockpit of a coursing airship. A better if more prosaic alternative is the tourist itinerary, especially if the visitor is august enough not to be allowed to leave India without seeing almost every important feature of the land.

Let us assume, the visitor enters this—to him a land of mystery and romance— by the usual portal, the gateway of India at Bombay. The city of Bombay is a new comer, a mere baby, as the age of cities goes in the immemorial East. Before the holy Benares and the historic Pataliputra, Bombay the Beautiful is a city of yesterday. Until the opening of the Suez Canal, the European ships coming round the extremity of Africa could more easily reach the Malabar than the Maratha or the Gujarat ports. Cochin and Calicut in the extreme south of India were hence for centuries better known to the Arabs and the Portuguese, the French and the Dutch and the English, than the little group of fishing islands off the mainland in the very centre of the Western Coast, which now proudly style themselves *Urbs Prima in Indis*. Bombay owes a goodly portion of her prosperity to the Canal linking up once again the Red Sea and the Mediterranean; for it made her the first port of call for European liners after rounding the base of the Arab Peninsula. Karachi is nearer; and ports on the Kathiawar and Gujarat littoral cheaper. But the magnificent system of railways which radiates from Bombay to the north, the East and the South, not only links up the island city with the principal centres of the Indian Government, but also gives her command of the vast hinterland in all directions behind the Ghats, which, in the days before the Railways, were inaccessible to the City of Bombay. She has a magnificent natural harbour, whose twinkling light dancing on the waves spread a gorgeous picture—a fit symbol of the India of Romance—before the mail-boat from Europe or America steaming slowly into her berth in the early hours of a winter morning. The modern city—this Queen of the West—was yet in the womb of time, when the great fleets of Arab and Egyptian traders were draining the wealth of the Roman Empire to pay for the fabrics of the Indian loom, or the marvels of the Indian mines. The decaying town of Broach is to-day a pitiable relic of the ancient Baruagaza (or Bhrigukaccha), in whose broad river a regular forest of masts was for centuries present to impress and bewilder the inland native. Even Surat, on the South, or Cambay on the North, have a history before which the lustre of Bombay pales like the evening star before a full-orbed moon. The ships and sailors of Surat and Broach and all the ports to the very land's end of India ventured in every sea and were known in every port in the East and the West from Java to Zanzibar. They had an ample, unfailing wherewithal for their business. The marvellous evergreen plain of Gujarat had tempted, a thousand years ago, the insatiate Sultan Mahmud of Ghazni, who wondered if it were not the Garden of Allah. He would have made it his home, could he have afforded to be so far away from the seat of his Empire. The produce of Gujarat alone may not have sufficed to freight the countless ships that thronged her harbours; but behind Gujarat lay the rich hinterland of Malwa and Rajputana and the home provinces of the most ancient as well as modern Empires in India. These, with their varied products of the farm and the forge and the loom and innumerable needs, kept the double stream of imports and exports flowing perennially through these ports, and kept for ever piling up the riches which made this land the envy and the temptation of the world.

Gujarat, including the large peninsula of Kathiawar, is mostly a low-lying plain. Mount Abu stands a solitary sentinel at the north end, loaded with temples and palaces. Their art was a marvel five hundred years before the Taj Mahal was

PLATE III

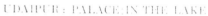

5   UDAIPUR: PALACE IN THE LAKE

6   MAHARANA OF UDAIPUR

7   KHYBER PASS (AERIAL VIEW)
(Photo: Royal Air Force)

8   A TRAIN IN KHYBER PASS (AERIAL VIEW)
(Photo: Royal Air Force)

PLATE IV

9   KOHAT CITY AND FORT—(N. W. F. P. AERIAL VIEW)
(Photo: Royal Air Force)

10   AERIAL VIEW OF FRONTIER LINES
(Photo: Royal Air Force)

11   MAHENJO DARO EXCAVATIONS—
'TANK BUILDINGS'' AND SURROUNDINGS
(Photo: Archaeological Survey of India)

conceived. But though Abu is 5000 feet high, it is cut off from the main range of the Aravallis, of which it is an outlying spur. This most ancient range in the land of the Rajputs stretches diagonally across Rajputana, dividing the desert from the habitable region, and marking the edge of the continent, beyond which ebbed and flowed the tides of a shallow sea in prehistoric times. The Ridge of Delhi marks the north-eastern limit of the range. In the plateau enclosed by the double range of the Aravallis on the North and the West, and the Vindhyas on the South, and watered by the Chambal and the Banas, lie the homes of the most famous warrior clans of India. Descendants of the Sun and the Moon, these are warriors by birth and temperament, who have not learnt to tame their wild spirit of adventure after a thousand years of ceaseless fighting. The canons of courtesy and the laws of chivalry they developed in their centuries of ceaseless strife, *inter se* as well as with the Musalman, cannot but move admiration in every age. Courage is contagious, and the freemasonry of the really brave is incomprehensible to the ordinary mortal; so that even if the Pathan and the Mughal could not thoroughly assimilate in five hundred years the real spirit of Rajput chivalry, the best of the Pathans and the Mughals failed not to pay their tribute of admiration to this supreme trait in their opponents. In the whole wonderful book of Indian History, there is perhaps nothing so touching, so eloquent, so exalting as the story of the succour by the Mughal Emperor Humayun of the distressed Queen Regent of Udaipur. His father had fought and vanquished the Maharana Sanga, the leader of the Rajput confederacy; and his still greater son was to fight and praise the force and courage and pride of the indomitable and immortal Pratap of Udaipur. He himself was, at the moment the call came to him, at grips with the rising might of Sher Shah in Bengal. But because a Queen in distress, his sister by the law of chivalry, though alien in faith and enemy in tradition, had sent him a call for aid against Bahadur Shah, the Muslim Sovereign of Gujarat, Humayun left the field in Bengal to rush to the rescue, risking thereby not only his life but also his empire. The modern cities of Udaipur, Jaipur, Jodhpur are but faint reminders of their past grandeur. But though the rushing automobile in eternal hurry may have replaced, even here, the gallant steed or the gorgeous elephant; though the siege-gun has rendered useless their walls, and the machine gun their incomparable warriors, the mighty spirit of an unforgettable past still hovers over the land. The martial figure of the Maharana of Udaipur is still unbent, in spite of the snows of eighty winters lying on this head. And though his sword and shield may be only symbolic, such symbols have a message of hope to a people conscious of their ancient heritage.

The great Indian desert lies to the north and west of Rajputana, on the site where once ebbed and flowed the waves of the ocean. It has ever proved an effective barrier to the invader. The sands of desert are piled in hillocks of 50 or 100 feet high, and march in rhythmic curves in obedience to the winds from the western seas. The cities of the desert—Jaisalmer and Bikaner,—testify to the bracing character of the climate in this hot, arid, desolate region. Housed in an inhospitable soil, these oases in the desert gather round them all the slender stock of human as well as vegetable life in these parts. Their massive ramparts present even to-day marvels of military architecture, which once made them proverbial for invincible security. "So constant and unceasing is the steady sun-glare of the desert," says the Imperial Gazetteer, "that a tradition (supported by a certain amount of evidence) relates that in days long anterior to the date of our introduction of the heliograph, bazaar prices of the wheat and grain in the Punjab were signalled by means of reflecting mirrors across Rajputana to Sind and Bombay all the year round."

The traveller in India on pleasure bent usually leaves Rajputana by the Delhi Gateway for the fertile plains of the Ganges Valley, without a glance at the desolate plains of the Indus Valley called Sind. Judging, however, from the remains now slowly being unearthed after their sleep of centuries, the civilisation of this arid valley is more ancient and amazing than that in the more historic provinces of this vast continent. A flat alluvial land, its wealth is the creation of the annual inundation of the great stream slowly wandering to the sea. Like the Nile in Egypt, the Indus compensates Sind for the absence of the regular monsoon, which is such a peculiar feature of the rest of the Indian continent. Like an ace of hearts, the province of Sind is based on the Sea and the Salt Marsh known as the Rann of Cutch; but the rain-charged current of air from the Arabian Sea sweeps over the plain without any resistance from a coastal or continental range of mountains, which would force it to part with its moisture to water the parched land. Right until it reaches the confines of the Punjab, the rain-laden wave has no inducement to exhaust itself. Even the great and wealthy land of the Five Rivers,—the classic *Sapta Sindhu* and the modern Punjab,—appears at first sight a flat, treeless waste of level plains, where wave upon wave of the same landscape rolls on to an ever expanding horizon. Lacking in the gifts of Nature, the provinces of Sind and the Punjab have been converted into an eternal envy for the rest of India by the ingenuity and enterprise of man. The marvellous system of irrigation based on the Indus and its tributaries are modern—only in the scale of their dimension. But, despite the gigantic irrigation works, which literally make millions of stalks of corn and blades of grass grow where previously not a single seed could thrive, the ancient forests of the Indus banks have become a thing of the past. The towering elephant and the ponderous rhinoceros no longer find a home in the valleys of these mighty rivers, as they no longer afford shade or swamp enough for these lords of the brute creation.

If the arid waste of Sind has, as yet, no attraction for the foreign visitor, the frontier abounds in marvels of defence and strategy which no one who may would care to leave unseeen. From Delhi north-westwards, through Sirhind and Patiala, to Lahore; and thence on to Peshawar along the Jumna and the Sutlej, between the desert on the south and the mountain on the north; the land is strewn with battlefields of ancient, medieval, as well as modern history. Every square mile of ground has its own tale of courage and carnage. The parent stream of all invasion started on this frontier where the big-boned, blue-eyed, light-coloured Pathan

PLATE V

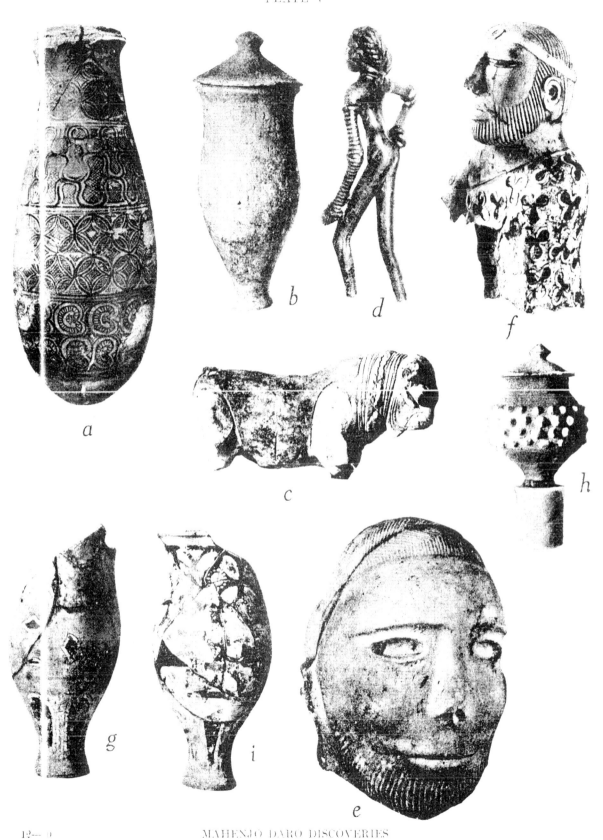

MAHENJO DARO DISCOVERIES

a, Painted Vase. *b,* Silver Vase containing Jewellery. *c,* Terra-cotta Bull. *d,* Copper statuette of Dancing girl. *e,* Stone head. *f,* Stone statue, stucco finished and painted. *g, h, i,* Polychromatic vases and urn.

(Archaeological Survey of India Photographs)

PLATE VI

21   MOUNTAIN SCENERY IN KASHMIR

22   THE JEHLUM AT SHRINAGAR, KASHMIR

jostles with the milder yet tenacious native of the Punjab. With the possible exception of the Gurkhas of Nepal, there are no braver or more fearless soldiers in the Indian Army than those recruited from the Rajputs and the Sikhs, the Jats and the Dogras, the Punjab Musalmans and the Pathan mountaineers, of this region of eternal warfare. India is at peace, for the moment, with all her trans-frontier neighbours. But it is not beyond the realm of possibility that the restless ambition of a successful adventurer in the yet unsettled land of the Afghans, or the missionary, even if mistaken, zeal of the more distant Russian, may once more force conclusions on the Indian frontier at any time. Hence it is that the entire organisation and distribution of the army in India, and the lay-out of the railways in the border province, are made with an eye predominantly to the frontier. At two points only— the Khyber and the Bolan Passes—is the land frontier of India on the north-west considered to be vulnerable. The highlands of Afghanistan, narrowing to a single, though lofty, ridge of the Hindu Kush, almost opposite to the valley of the Indus near Peshawar, open in several passes to the valley of the Kabul River flowing into the Indus. The most famous and frequented of these passes is the Khyber, crowned by the fort of Ali Masjid, some three thousand feet above sea-level. Peshawar, the ancient Pushkalavati, is a city of the plains on the further side of the Indus, serving as capital of the newly formed Frontier Province. Nine miles of slowly rising ground to the west of it is the entrance to the Pass at Jamrud, which forms the halting ground for the caravans between India and Central Asia. The Pass, beginning at Jamrud and passing by the crowning fort of Ali Masjid, descends into Afghanistan on the other side of the Hindu Kush at Landi Kotal; and through this has flowed in historic times wave upon wave of invasion into India with varying fortunes. For nearly a hundred years, however, the stream seems to have dried up, and the people of India are now immune from the danger they apprehended for centuries.

Five hundred miles to the south and west lies another indenture in the hilly barrier round the continent of India. An open plateau at the foot of the Afghan mountains descends into the low-land of Lower Indus in Sind through the Bolan Pass, named after the last gorge through which the plain of Sind is approached. This gateway, however, opens, unlike that of the Khyber Pass, almost opposite the great desert of India, which makes an effective and insurmountable barrier to any considerable invading force. The construction of the railway in Sind and the rest of the frontier district has ever kept in view the needs of military strategy for offensive as well as defensive purposes; so that the North-Western Railway, ordinarily choked in some months of the year with the heavy produce of the wheat fields and cotton belts of the Punjab canal colonies, is ever ready to transport troops and stores to Quetta in Baluchistan, which, with Peshawar, forms the only key-position to the gateways into India. To ensure the commercial success of this railway line, and to add to the material prosperity of the Sindi people, vast projects of damming the Indus at Sukkur, and flinging out a network of irrigation canals over millions of acres of until now barren soil are making rapid progress.

Sceptics are not wanting who question the commercial possibilities of the Sukkur schemes; and there are political pessimists who foretell the intensification of inter-provincial jealousies when one and the same river-system has to be drawn upon for the benefit of more than one province. But the rail-road is above these jealousies, and flings out one arm through the Bolan Pass forking out in two branches over the Mushkaf Valley, and over the more easy gradient of the Harnai Loop through the Pishin Valley. Quetta is itself on a plateau, a mile from sea-level, strongly fortified, overlooking and protecting the railway through the Khojak Pass into India. All along this hilly region, the watchful might of the Indian army is ever on the alert, ready to march at the first signal of disaffection into the heart of a possible enemy whether from Persia or Afghanistan. The coastal strip of Makran, though a conceivable source of invasion, is, ever since the disastrous march homewards of Alexander, regarded as utterly impracticable for such a purpose.

If the survey of the Frontier is interesting to the traveller for historical and political reasons, the view of the inland provinces along the river of the frontier is not an iota less interesting for its own peculiar reasons. But for the vast irrigation works, from the point where the Sutlej debouches on the plains from its home in the Himalayan gorges to the final merging of the last of the Five Rivers into the ever-swelling volume of the Indus waters, the Punjab partakes of all the natural characteristics of the hot and arid province of Sind. But the engineering triumphs of our days have converted thousands of square miles of her territory into one of the most wealthy and productive regions of the British Empire.

The Indus, a mighty stream of 1800 miles, and ranking among the dozen largest rivers of the world, rises in Tibet, almost due north of the sacred city of Benares, and flows north-westwards from its source till it reaches the further angle of the Kashmir Valley in the north-west. Here it suddenly bends southwards, and breaks through the Himalayas by the most magnificent gorge in the world. The venturesome visitor, if he ever reaches there, may stand on the right bank of the river and look across its roaring, yellowing waters to the titanic mass of a Nanga Parbat rising sheer into the air to the vertical height of four miles, double that of the Matterhorn. From there, the river cleaves its way to the plains of Peshawar and Kalabagh, through deep canyons, over a distance of 200 miles, receiving on its way its Afghan tributaries of the Kabul and the Kohat. The bed of the river in its lower reaches through the desert soil of Sind has ever in history been constantly shifting. Vestiges of ancient river-beds abound in the deltaic flats to the east of the Indus. By these ancient channels must have been watered and fructified the now dessicated region, under which lie buried and forgotten, perhaps innumerable cities of a vanished and amazing past, greater than the one recently dug up at Mahenjo Daro considered to be 5000 years old. At least one historic river—the Vedic and vanished Saraswati—is definitely traceable; and though in modern years the tradition may sound fantastic which says that the vanished river has turned on its own watershed, its dried up bed is even to-day an indelible proof of the vicissitudes of physiography.

PLATE VII

23   THE JEHLUM AT PANDRETHAN

24   THE CANAL LEADING INTO THE DAL LAKE

PLATE VIII

25   THE SUTLEJ IN ITS HIMALAYAN HOME

26   BRIDGE ON THE CHENAB IN KISHTWAR, FRONTIER OF KASHMIR

PLATE IX

27   A GENERAL VIEW OF SIMLA

28   THE CITY OF MUTTRA, ON THE JUMNA

PLATE X

29 TARA DEVI HILLS, SIMLA

30 BATHING GHAT, MUTTRA
(Photo: Indian State Railways)

31 GANGES CANAL, CAWNPORE
(Photo: Indian State Railways)

The vale of Kashmir—what a marvel of nature! The land of Romance and Lalla Rukh, it is made up of the valleys of the Jhelum and the Sutlej, rolling in endless vistas of snowy ranges and silver streams and pine-clad dales of unspeakable scenic grandeur. The Indian State of Kashmir is nearly a square block of territory, watered mainly by the Indus on the north and on the west, and the Jhelum winding its way round the capital, and flowing south-westward through the Punjab into the Chenab and thence to the Indus. Walled in on the north by the magnificent Mustagh Range—an extension of the Karakorum Mountains,—the Kashmir of the tourist and the holiday-maker, is not the land of the Indus, but of the Jhelum basin. This river rises in the western spurs of the Himalayas east of the vale of Kashmir, and flows past the city of Srinagar, washing its temple steps and lapping the piles of its wooden bridges, till it reaches the narrow outlet of Baramula. Here the surrounding hills ring it round, and the river bends southwards to the plains of the Punjab. The curves and loops of the Jhelum are so frequent that the pattern on the world-famous Kashmir shawl and carpet is traditionally said to be modelled on these windings of the country's principal river. Vast, inexhaustible stores of alluvial soil have been accumulating since countless ages along the passage of the river to make the unrivalled fertility of this glorious garden of India. The entire beauty of the land of Lalla Rukh is centred in the districts of the south and the west, where the gigantic *massif* of the Nanga Parbat looks serenely, like some ages-old Yogi lost in the contemplation of the riddle of the universe, across the valley of shadows, along the Indus banks to Rakaposhi; or where the purple waters of the Woolar Lake reflect the splendour of Haramukh. Not one, however, in every ten thousand of India's teeming millions, is able to visit Kashmir during a whole life-time to revel in the magnificence of Nature at her lavishest; but nineteen out of every twenty inhabitants of the plains of the Punjab and the Indus have to be thankful for their daily bread to these immense reservoirs of water in Kashmir, which fertilise perennially the otherwise uncultivable wastes of the plains.

Of the other rivers of the Punjab, the Sutlej (900 miles) is the most considerable. It may be taken to be the natural boundary of the land of the Five Rivers. Rising in the paradise of Sanskrit literature, the Kailasa mountain near Manasarowar, not very far from the source of the Indus and the Brahmaputra, the Sutlej flows south-westwards, cutting a gully of 4000 feet deep, between Himalayan Ridges, which make of the winding river channel a veritable mountain trough of giant dimensions. Emerging into the plains near Rampur, the river leaves Simla, the summer capital of the Government of India, and takes a more pronounced westward curve, meeting the Beas at Sultanpur near the famous battlefield of Sobraon, the Jhelum-Chenab-Ravi at Jalalpur, and the mighty Indus at Mithankot, some 900 miles from its source.

The geographical position of Simla is on the water-divide between the rivers of the Indus system on the west, and those of the Jumna Ganges system on the east. It overlooks, and, in a way, dominates the famous battlefields of the Sutlej, where the prize was often the mastery the entire continent. The Ravi, the River of Lahore, and the Chenab, the more northerly of the five rivers, have practically the same geographic characteristics of Sub-Himalayan streams,—mountain torrents cutting their way through deep gullies, flanked by gigantic mountain ridges for a good portion of their earlier course of rapids and cascades, and placid streams wandering through slowly falling plains to the parent stream. The vast network of irrigation canals from Kashmir to the confines of the Patiala State, from Bilaspur to the Indus at Sukkur, is a marvel of modern history, which, however, is not entirely without a respectable model and precedent in the past.

Returning from the Punjab, our traveller re-enters the Indo-Gangetic plain at Delhi. Though the court of the Viceroy of India and the assemblies of the Diwan-i-am are no longer held in the jewelled halls of the marble palace of Shah Jahan; though Indraprasth is a name, and Tughlukhabad a ruin; Delhi,—the scene of so many struggles and suffering, of so much splendour and glory,—is once more the seat of a mighty empire. The classic Jumna, the playground of Krishna, runs past the palace in the fort and the modern city—Shah Jahanabad—in a southward course. The Ridge of Delhi, where the last struggle for the mastery of India took place seventy years ago, is the last of the outlying spurs of the Aravallis; and lies to the west of the city, which is ensconced in the angle between the river and the Ridge. Agra, another or alternative capital of the Mughal Empire, lies a hundred miles south along the Jumna. Its fame as the seat of the most wonderful poem in marble, the most eloquent memorial of marital love, has almost eclipsed the memories of Agra as the most magnificent capital of the most cultured, refined, luxurious, voluptuous Emperor. Muttra, midway between Agra and Delhi, is the playground of Krishna and his Cowherdesses, whose memory lingers imperishably in the innumerable songs of the people, familiarising them with the woods along the Jumna in a way no post-card photograph, or painted landscape, could ever do. Rising at Jamnotri, not far from the mountains giving birth to the holy Ganges, the clear blue stream of the Jumna murmurs along its age-old song for an independent length, through hill and dale, of 860 miles to Prayag, on a narrow tongue of land near the modern Allahabad, to be merged, if not lost, in the Ganges. Like the rivers of the Punjab, but much earlier in point of history, both the Jumna and the Ganges have been canalised to spread immeasurable fertility in the districts along their banks. The Jumna receives only one tributary, the Chambal, from the central Indian plains; but its waters bestow no less wealth through its course.

From the delta of the Indus to the delta of the Ganges extends the most wonderful physical feature of the Indian continent. "Within it is not to be found a boulder (not even a pebble) to break the uniform regularity of its alluvial surface." The Holy River rises in a glacial hollow of the central Himalayas, known as Gaumukh or cow's mouth, and flows south-eastwards to the Bay of Bengal, a distance of 1550 miles, every yard of which is sacred to the Hindus. It is in the valley of the Ganges, and in the plains watered by its tributaries, that Indian history is at its richest. The chief kingdoms of history and mythology; the most

PLATE XI

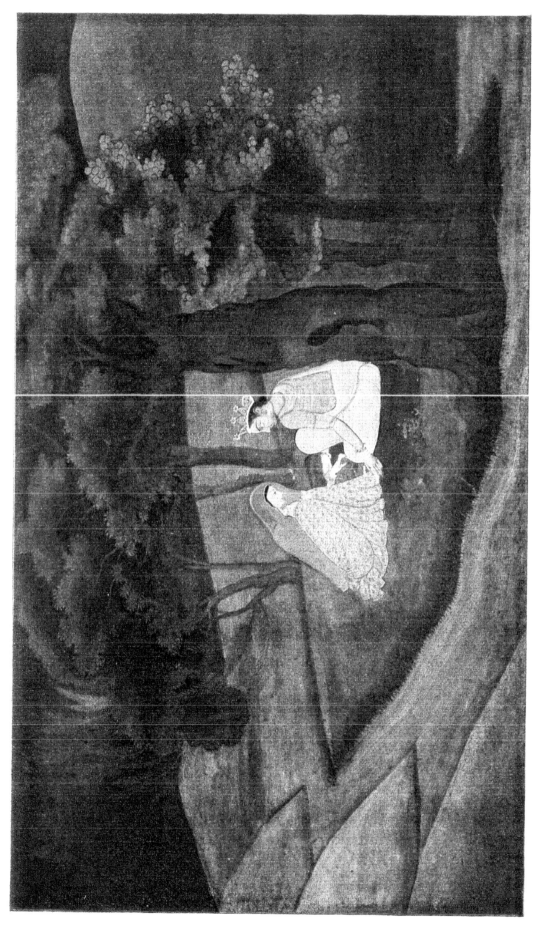

KRISHNA AND RADHA

(From No.1, Ritter's book. Studies in Indian Painting.)

ancient seats of learning and religion and civilisation; of art and industry and wealth, lie in these extensive regions. Thousands visit the holy Ganges every year from all parts of India; millions believe that to bathe in her sanctifying stream is to purify oneself from all sins, to die and be burnt on her banks is to get straight to paradise. While yet in its parent heights, the Ganges is a furious snow-fed mountain torrent for a little less than 200 miles, known as the Bhagirathi, and flowing over rapids and shoals and pools towards the plains on the south-east. At Hardwar it issues from the hills in a clear stream of crystal waters, to which every year the Magha Mela attracts thousands of pious pilgrims. There is only one other city on the Ganges,—the sacred and the learned Benares—which can rival the holiness of Hardwar for the Hindus. The Ganges irrigation also commences here. From Hardwar to Darjeeling, the foot-hills of the Himalayas and the plains and the jungles attached to them belong to the independent Gurkha kingdom of Nepal, which supplies the most famous soldiers of the Indian army. The Nepalese is Hindu by religion,—the Maharaja a Rajput; but by race a cousin of the Mongol. On the south and east, the districts of the United Provinces of Agra and Oudh,—the former a seat of Mughal magnificence, the latter the homeland of the classic Raghus,—and Bihar stretch in mile upon mile of brown, waving plains, studded with mud villages more ancient in history than the proudest modern capitals, shaded by lovely groves of mango and tamarind, banyan and nimb, that are gradually changed in the lower reaches of the stream into lines of tall bamboo, or the broad-leaved banana, or the coronated palm. The basin of the Ganges and its affluents differs from that of the Indus in that the entire region is here within the range of the monsoon current. At Allahabad, the Ganges is joined by the Jumna, while the Gogra and the Gandak from the hills of Nepal join it on the north at Chapra and Patna, the capital of Bihar. Near about the same place, the Son from the Vindhya mountains delivers its tribute. A broad shining stream of muddy turgid waters, the Ganges now flows in easy channels through a flat alluvial plain, broken only once in a length of 500 odd miles by the heights and slopes of the Rajamahal Hills. From Allahabad onwards, the fall in the land surface is barely 6 inches in a mile; while in the last 200 miles of the course the sluggish current has not force enough to carry all the silt it has brought from the mountains. The silt is thus deposited, and the river split into more than one channel as it nears the sea; while new land is formed to add to the available surface in the crowded delta.

The Delta proper of Bengal begins where the Hooghly branches off from the parent stream. Between that point and the basins of the Brahmaputra and the Meghna lie some of the richest and the most densely peopled land in India. A line drawn from Delhi to Patna and thence to Calcutta measures the length; and another from Bareilly to Agra,—or Lucknow to Allahabad—measures roughly the breadth of this crowded area, where there are something over 500 souls per each square mile of surface. In this region of over 50,000 square miles, there are only two mountain ranges of any considerable importance. East of Bengal is a range which divides Burma and the Irrawady Basin from the delta of Bengal. Deeply forested and copiously watered, its most prominent spur is named the Garo Hills on its western edge. The Assam Valley, through which the Brahmaputra trenches its way to the delta, lies between the Garo Hills and the Himalayas. Southward of the Garo Hills, the drainage forms another delta watered by the Meghna, which extends almost to the edge of the sea at Chittagong—second, but a very poor second, to the port of Calcutta. Opposite the Garo Hills on the South-west is another range—an offshoot of the central Indian mountain-system—the Raja Mahal Hills. Through the broad low-land portal between the Garo and the Raja Mahal Hills, the Brahmaputra and the Ganges bend southwards in parallel streams to the sea. It is in these parts that the record average rainfall of the world occurs every year.

The Brahmaputra is, like the Indus, a Himalayan stream. Rising on the eastern slopes of Mount Kailasa, this Daughter of the Creator (Brahma) flows through Tibet for half its length under the name of Tsan-po. Rounding the corner of the farthest Himalayas on the east, it enters British Indian territory near Sadiya, and changes its name to Digang. On the way it absorbs the Ditang and the Luhit, and the united stream once more changes style to be now called Brahmaputra. A vast sheet of silting water, broken by innumerable islands, and constantly shifting its channel if the slightest impediment of its own creation meets its course, the river rolls its way in majestic windings for 450 miles down the valley of Assam. It leaves the Assam Valley in another magnificent curve at the foot of the Garo Hills, changes the name yet again to *Jamuna*, and flows almost due south for 180 miles to meet the Ganges at Goalundo. Here the two deltas unite. Between this and the sea, fresh tributes are received from the Meghna, itself a mighty river, to swell the main stream.

Unlike other rivers, the Brahmaputra does not now allow its channel to be utilised for irrigation. But the same purpose is achieved by the tremendous annual floods in this river, which act like natural irrigation works on the adjoining lands. From the sea to Dibrugarh, its length of 800 miles is navigable; and though the railway has killed the river traffic in India, rarely is the river equalled anywhere else even now in its picturesque beauty of quaintly-rigged country craft crowding the surface.

The Tarai forest at the foot of the Himalayas, fringing the British districts to the north of Bengal and Bihar, is still the home of big game and paradise of the hunters, though deadly to man, owing to its everlasting malaria. In these yet unexplored depths lie buried many a remains of the most famous cities of the Buddhist period. The Siwalik mountains to their north-west are similarly rich in the fossil remains of a still more ancient ancestry of man and animal in India. In the *Sunderbuns* at the mouth of the Ganges—Meghna, there are gigantic creepers of gorgeous hues festooning the trees—themselves of enormous height and thickness.

The forests of the central highlands,—of the Vindhya and the Satpura mountains, of the Godavari and the Mahanadi Basin in the Deccan,—are radically different in

PLATE XII

33 THE AMAR SINGH GATE, AGRA FORT, ON THE JUMNA

34 TAJ MAHAL ON THE JUMNA

35 VIEW OF THE GANGES AT DANGULLY

PLATE XIII

36   THE GANGES AT DERALI

37   BENARES : TEMPLES

38   GENERAL VIEW OF BENARES

character. Sal and teak and tamarind and bamboo grow there; but they do not prevent the light of day streaming through the foliage. When their thorny shrubs have put out new buds and are gowned afresh in lovely verdure, these jungles display a strange riot of gorgeous colouring. The scarlet blossoms of the stiff-standing cotton tree, without any background of leaves, remind one strangely of the old-time red-coat soldier of the line; while the vermillion bunches of the velvet-leafed Dhak offer a rich contrast that in no way modifies the blinding glare of the summer sun.

The tourist's next halting place is at Calcutta. Eighty miles from the mouth of the Hooghly, this is the richest, the largest and the most crowded city in India, and second only to London, in the whole of the British Empire. But Calcutta cannot compare in its importance to the inner life of the people around to the great triangle of the holy cities on the Ganges—Benares, Patna and Gaya. Gaya is the Jerusalem of Buddhism, as Benares is the Rome of Hinduism. Millions of souls even to-day from Karachi to Tokio look upon this triangle as the centre of holiness and source of refinement. Calcutta is described as a city of palaces; it would be fitter to name it the haunt of bastis. The palaces of Calcutta, such as they are, are more often the offices and residences of alien commercial magnates, than the cultured homes of a native aristocracy of birth or brains. It is, however, the gateway for what wealth India still receives in the east, in exchange for the products of her fields and factories, mines and forests.

Leaving the low-lying plains of the Ganges and the Brahmaputra, the traveller might go by sea to Rangoon on the Irrawady, the port and practical capital of Burma, which, as already noticed, is not intrinsically a part of the Indian continent. Instead let him steam or sail along the coast of India south-westwards by Puri and Vizagapatam to Madras and Pondicherry, and thence down to the very last promontory on the Indian continent. Along this route lie the mouths of the Great River (Mahanadi), the mighty Godavari, the wealthy Krishna, and the holy Kavery. Southward from the valley of the Ganges, the continent slopes gently upwards till it reaches the Vindhya Range, running horizontally almost like a waist-line in the Mother's gown. The Vindhyas divide the watershed of the Hindustani from the Deccani rivers, the affluents of the Ganges from those of the Mahanadi. The Vindhya range is by no means so regular as the Ghats on the Western coast, or the Himalayas on the North and the East. But its elevated plateaux provide a most bracing winter and a tolerable summer, its irregular hills and their deep dark ravines and roaring torrents making in parts a scenic grandeur, rare in other regions of the country.

Let us now take, with our imaginary traveller, a voyage along the south-eastern sea-board of India from Calcutta to Cape Comorin. The first considerable river is the Mahanadi. It rises on the fringe of the Vindhyas, and, passing through the Central Provinces, enters the plain of Orissa near Raigarh to discharge its volume of water into the sea beyond Cuttack.

The Godavari, merging in the sea next to the southwards, rises in the far away Western Ghats, almost within sight of the sea, near Nasik, and flows in gentle

4

curves, in wide, shallow channels, through three political divisions of the country. The scenic magnificence of the Godavari banks and forests is famous since the days of the exile and adventures of Rama and Sita; and is repeated along its principal tributaries the Wardha, Penganga, and Wainganga. When it re-enters British territory from the Nizam's dominions, it receives the Indravati and the Shabari, classic names in the story of Rama, and develops into a broad channel broken by many an islet along its meandering course. In the unpioneered depths of the Mardian forests along the banks of the Indravati live the Ghonds, the most ancient perhaps of the aborigines of India, ruder or more primitive in their mode of living than even the Bhils of Dahod in the Narmada basin. Sixty miles from the sea coast, the stream of the Godavari narrows and deepens, thanks to the hills along the shores closing round, till at one point the river roars its way through a magnificent gorge in a mighty torrent barely 200 yards wide. The Delta of the Godavari is turned into a perennial garden by the great irrigation works watering some 780,000 acres of the most remunerative land. Past Rajahmundry, it flows into the sea by a variety of mouths between Point Narasapur and Coconada.

The Krishna rises near the Summer capital of the Bombay Government, Mahableshwar, forty miles from the sea. Receiving on its way the Bhima from the north and the Tunga-Bhadra from the Mysore State, the Krishna winds its way through regions similar to those of the Godavari. The great Bahmani kingdoms were cradled and nurtured in these parts, expanding farther to the south and the east on the downfall and decay of the now forgotten Empire of Vijayanagar. The river flows in a rapid stream over a rocky bottom, not permitting any irrigation works on a large scale, till it breaks through the Eastern Ghats at Bezwada on to the Madras Plains. Here an ancient anicut arrests the flow of the river, and two main canals carry its waters over an area of 226,000 acres.

The third great delta in the south-east corner of India is formed by the Kavery, the southern Ganges, the river of Tanjore, known as the Garden of South India. This river takes its birth in the mountains of Coorg, in the western corner of the great Indian State of Mysore. Tortuous in its course and rocky in the bed, the Kavery winds its early way between steep banks covered with rank vegetation. The enlightened and enterprising rulers of Mysore have constructed a dozen dams at various points in the course of the river to irrigate their lands, and have harnessed the stream at the holy island of Shivasamudram, near the borders of the Madras Presidency, where it forks and rushes down a perpendicular slope of 300 feet in two channels. The hydro-electric works there established are amongst the earliest and the most considerable in India, and are rapidly solving the problem of motive power for India.

Three other rivers,—the Pennar of Nellore, the Palar of Madras, and the Vaigai of Madura,—add to the wealth of the sea-board lands in the Southern Presidency. The population of these parts is easy-going, rice-eating, poverty-stricken and enervated, despite the fact that little more than a hundred years ago it was the

PLATE XIV

39   DALHOUSIE SQUARE, CALCUTTA

40   KALIGHAT CANAL, CALCUTTA

PLATE XV

41   WAL, NEAR THE SOURCE OF THE KRISHNA

42   THE KAVERI NEAR SERINGAPATAM   43 GARSOPPA FALLS, SHARAVAT

(42—43 Photo: The Palace Studio, Mysore)

PLATE XVI

THE GODAVERI AT NASIK

RIVER SCENE (KAVERI), TANJORE

PLATE XVII

46   THE ROCK, TRICHINOPOLY

47   THE MARBLE ROCKS OF THE NARBADA

ceaseless battle-ground for the Marathas and the Muslims from Mysore, and the European from overseas.

The traveller has now surveyed the whole of the region, commonly known as the Deccan. The southern half of the Indian peninsula is divided from the Indo-Gangetic plain by a thousand miles of mountains and forests along the Satpura and the Vindhya ranges, which thus form its northward boundary and escarpment. A land of open valleys and broad plains; of noble rivers and impenetrable forests; the country yet admits of good cultivation in the States of Hyderabad and Mysore, as well as in the alluvial plains of the Madras coast. The coast is poor in natural harbours, the best of them being little better than open, unprotected roadsteads, at the mercy of the first hurricane that blows. The rivers do not permit,—or at least are not encouraged to allow—of any navigation even in the level regions near their mouths. The mines of Golconda no longer yield the world-famed diamonds; but the gold veins in the Kolar fields in Mysore still testify to the fabulous wealth for which India was once famous among the peoples beyond the seas. Even now agricultural wealth in this region is second to none in the whole of the continent. There is no soil more remunerative to the ryot than the black cotton soil of the central highlands; while the weird, awful grandeur of the giant tors and bosses dotting the landscape of the Deccan makes the region unique in its natural aspect. The famous rock of Trichinopoly, or the great curved bull of the Chamundi Hill dominating the city of Mysore, are typical examples.

The Ghats on the west are serried rows of flat-topped, castellated hills, making a veritable rampart along the coast. The sturdy highlanders of these regions became, under the inspiring leadership of Shivaji and his successors, the champions and redeemers of Hinduism against the last of the Great Mughals. Their spirit breathes still in the regiments of Marathas forming no inconsiderable part of the Indian army; while their leaders maintain the traditions of sturdy independence and intense patriotism implanted in their blood in the days when the terror of the Maratha light horseman was spreading from sea to sea, and from Tanjore to Lahore. The lowland strip of coastal land at the foot of the hills—Konkan—is nourished by the sea-borne mists condensing on the crests of the hills, and streaming down the mountain gullies in copious rains during the monsoon months.

The rain-bearing current is squeezed of most of its moisture by the time it has passed the crests of the Western Ghats; so that the country lying under the lee of these hills is very poor in rainfall. The Bombay Deccan is thus peculiarly exposed to famine, where they badly need, but cannot easily construct, irrigation works. Even so, man has not remained wholly inactive; and though the Bombay Deccan works cannot compare in scope and grandeur to those of other provinces, they too have managed to reclaim or protect thousands of acres from perennial famine.

On the east, or Coromandel coast, the Ghats are neither so steep nor serried, nor quite so contiguous to the sea. The broad rivers of the Deccan have built up a wide margin of alluvial plain near the coast on the Madras side, where their waters help to raise the most abundant crops for a teeming multitude. The absence of the

South-west monsoon is made up for by the North-east current, bringing moisture from the Himalayas in December and January. These lowlands are the home of the palm and paddy; of magnificent temples and classic monuments; of indigenous culture and craftsmanship, where they have still managed to preserve the germ of our native art. The marvels of the Dacca muslin are dead, as also the beauties of Burhanpur silks; but Coconada still claims to make the finest khaddar to clothe the ardent and idealistic patriot of the Gandhi days.

The Eastern Ghats follow the coastline north-east from Madras at a distance of fifty miles from mountain-crest to sandy beach. Small and scattered and irregular, they are probably the stunted relics of a more magnificent range, contemporary, in prehistoric days, to the Aravallis of Rajputana.

In the extreme south, the districts of Tinnevelly and Madura present a new feature in Indian physiography. Shut off by the southern ghats from the sea-board States of Travancore and Cochin, they are mostly regions of treeless waste sloping gradually to the sea, their coast being fringed with groves of palmyra and cocoanut palms. The districts of Malabar are walled in by the closing range of the Western Ghats, now broken and irregular, till they merge in the highlands of the Nilgiris, which house on their lofty terraced slopes smiling tea-gardens and eucalyptus plantations and a variety of other exotic plants, that have turned the Blue Mountains into a multi-tinted garden of green. On a clear day, the western sea can be seen from the higher peaks near Ootacamund, the summer capital of the Madras Government. On the South, the Nilgiris fall abruptly down to a narrow gateway from the east to the western coast, the so-called gap of Palghat, through which a railway now winds to connect the east with the west. Malabar in the south-west corner of India is another Kashmir, but lacks the eternal snows and titanic peaks of the northernmost regions of India. For here are the same inlets and backwaters which serve the purpose of the lakes and rivers of the Kashmir Valley; the same cascades falling down steep sides of forest-clad hills, lit up with the iridescent hues of unending rainbow: the same clearness of complexion and regularity of features, at least among the superior strata of the Nair and Nambudiri men and women, with a much greater degree of personal cleanliness than in the lovely land of Lalla Rukh.

Our traveller has now completed the circuit of the continent, except a very small bit along the Narmada and the Tapti rivers. These are the rivers of Gujarat. Rising in the central mountains, they run in nearly parallel channels, between steep banks flanked by sharp heights and dense forest, till they emerge in the fertile plain of Gujarat. Unlike almost all other principal rivers of India in the north as well as the south, they are peculiar in flowing east to west. The Narmada is the western Ganga, almost equal in holiness to its more celebrated namesake; while the Tapti marks the northernmost limit of the Western Ghats. They both flow into the Arabian Sea past ports famous for centuries in the foreign commerce of India, and exhibiting, in themselves splendid specimens of the splendour that once was India.

CHAPTER II

THE PAGEANT OF A PEOPLE

History has no complete record of the peoples who lived in and loved this ancient land. The connected, chronological, reliable narrative, now available, takes us back only 3,500 years at most; but records not less significant or authentic than the written word, or tradition not a whit less reliable, carry on the story into dim vistas of the past for another thousand years or more. Every new discovery, however, of the relics and monuments in stone or marble, in wood or bronze or gold, serves only to deepen the mystery hanging over the story of human life in this country, till the very earliest beginnings seem to be shrouded in impenetrable mist and darkness. The actual commencement of the story of human life on earth is certainly untraceable precisely in every country; but whether it goes back fifty thousand years or five million years, lands like India appear to be inhabited since the very beginning. Evidence of language, even now spoken in some parts of India by certain tribes, shows a marked relationship with the existing speech in the farthest east, reaching so far away as the southern Continent, thereby indicating a most intriguing possibility, not only of the present Peninsula of India and the modern island of Australia being, at some remote date in the past, a single block of land; but also of their being inhabited by a common, or at least a connected, race of people. The Munda languages, spoken chiefly to-day in Chhota Nagpur and in some districts of Bengal, Orissa, Central Provinces and Madras,

> "are amongst those which have been longest spoken in India, and may, with great probability claim to be aboriginal. It is of importance to note that there exists a common element in them on the one hand; and in the Mou-Khmer languages of further India, in the dialects of certain wild tribes of Malacca and Australasia, and in Nicobarese, on the other, although the two sets of speech are not otherwise connected. This is best explained by the supposition that a common language was once spoken over further India and a great part of India."
>
> *(Imperial Gazetteer.)*

The race, if there was one, that originally spoke a common or connected language between the Vindhyas and the Australian continent is represented to-day only by a few straggling, backward tribes, who may justly claim to be the real natives of India, before whom the Indian home of the Aryan peoples is only a creation of yesterday; while even the more ancient and aboriginal Dravidian seems to be an invader of comparatively recent times. The Aryan invasion of India is some four thousand years old, though to-day the peoples of Aryan speech and descent inhabit the largest section of the country, and aggregate the largest proportion of the population. When they first came into the land of the Five Rivers, they already found there a people, who were, on the Aryans' own evidence, strong and civilised enough to merit the new comers' lasting hostility. They are known in the earliest hymns of the Rig-Veda as the *Panis* or merchants, and the Aryan looked down upon them, almost in the same light in which an English peer of Queen Victoria, — tracing his genealogy to some marauding companion in arms of the Bastard of Normandy, — looked down upon the honest tradesman or burgher with Saxon or British blood in his veins inherited from unrecorded generations of simple working men. "Let the *Panis*, who do not perform sacrifice and do not give gifts, sleep the eternal sleep," says one Poet, addressing the Vedic Goddess of Dawn (R. V. I. 124, 10); while another wonders why the mighty twins, the Aswins, tarry with the *Panis:* "Ignore them, destroy them," exhorts the Seer (R. V. II. 83, 3). Mr. Ramprasad Chanda, writing in the *Memoirs of the Archaeological Survey of India* No. 31, says: —

> "It appears to me that the aboriginal towns-folk with whom the Aryans came into conflict in the Indus Valley are called *Panis* in the hymns of all the books of the Rig-Veda. These are merchants, according to the commentator Yaska; and as the Vedic Aryan had no place in his social system for trade and traders (cp. R. V. 9, 112), the conclusion is not difficult that the much maligned *Panis* were the representatives of an earlier commercial civilisation."

Who were the traders, — despised by the agricultural Aryans, — by race? Were they the advance wing of the Southern Dravidian? Once again, if we rely on the existing speech, we find a most curious phenomenon that may well be related to throw considerable light upon this question. In the hills around Quetta there is a most curious linguistic island. The highlanders speak a dialect, Brahui, which is distinctly Dravidian in its origin. The speakers are, by ethnic characteristics, utterly unrelated to the true Dravidian of southern India; nor is there around them any other tribe or nation speaking a cognate tongue. Being isolated, the language has grown on its own lines independent of the other offshoots of the parent stock, though it lacks a literature of its own and is defective in cultivation. How did this language get into the highlands of Baluchistan? How did the whole Dravida race enter India? Are they the aboriginal natives of the old and vanished Lemurian Continent, now lost under the waves of the Indian Ocean, who, advancing from the South, not in massed bands perhaps, but as isolated adventurers, seeking commercial gain wherever they could find it, colonised each newly discovered and promising land? Even thus did the Phœnician trader, voyaging in the unknown recesses of the Mediterranean, come upon and settle in and colonise and develop into the mighty naval power of Carthage. Even so might the adventurous Dravidian merchant have led his caravans, or sailed his caravels through the Rajputana Sea into the Indus Valley, and thence into the mountain fastnesses of modern Baluchistan, to trade, to develop, and at last to own.

Whatever their origin or wherever their introduction into India, the Dravids are certainly the older inhabitants, older by centuries if not millennia. The evidence for an old, vanished mesozoic Indo-African continent, — in which India, Africa, Australia, and possibly also South America, formed one block of territory, — is by no means so slender or fanciful as to be negligible.[1] But even if we leave it aside as

---

1) cp. W. T. Blanford—*On the Ancient Geography of Gondwana-Land* in the Records of Geological Survey of India, Vol. XXIX.

PLATE XXI

MIXED TYPES (MOHAMEDANS—OUDE)

59   BHALI SOOLTANS
(Oudh)

60   PATHANS
(U. P.)

61 MOHAMEDAN LADY
(Allahbad)

62 GURKHAS KHAS TRIBE
(Mixed Type)

PLATE XX

TYPES OF PRESENT DAY ARYANS

55 BRAHMIN

56 RAJPOOT
(Indo Scythian Type)

57   KASHMIRI PUNDITS

58   BUJGOTEES
(Rajputs of Oudh)

PURE TYPES OF ARYANS: BRAHMINS AND KSHTRIYAS IN GROUPS

PLATE XVIII

ABORIGINES OF INDIA

48 MUNDA FEMALE

49 ORAON COLE

(Chhota Nagpur)

50 HILL NAGA (CACHAR)

51 SONTHAL

48-51, from Watson and Kaye's book "The People of India".

PLATE XIX

52 GROUP OF NAGAS
(Cachar)

54 RENGAM NAGA

53 COLE NATIONAL DANCE

an open question whether human life had come to be in those remote ages; and even if we consider it improbable that a continuity in race and homogeneity in type has been maintained during all these ages, the Dravidian even now continues to be a type by himself, distinct in all important particulars from the Aryan or the Indo-Chinese.

Evidence of the nature and the extent of this ancient, pre-Aryan, Dravid civilisation of India,—though abundant in the South in the shape of stone-circles and megalithic tombs containing cremated remains of the departed heroes,—came to light in the Punjab and Sind only a few years ago. The Harappa and Mahenjo-Daro remains in several strata indicate a very high degree of advancement.

> "Some of the material, presumably the oldest, evinces obvious parallelism to early Mesopotamian remains; the use of brick for building, the interments of contracted bodies in brick cist graves, the shell inlays, the mace-heads and pestles all have the most exact analogues in early Sumerian levels in the Tigris-Euphrates Valley. The beautiful stamp-seals engraved with figures of Bos Primigenius and (?) unicorns, and the curious symbols of their legends, likewise have good Sumerian counterparts, and so, to a less striking degree, have the clay models of rams and female figurines. Finally the painted pottery from the Indus sites is connected through Baluchistan with Elam and southern Mesopotamia, and more vaguely with Seistan and Transcaspia."[1]

The writer dates this connection between India and Western Asia anterior to 2880 B. C., when the cylinder seal was generally adopted in Mesopotamia; and quotes the authority of Dr. Hall *(Ancient History of the Near East)* to argue that the Dravidians of India resemble, in anthropological type, the Sumerians of Mesopotamia. Mr. Codrington, in his *Ancient India* (1926), considers the non-Aryan culture in India to be not only Dravidian but also "the original culture of almost all India;" and finds in it strange parallels to the ancient civilisation of the peoples on the Mediterranean shores.

> "The use of ruddle, gold diadems, trumpets and drums, phallic lucky images and of images in general are a few of the bonds between the two cultures; but above all in importance is the worship of the Great Mother, which is found universally wherever that culture is dominant, which must be called non-Semitic and non-Aryan."

That trade formed no small share of the Dravidian's activities, and adventure no insignificant trait of his character, is amply evidenced, not only by the passages in the Vedic hymns already sampled, but also by the Dravidian words occurring in the ancient Hebrew for certain purely Indian products like the peacock, or rice, or spices. The sea-borne commerce at least, if not the entire foreign trade, of India, was throughout the early recorded history,—and perhaps for centuries before the dawn of history,—indebted for its origin and magnitude to Dravidian enterprise, as is evident from innumerable tales of imperishable folklore, glimpsed by the modern cultured world in such stray creations as the *Jataka* fables. The Vedic Aryan was certainly a stranger to the mysteries of trade; and perhaps because, in his heart of hearts, he envied the enterprise of these sturdy little traders in the lower reaches

---

1) cp. Gordon Childe; *The Aryans*. p. 34. 1927.

of the Indus, he prayed to his tutelary deities for the destruction of these "price-makers," as even now perhaps some intelligent Zulu or advanced Maori might be praying in the unfathomed recesses of his inner consciousness for the speedy destruction of the European traders. To the Arab and the Jew and the Phœnician of the Old Testament days, as well as to the Chinese and the Ceylonese, the spectacle of the Dravid ships and sailors must have been as familiar as the Europeans became in the Indian waters in the age of the Great Mughals. The Dravidian was, however, gradually pressed back in recorded history by the advancing Aryan, whose instinctive race-snobbery is as much in evidence in the epic poem of *Ramayana*, as in any Kipling of our own days. Because the Aryan Valmiki pictures the denizens of the Deccan as monkeys, it would not be historically correct to conclude that the people of the far south in the epic age had not advanced beyond the stage of the Missing Link. On the contrary, there is the amplest evidence to show that the Dravidian Indians had reached a high degree of civilisation, perhaps rather rapidly as all commercial peoples are likely to do; were excellent ship-builders and experienced sailors; good carpenters and passing brick-makers; knew the mysteries of the starry firmament, and had unearthed treasures from the bowels of the earth; could build houses and towns, and even castles and forts, of a defensive value. They knew the mystery of painting and pottery, as shown by the discovery of painted pots in a village of modern Baluchistan, and repeated in the remains near Mahenjo Daro; and seem to have understood the place of fashion in dress and ornament, as evidenced by the fine blue glass-paste bangles, and the statuettes of a goddess wearing a high, out curving head-dress, which was to come into fashion in Europe in XV century A. D. What more could they need to provoke the undying hatred of the snobbish Aryan? Linguistically, these Dravidians might suggest a distant relationship with the primitive Mundaris, who may be remote cousins of the aboriginal Australians. But physically, ethnically, they are a far advanced race, with better brains, if not greater brawns, before whom, it is no wonder, the primitive natives — who have even now not emerged from the Stone Age — went down.

The Dravidians, however, yielded, in their turn, before the greater virility, if not the superior science as well, of the Aryans. These entered India at the close of the third millennium before Christ at the earliest. Who were the Aryans? What was their civilisation like? These are difficult questions, the attempts to answer which have, so far, been more tantalising than satisfying. There are many who claim the Aryans to have been natives of India from time immemorial; but their claim still lacks convincing evidence before the tribunal of history. There are others, who, relying on some astronomical passages in the oldest body of hymns now extant in the whole world, claim for the Vedas and their authors an arctic home and a 7000-year-old origin. There are others yet again, and these the latest and now most fashionable, who have studied the fauna and flora indicated by words of a like sound or a common stem in the various tongues collectively styled the Indo-Germanic languages, and have come to the conclusion that the homeland of all these peoples, when they were yet an undivided family, must have been somewhere between the

Carpathians and the Erzgebirge mountains and the Balkans and the Alps in Central Europe (cp. Dr. Giles in *The Cambridge History of India, Vol. I. p. 68*). These disquisitions would appear to a beginner in history only an argument for arraigning all history as a lying jade.

But, whoever the Aryans may have been originally, and wherever they may have originated, whether they were the Wiros out on a grand hunt from the hills and plateaux of Hungary, or the nomads in search of pasture for their cattle in lands more sunny than the Steppes of Siberia, they appear in the hymns of the Rig-Veda to be settled somewhere along the banks of the Five Rivers. They call their home *Sapta-Sindhu*, which might have been made up of the five existing rivers of the modern Punjab, plus the mighty Indus (Sindhu), and the vanished Saraswati or the Harau'vtis of the Avestan description; or perhaps they included the Kabul and the Kurrum and the Gomal rivers of modern Afghanistan, plus the minor rivers of the Punjab, without counting the final absorbent of them all, the ocean-like Indus.

Whatever their native home, they were a rollicking lot,—these ancient Aryans,—when they first came to this country, and as they appear in the solemn, stately spirited rhythm in the most ancient poetry of the world. A race of tall, stalwart, high-nosed, fair-skinned warriors and priests and peasants, they had the most wonderful genius for poetry. They deified and worshipped all the powers of nature they came to know in their new home; and were by no means averse to the pleasures of the table or of the chase, of dancing and dicing. Their mighty war-god, the thundering Indra, takes the pride of place over the still greater Varuna, who held the post of honour when the Indian and Iranian branches of the Aryans were yet one people and worshipped the same gods. In Greece, another branch of the same family witnesses an identical phenomenon in the gradual displacement of Neptune, the sea-god and father of all gods, by Jove the Thunderer, who heads the pantheon in the classic mythology. The Indian poet of the Vedic hymns made Indra in the image he was most familiar with, or which he most idealised. Drunk with Soma, and fed by welcome oblations of milk and meat and curds and ghee, he slays the dragon Vratra, sets at liberty the fairy princess Ushas (the Dawn), and brings home to the Aryan the much needed kine (rain-clouds). The Aryan's wealth was mostly in cattle, and horses; but though the cow is styled *Aghnya* (not kill-worthy), they did not eschew altogether her flesh or milk. Usually, however, the cow or horse flesh was eaten only after a sacrifice,—horse-flesh particularly to get the strength and swiftness of this most favourite animal of man in all ages.

The Aryans were, however, from the beginning excellent husbandmen; and no prayer is more intense, or more repeated, than that for rains and the success of their husbandry.

> " 'Oh Lord of the field, we will cultivate this field with thee. May the plants be sweet to us; may the rains be full of sweetness; may the Lord of the Field be gracious to us."[1]

---

[1] F. A. Steel—*India Through The Ages.*

The cry has been echoed in India through countless centuries, and is even now as fresh and intense as when it was first uttered in the solemn measure of the Rig-Veda, despite the achievements of modern engineering in irrigation.

So these Aryans lived and thrived in India for two thousand years, stringing their immortal odes to the gods of their hearth and home, and praying for the wealth of their field and fold. Their rhythm is impossible to render in its inimitable sweetness and simplicity in even the filial tongues of the Vedic Sanskrit. But a glimpse of the unrivalled grandeur of their poetic imagination may be had in attempts like these :—

> " Many tinted Dawn ! Th' Immortal daughter of Heaven !
> Young, white-robed, come with thy purple steeds ;
> Follow the path of the dawnings the world has been given,
> Follow the path of the dawn that the world still needs.

> " Darkly shining Dusk, thy sister, has sought her abiding,
> Fear not to trouble her dreams ; daughters ye twain of the Sun,
> Dusk and Dawn bringing birth ! O sisters ! your path is unending ;
> Dead are the first who have watched ; when shall our waking be done ?

> " Bright luminous Dawn ; rose-red, radiant, rejoicing !
> Shew the traveller his road ; the cattle their pasture new ;
> Rouse the beasts of the Earth to their truthful myriad voicing,
> Leader of lightful days ! softening the soil with dew.

> "Wide-expanded Dawn ! Open the gates of the morning ;
> Waken the singing birds ! Guide thou the truthful light
> To uttermost shade of the shadow, for—see you ! the dawning
> Is born, white-shining, out of the gloom of the night."[1]

Thus they lived and loved, and at times fought amongst themselves, no doubt, as brethren are wont to do. More often they warred with their dark-hued Dasyus, whose lands they gradually invaded and overran, till the whole of India from the Himalayas to the Vindhyas, from the Indus to the Ganges and Brahmaputra, became peopled by races of their descent. In the south, beyond the hills of the Vindhya and the Satpura ranges and the streams of the holy Narmada and the sacred Godavari, the Dravidians still held their own. But whatever may have been the intrinsic strength and wealth of their earlier civilisation, it yielded at every step before the steady onward march of the Aryan culture. If the Aryans were Indianised by residence in India, in build and stature and complexion, the Indians were Aryanised in thought and cult and even speech itself. The story of these two thousand years and more is a magnificent epic, rolling on and on in ever-increasing splendour and beauty, with glorious empires and mighty warriors and men like gods, now rising in one spot and anon in another, some conquering and colonising and building and beautifying wherever they went ; others preaching and teaching the truth man has ever yearned for, and ever missed. A full picture of Aryan India needs a vast canvas ; but a cinematographic glimpse may be attempted even in this restricted space.

---

1) F. A. Steel—*India Through The Ages.*

PLATE XXII

63   FRONTIER TRIBESMEN

64   KASHMIRI GIRL   65   AKBAR IN OLD AGE

Of all the races whose advent and acclimatisation in India we have reviewed, we can make three main groups, which, by intermixture, might be increased into any number of divisions: the original Dravidian, the predominant Aryan, the leavening Mongol. Of course, centuries of common life render it more than doubtful if we can find to-day an absolutely pure and unmixed type of any of these. The earliest—aboriginal—type, like the latest super-imposed group, may remain apart. But the principal racial groups mentioned above cannot but have intermixed in the past, and must produce many a mixed type. The outstanding racial characteristics have been thus summarised:—

(1) The pure Dravidian is small in stature, dark—almost black—in complexion, curly-haired, dark-eyed, long-headed and flat-nosed. The nose has always been regarded in India,—at least since the advent and settlement of the long and fine-nosed Aryans,—to be an excellent index of race. Sir Herbert Risley might well generalise "A man's social status in India varies in inverse ratio to the width of his nose." But the inevitable intermixing has made it increasingly difficult to rely on the nose as an unfailing index. Even when joined with eyes and hair, colour and stature, the index is seldom satisfying absolutely. The Dravidian has mixed on the one hand with the advancing Aryan, getting, in the process, an improvement in features and stature and complexion, and formed the Aryo-Dravidian type; on the other hand he has mixed with the Scythians from the north ("lower stature than Turco-Iranian, greater length of head, higher nasal index, a shorter nose") as exampled by the Marathas principally; as well as with the Mongols in the east, who have broad heads, yellowish complexion, scanty hair and low stature; nose fine to broad, face flat, eyes small and oblique.

(2) The Indo-Aryan, on the other hand, chiefly found in Kashmir, the Punjab and Rajputana, is tall, fair, dark-eyed, even as his ancestor of four thousand years ago. Long headed, and fine nostrilled and high-nosed, he is a type still in evidence in the home countries of the Aryans. He has mixed in innumerable sub-groups with the Dravidian and also with the other aborigines, with noticeable variation in feature and complexion.

(3) The peoples of the frontier districts show a greater affinity with the Turco-Iranian than with the Indian types. The characteristics of the former are: high stature, light or fair complexion, dark or grey eyes, broad head, medium nose in width, but high and long and plentiful hair; and the Pathans, Balochs, Sindis, and the allied peoples exhibit these features in the most conspicuous degree.

These various groups necessarily shade off into one another, and are often difficult to demarcate. Corresponding to these, their physical or ethnic differentia, there may be moral and intellectual differences as well. Let us study them through

their marks on the history of this country, and their quota to the enrichment of
the civilisation of this people.

      *   *   *   *   *   *

The Vedic Aryans lived in scattered hamlets or small villages, but their
descendants soon learnt the art of city-building, and the chief amongst them lived
in splendid capitals of gorgeous palaces, with parks and gardens and fountains
that never failed to call forth the envy of every intelligent and observant foreign
visitor. Look at his very likely contemporary picture of Ayodhya, the capital of
the Raghus:—

> " And his town like Indra's city,—tower and dome and turret brave—
> Rose in proud and peerless beauty, on Sarayu's limpid wave,
>
>   *   *   *   *   *
>
> " Altar blazed in every mansion, from each home was bounty given
> Stooped no man to fulsome falsehood, questioned none the will of heaven.
>
>   *   *   *   *   *
>
> Strong barred gates and lofty arches, tower and dome and turret high,
> Decked the vast and peopled city, fair as mansions of the sky." [1]

This may seem to the cold critical eye of the historian an over-coloured picture. If
so, let him consider the unbiassed description of the capital of the mighty
Mauryas by a Greek ambassador to the court of Chandragupta. The Mauryan
capital was founded in the fifth century before Christ, at the confluence of the
Ganges and the Son, on the site of modern Patna and Bankipore, and remained
the Imperial capital of India to the end of the Gupta dynasty—a period of close on
a thousand years. It was a long, narrow parallelogram, 9 miles by $1\frac{3}{4}$ miles. A
wooden palisade went all around the city, serving it for a rampart; and the defence
was further secured by a broad (200 yards), deep (30 feet), moat, which also did
duty as the common sewer. The rampart was at intervals pierced with loop-holes
for the guardians of the city to shoot through on an approaching or besieging
enemy; while towers or bastions, 570 in all, helped along the palisade as rallying
places for the garrison. The city opened upon the river by no less than sixty
gates, a wealth of exit greater than even that of the classic Delhi. Though an
Imperial seat of Government, the situation of Pataliputra forbade any but a
wooden rampart like in a Vedic Pur, as the heavy rain and tremendous floods in
the river would make as little account of stone or brick walls as of wood. Other
towns, however, more favourably situated on the crest of hills in the depths of a
forest, were fortified with much stronger and more durable defences, with battle-
ments, towers, covered approaches, and strong-barred gates, flanked by guard-
houses, for the defence of the city in war and its good order in peace.

The royal palace of the Mauryas at Pataliputra was a vast enclosure, made
chiefly of timber. Within, it was in no way inferior in size or magnificence to the
palaces of Susa and Ecbatana, or even to those of the Great Mughals two thousand
years later. Round the Royal palace stretched a noble park, in which peacocks—
prime favourites with Indian princes all through our history—preened themselves
for the delectation of the Prince and his consorts.

---

1) R. C. Dutt's *Ramayana*.

PLATE XXIII

A TODA GIRL

Painting by Rao Bahadur M. V. Dhurandhar

"There were shady groves and trees set in clumps and branches woven together by some special cunning of horticulture .... Birds are there free and unconfined; they come of their own accord and have their nests and roosting places in the branches, both birds of other kinds and parrots which are kept there and flock in bevies about the King...... In this Royal pleasance there are lovely tanks made by hand of men, with fishes in them very large and gentle, and nobody may catch them except the sons of the king, when they are yet children."[1]

So wonderful was the structure of this gorgeous edifice that the Chinese pilgrim, Fa-Hien, seven hundred years later, ascribed it to special divine creation.

The Emperor Chandragupta was served in basins and goblets of solid gold, some of them 6 feet in diameter, or copper plate studded with precious stones.

"When the king condescended to show himself in public, he was carried in a golden palanquin, adorned with tassels of pearls, and was clothed in fine muslin embroidered with purple and gold. When making short journeys, he rode on horseback, but when travelling longer distances he was mounted, like a modern Raja, on an elephant with golden trappings."[2]

As a pendant to this picture, let us take a leap of some seventeen hundred years and note, in passing, the testimony of another foreign visitor to another Imperial seat. Abdur Razzak, the Persian ambassador to the court of Vijayanagar, becomes almost dythrambic while speaking of the Emperor, Deva Raya II, and his palace. He records:—

"Over all this magnificent space were erected numerous pavilions, to the height of three, four or even five storeys, covered from top to bottom with figures in relief. * * * * Some of these pavilions were arranged in such a manner that they could turn rapidly round and present a new face; at each moment a new chamber or a new hall presented itself to the view." * * * * * * * * * *

"The throne, which was of extraordinary size, was made of gold and enriched with precious stones of extreme value. * * * * Before the throne was a square cushion, on the edges of which were sewn three rows of pearls. * * * * When the feast of Mahanavami was ended, at the hour of evening prayer, I was introduced in the middle of four estrades, which were about ten *gaz* both in length and breadth. The roofs and the walls were entirely formed of plates of gold enriched with precious stones. Each of these plates was as thick as the blade of a sword, and was fastened with golden nails."[3]

These, alas, are splendours of a vanished past; let us rather continue the outlines of the picture of society among the ancient Aryans. The early Aryans were a people divided amongst themselves by the narrowing sentiment of the family, the clan, the tribe, and united only in their common hatred of the native Dasyus whom they were anxious to overthrow. From the earliest days and in the earliest hymns we read of kings. It may safely be affirmed that the tribes of the Rig-Vedic Aryans were under kingly rule; they might have evolved more liberal and freer

---

1) Aelian—quoted in *Cambridge History of India*, Vol. I, p. 411-12.
2) Vincent A. Smith—*Early History of India*, p. 128. (Oxford, 1924.)
3) Sewell—*A Forgotten Empire*.

7

forms of Government. From the moment of its birth on the Indian soil, the Aryan royalty was hereditary, though the rules of descent are by no means definite. Election might have had its chance at times, or in a round manner, somewhat in the same style, perhaps, as the First Commanders of the Faithful may be said to have been elected. The story of Rama and Bhishma, parallelled many a time in more recent Rajput history, may be taken to illustrate the growing custom of primogeniture, though the historic precedents of the designation of their successors by the Maurya as well as the Gupta emperors implies a latitude of choice somewhat at variance with the uniform rule of primogeniture.

The chief—or at least the most emphasised—function of the Vedic King was to lead his hosts in war, and to perform sacrifices in peace. His companions were also more soldiers than statesmen, except, perhaps, the family bard, the Minstrel and Herald and Chaplain combined. So passionately, indeed, was military renown loved, that no great name in Indian history,—from Divodasa and Sudas of the Vedic days, and the Mauryas and the Guptas and Harsha of medieval times, to the last of the Great Mughals,—is without its resplendent halo of war-like fame. Even Asoka the Pious can scarcely be ranked as an exception. The thirst for military renown was tempered and refined by the laws of chivalry, evolved by an unbroken practice of untold centuries. A stratagem permissible to a general must not degenerate into a subterfuge degrading to an individual warrior. Alexander of Macedon, fierce warrior as he was, could not but admire the ringing challenge of the beaten Porus,— a foeman worthy of his steel.

> "With one, who has thrown away his sword, with one fallen, with one yielding, with woman and one bearing the name of woman, or with a low, vulgar fellow,—with all these I do not battle,"

says the mighty Bhisma, the first and greatest and strongest of the myriad warriors met on the epic field of Kurukshetra; and this code of the Warrior's honour was ever obeyed wherever Aryan chivalry was understood and practised.

When however foes began to swarm in the country, who could not understand, or would not respect, these refinements of War's high etiquette, the valiant vanquished marked their contempt of their conquerors by the awful rites of *Jauhur*. Rather than fall into the hands of these barbarians, women mounted the funeral pyre with every token of rejoicing; and their men, now safe from the sting of any outrage on their beloved, rushed out with one single thought to kill and be killed, without quarter asked or offered.

Another noteworthy trait of Aryan chivalry was in regard to their duty of asylum to the distressed.

> Their kingdoms may be lost; their capitals destroyed; their palaces ruined, their places of worship desecrated; but the princely Rajput would never refuse shelter to him who asks for it even though an enemy.

During the period of Aryan supremacy in India, the country witnessed many an Empire, before the size and wealth of which the modern British Empire in India

PLATE XXIV

A KASHMIR GIRL.

Painting by Rao Bahadur M. V. Dhurandhar

loses all its characteristics of awful grandeur. Setting aside the legendary grandeur of epic or Pauranic *Chakravartins*, we find the earliest known authentic empire of the Mauryas as extensive, as powerful, as prosperous, as the greatest that has since grown up on the same soil. Chandragupta, the first and greatest of the Mauryas, had served his apprenticeship under Alexander of Macedon. Graduating through the school of adversity, the Maurya,—perhaps a royal bastard like William of Normandy,—fought and won his patrimony in Magadha; cajoled, coerced or conquered his allies; vanquished in battle, as well as in diplomacy, the most considerable of Alexander's successors; and built up an empire, which stretched from the Oxus and the Jordan, through modern Afghanistan and Baluchistan, down to the barren coast-line of Mekran on the Arabian Sea, and to the mouths of the Ganges and the Brahmaputra in the Bay of Bengal. His more famous successor, the Emperor Asoka Vardhana, added only the coastal strip along the Coromandel Sea-board, which served to round an empire that for a hundred and fifty years was guarded by the might and governed by the wisdom of a succession of warlike, yet pious, rulers.

The Empires which took its place in the succeeding centuries never quite attained to the might or magnitude of the Maurya State. The sovereignty of the Kushan Kanishka extended, it is true, far beyond the limits of the Mauryan Empire, at its best. But it may be questioned if Kanishka could really be called an Indian, despite his capital at or near modern Peshawar, and despite his ardent Buddhism, which bade fair to eclipse the fame even of the great Asoka. The Kushan dominion from A. D. 40 to A. D. 220 was followed by the more truly Indian Empire of the Guptas, which was at its zenith from 308 A. D. to 455 A. D. and struggled on for another 75 years, more or less in the manner that the descendants of Aurangzeb struggled on after the end of the Great Mughal. The Gupta dominion is famous for the conquests of three successive warriors, who carried their standards to within sight of the southern seas. It was more famous still for that unparalleled blossoming of the literary genius of India, which has justly earned for this epoch the title of the Golden Age of Sanskrit Literature. The incomparable Kalidasa, courtly and cultured prince of dramatists as he was the dramatist of princes; the Astronomer-Royal and Master of Mathematics; and the Lexicographer Imperial—were all gems that stand towering for all time, and were eminent even amongst that brilliant galaxy of talent and genius that adorned the court of the Guptas. The Government of the Guptas was strong yet popular, not merely because it was native and sympathetic, but because it practised to its utmost the one great virtue of successful government in India: perfect toleration of all forms of belief, perfect freedom to all forms of worship, perfect aloofness of the State from all forms of ritual and symbolism. The Emperors were not without religion; but they were also not without enlightenment. And so they protected and cherished and governed all alike,— the Brahman and the Buddhist, the Jain and the Charvak. They felt, if they did not avow, the futility of man striving to solve the riddle of the universe, to determine the aim of being, to define the purpose of life.

"But leave the Wise to wrangle, and with me
    The quarrel of the Universe let be:
    And, in some corner of the Hubbub coucht,
    Make Game of that which makes as much of Thee.
"For in and out, above, about, below,
    'Tis nothing but a Magic Shadow Show
    Play'd in a Box whose candle is the Sun,
    Round which we Phantom Figures come and go."

Their less worthy successors suffered a decline in Imperial possessions as well as splendour, till early in the seventh century rose the great Shiladitya or Shri Harsha, with his capital at Kanauj. His conquests extended the Empire in the East almost to the borders of Assam, and on the west to the shores of the Arabian Ocean. The King of Kamarupa—modern Assam—was his ally, even as the Nizam to-day is the ally of the King-Emperor. The friendship and obedience of the King of Valabhi—Gujarat—was secured by the charms of the Emperor's daughter given in marriage to a grateful prince. The fame of Harsha has been immortalised by the greatest novelist of classic Sanskrit,—a master-craftsman, whose versatile genius scintillates through countless pages of his patron's biography, as much as through the deathless story of Kadambari. The Emperor was a creative artist, himself, of no mean genius. His appreciation, therefore, was doubly welcome to the lesser stars of the Imperial firmament, because he could enter fully into the adoration of the tuneful muse. A warrior in camp and a statesman at court; a poet in his palace and a devotee in the temple; a refined diplomatist and a respected despot, he was a worthy successor to the glories of the Mauryas and the grandeur of the Guptas.

For five hundred years after Harsha, the history of India,—even of Hindusthan proper,—is either unknown or uninteresting. In the interval before the Muslim invasion, there are, indeed, individual peaks and isolated eminences, all the more impressive because they seem to be solitary specimens of loftiness of soul or grandeur of purpose. The exploits of a Siddha-Raj of Gujarat might claim our admiration, as the courage and misfortunes of a Prithwi-Raj claim in turn our wonder and our commiseration. But to the student pursuing the thread of continued solidarity, the imperial idea does not seem to blossom forth until the throne of the Mauryans and sceptre of the Guptas had passed into the hands of a new race.

*   *   *   *   *

With the advent of the Muslims, a few surface changes seem to be manifest. These new-comers were alien by race as well as by religion, by culture and civilisation as well as by tradition and temperament. It is only when we review the consequences of their conquest and assimilation in India, in the dispassionate atmosphere of centuries after the event, that we may be able at all to claim to be rendering them justice. The vision of contemporaries is bound to be narrow, their outlook prejudiced, their judgment too much biassed in the clash of continued conflict, perhaps with its open festering sores, to be able to be just, impartial, and trustworthy on

PLATE XXV

A GOND WOMAN

(Painting by Rao Bahadur M. V. Dhurandhar)

all points. The cultured and poetic, even though bigoted and iconoclastic, Arab never really found a footing on Indian soil, though the sovereigns of India who reigned at Delhi for six hundred years claimed the Prophet of Arabia as their Light in this world and intercessor in the next. But what the gentle, refined, chivalrous Arab could not accomplish, the convert to his sword had little difficulty in achieving. The fierce, untutored, half-savage hordes, which the iconoclastic zeal of Mahmud of Ghazni, or the more constructive statesmanship of Shahabuddin, led into India, proved lucky as they were fanatical, ferocious and determined. After a couple of centuries of struggle and vicissitudes, and thanks chiefly to the internecine jealousies of the contemporary Indian potentates, the Muhammadan power was at last established at Delhi in the closing years of the twelfth century of the Christian era. From Delhi, the new power rapidly spread, till, within a hundred years of its establishment, it had overrun the entire continent from north to south, from east to west. A mosque was built by an ennobled slave and enterprising general of Alauddin Khilji on the Southernmost extremity of India to mark the triumph of the Crescent, even if it did not mean an equal spread of the Quran. And though raids like these could scarcely be dignified by the name of permanent conquest, the cry of the Muezzin, acknowledging the one God as the only God and Muhammad as His Prophet, was destined thenceforth to resound through all the centres of the Indo-Gangetic plain. Hindu India was not destroyed; Hindu creed and culture could not be annihilated; Hindu power and pride could not be extinguished altogether. On the contrary, driven to be on the defensive, Hinduism unconsciously arrested the process of development; and reinforced itself by a timely alliance with the sentiment of self-preservation, which thenceforward mobilised all that was virile and living, the ideals as well as the forms, the philosophy as well as the ritual, of a people on the defensive.

Islam began aggressively; continued to act on the offensive, and has remained in the country by assimilating all that was worth acquiring and adopting in the Indian civilisation and organisation. It failed to Islamise India. But the magic spell of this ancient land fell upon Islam, and Islam was Indianised in art and culture, in social grouping and political structure. Caste, for instance, is the most outstanding peculiarity of the Indian—the Hindu—social organisation. Nothing can be more foreign to the genius of Islam,—or of Christianity, for the matter of that,—than caste. And yet the Musalmans in India are as minutely split up into castes as the Hindus in any part of India. Even idolatry,—in the guise of deification of saints and heroes,— is not altogether unknown in Islam as practised in India to-day. If the Muslim has been Indianised in these essential matters, need we at all question the prevalence of the process in the less important concerns of dress and manners; of food and furniture?

The submission to this unspeakable magnetism of India was, in fact, the measure of the real greatness and success of the Musalman dominion in this country. Though the Afghans and the Turks, who gave us the early Musalman rulers, came rapidly under this spell, they were not so completely acclimatised and assimilated as the

8

Mughals. It may be regarded as an accident or a mystery of history that the race of Timur should have bred a cultured soul and a poetic statesman like Babur. But given Babur—the warrior-poet and the philosopher-emperor,—it is not surprising that we should have Akbar the Great, Jahangir the Æsthetic, Shah Jahan the Magnificent, and even Alamgir the Annexationist. Art and literature; science and philosophy; industries and commerce, had never flourished in India as a whole quite as much as in the 150 years of the Great Mughals' rule, with the possible exception of the Gupta Empire of a thousand years before. Akbar was the greatest of the Mughals, and perhaps the greatest of all Indian rulers for a thousand years, if not even since the days of the mighty Mauryas. But, without detracting in the least from the genius of the man or the inheritance of his birth, it may yet be said that Akbar was so great, because he was so thoroughly Indianised. His genius perceived the possibilities, and his courage undertook the task, of welding the two communities into a common nation by the universal bond of common service and equal citizenship of a magnificent empire. Akbar was born a master of men, and bred an autocrat in an age of despotism. It would be unjust to criticise him by the canons of another age, or from the standpoint of other ideals. Within the legitimate limits of a most searching criticism, there is much,—very much, indeed,—in his life and outlook and achievements, which must demand our unstinted, unqualified admiration, and little that could merit just censure. His successors were, indeed, not of his calibre. But the wonder is rather that such a high average of talent should be maintained by such a number of succeeding sovereigns of the same family. Even Alamgir, the last of the Great Mughals, who is blamed by many historians, by a sort of *post factum* wisdom, for the Decline and Fall of the Empire of the Mughals, was great in his own way, had his own strain of lofty ambition, his own conception of imperial solidarity. If events have proved his policy to have been mistaken at times, we must remember, in judging him, the tradition and environment in which he lived. The fact of conquest and annexation, even of Musalman kingdoms, could not possibly be a fault, and much less a crime, in the eyes of a scion of the warrior House of Timur. And the overthrow of the Shia power in the Deccan must needs appear a meritorious act in the eyes of a strong Sunni like Aurangzeb, especially as he could justly claim, for his reign at least, to have extinguished the Maratha menace after the defeat, capture and death of Sambhaji Maharaj. Aurangzeb may have lacked, in his personal character, all that is amiable or attractive. We may censure him as a son, condemn him as a brother; we may accuse him as a master, and arraign him as an associate; we may doubt his sincerity, question his loyalty, condemn his fanaticism. But we cannot deny his courage as soldier, talent as commander, acumen as statesman, devotion, simplicity, and, withal, greatness as Emperor.

* * * * * * * * * * *

Thus flits the pageant of the Indian people on the stage of history. The story is too vast, its parts too intricate and complex, to be effectively summarised as we have here sought to do. The glimpses here given are but the outstanding features from an endless, deathless story; but even these few glimpses would suffice to give some idea of the greatness and glory, the splendour and magnificence that was India in the past.

*　　　*　　　*　　　*　　　*

In the panorama of the Indian people we are here picturing, the ups and downs of the last two hundred years are relatively unimportant. The Maratha outburst is only a Hindu resurgence, short-lived, though wide-spread; neither deep nor abiding, perhaps, but still significant, if only of the undestroyed and indestructible vitality of the Indian race. Greece and Rome and Egypt have vanished from the face of the earth, their gods a myth, their people a name, their civilisation,— mostly ruins. But India still lives. She may be eclipsed; she may be oppressed. But she has an immortal soul, an invincible spirit that will not yield. The soul of a people cannot die.

CHAPTER III
HEROES AND SAINTS

In a history so long as that of India, and for a people so mixed and varied as the Indian, there could be, of course, no paucity of the stories of saints and heroes that charm our infancy, fire our youth, and are our support in an age of decline and decay. There is a veritable *embarras de richesse* in the selection of suitable illustrations of heroism or goodness, both of men and women, which would show, in their endless variety, something that may fairly be called India. Heroism is native in every people; so that in the heroes of our history it would be absurd to claim a pride of exclusive proprietorship. Even goodness is not the peculiar privilege of any one people or any single age; though its forms are infinitely varied, and the conception of true saintliness may often differ from country to country and from time to time. The Heroes and Saints of India still await a greater than Plutarch to sing their praises in bewitching strains and divine rhythm. We shall here select only a few outstanding examples of heroes and saints, who, without owing very much to their birth or environment, are yet entitled by their achievements to rank among the master-builders of national life and character.

The heroes of the earliest age of Indian history are vague personages, so mixed up with their prototypes the idealised and deified personalities, that it is impossible to segregate and consider apart their human achievements. The one great event of the earliest Vedic Age, which is at all historical, is the war of the Ten Kings. The leader of the Bharata tribe in this conflict was King Sudas, of the Tritsu family, whose family priest was the celebrated Vashishtha. The classic strife also, between the rival sages, the Brahman Vashishtha and the Warrior Vishwamitra, makes its appearance on the stage of Indian history for the first time in this war. Revenge, said the ancients, is the food of the gods. It was to avenge his wounded vanity that Vishwamitra, superseded in his pontificate with the Bharatas by his hated and unapproachable rival Vashishtha, effected an alliance of the Ten Tribes against the undutiful Sudas. But, unlike the later similar alliance made for the Maurya hero, Chandragupta, by his immortal guide, friend and philosopher, Vishnugupta, better, known to history as Chanakya, this Vishwamitra was doomed to disappointment. Sudas defeated his enemies in a mighty battle on the banks of the Purushni, the modern Ravi. Little,—a very little—more is known of this mighty warrior of the Vedic Age, except that his was a life of incessant warfare, and a career of unbroken victories. Immediately after this battle of the Ravi, he had to rush back,—almost like Hindenburg rushing from the Western Front to fight the magnificent battles of the Masurian Lakes,—to the other extremity of his kingdom, to fight and defeat on the Jumna another alliance of three other clans, who were made uneasy by his growing dominion.

Shadowy and legendary as this personality is, Sudas seems to have sprung from an illustrious warrior stock. His father,—or perhaps grandfather, Divodas,—was no less a warrior and conqueror. He had won by his mighty exploits the cognomen of the "Servant of Heaven," and the "Slayer of Kine for Guests" *(Atithigva)*, somewhat perhaps in the style of Clovis's title of the Eldest Son of the Church, or Henry VIII's *Fidei Defensor*. He fought all round and everyone, just because war was the breath of his nostrils. He fought and beat the Aryan tribes of the Turvacas, Yadus, and the Purus, with as much zest as he fought the non-Aryan Dasa, Shambara, or the Panis, the merchants of the Indus Valley. But of solid achievement or Empire-building, as the result of these wars, we have little evidence worth the name.

The gods of the Vedic age, were, perhaps, none other than deified heroes, who had once worn a mortal shape, but the grandeur of whose achievements had so dazzled contemporaries as to find them a special niche in the Pantheon for all generations to come. Indra and Mitra, if not Varuna and Agni, seem little better, at least in their personified aspect. Though dual or multiple gods,—like the Earth-and-Sky, or the Maruts,—not to mention the single, but elusive, yet fascinating personality of the Goddess of Dawn, may suggest greater resemblance of the entire Pantheon to deified powers of nature, one regrets to relinquish the amazingly personal magnetism of these human—all too human—beings. One-fourth of the hymns in the Rig Veda are in honour of Indra, the mightiest, but also the most human, of the gods. A mighty fighter,—big of bone and large of limbs, golden-haired, broad-chested, mace-bearing hero,—he loves to drink Soma; and is not above loudly singing his own praises. His greatest exploit is the conquest of the demon *Vritra* who had imprisoned the cows (rains), a common calamity even now to the countrymen in India. It is but in the fitness of things that against this common curse of the nation the greatest of the Gods should engage in ever-renewed strife. His mighty thunderbolt, that none may withstand, cleaves the Demon into two, and the ever welcome rains are free to fructify the parched fields of the Aryans.

In marked contrast with the rollicking fighter, is the calm, serene, steady image of Varuna, second only to Indra in importance in the Vedic Pantheon; and that, too, if we reckon by the number of hymns dedicated to him. He is the presiding deity of the sacrifice, the genius of law and order in the universe. Endowed with all the human features, he is yet the author of heaven and earth, the creator of the sun, the father of fire, the parent of air. The moon and the stars shine by his orders; rivers flow at his command, while the ocean marks for ever the limits laid down by him. His dominion is universal; his omniscience is unquestioned. But his greatness is of the mind, and not of the brute force that Indra personifies. Nowhere else in all the hymns of the Rig Veda do we find that note of real trust in the Divine adored—that veritable *cri de coeur*—as in the hymns of Varuna.[1]

---

1) *Hymns from the Rig-Veda*—by Macdonnel, with changes.

"Who is, O Varuna, Thy constant kinsman?
Once dear, though sinful now, he claims Thy friendship.
As guilty, make us not, O Wise one, suffer!
Do Thou, O Sage, grant shelter to Thy praiser.
O make us in these earthly homes abiding.
Find favour now in Aditi's lap residing!
And may from his chains Varuna release us.
Ye Gods—for ever more protect and bless us."

It would take us too far afield, if we strayed to cast even a glance at the minor gods of the Pantheon. The goddesses in the Vedic Age are few and insignificant, probably because in the Aryan society woman's less spectacular virtues could not arrest attention. Indrani—the wife of Indra—is little better than a charming plaything of the warrior god. Not so, however, the ever young Goddess of the Dawn— Ushas. This Aurora of the Vedas is ever fleeing the Sun in his golden chariot, drawn by fiery steeds, in endless pursuit of an unattainable and yet unrelinquishable ideal. This Goddess of Youth is the spirit of childhood, innocent as insouciant, clothed in spotless raiment, bright and filmy. Like some heavenly dancer, she has sworn eternal war with the spirit of Darkness and all its brood of nightmares, ghosts and evil thoughts. "Daughter of Heaven", she is the longed-for bride of the Sun, and yet his mother, because to the world of mortals she is ever the harbinger of his light and warmth. The humble, homely god, Agni—the deity of every Aryan home—is also her lover, whom she kindles into life afresh each morning on every hearth as soon as she appears.

More human, though still shadowy in point of history and achievements, are those great High Priests of the early Aryans, who first composed the Vedic hymns. The sacred books of the Hindus represent the Seven Sages, the first Seers of the eternal Rig—as the mind-born sons of Brahma, the God of Creation. These seven, whose names are not identical in every list, are immortals, now residing in their stellar mansions in the constellation of the Great Bear. Gautama, Bharadwaja, Vishwamitra, Jamadagni, Vashishtha, Kashyapa and Atri are the Seven most commonly given. Their doings are, in general, fabulous and incredible. But the frequently mentioned and long-continued duel between Vashishtha and Vishwamitra obviously embodies a substratum of historical truth that cannot be denied an element of grandeur. Vashishtha is reputed to be the author of the seventh Mandala in the Rig Veda, while Vishwamitra is credited with the composition of the third. According to classic mythology, Vashishtha had the advantage of birth, being born a Brahman; though a hymn in the Vedas considers his birth to be the result of a passing fancy of the Gods, Mitra and Varuna, for the heavenly nymph Urvasi. Vishwamitra, however, has a less romantic origin, and was better endowed with worldly wealth. Born a king's son, he had no difficulty in attaining to the dignity and powers of a Royal Sage, when he was so minded. But the boundless ambition of this determined, austere, unswerving Kshatriya would not be satisfied with that rank. He would rather be first in hell than second in heaven. Sudas, the Vedic King, seems to have

PLATE XXVI

9 BRAHMĀNAM ĪSHAM KAMALASANASTHAM

(The Prince of Wales Museum, Bombay)

50 KRISHNA

Hiding on a Tree with the Clothes
of the Gopis

71 VISHNU

On Garuda with Shri Devi and
Bhu Devi

72 PARVATI

(Wife of Shiva)

73 KRISHNA

Dancing on the Kaliya Serpent

(No. 74, The Government Museum, Madras)

74 SURYA

On Chariot

been his first protege and experiment for displaying his vast powers. But that prince preferred the priestly Vashishtha for his Primate, and was justified in his choice by the end, in which he defeated the Ten Tribes whom the furious Vishwamitra had allied against him. This much appears to be sober history. The rest, even if it is grounded in fact, is so highly embroidered by fancy, that, in these days of hard-headed materialism, it will be summarily dismissed as incredible. The moral, however, is perfectly clear. Vishwamitra was determined, as he was daring. He is beaten again and again; but he holds on in grim determination, till at last he achieves his mighty ambition.

Equally fabulous is the origin of Vashishtha's uterine brother, Agastya; but the latter's role is much more modest. A renowned sage, and an author of several hymns in the Rig-Veda, his credit must needs have a dose of the marvellous. If the legends of his drinking the ocean, and beating back the Vindhyas to make him a pathway to the unknown South, have no foundation in fact, he seems to have been the first of the great Aryan Seers to cross the mountains and reach the ocean on the south-western coast. The Ramayana speaks of him as living in a hermitage on Mount Kunja, south of the Vindhya mountain; and, if we may read this legendary lore in a historical perspective, he seems to have been the first to Aryanise the Deccan. He is held to be the first teacher of science and literature to the Tamils, whose language he took a great share in moulding.

*   *   *   *   *   *

The ideals and conditions of the Vedic age become sensibly modified in the mould of Indian environment by the time we come to the epic age. The personages of the Epics are distinctly Indianised, even though they still mark the original type very clearly. Take the instance of Ramachandra, the hero of the *Ramayana*. A warrior born and bred, he is as different from the Indra of the Vedas as could possibly be imagined. A dutiful son, a loving brother, a devoted husband, he is unavoidably a good king, a gentle knight, a noble friend, a generous foe, whose human perfections seem to be so complete that one is not surprised at all when one is told he was the essence of Godhead incarnate. A man, he has all a mortal's share of sorrow and suffering, of trial and hardship; but these serve to bring out his indisputable humanity. The eldest born of King Dasharatha of Ayodhya, the modern Oudh; and renowned in his youth by his great exploit of breaking the bow of the Great God Shiva at the time of Princess Sita's choice of a husband, Rama yet experiences the mortal's lot of disappointment on the very eve of realisation. On the day he was to have been anointed Heir Apparent, his father is compelled by his stepmother to exile him for a period of 14 years, and give the dignity of the Crown Prince to her own son Bharata. Kaikeyi, the petted queen of Dasharatha, was only asking payment of an old bond—the fulfilment of a promise her lord had made to her in a moment when her pluck and courage had stood him in excellent stead. Dasharatha could not refuse her without being forsworn, though it killed him to comply. And Rama was not a Prince to commence his new role by making his father be forsworn. So to the forest he would go, though his own mother weep, and his father swoon, and his peoples break their hearts. Only Sita,—his wife and Queen,—will not be denied, and Lakshmana his devoted brother. Rama tried to dissuade Sita from accompanying him into the forest, but the high-souled Princess would have none of it:—

"Lightly I dismiss the counsel which my lord hath lightly said,
For it ill becomes a warrior and my husband's princely grade!
For the faithful woman follows where her wedded lord may lead,
In the banishment of Rama, Sita's exile is decreed."

The brother's devotion is even more touching, though the wife's has come down to us for all these countless generations as the model and the ideal of wifely devotion. Anyway, these three went into exile; and the story of that exile is perhaps the most touching portion of the poem. The plot thickens, and the action quickens, and the drama moves on to its inevitable *denouement* when the sister of the demon king, Ravana of Lanka sees Rama and falls in love with him. Denied by him as well as his brother, she flies into a rage, and rushes to fetch Ravana to avenge her wounded vanity. Hell hath no fury like a woman scorned; and Surpanakha was true to type. But Ravana,—mighty, ten-headed warrior as he was, and lord of all the demons,—dared not touch Sita while Rama or Lakshmana were by. And so he devised the ruse, with the help of a Rakshasa sage Marichi, of a golden deer, which Sita had but to see to covet. Sita was a veritable woman in her love of the beautiful; and though common sense told Rama a golden deer was impossible; and that, even if real, it must conceal some plot, he could not refuse the prayers of Sita to kill it and fetch its skin. Thereupon Rama leaves her in charge of Lakshmana. Ravana durst not brave even the cadet of the Raghus; and so he instructs his tool Marichi to cry for Lakshmana, as the arrow of Rama pierces him, letting Sita fear her husband was worsted. Lakshmana would no more believe that it was Rama's veritable cry for succour than Rama himself had believed that there could be a real, live, golden deer! But Sita's reproaches became atrocious; she charged Lakshmana with coveting the wife of his elder brother as the only reason for his indifference to the safety of Rama! Poor Lakshmana could bear it no longer. He drew a charmed circle to protect Sita, and left the cottage in search of his brother. All that was, however, of little avail against the wiles of Ravana and the impulsive hospitality of Sita. She left the charmed circle only for a moment to give alms to a mendicant who came begging at her door. But that moment was fatal. The mendicant was Ravana in disguise, who bore her away to his capital in the far, far south, girt by the seas and guarded by the demons.

The martial strain of the narrative henceforth gathers force at each step, till the end comes, in which the proud Lord of Lanka is laid low in the dust; and Sita is restored to the arms of her husband. The new personages who ally themselves with Rama in his struggle with Ravana are, in sober history, the aborigines of the Deccan. Some of them have become, like Hanuman, household names in India ever since. Rama, too, shows himself every inch a king to friend and foe alike,—to Sugriva, Hanuman and Vibhishana, no less than to Indrajit, Kumbhakarna and Ravana himself.

Only to Sita is he less than just; for had she not been defiled by the polluting touch of Ravana's arms—even though against her will? But the God of Fire is at hand to vindicate and purify the Daughter of the Earth, and silently rebuke even the god-like Rama for his doubts.

> "Wherefore spake you not, my Rama, if your bosom doubts my faith,
> Dearer than a dark suspicion to a woman were her death?
> Wherefore, Rama, with your token came your vassal o'er the wave,
> To assist a fallen woman, and tainted wife to save?
>
> "But a woman pleadeth vainly when suspicion clouds her name.
> Lakshman, if thou lov'st thy sister, light for me the funeral flame.
>
> "If in act and thought" she uttered, "I am true unto my name,
> Witness of our sins and virtues, may this Fire protect my fame!
> If a false and lying scandal brings a faithful woman shame,
> Witness of our sins and virtues, may this Fire protect my fame!"
>
> Slow the red flames rolled asunder, God of Fire incarnate came,
> Holding in his radiant bosom fair Videha's sinless dame,
> Not a curl upon her tresses, not a blossom on her brow,
> Not a fibre of her mantle did with tarnished lustre glow!
>
> Rama's forehead was unclouded, and a radiance lit his eye
> And his bosom heaved in gladness as he spake in accents high:
> "Never from the time I saw her in her maiden days of youth,
> Have I doubted Sita's virtue, Sita's fixed and changeless truth."

The God in Rama may have known all along the purity of Sita, but the man in him was weak enough to doubt. His weakness is the more evident when, once more, crowned and reigning in his own native land, he exiles the pregnant Sita, because a citizen had voiced his suspicions of the Queen. Once again Sita's purity is proved, years after, when her twin-born sons are reciting the *Ramayana* as minstrel boys at the great sacrifice; but the long-suffering daughter of the Universal Mother would have no more of earthly bliss, and is absorbed at last into her parent earth.

The Golden age of the Aryan heroes passes away with the days of Rama and his brothers, who probably flourished late in the second millennium before Christ. Men cease to be the models of truth and simplicity and sincerity, and single-hearted devotion to whatever was their aim in life. Women also decline from the lofty standard of Sita's ideal of love and devotion and unsullied chastity of mind and body. The age of Sitas and Savitris is over; and there is even greater moral distance between them and the Kuntis and the Draupadis of the *Mahabharata* fame, than between Rama and Krishna, or the Pandavas and the Kauravas. Rama is moral perfection embodied, *a preux chevalier sans peur et sans reproche.*

10

Krishna also is mighty; and if a baffling genius for diplomacy of the most tortuous kind must claim our admiration, he too is great. He is greater even, as the author and teacher of that quintessence of the Hindu philosophy known as the *Bhagavad Gita*. But though that work preaches unruffled serenity born of utter peace, Krishna himself is far from a model of lofty motives and unblemished character. He is the Indian Gay Lothario, whose flirtations with the women of Vraj are but poorly extenuated by any hint of his divine personality, whom naught can bind or besmirch.

The God Vishnu incarnate, Krishna was born man for the purpose of destroying the demon Kamsa, his own maternal uncle. His parents were in prison when he was born, as his uncle had been warned of the fatality. But the bars broke, and the guards slept, and the city-gates opened, and even the mighty Jumna in flood gave a safe crossing to Vasudev to place the child with the chief cowherd, Nanda, on the other side of the river, and return with a fresh-born female babe of Nanda's wife, Yashoda, to satisfy Kamsa. In Gokul, the home of his boyhood and youth, Krishna's endless pranks as a merry little mischievous imp of a child, and his wonderful dancings and amours with the simple cow-herdesses have ever since remained the inexhaustible theme of countless generations of Indian poets and singers and dancers. More serious exploits, however, giving promise of the man to come, are not wanting even at this stage. His fight with and destruction of all the demons sent by Kamsa to kill him culminated in the death of Kamsa himself, and the restoration of the throne of Mathura to its rightful king, Ugrasena, Kamsa's deposed father. Of the splendid series of wars and conquests, of alliances and manœuvrings; of the winning of Rukmini, and the founding of Dwarka on the shores of the Arabian Sea; of the glorious fight in the Kurukshetra between the Pandavas and the Kauravas; of the last sad scene of life's closing tragedy, from which even men like gods cannot escape, and in which Krishna saw his mighty empire vanish in the fault of a single day,—in a drunken orgy,—and the divine founder of the Empire laid low in the dust by a chance arrow of the humblest hunter,—of all these there is no space to speak. But the moral is irresistible, unmistakable, unforgettable. None knew when He was born, and none was by when He was sped to his eternal rest!

Legendary embroidery apart, Krishna seems to have been an epic hero, who perhaps embodied the first great mixture of the Arya and the aborigines. A Yadava, he was of the Yadu race, famous even in the Vedic age; but his dark complexion suggests a mixture of blood, not at all unlikely in sober history. Taking the story of his conquest of Kalinga, and also of his establishment of a capital on the shores of the Western Sea, the inference may safely be made of a slow infiltration of the Aryan influence to the south by his time.

Apart from the semi-legendary personality of Krishna and his brother, the heroes of this other epic of the *Mahabharata* have both lost and gained somewhat in stature, since the days of the *Ramayana*, and more still, since the days of the Vedas. The world of men has grown infinitely more complex. It is impossible to have a

PLATE XXVII

RAMA'S DEPARTURE

From N. C. Mehta's book "Studies in Indian Painting"

HANUMANA

75 The Government Museum, Madras

straight choice always between clear good and positive evil. No one in the *Mahabharata* is utterly blameless. Even Yudhisthira, the personification of Righteousness, has to tell one little lie at least to save his army, and lead his ancient preceptor Drona to believe that the latter's son was killed, when really only an elephant of that name had been destroyed. The war of the Pandavas and the Kauravas was as much a struggle with mortal weapons, as mental wiles. The side that prevailed could scarcely claim their victory to be a triumph exclusively of truth and justice.

Three grand personalities, at least, stand out prominently in this story;—each a type of manly virtue then prized most among the ruling class; each a hero whose like the world has seldom seen. Bhishma, the eldest of all the warring cousins, was the first-born of King Shantanu of Hastinapur, who had taken the goddess Ganga to wife. The nymph had her own purpose to serve; but the king was a mortal after all, and could not resist, in spite of his promise, asking his wife who she really was, when he had seen one after another, seven of their children consigned to a premature grave by their inhuman mother! The nymph, rather than answer, disappeared, and left the king with the eighth child, the mighty Prince Bhishma! When he grew up to the estate of manhood, his father again fell in love with a fisherman's daughter, who would not smile on the king's proposals, unless and until the infatuated monarch had promised that his throne and sceptre should descend to her offspring in preference to the Crown Prince, Bhishma. Not content with the royal word, she insists on Bhishma publicly renouncing his rights, and even taking a vow of perpetual celibacy to guard against any chance of a civil war. Bhishma, like Rama before him, makes his grand renunciation to keep his father's royal pledge, even as others of his race have done time and again in more modern times—a renunciation more difficult than that of the Buddha himself, because Bhishma had to be in the world and yet not of it. When his father died, leaving an infant son and heir, he had to assume the regency along with the Queen Mother! He did his best to bring up his brother as befitted a king. He won for him 3 brides, daughters of the King of Benares; but they could not keep the boy-king from the common curse of princes in that position. And so the boy faded away into nothingness; and the Regent and the Queen Mother had to seek afresh to provide heirs for the kingdom. The Queen now repents of her having forced Bhishma to take the vow of celibacy, and she even suggests that he should raise issue on his half-brother's relicts. But Bhishma would not fail his oath, though earth may lose her scent and water its moisture and the sun his glory. Then they found another to take his place; but the latter came to the Princess in such a horrid form that the poor bereaved Ambika would not even look at the monster; and so her son Dhritarashtra was born blind, and unfit for the kingly role. The other widow of the late king then made an effort to save the royal line from extinction; and though she paled at the sight of her companion on that fateful night, she endured, and in the fullness of time gave birth to Pandu,—the Pale Prince,—who became heir to the throne.

It is the sons of these two brothers, born of different mothers, who are the heroes of the *Mahabharata*. The blind Dhritarashtra had a hundred sons, the Kaurava brothers; and the Pale Prince had five, who are the seeds, respectively, of Dharma, Vayu (wind), Indra, and the two Ashwins. Pandu died young, and his blind brother Dhritarashtra was installed Regent, Bhishma continuing still faithful to his trust as the first of the King's subjects, and yet a sort of grandsire of them all. As the story develops, Bhishma watches with rising dismay the bad faith and the duplicity of the Kaurava Princes to cheat the sons of Pandu of their due. His heart must have throbbed with high delight at the triumph upon triumph of his best-beloved Pandu Prince, Arjuna. But, when the Civil War comes at last, he has to range himself on the side of the Kauravas, because he had ever remained the first of the King's subjects; and, for the moment, the first of the Kauravas was King. Commander-in-Chief of the Kaurava hosts, none could beat him, and few withstand his mighty blows. For ten days he battles; and the Pandu host has little chance of success, though led by the greatest warrior of the age, and guided by the God of Gods himself! At last they discover a way to kill the old lion. When the warring forces were withdrawn for the night on the ninth day, the Pandu Princes went to Bhishma's tent; and, on Krishna's advice, asked him the means of his own destruction. With a smile and a sigh the hero named Shikhandin—the man born woman—none other than the eldest and the noblest of the Benares Princesses, whom in his youth Bhishma had won for his feeble brother, but whom he had let go because she had confessed to a prior attachment. Slighted by the man whom she had preferred to the King of Hastinapur, Amba had returned to Bhishma,—only to be refused! And so, in despair, the noble lady had devoted herself to austerities, which at last had won her the boon of being the death of Bhishma in her next birth. She was, accordingly, reborn a woman, but changed into man, and was fighting in the Pandu host. Because Shikhandin was born a woman, Bhishma, the unflinching celibate, would not even look at her; for he battles not with him who had laid down his arms, or is fallen, or flying, or with a woman, or with low and vulgar people. Here is a complete code of chivalry in a nutshell. The hard-pressed Pandavas had to take the hint; and wound the old hero to the heart next day by Arjuna preceded by Shikhandin. The latter's arrows would have been less than a flea-bite to the seasoned veteran; but when his best-beloved Arjuna's arrows searched out and pierced his vitals, Bhishma at last fell! Even when he lies low on the field of battle, his warrior's heart would wish for no other couch but that of the arrows on which he was lying, nor any other pillow but what Arjuna's mighty bow could wing him through the head. Not even Arjuna, his own best-beloved Pandu Prince, approaches Bhishma in kingly courtesy and princely generosity.

Arjuna, the son of Indra, has been the *beau ideal* of the Hindu warrior for all these ages. But his exploits, marvellous as they are, sometimes feel almost monotonous. There is no chance for anyone against him—the friend of Krishna and the favourite of Indra. Even the Great God Shiva finds it difficult to beat him in a hand-to-hand fight. Krishna is always his friend, whether it is to abduct his own sister Subhadra, or to second him by moral support in the Great War. The only break is in that year of concealment, the last of the exile resulting from the defeat at dice of the Emperor Yudhishthira. Arjuna becomes a eunuch to give fulfilment to an old curse, lies concealed for the fateful year in the zenana of King Virata, teaching the inmates music and dancing, and all the arts of refined womanhood. At the end of the tale, its innate drama once more wakens into sudden life. Arjuna and his brothers disclose themselves to save the cattle of King Virata, that the Kuru Princes were stealing away. The disclosure forces the main issue whether the Pandavas are to have any share of their patrimony or of their own conquests. There are messages galore and negotiations, and all the elaborate apparatus of seeming to be anxious to avoid bloodshed; but all the while everybody knows that a fight there must be,—and a fight to the finish.

So the great battle is staged, and a slaughter grim and grand takes place. Arjuna is the hero of the fight. He cannot beat the fierce old war-dog Bhishma, or even his own uterine brother, Karna, without a base ruse. But he is not himself actively concerned in all the series of ruses and manoeuvres that finally wins him the war. On the contrary, on the very first day of the war, he utters sentiments to which not even the most exacting moralist could possibly take exception. It is a little trying to see the hero, after all those years of fighting and striving for mastery, holding forth in trite little sayings that could have been new to no one. But one overlooks his repugnance in the eleventh hour to fight his brethren, on account of the wonderful sayings of Krishna, his divine charioteer, embodying the quintessence of Hindu philosophy in language of ineffable beauty and unrivalled simplicity. When Bhishma is killed, thanks to the interposition of the Indian prototype of the Chevalier d'Eon; and Karna quits the scene, by being first deprived of his invulnerable body armour and then destroyed by what was a foul blow by all the codes of their chivalry, Arjuna, of course, remains the peerless hero, the ideal of Hindu chivalry, the model of manly grace, beauty and virtue.

In marked contrast to this favourite of fortune, is his own eldest brother Karna. He is all that Arjuna is, or would be; and a great deal more. For Arjuna has the advantage of birth at least, while Karna has throughout his life to battle against a supposedly inferior origin. He is the child of the Sun by Kunti, the mother of the three Pandavas; but being born before marriage, his mother had no alternative but to leave him on the banks of the Jumna at the moment of his birth. A charioteer finds him, and brings him up as his own son; but his handsome figure and princely bearing ever give the lie to his seeming origin. Early in their career, Karna and Arjuna discover themselves to be the only match for one another. But at each regular trial of strength,—until the final catastrophe,—Karna is denied the full test by a pitiless fate. Drona, the incomparable teacher of the art and science of War, would not teach him the lore of the Princes—because of his birth. Karna dispenses with a teacher, and learns by himself. When the Royal Tournament is held to display the accomplishments of the Princes, Arjuna will not meet Karna in single combat, again because of his birth. In the self-choice of Draupadi for a husband,

Karna is ready to accomplish the task set to the assembled princes; but again his birth is flung into his teeth, and Arjuna is allowed to carry off the prize. The soul of the noble Karna revolts at, but is unsullied by, the ruses and subterfuges of his friend and King, Duryodhana; for Karna trusts absolutely in the invincibility of his own strong arm. When at last the War comes, he, proud and peerless, is a veritable tower of strength for the Kaurava cause. When Bhishma has gone the way of all flesh, and Drona has fallen, Karna takes the baton of command. Long before this, he has known of his real birth; and that it wanted but a word of their common mother to make the rival champions forget their hostility. But Karna is too noble to bring a blush of shame to the cheek of the mother who gave him birth; too chivalrous to forget the father who had adopted him and brought him up; too noble to flee from a sinking ship; too proud to avoid the one and only chance of proving his valour before his only match, by acknowledging that man his brother. And so poor Kunti, mother of the greatest warriors ever born, has to remain content with the reflection that whatever happens,—whether Arjuna falls or Karna,—she would still have her *three* sons. Karna, too, is under no illusion about his doom. He fights with all the courage of his birth and breeding,—knowing, however, all the time that his best weapons are to be taken away from him, or misapplied. Thus, he was born with a body-armour, the gift of his father, the Sun; while he was covered with that breast-plate, no mortal arrow could ever pierce to his vitals. But generous as he was brave, when his own mother,—or is it his rival's father?,—begs of him the armour that covers him, off it comes to satisfy a mendicant. There cannot be a more sublime gift than this,—or one more tragic. The unprotected hero goes to fight—to meet certain doom. There is hope still. He has a lance that the Prince of Gods has promised will take one life without fail. Karna keeps it to throw it at his only rival Arjuna. But Duryodhana, his liege lord, is frightened by the havoc of Bhima's demon son on the Kuru forces; and so the King begs, and urges, and at last commands the Marshall of the host to use his lance against that champion. Karna yields against his better judgment; and that danger is over for the moment.

But now the Pandava host presses him on all sides. His own son is killed, even as Arjuna's heir had been done to death on a previous day. The conquering Arjuna, spurred by revenge, showers a ceaseless hail of arrows on Karna. Even then the hero faints not, nor blenches. He rushes in the very heart of the fray with redoubled fury; but his chariot-wheel sticks fast in the bloody mud at the crucial moment. A past-master in all that appertains to the art of war, he jumps from his seat to release the wheel, and asks Arjuna, as honourable chivalrous warrior, not to shoot while he, Karna, was on the ground and without weapons. But Arjuna is maddened by the recollection of the death of his son Abhimanyu, who had been killed in the presence of Karna, in a similar predicament. Well might he taunt Karna, where was Karna's chivalry when the lad had been done to death in that dastardly manner! He would have been greater if he had withheld that taunt; he would have been great beyond compare if he had forborn the foul blow. Fate willed otherwise. Arjuna shot, and Karna fell pierced to the heart!

PLATE XXVIII

A VILLAGE BEAUTY

(From N. C. Mehta's book "Studies in Indian Painting")

These three heroes are unmatched throughout the magnificent epic. But even they rise not to the simple faith and dauntless courage of Rama and his brother. Amongst women, also, the decline is noticeable. Kunti, the mother of the Pandavas, is honoured and upheld. But her amours with the Gods cannot be glossed over by any amount of sophistry. Draupadi is a nobler soul—a perfect warrior's bride. She is even shrewd and deep in a way that Sita could never have attained to. But the love of Sita for Rama remains unparalleled throughout the *Mahabharata*. There are noble and high souled dames in plenty in this poem too; but the very fact that the poet has to interpolate the legend of Savitri to point his moral is enough to prove the change at least, if not the decline, in the ideal of womanhood. Savitri was married by her own choice to Satyavan, though she knew her husband had only a year to live, and though his parents were driven from their kingdom and blinded. But she remained a devoted wife and faithful companion all through the brief year. And when at last Satyavan died, and the God of Death came to claim him from the charge of the chaste and true Savitri, she begged him and pursued him to his very home, and one by one persuaded him to grant her requests,—the restoration of sight to her parents-in-law, their kingdom, and a son of herself, without stain on her troth as wife and woman; which at last compels Yama, the God of Death, to restore the life of her deceased Lord.

*   *   *   *   *   *

Of the Saints in the epic age, let us mention Hanuman and Narada, Vidura and Vyasa. The claim to rank Hanuman as a saint rests more on popular tradition than on historical evidence, such as it is. The former makes of him a perfect devotee of Vishnu in the form of Rama. So much, indeed, was he devoted to Rama that, according to a most popular legend, when, on her husband's restoration to the throne of his fathers, the Queen, Sita, gave him a pearl necklace in reward of his invaluable services, he broke open every one of those priceless pearls, and, after looking into the interior of each, threw them away. The Queen was surprised,—perhaps hurt. She asked for an explanation. The great *Bhakta* (devotee) answered, "They had not got the name of Rama inscribed upon any of them". Sita, amazed, asked if Rama's name was inscribed on his own heart. Hanuman, in reply, tore open his breast with his claws, and showed his bleeding heart with the name of Rama blazing upon it. He was a monkey chief by birth, son of Anjana, by the God of Wind, an elder half-brother of the Pandava Bhima,—in sober history, perhaps, an aboriginal chieftain. Ever since he met Rama, distracted by the loss of his queen, he served and helped the King with infinite valour and unrivalled devotion, as a spy and messenger, as a warrior and ambassador; and the Rakshasas of Lanka knew to their cost the might of this Prince of Monkeys.

Narada's claims to saintliness seem to be much better founded. He was one of the Vedic Rishis—a composer of several Rig-Vedic hymns. In real history he probably belonged to the Kanva family, though legend ascribed his origin to Brahma, the God of Creation. On his father, Brahma, advising him to marry, he denounced his father, as a false teacher, because devotion to Krishna was the only true means of happiness. Narada is also remembered as the father of Music in India, and as the inventor of the flute. A prince of wits, Narada is also famous in popular story as a mischievous imp on account of his innumerable pranks in setting people at loggerheads; but these are much too legendary to justify a specific mention.

The name of Vyasa is applied to several; but the most famous is the compiler of the Vedas, in their present permanent order. He must have flourished somewhere about the seventh century B. C. Another Vyasa—if not the same,—is also the reputed author of the *Mahabharata*, and contemporary of the chief personages of the epic.

*   *   *   *   *   *

In the next age,—the middle Aryan or Hindu period, stretching from about 700 B. C. to 1200 A. C.,—there is no lack of heroes or saints either. Leaving aside for the moment great founders of world-religions or vast empires,—like the Buddha or Chandragupta Maurya,—we still find heroic personages in every province of which we have as yet unearthed an authentic history. It is impossible,—as it would be invidious,—to select. But take the case of Porus, the heroic enemy of Alexander of Macedon. Prepared by all accounts to meet an invincible foe, and aware of the disaffection in his own ranks, he yet determined to face and withstand the advancing tide. He was out-manoeuvred,—perhaps betrayed,—and out-fought. But his spirit remained indomitable as ever. Wounded and wearied, he was led into the presence of his enemy, who gazed in wonder upon that tall, martial form, every inch a king and a hero, and looking straight before him unquenched by the fortune of war. Alexander asked him what treatment he would have. Porus cared not if it was a cheap sneer, or a vulgar display. He answered promptly: "That of a king." The Macedonian was impressed, and Porus received from him a truly Royal treatment.

The Muslim conqueror of the last of the Hindu kings of Delhi had neither the chivalry nor the perspicacity of the Greek. Prithwi-Raj Chauhan, the last of the Hindu sovereigns, the Prince and warrior and lover in excelsis, has a most romantic history. Born to the throne of Ajmer, he was called to that of Delhi by the preference for him of his maternal uncle, over his cousin Jaychand Rathod of Kanauj. A dauntless warrior himself, he was the prince of a band of mighty fighters,—brave and fearless and invincible,—whose fidelity and allegiance to their Chief is even now the model of feudal loyalty; whose love of country and religion, whose instincts of chivalry and devotion to their warrior traditions, made Prithwi-Raj the fittest guardian of the gate of India, at that time. The Chauhan Prince inflicted more than one crushing defeat on the Ghouri leader. But the high traditions of Rajput chivalry would not permit him to war with the vanquished; and so when Shahabuddin was once defeated and captured a prisoner, Prithwi-Raj must needs set him at liberty. He did not despise his enemy; nor did he fear him.

The curse of India, however, has always been internecine dissension. During 1500 years, from the Maurya Empire to the Chauhan debacle, there have, of course, been many ambitious princes and conquerors within India herself. But while the conquerors and the conquered, themselves of the same race or religion, were strong enough to settle their quarrels without the help of an outsider, India remained free from any large, lasting foreign invasion and conquest. Even Alexander of Macedon was, in the true perspective of history, a mere raider, a dazzling meteor, whose rise and blaze and fall was a matter of two short years at most. Darius and Cyrus of Persia may have been greater, more permanent conquerors; but it may be doubted if the Persian influence was of an abiding or pervading character. It is, therefore, a wrong view of Indian history to regard that country as being for ever a helpless prey to the first invader. It is only when internal dissension has coincided with foreign aggressiveness, that the path of the invader has been made easy to conquest and settlement. The Ghouri conquest was facilitated by the spite of Jaychand of Kanauj against Prithwi-Raj of Delhi. Jaychand had, indeed, good reason to feel aggrieved. Prithwi-Raj had ousted him from the throne of Delhi, and had wounded him in the most vulnerable part of his being. In revenge, Jaychand omitted Prithwi-Raj from the list of Princes invited to compete for the hand of his daughter Samyukta. Allied with Bhima-Deva of Gujarat, Jaychand felt he could very well afford to ignore Prithwi-Raj. But he counted without reckoning with either the daring of Prithwi-Raj, or the fancy of his daughter. She was in love with the beau idcal of Rajput chivalry, the hero of a hundred fights. The mystic telegraph of love was at work. Prithwi-Raj came in disguise to win himself this peerless Princess, even as Arjuna had been on a similar quest to win the princess of Panchala. Jaychand had made a golden image of the King of Delhi, and stationed him, as his doorkeeper, at the very lowest place in the *Mandap.* The Princess, however, went the round of the assembled Princes without throwing the garland she carried—the symbol of her choice—on any one, until she came to the golden image of Prithwi-Raj. On him she placed the garland. That moment a mail-clad horseman seized her, placed her in front of him, and, with sixty choice followers—the bravest of the brave—flew on the road to Delhi. The disguise was off. Jaychand was humiliated in his own court, as never a Prince had been these thousand years. He let loose his whole army in pursuit. But Prithwi-Raj and his heroes had not won in vain the first place amongst the Indian chivalry of the day. Two by two they held the road against the advancing host, while the rest flew on towards the sheltering walls of Delhi. Two by two they met and fought the champions of Jaychand and stayed their onrush. Two by two they met their death, dyeing the banks of the Jumna with their blood, falling with their face to the foe, and with never a scar on their back. It is a hundred leagues from Kanauj to Delhi; but the Prince and his bride reached the capital safely at the cost of sixty of the bravest and noblest of that peerless band of Knights.

Baffled rage and wounded pride made Jaychand seek the aid of a stranger to revenge himself. Prithwi-Raj, though sadly missing the heroes of the greatest adventure of his romantic life, was not without his allies. The Maharana of Mewar, his sister's husband, and the head of Rajput royalty as the descendant of Rama, came to Delhi: and fought in that fatal battle of Panipat where India lost for ever the Hindu sovereignty of the land. It was a gallant fight, bravely fought. Prithwi-Raj the lover was forgotten in Prithwi-Raj the warrior. Samyukta herself buckled on his mail, girt on his sword, and hastened him to the fight, as only a Rajput Princess can. When the end came, she burnt herself alive rather than fall in the hands of the sacrilegious conqueror, though her husband was a living but wounded prisoner in the hands of the Ghouri. The brave Maharana was killed,—the first of a long line of devoted kings, destined to fight the Muslim for 500 years thereafter in defence of the ancient gods of India. Prithwi-Raj was, according to some, killed after the battle by his savage foe, a stranger to any notion of chivalry. It is, perhaps, nearer the truth than that other story, which describes him as blinded and starved but still undaunted in his prison, until his faithful bard,—another Blondin to another Coeur-de-lion,—should come seeking him in the enemy's camp. Shahabuddin was so wonder-struck by Chand Barot's tales of Prithwi-Raj's mastery of archery that he would have an immediate exhibition on the spot. A mark was fixed; the blinded Prince was brought forth, and armed with his unfailing bow. The Bard was told to give him directions as to the nature and distance of the target. In a flash Chand told Prithwi-Raj,—ready with the bow-string drawn to the ear,—the distance and direction of the Sultan on his throne watching the exploit. The shaft was loosed, and the Sultan fell; and before his nobles could realise the last act of a heroic life, the Prince and the Bard had thrust their daggers into each other's hearts!

*   *   *   *   *   *

But though Prithwi-Raj was dead, his memory lingered. Countless Rajput heroes of lesser renown have emulated his exploits age after age, until even the conquering Musalman came to appreciate the nobility and grandeur of the Rajput's code of war. Let us give but one specimen—the story of Bhim Singh of Chitor and Princess Padmini. He was a cadet of the Maharana, and was appointed Regent, when his father died, to watch over his nephew, the minor Maharana. Padmini was a Princess of Ceylon, a peerless beauty, married to perhaps the most famous warrior of the age. Alauddin-Khilji, a great warrior and conqueror in his own way, who first carried the Crescent banner into the Deccan, came to hear of her unrivalled loveliness. In his insolence, the Sultan ordered Bhim Singh to surrender his wife. There can be only one reply to such a demand; and when he got it, Alauddin led a vast host into the land of Mewar. The defence was concentrated at the capital-fortress of Chitor. Alauddin had met his match,—at least in courage and the science of war. He could not possibly take Chitor by open warfare. So he had recourse to his usual duplicity. He was going to raise the siege, if only his one desire was

PLATE XXVIII A

KRISHNA WITH GOPIS

From N. C. Mehta's book "Studies in Indian Painting"

granted—a glimpse of only a reflection of the far-famed beauty. It was a little thing to grant; and Bhim Singh, unequal to Alauddin in his wiles, readily consented. Alauddin came up to the fort, and was received by his gallant enemy in the hall of his palace, where the peerless Padmini passing by, though herself unseen, was reflected in one of the mirrors hung against the wall. The Sultan was content, and began to take his leave. True to the traditions of Rajput hospitality, Bhim Singh accompanied his guest to the last outpost of Chitor, despite the warnings of his nobles. When the last gate was passed, and host and guest were bidding farewell, Alauddin whistled, and his concealed guards sprang upon the Rajput Prince. Taken unawares, the latter was overpowered, and carried to the infidel camp.

Secure in his camp, Alauddin now sent a message to the guardians of Chitor, either to deliver the Princess in his hands, or to suffer their gallant commander to be done to death. When the Chitor chiefs had met in council to consider this strange demand, they were delivered from their dilemma by a woman's wit. The Princess offered to go of her own accord as a ransom for her lord, provided the Sultan agreed to receive her with the pomp and ceremony befitting her rank and birth. This was an easy condition; though Padmini desired to be accompanied by 700 of her hand-maidens in palanquins. The agreement was soon made, and the princely cortege reached Alauddin's camp. The monarch was overjoyed, and granted easily one last prayer of Padmini for a final half-hour of farewell with her lord.

That was all she needed. The 700 pretended maidens jumped from their palanquins, each a warrior armed to the teeth; and the twenty-eight hundred palkhi-bearers were no less. A fierce yell of dismay, a resounding cry of "Har! Har! Mahadev!" and the clash of arms had begun. While the bloody carnage went on, Bhim Singh and his queen rode to Chitor, their rear-guard held by the warriors who had accompanied the Princess in disguise. Once within the fort, there was no hope for the Delhi sovereign to win back the prey that had slipped so bravely and so wonderfully from his grasp. He had to confess himself beaten, and so went his way, shamefaced and crest-fallen and smarting at the clever way a woman's wit had outwitted him.

A few years later, Alauddin again returned to conquer the heroic land of Mewar; he was met by the same men, the same courage, the same resistance,—but not the same result. Chitor was doomed. The last charge was led by Prince Bhim Singh, and at the same time every noble dame in Chitor passed into a walled up place, with the heroic Padmini bringing up the rear, to be burnt alive. When the conqueror at last forced his way into the smoking ruins of Chitor, his savage mood expressed itself in an immediate order to raze the fort to the ground. Only one building was sacred even in his savage eyes, and that was spared,—the palace where he had once seen Padmini in life !

*   *   *   *   *

The history of Mewar is a series of thrilling exploits, matchless in their courage, heroism and self-sacrifice. We can only select one more for special mention;

though the choice must not imply any diminution of the glories of Hamir; or the splendours and conquests of Kumbha. Kumbha, indeed, (1419-1469) was, in many respects, the greatest of this long line of warrior kings. Victor over the allied Muslim kings of Malwa and Gujarat in a pitched battle, he fully maintained the reputation of his house for martial renown. Conqueror of the Malwa king,—a prisoner in his capital,—he displayed at its best all that high-bred Rajput courtesy to the defeated, which their Muslim opponents had yet to learn. But as a poet, perhaps inspired by his famous wife, the poetess Mira; and as scholar, translating the classic work of Jayadeva, *Gita Govinda*,—he stands unique. Maharana Sanga, the protagonist of Babur, was no less heroic, even though less fortunate in war. But their descendant Pratap surpassed both in fame, probably because of the greatness of his enemy, perhaps also because of the contrast he makes with his father—the cowardly Udai Singh. When Akbar first invaded Mewar in 1567, the reigning Maharana fled from the fortress-capital that had witnessed so many stirring scenes of Rajput chivalry. The burden of defence fell on Salumbar, the first of the Mewar nobles. After months of arduous, unrelaxing siege, with all the appliances that the amazing genius of Akbar could devise, the first stage was reached by a massed attack at the Sun Gate, where the commandant was himself in charge. Salumbar fell mortally wounded, and the command passed on to another noble, Patta of Kelwa, a seasoned warrior at the ripe age of sixteen. He went to take one last look at his newly married bride, and seemed to waver because of his love for her. She said nothing; but when he left the palace to join his forces, she followed as a youthful warrior sheathed in complete mail. Wherever that day her young lord moved in battle, there was her guardian lance in unflinching attendance. Sheer bravery was, however, no match against the science of War, the force of numbers, and the cunning of the most consummate commander of his age. Patta fell, and with him his brave bride, clasped on her husband's bosom, as never perhaps she had been clasped in life. A third noble—Jaymal of Bednore—now took command; and would have perhaps made good the defence, had he not been picked off by Akbar's own bullet at night. To the Rajput's idea of honourable war, this was a foul blow; for it was the time of truce, and Jaymal, though clad in steel, was far from expecting a shot. Akbar, however, made what amends he could, by erecting two noble statues on elephant on each side of the principal gate of his palace—representing Jaymal and Patta of Chitor.

But while the great nobles of Chitor were dying one after another in vain defence of the capital; while their wives and daughters were cheerfully offering the supreme sacrifice of Rajput heroism, the recreant head of the House of Mewar lived in a new palace he had built on the shores of a lake. On his death, his second son Pratap, the most famous of a very famous line of warrior-kings, succeeded to a kingdom without a capital, without an army, without a treasury (1576). He had, however, something more than all these, a dauntless spirit. He summoned his vassals to his standard, affronted the most favoured Rajput general of Akbar, the celebrated Man Singh; and fought the Imperial forces at the historic pass of Haldighat.

Of 22,000 troops that had obeyed the Rana's call to arms, only 8,000 survived the slaughter. The Rana himself had come to the fight in the full insignia of his Royalty; but rather than that life so precious to Mewar and to Hindus be sacrificed in a vain struggle, a noble seized the Royal umbrella, and rushed with it to another part of the field, thus attracting the fury of the Mughal attack on his devoted head. Another noble forced Pratap to quit the field when the day was lost. In his reluctant flight, on his no less famous charger, the Rana was pursued by two Mughal warriors, and his own disaffected brother Sakta Sinh. Blood, however, proved thicker than ambition on that tragic day. Sakta charged his companions and wounded them; and then called to his brother, and gave him his own fresh charger to continue his flight into the sheltering hills of Aravalli. For years the Rana lived in the hills, — an implacable foe of the Great Mughal. From his mountain abode he issued his orders to his vassals and to his subjects, — the former to join him, the latter to cease cultivation so as to starve out the Imperial garrisons. For twenty years he warred in this way, — the hero of every Rajput heart, even those in Akbar's service. The latter could, perhaps, have crushed him had he so willed. But he was either too generous not to admire Pratap for his heroic resistance; or too politic to risk his own Empire by alienating the main pillars of his power. Pratap lived to fight another battle, and to re-conquer, before his death, practically his whole realm of Mewar, with the exception of Chitor. He felt that lack terribly; and the vows of self-denial he had taken until Chitor was conquered are even now observed by his descendants. For Chitor is still in ruins, and outside the Maharana's dominions!

Mewar remained the most prolific breeding ground of heroes throughout the reigns of the 5 Great Mughals. Amar Sinh, Karna Sinh, Rai Sinh, in direct succession after the immortal Pratap, maintained to the full the glories of Mewar. The last-named added to the trophies of a warrior the laurels of a statesman. His spirited espousal of the cause of Ajit Sinh, the infant king of Marwar; his romantic marriage with the Princess of Kishangarh, with all the glamour and poetry of the marriage of Samyukta and Prithwi-Raj; his determined fight in the field against Aurangzeb, make a classic chapter in the stirring annals of Mewar. But even his exploits are eclipsed by the heroism and devotion of the Rathor Chief, Durga Das. Maharaja Jaswant Sing of Jodhpur, Aurangzeb's viceroy of Afghanistan, died at Jamrud in December 1678, A. C., leaving no son to succeed him. But his Queen, a Princess of Mewar, was *enceinte* at the time of his death; and, following well-established precedent, she refrained from mounting the funeral pyre. Soon after, a son was born to her. In his name, and on his account, she claimed the kingdom of Jodhpur from the Emperor. But the perfidious Aurangzeb had already bestowed it on another Rathor Prince, — a willing tool in his hands. When the infant heir of Marwar and his mother reached Delhi, the Emperor would not let them pass. He wanted to assume the guardianship of the Prince, to bring up the latter in the imperial harem. The envoys of the Queen, — Durga Das Rathod, Ranchhod Das Rathod, and Raghunath Bhatti, — were horror-struck at this glimpse of the Emperor's intentions; and left the Presence to recount their audience to the Queen. Aurangzeb had left them no time to deliberate. Hardly had they finished telling the Queen about the Emperor's views, when a force of the Imperial Guards was heard to approach the palace. Durga Das evolved a masterly plan of action. With a hundred chosen warriors, the Bhatti was to create a diversion by charging upon the Imperial Guard, and hold the gates of the palace as long as they could. In the Queen's chamber, a slave-girl was to be left impersonating the Queen, with an infant borrowed from a neighbouring milkman. When the shock of battle between the Bhatti and the Guards was first heard, Durga Das left the palace from the back-gate with the remaining clansmen, the Queen riding in the midst of her gallant escort with the baby-prince at her saddle-bow. Of the 100 led by Bhatti, 70 fell in the Battle of the Gates, never to rise again. The Kotwal rushed over their dead bodies into the palace,—into the chamber of the Queen,—to find a substitute! The ruse was soon discovered, and pursuit resumed, after the masquerading slave-girl and the milk-man's child had been sent on to the raging Emperor. Nine miles from Delhi, on the road to Jodhpur, on the banks of the Jumna, the pursuers came up with the pursued. Once again Durga Das divided his slender force. Forty picked lances galloped on with the Queen over the bridge; with 50 more Durga Das held the Imperial Guard, 300 strong, at bay. Never did a Horatio or a Bayard defend a bridge more gallantly than these Rathod warriors. Every mother's son among them was fearfully wounded, and forty-five killed in this Battle of the Bridge, which lasted for one brief hour. But that hour had done its work. The Imperialists were checked, daunted, and thrown back; and Durga Das resumed his gallop after the Queen with only five companions. But so wondrous had been his exploit, that every Rathor,—every Rajput,—heart had been stirred; and when the Queen reached the gates of Jodhpur she was at the head of a considerable army. The Mughal Governor fled before the avenging Durga Das had arrived; and the son of Maharaja Jaswant Sing entered the capital of his ancestors,—an acknowledged king.

* * * * * *

These are all Rajput heroes,—all of the native Indian faith. Let us not forget in this list the names of those other heroes, who, though professing another faith, still add lustre by their exploits to the story of Indian heroism. We can scarcely claim Muhammad-ibn-Qasim, the first Muslim invader and the conqueror of Sind, as an Indian at all. But his name cannot but recall the memory of that heroic Queen of Dahir, who first gave an example of the unrivalled sense of honour of the Rajput dame. When Dahir was defeated and killed by the Arab commander, the latter found the gates of the capital still barred; and the Queen Regent, armed and determined, in command of the defenders. Muhammad was foiled in all his attemtps to storm the city, and so he sat down to besiege it with all his equipments of catapults and battering rams, which left no alternative to the defenders but to surrender, or to die. They chose the latter. Throwing open the gates, the nobles and clansmen rushed out with the Queen at their head, charging the Muslims with

PLATE XXIX

78   SIEGE OF LANKA
(From Coomaraswamy's "Rajput Painting")

79   ARJUNA BEGGING KRISHNA'S
HELP IN THE GREAT WAR
(The Prince of Wales Museum, Bombay)

80   VYAS MUNI
(Author of the "Mahabharata")

81   RAI PITHORA
(Prithvi Raj, Last Hindu King of Delhi)

PLATE XXX

82   MAHARANA PRATAP   83   MAHMUD OF GHAZNI

84   EMPRESS RAZIA   85 CHAND SULTANA OF AHMEDNAGAR

(Prince of Wales Museum, Bombay)

such fury, that, but for their numbers, they would have retrieved the day. The charge, however, failed. The heroic queen fell fighting to the last, along with her devoted band of followers.

If we cannot claim Muhammad-ibn-Qasim as a hero of India, still less can we claim Mahmud of Ghazni,—the Iconoclast,—or Shahabuddin of Ghor. They were essentially raiders, though Shahabuddin certainly had in him the mettle of an Empire-builder. In fact, the real sway of the Muslims in India begins with him. His courage and generalship, and astute diplomacy are beyond question; and though to the Hindu mind a perusal of his life and achievements would not acquit him of unworthy, unchivalrous action, the historian would be amply justified in discounting that feeling against the resolute persistence of Shahabuddin's fixed goal of permanent conquest of India. His slave and successor, Qutb-ud-din, is, however, the first Indian Emperor of Muslim persuasion. A matchless commander himself, the Ghori Prince was quick to perceive the gifts of his slave, whom he, therefore, rapidly raised to high rank in his army. When Delhi had been conquered and Kanauj had fallen, Shahabuddin could find none better to hold the viceregal sceptre in India than his erstwhile slave. Qutb-ud-din carried the standard of the Crescent to Bengal in the East and Gujarat in the South-west, though in the latter he did not feel it safe to remain much longer. It was on his return from the capital of Gujarat that he met with the one great defeat of his life,—all the more humiliating because inflicted by a woman and a child. The Queen of Mewar, Korumdevi of Gujarat, guardian and Regent for her infant son, Maharana Karna, called all the vassals of Mewar together in the name of her son, and with them inflicted such a defeat near Amber on the Afghan forces, that they fled in disorder to Delhi, and left the entire camp and war material in the hands of the triumphant Rajputs. Qutb-ud-din fought bravely and desperately in the battle; but he was wounded; his army demoralised; and defeat inevitable. What he lost in Rajputana, however, he made up for by gaining in Bihar and Bengal, where Muhammad-ibn Bakhtyar, a soldier of fortune, was appointed Governor under the Viceroy. In Bundelkhand Qutb-ud-din met another Hindu heroine, Malundevi of Kalanjar, under whose inspiration the cowardly Paramar put up a most vigorous resistance. The battle under the walls of Kalanjar was, perhaps, the most fiercely contested field Qutb-ud-din ever fought. But he was victorious at last. Their gods seem to have deserted the Hindus; for the great Chandel dynasty of Bundelkhand came to an end after 1203, having flourished for nearly 400 years. Two years later, Shahabuddin himself was killed by a band of revolted Gakkars while sleeping in his tent at Rohtak; and, after a short interval, Qutb-ud-din was proclaimed Sultan of Delhi by the successor of his late master at Ghazni.

This is not the place to record the achievements of the successive Turkish and Afghan Sultans of Delhi. But we must pause to name at least Altamsh, the son-in-law and successor of Qutb-ud-din, and his famous but ill-fated daughter Raziyya. Altamsh was a worthy successor of the founder of the Slave dynasty. He added Malwa to the Empire, and captured the impregnable fort of Mandu, which had baffled even the irresistible Mahmud of Ghazni. On his death, his son Rukn-ud-din ascended the throne; but he was a wastrel and an incompetent. The real power lay with his mother, once a slave-girl of Altamsh. Her cruelties made her abhorred; and the nobles of Delhi at last rose in revolt, and asked the Princess Raziyya to assume the reins of government. Brave and accomplished as she was beautiful, she had been the constant companion and the most trusted adviser of her father, who had once even appointed her Regent during his absence from Delhi. Her brother, the shadow-emperor, demurred and opposed; but he was betrayed and surrendered, and was executed by order of the Empress. For $3\frac{1}{2}$ years she ruled the Empire,—as a firm, wise, and just ruler. But the woman's penalty of youth and beauty was inevitable in a court unfamiliar with the lofty traditions of Rajput chivalry. Raziyya's name was linked by the tongue of scandal with that of a slave in the palace. The nobles rebelled, led by Malik Altuniya of Bhatinda. He could not resist the spell of her youth and beauty when betrayed and carried into his camp; but her own brother Bahram, head of another party, was less susceptible and less merciful. She and her husband Altuniya were beaten in the field, and were beheaded after a month's imprisonment. Her only fault, as Firishta well says, with a touch of inexpressible pathos, was that she was a woman!

Alauddin-Khilji, the second Emperor of the second Muslim dynasty, styled himself a second Alexander. But his beginning as well as his end were bloody; and this whole life and reign unredeemed by a single trait of nobility or generosity, or lofty chivalry towards the vanquished. Courage he had in abundance; and even the talents of a general. But his conquests, though many and amazing, were stained with treachery and cruelty, that necessarily deny him the title of a national hero.

It would require too much patience, and too vast a screen, to watch the film of that procession of history, which is concerned with the 2 last centuries of the Pathan dominion. We cannot even pause to speak of the great Maharana Sangram Sinh, who had rallied all Rajputs under the sun banner of the Sisodias to make one more attempt to wrest the throne of Delhi from the defiling 'Toork'. Not, indeed, because he was eventually beaten by the superior generalship of Babur; but because the rest of Sanga's career of conquest and ascendancy would, if narrated, take us too far out of the perspective of history. Even the inspiring figure of the last of the Pathan heroes,—the Lion-hearted Sur,—must be passed over in silence, the rather because he finds a more fitting niche in our Hall of Emperors. But we must let the procession halt for a brief while, to enable us to gaze upon the grand, awful, tragic figure of Bairam Khan, the Guardian and Prime Minister of the greatest of the Mughals. Bairam was a faithful follower and a loyal soldier of the Emperor Humayun. Gifted with all the virtues and vices of his race and his age, he was brave and bigoted, faithful and self-willed, loyal to the core, yet headstrong. He had followed Humayun in all his wars, and also in his exile. Returning with his master, he fought with Prince Akbar the historic battle that conquered the empire of India. The restored Emperor, brave and chivalrous and generous to a fault, was not destined to enjoy his triumph for any length of time; and his son, the boy-Emperor, was left under the ministry and guardianship of the staunchest friend of his father. Bairam was as sagacious in generalship as he was peerless in personal bravery. He fought and won another yet more historic battle for his new sovereign; but tarnished his glory, at least in the mind of his Imperial pupil, by the double execution of Tardi Beg before the battle, and of Hemu, the helpless and vanquished enemy, after. The sensitive soul of Akbar recoiled with horror from such a savagery committed in the name of religion. But he was yet too young, inexperienced, insecure to show his Minister who was the master. For four years he bided his time. When at last the hour of doom struck, by a masterly manœuvre he unhorsed the Minister in a single charge. Politely exiled by his sovereign, Bairam at first obeyed, then rebelled, and was eventually conquered. The star of Akbar was rising. The vanquished Minister was received in audience. But instead of reproaches or humiliation, the son of Humayun only remembered the services of Bairam Khan to the House of Timur. Covering him with the Imperial mantle, he offered him the choice of active service in the field or in the Council, or a dignified retreat. Bairam chose the latter, and started on his pilgrimage to Mecca. But fate again intervened. An old enemy revenged himself upon the great *Khan-i-Khanan* as he was visiting a temple in the ancient capital of Gujarat, before taking ship for Arabia at Cambay; and Bairam Khan was no more!

Another figure, still more romantic and tragical, is that of the heroic Queen Regent of Ahmadnagar. The young king had succeeded to his father's throne after a series of revolutions; and his great aunt was the only person capable of holding the reins of government loyally for the king's benefit. But the disaffected Minister of his predecessor had already invited the aid of the Mughal Viceroy of Gujarat,— Prince Murad,—the second son of the Emperor Akbar. With the fall of the plotting minister, there was no justification for a march on Ahmadnagar. Prince Murad and his Mughals, however, had no intention of letting the prey escape from their grasp so easily. Arrived at Ahmadnagar, they were surprised to see the gates barred against them. The beauty, grace and magnetism of the heroic Queen had silenced the discordant note of faction within the city; and the natives as well as the foreigners in the State strove only to show who made the greatest sacrifice in the cause of the city. It could not be carried by storm. The Mughals therefore sat down to besiege it in real earnest, and laid mines under the walls and bastions of the fort. From one of these the dauntless Queen, clad in armour and acting the common soldier, removed the powder with her own hands. But the two others exploded before the same treatment could be applied to them. The Mughals, sure of an easy capture, delayed assaulting till the next morning. They were too late. The night sufficed the tireless Queen to fill up the breaches. The Prince was impressed by the courage of a woman, and the native chivalry of his race and breeding was aglow. He held a solemn Durbar, and formally conferred on the heroine the title of Sultana, already a Queen in her own right. Negotiations were

14

opened while this mutual admiration was at its height, and a treaty, honourable to both sides, was signed. The young Prince Bahadur was recognised King of Ahmadnagar, under the regency of his aunt, and acknowledging the suzerainty of Delhi. But the peace was short-lived. No sooner had the sense of a common danger worn off, than the internal turbulence of the Ahmadnagar nobles broke out afresh. Berar was invaded by the Ahmadnagaries, and Akbar's patience was exhausted. A strong army under Prince Danyal and the Emperor's most valued friend, Abul Fazl, was despatched to conquer. The Regent displayed all her wonted heroism; but her resources were exhausted, her troops demoralised, her councillors disaffected. It availed her little to use her own jewellery for charging the guns, when shot and shell were exhausted. Akbar's lieutenants would not, however, be too harsh on a woman—especially such a woman! And so Abul Fazl offered terms to the beleagured sovereign, far more generous than he or his council had a right to expect. But the moment the warrior-Queen pleaded for the acceptance of those terms, her doom was sealed. A disaffected eunuch ran out of the council-chamber, and told the troops their Queen was betraying them. The soldiers rushed into the council room; and, deaf to all appeals, forgetful of all the memories of her past sacrifices, unmindful of her age and sex, they put the noble, valiant, Queen mercilessly to death. So died Chand Sultana,—the noblest and the greatest of the heroines in the century of Akbar!

Other heroes there are, too, who have a claim to a recognition even in this brief review. But if any of them cannot find a place in the gallery of the Founders of Dynasties or builders of Empires,—like Hasan Bahman Shah, or Shivaji Maharaj,—they have to their credit deeds of heroism not essentially dissimilar to those instanced already; and as such there is little need to crowd still more this already over-crowded canvas. The picture, however, as unfolded so far, is rich in glowing tints of a most variegated description; and must, therefore, satisfy fully the most fastidious demands of national vanity. The types selected in this review have been chosen because of their undying influence upon the ideals of a nation, and the character of its people in successive generations. There are others still who have made these ideals live, and built out of the raw material afforded by these their mighty empires on the soil of India. These we review in the next chapter.

PLATE XXXI

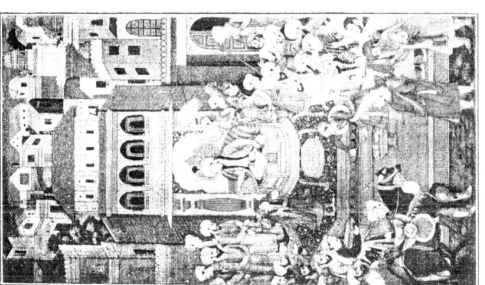

57 NUR JEHAN ENTERTAINING THE EMPEROR
JEHANGIR AND HIS SON

From the Collection of Bibi Abbas Ali, London(?)

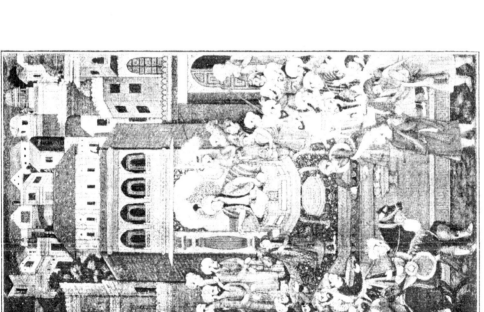

56 HUMAYUN'S ACCESSION DURBAR

PLATE XXXII

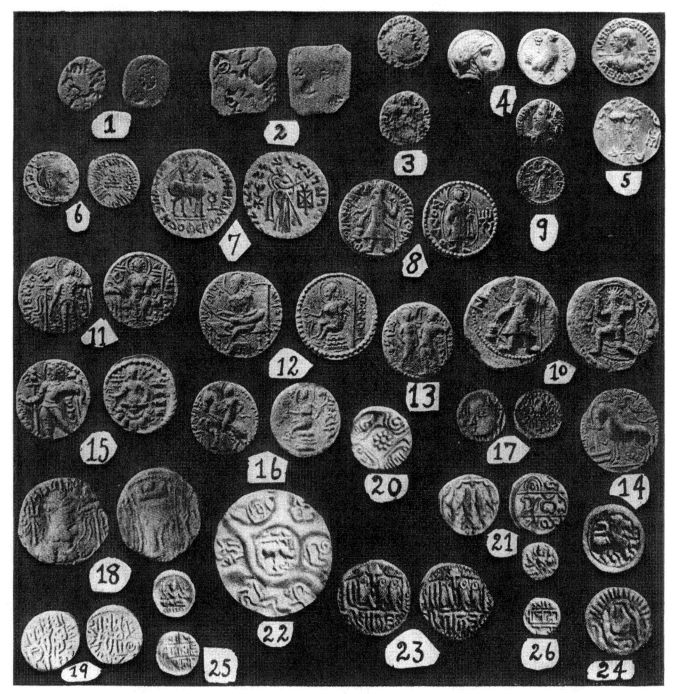

COINS OF INDIA

1. Round Punch-marked coin.   2. Rectangular punch-marked coin.   3. Mathurā: Rajuvala.   Sophytes (Saubhūti).
5. Menander.   6. Western Kshatrapa: Damasena.   7. Gondopharnes.   8. Kanishka.   9. Kanishka.   10. Kanishka.
11. Samudragupta. Standard type.   12. Samudragupta. Lyrist type.   13. Samudragupta: Chandragupta I. type.
14. Samudragupta: Asvamedha type.   15. Chandragupta II. Archer type.   16. Chandragupta II. Horseman type.   17. Silāditya
(Harshavardhana) of Thāneśar.   18. Mihiragula.   19. Delhi and Ajmer: Prithvi Rājā.   20. Padma-tanka.   21. Pāndya.
22. Eastern Chālukya: Rājarāja.   23. Chola.   24. Pallava or Chālukya (?).   25. Vijayanagar: Krishna Deva Rāya.
26. Vijayanagar: Harihara. II.

(From C. J. Brown's book "Coins of India")

CHAPTER IV

MAKERS OF HISTORY AND BUILDERS OF EMPIRE

"With the Maurya dynasty," it has been well said, "begins the period of continual history in India." We may, therefore legitimately commence the film of Indian Emperors and nation-builders with the Mauryan hero, never forgetting that the ideal of a homogeneous, solid empire is by no means foreign to the soil of India.

CHANDRAGUPTA MAURYA

Chandragupta Maurya (320 B. C. to 293 B. C.) reigned over territory far larger, in point of area, than even perhaps the present Empire of India. A contemporary of Alexander of Macedon and his successor in the former's Indian conquests, the Mauryan hero must have gathered not a few useful hints on the art of fighting when he was a visitor, or a suppliant, in the Greek Camp. He was not slow to use this knowledge, when the hour came, against the Greeks themselves. To one, however, who had, in his day, been the commander-in-chief to the greatest power in India, the Magadha realm of the Nandas, the invaders had, perhaps, not much to teach in the science of war and the art of fighting. What little his own experience had left unprovided must have been supplied by that inimitable master of all social sciences, who is variously known by tradition as the Brahmana Vishnugupta, the *Acharya* (Teacher) Chanakya, or the author Kautilya. It is a most reprehensible terminological inexactitude to style him the Indian Machiavelli. The parallel is suggested, no doubt, by the plot of a Sanskrit drama *Mudra-Rakshasa*, of which Chanakya is the real hero. The play was written nearly a thousand years after the events it deals with, and represents as facts what are little better than a poet's wild fancies.

The facts of cold-blooded history, as far as we can gather them, are somewhat like these. Chandragupta Maurya was a scion of an ancient race dwelling at the foot of the Himalayas, and an off-shoot of the holy race of the Sakyas, from which had sprung earlier the immortal Buddha. Perhaps he owed his rapid rise to the post of the War-Lord in the Magadha Empire to a bar sinister of royal origin. Certain it is, however, that he was disaffected with the Nandas, and driven from their service, at the time the overweening arrogance of the Magadha monarch had insulted a great sage and scholar, who had enough of the old Vishwamitra in him not to take the insult tamely. The disaffected soldier joined hands with the disgruntled sage; and at last obtained the aid of the redoubtable Porus, or some other lieutenant of the Macedonian. In an incredibly short time the Nandas were overthrown and their very memory uprooted, thanks chiefly to the wonderful sagacity of Vishnugupta. The allies were either bought off, or disposed of in some other way; so that, by the time Seleucus of Babylon was ready to try conclusions with the Indian, Chandragupta was master of India from the mouth of the Ganges to the mouth of the Indus, from the Narmada to the Jhelum and the Kabul. History does not tell us when precisely he acquired Malwa and Bundelkhand, Gujarat and Kathiawar, Sindh and the Punjab, besides the provinces of the Ganges basin. But history is quite clear about when he acquired the provinces of the modern Afghanistan and Baluchistan. These were obtained from Seleucus, perhaps as a dowry for his daughter given in marriage to the Maurya. In exchange the Maurya gave only 500 elephants to the Greek.

The Maurya Empire thus extended over a vast area. It is, however, an inaccurate picture of life in the Maurya Empire which would represent the Sovereign, not only as the Lord paramount, but as the uncontrolled, absolute master of the life and property of every one of his subjects. Though free from the modern restraint of a Parliament, the absolutism of the Mauryas was subtly checked by the structure of the society itself, in which the several strata or castes had a definitely assigned place; and of which one at least was even superior to the King himself. Besides, the King governed with the help of a large, well-ordered, bureaucracy, with a very precise hierarchy. These were all his servants and the ministers of his will; but in the nature of things they must nevertheless have formed an effective, though indirect, check on the royal authority. The nobility of the sword had its own power and influence, which was not the less considerable because it was not evident on the surface. And, finally, there were civic dignitaries,—let us call them mayors of towns and presidents of guilds,—who must also have provided no mean curb on the absolutism of the Prince. Some of these civic notables were considerable merchants, whose private wealth would not compare unfavourably with the King's own majesty.

The king's personal habits reflected in equal measure the splendour of his great position, and the simplicity of a man who was by training and temperament averse to ever-lasting luxury. Within the inner apartments, Chandragupta, like Akbar, passed very few hours each day; but, while there, he was guarded by a body of foreign amazons, who had been purchased for the purpose. Every day, however, when not engaged in war or the chase, the Emperor appeared in public to hear causes of complaint in person, to give audiences, or to consult with his ministers on a thousand matters of imperial importance. So much, indeed, did the duties of his post absorb the time of the Prince, that he was probably among the hardest worked men in his empire. The Emperor's only luxury in personal habits was massage, in which he seems to have indulged even while hearing cases in court, or giving ceremonial audience; while the only display of ceremonial magnificence was the hair-washing festival, probably held on the Imperial birth-days, when the nobles and grandees made considerable presents to the sovereign.

THE EMPEROR ASOKA

The Empire of Chandragupta passed in peaceful succession to his son Bindusara, and his grandson Asoka. The second Maurya must certainly have made additions to his father's dominions, though no definite accounts of his reign and conquests are available. The third and the most famous, if not also the greatest, made only one conquest, the country of the Kalingas,—the modern Coromandel coast. But his fame rests rather on his being the Imperial propagandist of Buddhism. The Buddhist Constantine was all the greater than his Christian prototype, because he did his very best to enforce in his own personal life as well as in his Empire the tenets of his creed. His famous rock edicts are veritable sermons in stone. From the foot of the Hindu Kush to within sight of the Nilgiris; from the Arabian Sea to the Bay of Bengal, he preached Buddhism and the doctrine of universal mercy. If Chandragupta was a man of blood and iron, Asoka was as clearly a man of peace. He had even taken the minor vows of a Buddhist monk. And yet so mighty was the Mauryan name, and so firmly established the tradition of law and order in this vast Empire, that in his long reign no internal rebellion or foreign invasion of any dimensions worth speaking occurred at all. Against all accepted ideals of kingliness in India, Asoka openly asked his subjects to abandon the notion of conquest by force of arms as the only work fit for a king; while he laid down the "Law of Piety" as the only way to attain salvation. The following tribute from the historian of *Ancient India* would suffice to give a fuller outline of the pious Emperor.

"Asoka did not attempt to destroy either Brahmanical Hinduism or Jainism; but his prohibition of bloody sacrifices, the preference which he openly avowed for Buddhism, and his active propaganda undoubtedly brought his favourite doctrine to the front, and established it as the dominant religion in both India and Ceylon. Still, notwithstanding many failures, fluctuations, developments and corruptions, Buddhism now commands, and will command for countless centuries to come, the devotion of hundreds of millions of men. This great result is the work of Asoka alone, and entitles him to rank for all time with that small body of men who may be said to have changed the faith of the world."

KANISHKA

With the death of the saintly Asoka, the days of the Mauryan glories were ended. The heirs and successors of Chandragupta and Asoka were feeble voluptuaries, lacking the strength to maintain the splendours of their forbears. Their distant satraps and disaffected feudatories neglected, ignored, and eventually defied the Imperial *firmans* from Pataliputra. A host of independent principalities cropped up within what had been a solid Empire, till, once again, a mighty genius came on the field to conquer or subdue, to annex and consolidate, the immense mass into a single whole. Such a one was Kanishka the Kushan, more than 250 years after the immortal Asoka.

Very little is known, authentically, of the origin of the Emperor Kanishka to enable us to claim him justly as an Indian Prince. By his conquests, and his creed, he was decidedly Indian,—more even than Babur. His capital was at what is now called Peshawar; his favourite pleasure-haunt was the vale of Kashmir, where he seems to have founded a city; his empire extended to the shores of the Arabian Ocean and to the heart of Magadha. What exactly were his own additions to the earlier conquests of his Kushan predecessors, it is difficult to say. He was, however, the most considerable and powerful Central Asiatic potentate of his day, able to deal with the Roman Empire on terms of equality and independence. His own conquests in Asia included Kashgar, Yarkand and Khotan, which, with the Parthian, Afghan, Baluch conquests and annexations of his predecessors, must have formed a very vast, solid block of territory in West-Central Asia. In India he was certainly the master of the Punjab, Kashmir, the Indus valley down to the mouth of the river, Malwa, Gujarat, and the peninsula of Kathiawar; and the Indo-Gangetic plain, probably extending as far as the eastern confines of the Mauryan Magadha.

This was an empire, not a whit less glorious or extensive than that of the greatest of the Mauryas. Like Asoka, however, Kanishka too, was touched by the subtle appeal of the Religion of Mercy. At some date in his career, Kanishka was converted to the Law of Piety; and, ever since, fact and fable alike conspired to make him a second Asoka,—a Buddhist Charlemagne. If he did not, like Asoka, actually assume the yellow robe of the Buddhist monk, he was yet too active a patron of Buddhism not to concern himself with a new and Authorised Version of the Law of the Sakya saint. In his reign, a great Æcumenical council was held in Kashmir, at Kundalavana near the capital, under the presidency of the Pontiff Vasumitra, and the guidance of the greatest Buddhist scholar and divine of the age,—Ashwaghosha. 500 theologians, prelates, and scholars participated in the protracted labours, which resulted in the authoritative promulgation of the true apostolic canon, engraved, for further security and permanence, on copper plates deposited in a special cupola, built by order of the Imperial patron for the purpose, where they may even now be lying concealed for all we know. The resemblance to the Catholic Apostolic Church of Christ in the West may be further completed by the story of the conferment of the Kingdom of Kashmir on the Buddhist church. The donation was first made by Asoka, and Kanishka seems only to have confirmed it.

THE GUPTAS

If we may place the reign of Kanishka between 78 A. C., and 120 A. C., a period of another two centuries of decline and dismemberment had to follow before the Imperial idea was reborn in India.

The fourth and fifth centuries of the Christian era may well be regarded as the Golden Age in the early history of India. The mighty Gupta Empire, rivalling in extent and splendour the magnificent fabric of Mauryan creation, was formed, extended, consolidated and maintained between 320 A. D. and 455 A. D. Chandra-Gupta, the first of this line of long-lived emperors, was the scion of a petty local prince in Magadha; but on his marriage to Kumara Devi,—a Princess of the Lichchavis, who were a famous clan at the time of the Buddha,—he was immediately raised to the status of a great power in eastern India. He himself had little time to build up a great empire by his conquests; but he was skilful and far-sighted enough to utilize the suzerainty of his Queen's people over the ancient Imperial capital to reduce the whole of the home provinces of the Mauryas to subjection.

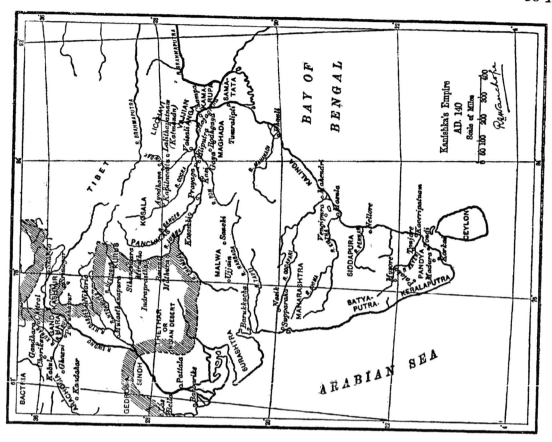

Kanishka's Empire
AD. 140
Scale of Miles
0 50 100 200 300 400

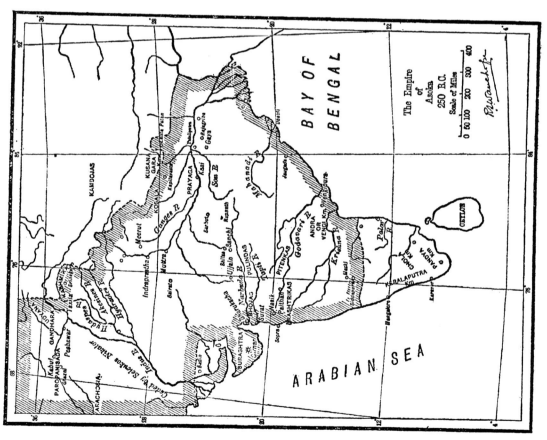

The Empire
of
Asoka
250 B.C.
Scale of Miles
0 50 100 200 300 400

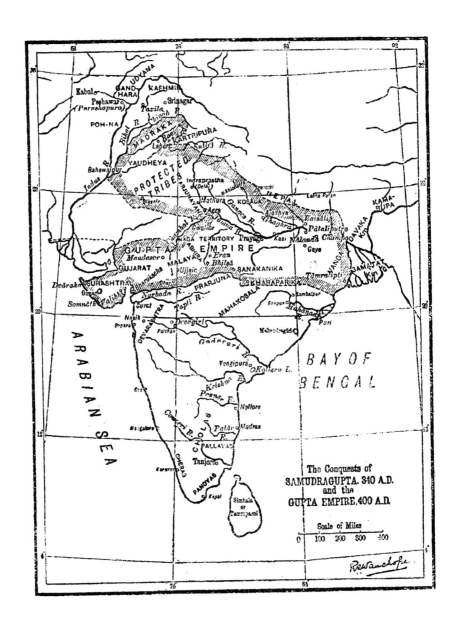

The Conquests of
SAMUDRAGUPTA. 340 A.D.
and the
GUPTA EMPIRE, 400 A.D.

Scale of Miles
0   100   200   300   400

His reign is further memorable for the great importance and reverence to his Queen,—the Lichchavi Princess,—after whom his much more famous son Samudra-Gupta is only too proud to be known; and in whose name coins of the realm were struck by her grateful and devoted husband, even as that prince of lovers, the Emperor Jahangir, some 1300 years later, minted his coins in the name of his Empress Nur Jahan.

Samudra-Gupta, son and successor of Chandra-Gupta and Kumara Devi, was a born conqueror. His father seems to have been of Buddhist persuasion, but this "Indian Napolean,"—as Vincent Smith justly calls him,—was a confirmed but widely tolerant Hindu. The sculptured records of his conquests, embossed in the flowery style of a court panegyrist, had ample basis in sober earnest to justify all the seeming vaingloriousness of style and bewildering magniloquence of expression. His father's sway had hardly penetrated beyond the confluence of the Jumna and the Ganges at Allahabad on the west, and on the south up to the Son basin. Not content with this, he carried his victorious arms to the further bank of the Indus on the north-west corner, making the Chinab the permanent frontier of the Empire on that side; subjugated all the semi-independent tribes of the Doab and of Rajputana; annexed the Punjab, and, together with Bundelkhand and the regions of the home provinces, stretching up to the foot of the Himalayas on the north and the mouth of the Ganges on the east, made a consolidated Empire of Hindustan proper, which was not much inferior to that of Akbar. On the south, he had vast ambitions, and actually carried out a tremendous Cæsarian march, which, beginning with the regions around Chutia Nagpur, passed along the eastern coast, and went as far south as the modern Conjevaram. Thence he turned backward through the plateau of the Deccan proper along the Western Ghats, conquering and subjugating wherever he went. It was a mighty progress, an unbroken triumph from beginning to end, lasting for perhaps over two years, and testifying during its course to the marvellous organisation of transport and commissariat, of ordnance and general discipline, which kept intact and ever victorious such a huge host, marching over hills, through dense forests, across mighty rivers, along altogether unfamiliar and unfriendly regions. For a thousand years before or after him, there was none to emulate this unparalleled feat. His importance may be illustrated by the instance of a peaceful embassy from King Meghavarna of Ceylon. Whatever justification Samudra-Gupta had to regard the rich presents of gems, etc., which the Ceylonese embassy brought him, as the tributary offerings of a vassal Prince, the fact is indisputable that the worshippers from Ceylon at the Holy of Holies of Buddhism had to seek and obtain the sanction of the Indian Emperor before they could build there an appropriate college of their own.

The unique glory of Samudra-Gupta lies in his bewildering versatility. Conquerors there were before and after him. Soldiering was the sacred, traditional, hereditary occupation of kings in India from time immemorial: so that excellence in this department of king-craft will not by itself call forth our unstinted admiration. Wisdom, foresight, toleration of all the several creeds have been the distinctive marks of outstanding kings in Indian history from the Mauryas to the Mughals; and in that aspect, also, though Samudra-Gupta was great, he has mighty rivals in Akbar and Asoka. In his patronage of arts and sciences, too, the greatest of the Mughals would easily equal, if not eclipse, him. But where the greatest of the Guptas stands unrivalled is in his own mastery of the Fine Arts. The flute seems to have been as familiar to his hand as the sword and the lance; while the making of verses came to him as naturally as the formation of military manoeuvres in the field. Even his celebration of the famous *Ashwamedha* or Horse Sacrifice may be taken to indicate that love,—that mastery of history,—in which some may have equalled, but none surpassed, him.

Chandra-Gupta II (378-413 A. C.), his son Kumara-Gupta (413-455 A. C.), and grandson Skanda-Gupta (455-467 A.C.) were worthy successors of the great Samudra-Gupta. The first of these even maintained his family tradition of conquest and annexation by over-throwing the western Satrapies of Malwa and Kathiawar, incorporating these rich and wealthy provinces in the Empire, and so extending it from sea to sea throughout the breadth of India. The Gupta Empire recalls in almost every prominent incident the later Mughal Empire. If the glories of the Mughals lasted a hundred and fifty years (1556-1707), those of the Guptas endured for a like period (320-467 A. C.). If the Mughal Empire went on tottering for another century and a half after its zenith had been passed, so did the Gupta for even a longer period. The last of the great Guptas had almost an indentical difficulty with the last of the great Mughals. For the Hun invasions may not quite unfitly be compared to the Maratha outbreak of a later age. Skanda-Gupta was at first victorious and stemmed the tide of invasion effectually. But in the last years of his reign he was weary and weakened, and the Hun menace had to be swept away from India by other races in the Empire. The Gupta age, finally, was an age of tremendous revival in the intellectual world. Some of the finest contributions to poetry and philosophy, to architecture and painting, to all the graces and amenities as much as to the arts and sciences of civilised life, were made in this Golden Age of Indian History. The kings were themselves great patrons of poets and artists, refined and cultured enough to appreciate to a nicety the value of the works of art they patronised. The name of Kalidasa,—the immortal laureate of Sanskrit drama and classic poetry,—who is now generally believed to have flourished in this age, would alone suffice to give point to this remark; while those of his other great contemporaries, the famous *Nava Ratna* of the Court of Vikramaditya, will be enough to establish the claim of a Golden Age made for this period. "Probably, India has never been governed better, after the oriental manner, than it was in the reign of Vikramaditya."[1]

SHRI HARSHA (606-647 A. C.)

Another interval of 150 years had to pass before the glories of the Gupta Empire could once more come to bloom. In marked contrast with the mighty Mauryas and

---

1) Vincent Smith.

the glorious Guptas, the reign of Harsha of Kanauj stands out alone, like a solitary boss in the midst of an otherwise level plain. A younger son of a local raja of Thaneshwar, the classic Kuru-Kshetra, Harsha was induced to succeed to the throne of his elder brother with some difficulty. When, however, he finally made up his mind to accept the invitation of his nobles and grasp the sceptre, he lost no time in avenging the dastardly murder in Malwa of his beloved elder brother and sovereign, Rajya Vardhana. Malwa was his sister's husband's country; but the king and queen were overthrown; and first Rajya Vardhana, and afterwards Harsha Vardhana, marched against the country to avenge the insult and annex the territory. With Malwa was involved a local king of Bengal, who was overthrown by Harsha, and his dominions annexed to the Empire of Kanauj. The Gujarati kingdom of Valabhi was brought into subsidiary alliance by the marriage of the Valabhi Prince to a daughter of the Emperor. Saurashtra and Kachchh were part of the Empire; while, at the other end of India, Kumara of Kamrup,—the modern Assam,—was a feudatory of the suzerain of Hindustan. Part of the Punjab and the whole of Central India, and the Indo-Gangetic plain up to the Brahmaputra, were under the direct government of Harsha. The Emperor entertained, of course, still vaster ideas of conquest and annexation on the south. But his host was met on the banks of the Narmada by another equally mighty sovereign, the famous Pulakeshin. He successfully withstood the Emperor of the North, and forced him to abandon his ambition of conquering the Deccan.

Harsha, however, had to keep on the alert for 30 years after his coronation. Though, like Asoka, he had adopted the Law of Piety, he was not able to doff the armour till towards the close of his long reign of over 40 years (606-647). At the height of his power and splendour and glory, the famous Chinese pilgrim Hiuen-Tsang visited the Empire, (630-644), and was accorded the honour of expounding the Canon in the Imperial Presence. The widowed Queen of Malwa, sister of the Emperor, sat in open Court with her brother; and failed not to express her unstinted praise of the Master when he had done.

The Emperor was a constant traveller, and his Imperial camp was, during his tours, surrounded by as many as 18 camps of vassal kings. In his own camp there were 4 courts, and the Emperor gave public audience in the fourth, "seated on a throne of pearl-like stone, with his feet resting on a foot-stool of sapphire and ruby." (Mukerji.)

As an example of the wealth and munificence of Shri Harsha, take the following:—

On the occasion of a grand Kumbh Mela at Prayag, 1000 Buddhist priests received each 100 pieces of gold, one pearl, one cotton garment, besides an enormous quantity of food and drink. For 20 days thereafter Brahmans received gifts, and 10 days thereafter other heretics, besides the orphans and the indigent, gifts to whom occupied a whole month. "By this time the accumulation of five years was exhausted. Except the horses, elephants and military accoutrements, nothing remained. The king freely gave away his gems and goods, his clothing and necklaces,

16

ear-rings, bracelets, chaplets, neck-jewel, and bright head-jewel." Not even his own personal clothing was excepted, so that when on the final day of the assembly he had to offer worship, he had to borrow a second-hand garment from his sister, Rajyashri! Verily, a record of personal charities!

Harsha was also a great, munificent, discerning patron of learning and the Fine Arts. Himself a dramatic poet of no mean order, he was able justly to appreciate the merits of men like Bana Bhatta, or the scholarship of men like Hiuen-Tsang. For more than a thousand years after the death of the Buddha, India remained not only the Holy Land for countless millions of men, but also the focus of the universe for arts and learning. Emperors, like Harsha, or still more the Guptas and Kanishka, who came under the influence of that Messenger of Mercy, were themselves keenly interested in the Scriptures; and able to facilitate the researches of such scholars without a trace of narrow-mindedness, bigotry, or parochialism, that later came to disfigure Indian Royalty.

* * * * * *

The history of the next five hundred years is not altogether a blank. The impulse given to the national spirit under the cultured Guptas continued all throughout the period until the advent of the Musalmans. The annals, however, of towering personalities of Imperial or epoch-making proportions seem to be quiet during these five centuries. The Musalman invasions of India did, no doubt, commence in the eighth century under the Arabs. But they are little better than sporadic raids, whose purpose of loot was but faintly tinctured with any intention of permanent settlement. Religious fanaticism and proselytising zeal marked the Muslim raiders from the start; and, in this respect, their influence, when it came to be considerable, was in marked contrast with the settled policy of perfect religious freedom and toleration that had distinguished all the early Indian Empires, whether Hindu, Buddhist, or Jain. The Arab Khalifas were, indeed, a highly cultured line. But by the time the Muslim wave of conquest reached India, the Arab influence was definitely on the wane; and the standard of the Crescent was borne by men hailing from the wilds of savage, dreary, inhospitable Turkestan. Until, therefore, they had received the sobering, humanising, civilising touch of more cultured peoples, it would be absurd to expect from them those graces which make the greatness of empire-builders still greater.

Of the Muhammadan conquerors, then, we need hardly touch upon Mahmud of Ghazni at the end of tenth century, and Shahabuddin of Ghor in the twelfth. Mahmud was, in India at least, frankly a raider, whose object was loot, and whose ambition idol-breaking. Patron of Firdausi and master of Alberuni, we scarcely recognise him in India, throughout his twenty-four expeditions, as being even on nodding terms with culture, grace, or beauty in human existence. Shahabuddin of Ghor was, in himself, perhaps, less cultured than his great predecessor. Certainly, his court had none of the splendours which the poetry of Firdausi and the scholarship of Alberuni lent to that of Mahmud. But lacking in these, Shahabuddin

PLATE XXXIII

90 PULAKESIN II RECEIVING THE PERSIAN AMBASSADOR —
AJUNTA FRESCOES

89 INSCRIBED PILLAR OF SAMUDRA
GUPTA OF BHITARI
(Photo. Archaeological Survey of India)

91 BABUR   92 HUMAYUN

(91-92 Bahadur Singhji Collection, Calcutta)

PLATE XXXIV

94   AKBAR'S MOTHER
HAMIDA BANO BEGUM

93   AKBAR

95   NUR JEHAN

96   JEHANGIR

(93 and 95: Bahadur Singhji Collection, Calcutta)

appears yet, in India at any rate, to have been gifted with a nobler imagination and actuated by a loftier ambition. He compares unfavourably, in Indian eyes at least, with his Hindu antagonists in point of chivalry, if not in regard to personal courage. But success having once crowned his arms, he speedily recurred to that dream of empire, which had captured the imagination of every Indian hero through the countless generations of our history. He did not, indeed, make India his home of adoption; nor had he time or inclination to assimilate Indian civilisation or Hindu culture. Probably he saw in the latter nothing but abomination. But the elements of greatness, which are accepted as such commonly by mankind, he certainly had; and his Indian career of conquest and annexation exhibits them in a noteworthy measure.

His slave and pupil, his lieutenant and viceroy, Qutb-ud-din was, of course, the first real founder of Muslim dominion in India. Lacking not a whit in personal courage or generalship, as compared to his teacher and sovereign, Qutb-ud-din had his own trait of greatness in the perfect fidelity to the master who had raised and ennobled him, and put him in the way of further greatness. Fanatic he probably was. But as his conquests expanded; as it became more and more evident to him that his home and that of his successors was to be in India; as he made a first-hand acquaintance with the spirit of the people in adventures like that with Maharani Korumdevi of Chitor at Amber, he seems to have realised the futility of the ambition to convert the whole of India to Islam. We have to wait 4 centuries before the perception could arise that since India could not be Islamised, Islam might be Indianised. In his own way, however, and with the unavoidable limitations of his age and conditions, Qutb-ud-din must be recognised to be a great soldier-statesman, surprisingly successful in the task he had taken in hand, with very little violence to his own conscience, and no outrage upon the then current ideals of mankind.

The Slave Dynasty has two other Emperors, at all comparable to Qutb-ud-din. Altamsh maintained the traditions of conquest of his predecessors, and Ghiyas-ud-Din Balban added the ornament of culture and refinement, to which they were strangers. In his day, while the savage Mongols were ravaging the rest of Asia, the Court of Delhi was the most splendid and cultured all through Asia. Fifteen Muslim kings from Central Asia, and the great Persian poet, Shaikh Sadi, were refugees at Delhi, where they were treated with that high-bred courtesy which henceforth becomes a distinguished trait of the Indian Musalman.

A tribute may also be paid in passing to that Prince of Peace, the Emperor Nasir-ud-Din Mahmud, who was the first crowned head to show the more refined and lovable side of the Muslim ruler. A son of Altamsh, yet prisoner himself for a long while, he had been schooled in adversity. Never forgetting the lessons of his youth, he maintained the same rule of rigid simplicity for himself and his household. This is probably unequalled in the annals of Imperial Delhi, unless we think of the mighty Aurangzeb and his own personal, marvellous, simplicity, in the midst of a blazing profusion and almost criminal extravagance. Nasir-ud-Din is said to have lived entirely on the proceeds of the Quran he copied and sold. His wife, the

Empress,—the only partner of his life,—had to cook his food and run his house, as any lady of the middle class, for the Emperor. He refused to employ any servant for his personal comfort out of the public funds, a rare conception of the duties of kingship.

Alauddin Khilji is the next considerable figure on the Imperial stage. A hardy warrior, his laurels in the field were tarnished a great deal by his record of ingratitude and treachery, unsurpassed by any ruler before or since. Kingship is, indeed, a sad craft, which makes men often forget their bonds of natural affection. We have, however, met him in another connection, and must, therefore, pass on to the next imperial race at Delhi.

Of the Tughluqs who succeeded the Khiljis, there is very little to record beyond the madness of Muhammad, a living paradox, if ever there was one; and the peaceful, but prosperous and uneventful, reign of Firozeshah, the founder of yet another Delhi. In the anarchy and disorders of the closing years of the Afghan dominion, no towering personality meets the eye until we come upon the greatest of them all,—Farid, better known to history as Sher Shah Sur. In almost every instance he seems to anticipate the glory and splendour of the greatest of the Mughals. A prudent soldier, his personal bravery was beyond question or cavil, since it could be so well appreciated by Babur, the bravest of the brave. But the soldier in Sher Shah never ran away with the farsighted, deep-thinking, broad-minded statesman. His rise from the position of a petty Jagirdar to the seat of Empire is evidence enough of his daring and sagacity, of his skill and judgment and enterprise. Had Babur lived, it is difficult to say what would have happened to the lion of Bihar and Bengal. Perhaps Sher Khan made the same mistake that the Maharana Sanga of Mewar had made in inviting Babur's aid for the destruction of the Afghan Sultanate of Delhi. They seem to have believed that Babur, like his ancestor Timur, would fight their fight, get his pay or loot for the fighting, and then leave India on some other wild goose chase. If so, they were both undeceived, the Maharana to his own undoing, Sher Shah, more fortunate, to his remarkable accession of power. For, Sher Shah knew his strength,—or the lack of it,—too well to stake his life and hope on the cast of a battle, especially with a warrior and commander like Babur. Like Chandragupta Maurya in the Macedonian camp, he had for a while served in person under Babur; and formed his own opinion of the daring genius and iron will of the first of the Mughals. Escaping from the Mughal camp, he busied himself with more immediate methods of personal aggrandisement, which made him, soon after the death of Babur, a formidable opponent to his son and successor Humayun. The new Emperor had all the courage and the poetry of his father. He certainly excelled Akbar,—his son,—in culture, and even Babur in chivalry. But he lacked, in the earlier years of his rule at least, that tenacity of purpose,—that iron strength of will,—which made the greatness of Babur. Humayun was, therefore, easily able to conquer in a pitched battle. But where the fight depended on something more than personal courage, he had to yield before the superior talents of Sher Shah. When once the Mughals had, as they thought, been expelled, Sher Shah was crowned Emperor of

India; and, during his brief reign of five years, did everything to mark him out as amongst the greatest of the Indian Emperors. The achievements of those five brief but crowded years of military triumphs, as well as civil administrative feats, make Sher Shah dispute almost evenly the supreme place with Akbar himself in the annals of Musalman India. He not only gained battles, but built roads and rest-houses; instituted the public post; constructed or renovated irrigation works; re-organised the public services; settled land revenue and fixed the canons of its assessment; reformed the mint and determined the ratio between gold and silver; revised the principles of Imperial taxation; patronised art and literature; and altogether gave every proof of his ability as well as intention to string together and consolidate the vast fabric of his dominions into a single, solid nation. But envious fate denied him the time needed for accomplishing a tenth of his self-imposed task. He was cut off by an accidental shot in the heyday of his career; and the dream of Sher Shah was left for the greatest of the Mughals to convert into a reality.

* * * * * *

Before, however, we speak of Akbar the Great, let us cast a glance in passing at another Empire-builder working on another part of the stage. Historical research has dealt rather meagrely, so far, with the fortunes of the heroes of the Deccan. The authors of the great Pandya, Chola, Chalukya Empires of the far, far South, are shrouded in impenetrable mists; and we know of a Pulakesin only by his opposition to and defeat of a more fortunate Shri Harsha from the North. But, notwithstanding the paucity of information, we can easily distinguish the outstanding figures of the founders of the great Hindu and Muhammadan kingdoms that, for nearly two centuries, were to dispute the country among them. The raid of the famous renegade general of Alauddin Khilji had terrorised, but not subdued, and much less annihilated, the Malayalis, the Kanarese and the Telugus,—descendants of that mighty race which had peopled India before ever an Aryan invader had set foot in the country. They at last found leaders in two brothers, feudatories of the Hoysala kingdom, who established a settlement at Kishkindha,—the epic capital of Sugriva, the monkey ally of Rama,—on the right bank of the Tungabhadra, in the margin of territory between the modern kingdoms of Mysore and Hyderabad. Bukka, succeeding his elder brother, became the ruler of this straggling settlement of mud huts, destined soon to blossom forth into the famous Empire of Vijayanagar. For to this settlement flocked, as to an asylum, all those who wanted to escape the tyranny and bigotry of the Muslim invaders; and with their help, the united strength of the Hindus was enough, not merely to stem back the tide of invasion and forcible conversion, but to open up a new chapter in the Hindu history of the south, lasting over 200 years, full of achievements of wealth and splendour, second to none in the entire continent.

While the foundation was being laid for the Hindu Empire of the farther South, a new Muhammadan power, independent of Delhi, was also coming into existence on the plateau of the Deccan. According to a common legend, Zafar was a humble

17

Musalman in the service of a Brahman called Gangu. In tilling his master's fields, he one day came upon a secret hoard, which, instead of appropriating for his own purposes, he took to his master. The latter was struck by this remarkable piece of honesty, and rewarded him by educating the servant with his own sons, and eventually obtaining for him a post in the Tughluq service. Once launched, Zafar's native talents carried him from post to post in a rapid succession of triumphs, that culminated in his being placed in command of an army corps operating in the south. The reigning sovereign, Muhammad Tughluq, had exasperated his people by his innumerable freaks of incredible folly, cruelty, ambition, or insanity; and so, when the fateful hour struck, the man also was at hand. The army proclaimed Zafar their Chief and Emperor; but the prudent adventurer, rather than grasp at the shadow of Imperial name in the North, chose the substantial security of the remote south. Zafar Khan was easily able to suppress opposition of the loyalists, and to secure himself in the Deccan—being proclaimed king as Ala-ud-din Bahman. This Empire, founded by an ex-slave of a Brahman, lasted for 340 years, and comprised, at the height of its prosperity, practically the entire peninsula of the Deccan.

*   *   *   *

The Mughal Empire was founded in India by Zahiruddin Muhamad Babur, to whose career we have made more than one reference already. A dreamer and yet a warrior of awful prowess; a poet and yet a statesman of consummate ability, foresight and sagacity; he was born of the turbulent race of Timur, cradled amidst the untamed beauties of Samarkand, and rose to manhood amidst the endless vicissitudes of fortune, that made him a seasoned warrior and a finished general at the ripe age of twenty-five. The character of the man shows clearly through every page of his early, varied, romantic career. Three times he took and thrice he lost Samarkand, the metropolis of Central Asia; but not all the blows of fortune succeeded in dimming his ardour for war, or his appreciation of natural beauty. A jolly toper, a gentle poet, a doughty soldier, he was every inch a knight of romance. But the gay insouciance of a poet-philosopher masked the keenness of one of the greatest strategists of his age. The story of his inroads upon India is better left for the historian to edit out of the Emperor's own memoirs, and from the voluminous material compiled by his son and daughter. Suffice it for us to note that he excelled all the previous invaders of India,—of his race and lineage particularly,—in the ease with which he arrived at the decision to make India his home and the heart of his Empire. His own immediate followers were against a permanent settlement in India, where they missed the snowclad mountains of their native wilds. But overlooking this advantage, he was yet able to see the immense possibilities of an Empire in India. By his firmness as much as by his eloquence, he was able to persuade his followers to stay on and share in the vast and rich empire he was hoping to build up. They stayed; and, before Babur died, they were masters of the Punjab and the country between the Ganges and the Jumna. After he had vanquished Sanga in the field, and taught his Afghan allies the weight of

PLATE XXXV

97   SHAH JEHAN

98   MUMTAZ MAHAL

99   AURANGZEB

By kind permission, Raj of the Scindia Collection, Calcutta

100   SHIVAJI

By kind permission, Prince of Wales Museum, Bombay

PLATE XXXVI

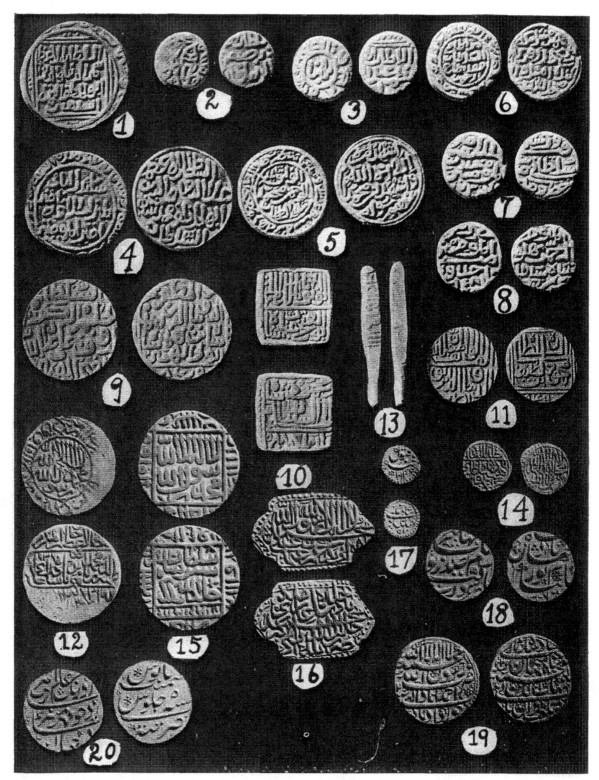

COINS OF INDIA

1. Altamsh.   2. Raziya.   3. Ghiyāsu-d-dīn Balban.   4. ʿAlāu-d-dīn Muhammad, Delhī.   5. Muhammad bin Tughlaq, Delhī.   6. Muhammad bin Tughlaq: Forced Currency, Tughlaqpūr.   7. Fīroz Shāh, Delhī. 8. Bahlol Lodī, Delhī.   9. Bahmanī: ʿAlāu-d-dīn Ahmad II.   10. Mālwā: Ghiyās Shāh.   11. Gujarāt: Mahmūd Shāh III.   12. Bābur: Lāhor.   13. Bijāpūr: Aʿdil Shāh, Lārīn.   14. Humāyūn.   15. Sher Shāh, Āgra.   16. Akbar, Āgra.   17. Jahāngīr.   18. Jahāngīr: with Nūr Jahān, Sūrat.   19. Shāh Jahān I. 20. Aurangzeb.

(From C. J. Brown's book, "Coins of India")

his sword, he settled down to plant gardens at Delhi and Agra, to grow his favourite melons of Kabul on the soil of the Doab. His sword was, indeed, held always loose in the scabbard. But the promise of his still growing greatness was nipped in the bud. His death was a fit end to his career of romantic adventure. His favourite son lay stricken before the Emperor's eyes. Rather than live himself and let Humayun die, Babur prayed to God to spare his son, and to take him instead. It was a rare prayer, and was soon answered. Humayun recovered, and Babur fell ill—never to rise again.

The Empire he left was divided by his dutiful son, the chivalrous heir of a knightly father, among his faithless and treacherous brothers, despite their character. His own share Humayun had to dispute with his erstwhile allies or feudatories. But undismayed by the troubles that beset his own throne, Humayun was ever ready to run to the rescue of the distressed. His succour of the widowed Queen and the orphaned King of Udaipur, against his own co-religionists, is amongst the noblest of his achievements. He conquered Gujarat for a while, but was himself driven out of his Empire by the superior genius of the Sur. But even in flight and adversity, the romantic ardour of his father's son knew no restraint. In Sindh he saw, at a feast given by his step-mother, a fourteen-year old girl, the most beautiful daughter of a Persian teacher of religion. To see her was to love her. Humayun asked her hand in marriage; and though Hindal, his brother, opposed, the union of two devoted hearts was soon followed by the union of their hands in holy matrimony. Their love lasted while Humayun lived; for Hamida Banu Begum was courageous as she was beautiful, devoted as she was high-souled. Akbar the Great was born of this union.

The story of Akbar is told too often to need repetition even in a summary form. His birth and infancy; his accession and first victories; his struggles with the companions of his father and the grandees of his court; his conquests and annexations in the full bloom of manhood; his organisation, civil as well as military; his search after Truth; his love of the refined and the beautiful in art as well as nature; his delight in music; his appreciation of painting; his patronage of poets and men of letters; even the minute details of his personal appearance, temperament and habits, are portrayed in Mr. Vincent Smith's masterpiece so vividly, that the reader cannot but recognise in Akbar as it were a personal acquaintance. But without transgressing on the province of his biographer; without repeating tales which no amount of repetition would stale to Indian ears; we may yet mention a few details illustrative of the splendour and magnificence of the court of the greatest Emperor of India since the Imperial Mauryas and the renowned Guptas. His great-grandson ruled, it is true, a larger extent of territories; and had probably a correspondingly larger revenue. But it was Akbar who had laid the foundation of that Empire, and built the greatest portion of it. Succeeding in 1556 to a shadow sovereignty, Akbar was for four years afterwards under the domination of the powers behind his throne. It was, therefore, within a period of less than twenty years (1560-1580) that he accomplished the bulk of his conquests, and settled and consolidated the vast empire stretching from Sindh to Bengal, and Kabul to Gujarat. His later years were not altogether free from warfare; but by 1580 he had given such unmistakable proofs of his transcendant genius, that we may regard the achievement of his imperial ambitions as complete by that time.

How far did he succeed in his task? At the time of his death in 1605, Akbar left, in Agra fort alone, hard cash to the tune of £ 20 million; and if we add up the treasure in all the other provincial capitals, the cash alone aggregates £ 40 million, equal in purchasing power to £ 200 million or more in modern money.[1] And this after fifty years of constant alertness, and splendid, magnificent living beyond the dreams of splendour of any days before or since Akbar!

For an empire founded on conquest, Akbar's stores of military material and weapons seem disproportionately small. But in this, as in many other matters, Akbar's genius set his own standard. He was in marked contrast in this to the earlier emperors. Akbar, unlike the Mauryas or the Guptas, was content with a relatively small standing army, trusting to special levies for any particular expeditions, and depending on the *aides* of his nobles and feudatories for a general strength fully sufficient for the defence of the Empire, its order and security. The military *noblesse* of Akbar was a hierarchy, ordaining the several ranks according to the varied strength of the contingent—horse and foot—which the holder was expected to supply, or entitled to command. It was not a hereditary aristocracy; but, as the biographies in the official list of the *noblesse* show, there was already a a seed of such a development in the policy of Akbar and his successors. The salaries payable to the various officers in this military hierarchy compare magnificently with those under the Mauryan Empire, where the heir-apparent was allowed only 48,000 *Panas* per annum,—not much more than Rs. 4000 a month in actual money, and probably not much more in real value either. In the days of Aurangzeb, a hundred years after Akbar, the allowance of the undesignate heir-apparent was

---

1) The following is an inventory of that treasure:—

Gold coin	...	...	...	...	Rs.	9,75,80,000
Silver coin	...	...	...	...	,,	10,00,00,000
Bronze coin	...	...	...	...	,,	7,66,666
Diamonds, rubies, emeralds, sapphires, pearls, etc. (gems)...			...	,,	6,05,20,521
Wrought gold (including jewels)	...	...	...	,,	1,90,06,745
Golden furniture (Plate and images of animals)		...	...	,,	95,07,992
Wrought silver: Goblets &c.	...	...	...	,,	22,25,838
Brazen vessels	...	...	...	...	,,	51,225
Porcelain	...	...	...	...	,,	25,07,747
Cloths, silks, cotton goods	...	...	...	...	,,	1,55,09,979
Woollen cloths	...	...	...	...	,,	5,03,252
Tents, hangings, umbrellas, rugs	...	...	...	,,	99,25,545
Books	...	...	...	...	,,	64,63,731
Engines of war and Ordnance Stores	...	...	...	,,	85,75,791
Weapons	...	...	...	...	,,	75,55,825
Harness	...	...	...	...	,,	25,25,646
Housings, cloaks and royal arms	...	...	...	,,	50,00,000

Total Rs. 34,82,26,503

Rs. 2 crores per annum from the Imperial Treasury. The widowed consort of Jahangir — Nur Jahan — was allowed by Shah Jahan Rs. 16 lakhs for the purely personal expenses of a retired widow. In the footnote is a table of salaries[1] under Akbar of the highest officers in the Empire. Even if these were not paid all the year round, they indicate a very high rate of pay, especially when viewed in relation to the purchasing power of the rupee in those days. No wonder that, as one of the English travellers in the seventeenth century remarks, the provincial governors were able to maintain a right royal state. The Subahdar of Gujarat, according to this authority, had a total annual expenditure of Rs. 1 crore! though, very probably, by far the larger proportion of this was derived from the private estates of the Viceroy. Akbar had discovered the principle of making up a splendid court and a brilliant aristocracy without any danger to the sovereign, in affording the nobles opportunities of honourable and dignified employment away from their homes, somewhat on the same lines as were followed in France under Louis XIV.

Akbar's passion for organisation, — a veritable mark of genius, — shows itself again and again in the minute regulation of every detail of life in his Court and his harem, his army and his administration. The continuance of his Empire for a century and a half in its pristine glory was in no small measure due to this perfect regulation and careful organisation. The harem, — that most sensitive, delicate and even dangerous point in an oriental monarchy, — was a marvel of ordered ease and luxury. Five thousand women dwelt within it, and each had her own separate state and quarters. The Camp of the Emperor on march was another such wonder, which never failed to excite the most unstinted admiration of the European travellers. It is impossible to give even a specimen of the myriads of regulations made by Akbar. The student who wants fuller details must be referred to the fountain-head of all information about Akbar's institutions, — the *Ain-i-Akbari*, the Mirror of Akbar. Let us conclude this sketch by a quotation from V. A. Smith, summing up the character and achievements of his hero.

> "The practical ability displayed by Akbar as soldier, general, administrator, diplomatist and supreme ruler, has been shown abundantly by his whole history, and does not need further exposition. The personal force of his character, discernible even now with sufficient clearness, was overpowering to his contemporaries. He was truly, as the Jesuit author calls him, "the terror of the East." In the later years of his reign, when all his old friends had disappeared, and he had been spoiled to a certain extent by more than four decades of autocracy, it is probable that he was feared rather than loved. The dread of him, even at an earlier time, was so potent that he felt himself free to flout and insult the most sacred feelings of his Muhammadan subjects, and to continue in the course of conduct for more than twenty years. As early as 1582 Monserrate noted with surprise that Akbar had not been killed by the Musalmans. It is true that his innovations provoked rebellions, but we never hear of their resulting in direct attempts

1) Commander of	Horses	Elephants	Beasts of Burden	SALARIES Rupees per month		
				1st Class	2nd Class	3rd Class
5,000	340	100	260	30,000	29,000	28,000
1,000	94	31	67	8,200	8,100	8,000
500	30	12	27	2,500	2,300	2,100
100	10	3	7	700	600	500
10	4	—	—	100	82½	75

on his life. His grand personal qualities seem to have shielded him from the violence of the assassin. We read of only one attempt to murder him, and that occurred when he was twenty-one years of age, and was still a zealous Muslim, but had given deep offence by invading the honour of families.

*   *   *   *   *

In the tale of the Great Mughal Emperors, there is at least one grand, noble, heroic figure of a woman that cannot be passed over in silence. Nur Jahan was not a heroine of the harem. She was the guardian angel, the inspiring genius of Jahangir, as she was the adored wife of his bosom, the beloved consort of his reign. The son of Akbar lacked many a trait of his father's towering personality; but his deficiencies were eclipsed by the dazzling qualities of his Empress. Their love is a fit tale for an inspired bard. The luckless child of a Persian immigrant, Nur Jahan was abandoned at birth in a desert by her parents; but fate had destined her for higher things. She was saved and returned to her parents. Her father obtained honourable employment under Akbar. The daughter, dowered by peerless beauty and still more matchless graces of the mind, was a frequent and welcome visitor to the Imperial *zenana*. Prince Salim once saw her in the palace garden for one brief fleeting moment,—and for ever lost his heart to the lovely Persian. His father, however, would have no such *mesalliance;* and so she was married and exiled to a distant province of the Empire. It was only when Salim had ascended the throne, that he could gratify the dream of his youth and manhood. Her husband was bidden to the court of the Imperial viceroy in his province; but Sher Khan, too, was worthy of her who had loved him so well and truly. Refusing to be a complaisant coward, he died the death of a warrior in the field; and his widow was brought to the court of the Emperor. But the Master of India dared not take liberties with the idol of his heart. Lord of life and death to countless millions, he was yet a humble suppliant at the feet of the matchless Persian. For four long, cruel, desolate years he waited her self-imposed widowhood. At last, when she had consented to accept his homage, he raised her to his throne. Alone among the women in Indian history, or with the possible exception of the first Gupta Empress, Nur Jahan was a consort regnant. Even coins were minted in her name jointly with her husband's. If the *Khutba* was not recited in her name, also, she was amply compensated by the perfect sovereignty she exercised over her husband and his Empire. Jahangir was a changed man under the dear, delicious influence of his adored Empress. For fifteen years she ruled the realm, commanded the armies, made and unmade the fortunes of many a grandee. Her power was more legitimate, her influence more beneficial, her policy more impersonal, than that of any woman that can at all be compared to her. When at last misfortune overtook her; when a rebellious general and an undutiful son beset her lord, she acted the heroine to perfection in a stricken field. Foiled in battle, she shared the gilded captivity of the Emperor to the day of his release wrought by her woman's wit. Her day was done when Jahangir died, and the closing years of this wonderful

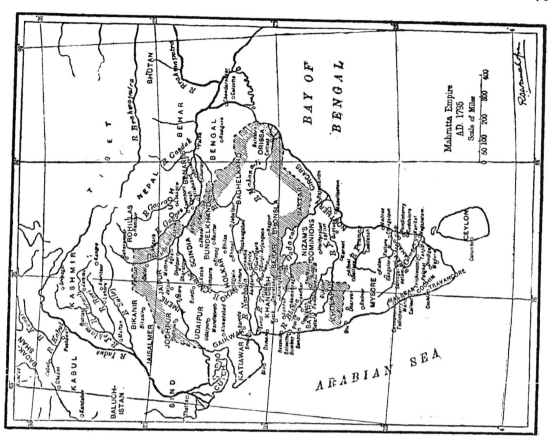

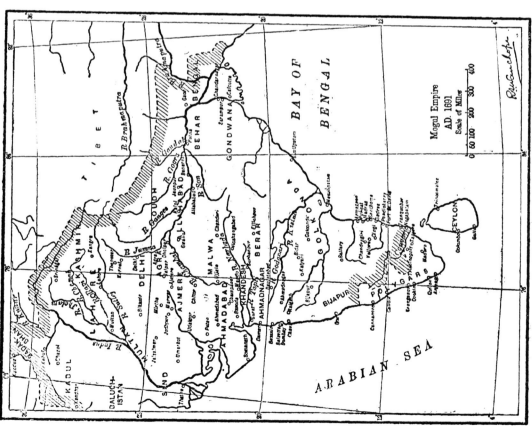

woman mark her to be even more high-souled in her retirement than ever she was at the height of her glory.

* * * * * * *

The descendants of Babur and Akbar maintained the Mughal Empire for a hundred years after the death of the latter, in all its strength and splendour, extent and integrity. The last of the Great Mughals, Aurangzeb Alamgir, even made considerable additions, carrying the imperial sway of the House of Timur from sea to sea to the farthest extremity of India. It would be difficult to find in any other country a succession of kings of the same House, for close upon two hundred years, of such high level of ability. But, with the exception of Babur and Akbar, the sovereigns of this line can scarcely be ranked as the makers of an empire or the builders of a nation. *Grand Seigneurs* in every sense of the term, Jahangir and Shah Jahan, even Humayun and Aurangzeb, cannot compare in constructive greatness to Akbar, or in the conqueror's renown to Babur.

After Akbar, again, first class Empire-builders fall into decline. Shivaji, the Maratha chieftain, was certainly a man above the biggest of his time; and, if he must be denied the title of an Empire-builder, the fault is not his own, but rather that of his immediate successors. His very insistence on Hinduism was, though not a pose, the inevitable result of the circumstances of his time. Aurangzeb, the third in descent after Akbar, had reversed the policy of real national solidarity of the greatest of the Great Mughals. The Hindus of the north were powerless, purposeless, or leaderless to make a stand against the suicidal fanaticism of the Emperor. Shivaji hence raised the standard which seemed to be threatened with annihilation. The son of a Bijapur *jagirdar*, he early imbibed a passion for liberating his suffering co-religionists from the tyranny of the Musalman. Illiterate in the same sense as Akbar, he was nevertheless well schooled in the peculiar requirements of his vocation. Step by step he rose by his own daring exploits to be the champion of defiant and assertive Hinduism, acknowledged as such by Aurangzeb himself. The latter tried both force of arms and duplicity to vanquish or ensnare him. But his daring overcame the armies of the Mughals, and his genius rescued him from their prison. His escape from Delhi was much more ambitious, extensive and dazzling. Crowned in regal splendour at his capital, he was recognised by all the powers around him,—native as well as foreign,—as an independent sovereign, the idol of the Hindus, the pride of the Marathas, the dread of the Mughals. Like Akbar, he, too, was no mere military adventurer. His greater glory shows in the splendid semblance of organised, constitutional rule that he strove to establish in his dominions. Read it how you like, it is a marvel how an illiterate peasant of the Ghats could evolve—could even think of—such a wonderful structure as his Cabinet, so much in advance of his age, so much at variance with his tradition!

The immediate successor of Shivaji was more unfortunate than incompetent. Shambhaji lacked not the daring that had distinguished his great father. But he was dissolute, slovenly, thoughtless. He shows at his best and noblest as a prisoner in the hands of an enemy that knew, and showed, no mercy. Shahu, his son, though brought up in the enervating atmosphere of the Mughal *zenana*, lost none of the passionate devotion to the faith of his fathers; and though he lacked the genius of his grandfather, he missed no opportunity, when it came to him, to raise once again the standard of Shivaji. But the custody of the Maratha fortunes was destined to pass to a line of great Brahman Ministers, who came within an ace of resuscitating the Hindu Empire throughout the continent of India in the eighteenth century. The Peshwas of Poona were nominally only the chief ministers of the descendants of Shivaji,—almost in the same way that the Mayors of the Palace in France served the descendants of Charlemagne. Baji Rao I, and his luckless but no less brilliant, daring, and gifted son and namesake, pushed the Maratha dominion to the extremities of India, north, south, east and west; and though they were beaten in the Battle of Panipat by the Afghans in 1761, the conqueror did not care, or dare, to remain permanently in India. The Maratha sovereignty was thus really unaffected by this terrible, but temporary, set-back. What really defeated, and undid the work of Shivaji and the Baji Raos, was the old, old curse of India— internal disunion. The great Satraps of the Peshwa,—the Scindhias, Holkars, Gaekwars, and Bhonsles,—failed to respond to the call of national solidarity in their suicidal search for personal aggrandisement. A Maratha Confederacy was created by the genius of the great, brilliant, pathetic Nana Fadnavis in the closing years of the eighteenth century; but was undermined by the perfidy, or ambition, of its most prominent members; broken by their incessant rivalries; destroyed by the weakness and vices of the last of the line—perhaps the last of the Hindus—as well.

*   *   *   *

There is no need to be tragic. The race of the Hindus is not ended, nor their spirit gone. A new breath of life is already seen to revivify the body of an ancient nation, which is all the more promising because it makes for a rational—not sentimental—solidarity among the myriads of India. The pangs of a new birth may not permit the picture to be uniformly pleasing to the eye of the contemporary; but contemporaries never see all the shades and nuances of the drama of their day. And hope is eternal in the human breast.

CHAPTER V

POETRY AND DRAMA

The literary treasures of India are the oldest in the world. Their beginnings reach far back into those dim recesses of the past, where history is yet only a fairytale, and biography a myth. The Vedic hymns—particularly of the Rig-Veda—are, indeed, not in the same tongue that holds the amazing treasures of the classic Sanskrit. But the difference is of absorbing interest and material importance only to philologists and archæologists. To the average reader of the classic Sanskrit, the Vedic hymns have a quaint, archaic flavour, all the more pleasing because of their wonderful capacity to embody sense in sound. The classic Sanskrit language is really the same high-born Vedic lady, dressed in more gorgeous clothing, adorned with more polished ornaments, embellished by more perfect art in the parure and allure of a veritable *grande dame.*

It may be open to question if the Sanskrit language, as regulated and fixed by Panini in the 4th or 5th Century B. C., was always the language of the people as a whole. It may be questioned whether the source and origin of the great mass of literature in epic or classic poetry, drama or story, or even the grand treatises on every branch of moral and mental philosophy, metaphysics and logic, law and social organisation, on dramaturgy, poetics, and mathematics—were always and from the beginning in the Sanskrit language as we find it now. But whether or not the various popular dialects co-existed with the parent stock of the speech we call Sanskrit; whether or not the seed of all the immense, varied, wonderful mass of literature we find in that language even to-day in spite of the countless ravages of time and of savage barbarians, came into it from the less refined, less scholastic, but more popular dialects,—it is nevertheless undeniable that the combined mass of the still surviving literature in the Sanskrit tongue makes even to-day one of the most precious treasures of mankind, amazing in its richness, bewildering in its variety, unequalled in its polished perfection.

It is, indeed, highly probable that the mass of the people, even in the days of the Vedic Aryans, spoke a language which was less refined and less systematized than the speech of the cultured Seers of the day. The language of the peoples not of Aryan stock, who remained in possession of a considerable portion of the peninsula, must also have had its influence upon the speech of the new-comers, as spoken whether by the cultured or the common. Whatever its origin, the Sanskrit literature is older, and grander, and more stirring, than that in any other language now surviving. Of the authors we know next to nothing. They were legendary figures, and their life and achievements are impossible even to glance at in the absence of any reliable records. We shall therefore confine our appreciation only to their works.

"The Vedic language as we find it in the Rig-Veda and the latter *Samhitas* is already a poetic and hieratic language, which was doubtless different even from the speech of the priests in ordinary life, and still further removed from that of the ruling and subject classes, not to mention the slaves or aborigines. The language of the *Brahmanas*, the *Aranyakas* and the *Upanishads* is equally a hieratic speech; it represents the language used primarily by priests at sacrifice, then in speculations based on the sacrifice, and extending ultimately beyond its immediate limits, not the language of every-day conversation either among the priests themselves or in intercourse with others. It is undoubtedly a general continuation of the language of the *Samhitas* in so far as it is descended from the prose of the Samhita period; indeed, while we have no prose as old as the Rig-Veda, there is no reason to doubt that the prose of the *Samhitas* of the Black *Yajur Veda* is contemporaneous with the later verses, of the texts. In the grammar of Panini (composed about the 4th century B. C.) we find the norm laid down for the spoken language—*Bhasha* of his time in the higher circles of society, a fact which explains the failure of the norm of Panini to conform to any texts which are preserved to us, though it has obvious affinities with the language of such *Brahmanas* as the *Aiteraya.*"

The pride of place, in point of antiquity at least, belongs, of course, to the Vedic hymns.

Among the four Vedas, the Rig-Veda (Veda of Verses) is the most ancient. The greatness and importance of this is inestimable, whether we look upon it as a store-house of data for ancient history, a mine of information for early theology, or a treasure house of facts of Aryan society, its structure and regulation. But its richness as a piece of artistic creation, of the poet's eye "in a fine frenzy rolling," is still more incalculable. The music that vibrates in every line of these thousand odd hymns is impossible to render in any other tongue, even including the purest, most refined, most beautiful daughter of the Vedic Sanskrit herself. Regarded in India as the most sacred of its treasures by the Indian people, the Vedas have been preserved in sound and sense with the most marvellous fidelity to the original. The great peculiarity of the Vedic accent has been maintained intact, thanks to the absolute necessity of reciting the sacred texts at the several sacrifices with absolute, perfect, meticulous correctness. This accent is musical in its nature, depending upon the pitch of the voice in pronouncing every syllable of each verse; and so differentiates that speech decisively from all the later languages, including the classic Sanskrit.

Of the literary beauty of the oldest of the Vedas, a by-no-means over enthusiastic English scholar says:—

"Regarded from this aspect alone, its value is considerable. As is to be expected from its great antiquity, its diction is simpler and more natural than that of post-Vedic Sanskrit. Its hymns as a whole are composed with a surprising degree of metrical skill and command of language. Their poetry is often impaired by conceits and mysticism, particularly where the two specifically ritual deities—Agni and Soma—are concerned. Yet the hymns contain much genuine poetry, often expressed in beautiful and even noble imagery."[1]

---

1) cp. A. A. Macdonell. *India's Past*. p. 39. (Oxford, 1927.)

It is impossible to select examples which could appeal to ears unused to the majestic sway and wave of the Vedic verse. But those familiar with the masterpieces of great musical genius easily recall how the creations of true genius in music can make sound blend in perfect harmony with the sense. There are war songs in these Vedic hymns, which, in the form of weird incantations of the royal bard, suggest the fierce blast of the trumpet, the rushing of the chariots, the shouts of rage and triumph of the warriors, in the changing rhythm of the verses, in the most marvellous choice of words suiting exactly the sense to be conveyed.

> "Let the might and the power of the prayer be now increased, as also the warrior's sway of whom I am the family priest. I lengthen his warrior rule by the incense-smoke rising to heaven. I shatter his foeman's arms. Let those who rage against the mighty king sink low. * * * Heroes advance and conquer; let your arms be fierce. Strike, strike home your pointed arrows; on the weak bowmen, strike with fierce weapons the powerless foe."[1]

In the very last verse rousing the host to advance and conquer, the bard is himself carried off his feet by the fierce passion in his own verses, and repeats over and over again the harsh sounds that thrill through the last two resounding lines, calling on the Aryans to annihilate the enemy.

> Prétā Jáyatā nara ugrá vāh santu bāhávah.
> Tīksnésavo abaládhanvano hata ugrá-āyudhā abalān ugrábāhavah.

The poets of the Vedas are equally felicitous in expressing the longing of the human soul to pierce through the unknown, and to grasp the infinite. The intense pathos of the following line is inexpressible in the most faithful, the most exact translation.

> Párā hi me vimanyavah pátanti vásya-iṣtaye
> Váyo ná vasatir-úpa.[2] (R. V. I. 25, 4.)

"And still my wearied mind turns to thoughts of wealth, even as a bird flies to its nest."

But the true end of the struggle is found in the one verse handed down from Vedic times and murmured by all orthodox Hindus to-day, as they wake every day to find the reality of the world rise up around them, and ever know that beyond this reality is that which they still yearn to know.

> Om! Tát Savituh várényam bhárgó
> dévásya dhīmahi
> Dhiyó yó nah prachódyāt.[3]

Once heard in the land of its birth, once heard from the lips of those who have caught its elusive music,

---

1) *Atharva Veda* III., 19, 7.

2) R. V. I., 25, 4.

3) "Let us meditate on the to-be-longed for Light of the Inspirer; may it incite all our efforts." R. V. III. 62, 10.

"It rings for ever after as India's noblest tribute to the divine, as an acknowledgment of submissive resignation to the decrees which bid man keep his soul in patience, until the day dawns when all things shall be revealed."[1]

To the remaining three Vedas it is unnecessary to devote much space. The *Sama* and the *Yajur* are nothing but the redactions of the great Rig-Veda, the former almost wholly, and the latter nearly a third, derived from the main stock. They deal with the ritual attendant on the several sacrifices. The hymn was the prayer without which sacrifice would be of no avail. The prayer must be recited and intoned with absolute exactness in voice and sequence of the sounds by the Priest. A single syllable mispronounced, a single letter misplaced, and the entire magic of the rite would go. Hence, the practice of learning the Vedas by heart, guaranteeing perfect accuracy in intonation and accentuation.

The *Atharva Veda*,—the fourth and last,—is more original and interesting. It is obviously the product of a society far more sophisticated than that of the Rig-Veda. For, besides an amount of pantheistic and theosophic matter, it deals in magic spells to remove disease, to vanquish foes, to bring good luck in love and in gambling. Here is a specimen from a hymn intended to secure a woman's affections by the aid of the God of Love:—

"With longing feathered, tipped with love,
  Its shaft is formed of mixed desire.
With this his arrow levelled well
  Shall Kama pierce thee to the heart."[2]

A considerable portion of the Atharva and Yajur Veda is written in prose, and its bulk is a little more than half the Rig-Veda.

Let us here note, in passing, the origin of the art of writing in India. The Vedic hymns were distinctly *spoken*, not *written* compositions. They were handed down from generation to generation by oral tradition, and so could dispense with a written form. Exactly when the art of writing first arose, or came into India, cannot be said with any degree of precision; but scholars are agreed that the eighth century B. C. must be taken to have witnessed the birth or introduction of the science in India. Basing their arguments on the fact that no written records are available, whether in actual manuscript or inscriptions like those of Asoka in the 3rd Century B. C., the modern Western scholars have argued that the earliest written records of India must have been for the use of traders' books only, migrating thence to legal documents, and coming to be used, last of all, for the transcription of sacred and profane literature. Allowing that no written records earlier than Asoka's inscriptions have still been discovered; and admitting that the completion and perfection of the literary language by definite rules of grammar was not accomplished until about the 4th or 5th Century B. C.,—the date assigned

---

1) *A Literary History of India* p. 61. by R. W. Fraser.
2) *India's Past.* p. 42. A. A. Macdonell.

to Panini,—it does not by any means follow that the art of writing was not known in India till about the eighth century B. C. The Vedic was a spoken, in contradistinction to a written, tongue; and the classic Sanskrit, with all its elaborate rules of grammar and letter combinations in words, may not have been formed much before Panini. But the fact that there are distinct marks, of the nature of inscriptions, on the seals discovered recently in the Indus Valley, must be enough to conclude that writing of some sort must have been known and used, if not amongst the Aryan invaders, then among the Dravidian natives, long before the 8th or even the 18th century B. C. The script used here is of course lost; and its deciphering must take time. But the art as known and practised amongst the native Dravidians must have provided material for the self-confident Aryans. Their own script,—or the variety of it which we now know to be the most ancient,—was derived from the Phœnicians. As used by the Aryans in India,—and particularly after the grammarians had settled the sound values, and the order of the letters according to the organ used in pronouncing them,—the script became materially different from the old Semitic alphabet.

The script, it may be added, is of two varieties,—Brahmi and Kharoshti,—both derived ultimately from the same Semitic source. The former is traced back to the Moabite inscription of circa 850 B.C., and is considered to be the parent of all modern Indian alphabets. Kharoshti, on the other hand, was, when it entered India, of Persian origin, written from right to left. Asokan inscriptions are in that script; and, though during the interval the alphabet is enriched to suit the more numerous sounds in the Indian tongue, its affinity with its sister scripts of Semitic origin is unmistakable.

*　　　*　　　*　　　*　　　*

The literature of the Buddhists, as we now possess it, does not go beyond the 3rd century B. C. The *Katha Vattu* of Tissa, son of Mogali, is the earliest extant written record, and dates from 250 B. C. The Third Œcumenical Council of Buddhism was held in or about 241 B. C., when the *Pitakas*,—or the Baskets,—of the Canon were completed. The three Baskets contain, respectively, Metaphysics *(Abhidhammapitaka)* as recited by Kashyapa, the most learned of the Buddha's disciples; the Canon or Rule of Ecclesiastic Life *(Vinayapitaka)* as recited by Upali; and the *Suttapitaka*, or aphorisms and parables given to his most favourite disciple,—Ananda,—by the Buddha himself. This *Suttapitaka* has 5 divisions called the *Nikayas*, containing the speeches and dialogues of the Blessed One. Says Mr. Rhys Davids:—

> "In the depth of philosophic insight, in the method of Socratic questioning often adopted, in the earnest and elevated tone of the whole, in the evidence they afford of the most cultured thought of the day, these discourses constantly remind one of the dialogues of Plato."

To this may be added the *Questions of King Milinda*, a compilation of some learned Buddhist dating from about 125 B. C., and pronounced by the greatest of the modern Buddhist scholar to be a "Masterpiece of Indian prose, and indeed the best book of its class from a literary point of view, that had been produced in any country." It ranks in authority next after the *Pitakas*. The author, a thorough-going rationalist, works out remorselessly, and with inexorable logic, a perfect system of negative dogmatism, denying soul, God, and a future for the liberated.

Later works of a Buddhist origin include the *Vissuddhimagga* of Buddhagosa (c. 400 A. D.) setting forth the *Hinayana* ideal of the Arhat; while the same writer's *Athashalini* is a most valuable commentary on the *Dhammasamgani*. The Chronicles, called the *Dipavamsa* and *Mahavamsa*, are of historical rather than philosophical importance; but they indicate the shifting of the centre of interest in Buddhist philosophy from the country of its origin to other lands and alien peoples.

Poetical writings of great Buddhist scholars like Ashwaghosha, the Court Pandit to the Emperor Kanishka, once head of the Buddhist University in Magadha, break the tradition of the Master, inasmuch as they begin to be composed in Sanskrit in preference to the language of the people. If we include writers like these among the glories of Buddhism, we shall have to carry the literary history of the Buddhists beyond the reign of the Emperor Harsha, who was himself no mean scholar, poet, and dramatist. We must, therefore, leave this brief survey at this point with the remark only, that while it was in the heyday of its popularity, Buddhism added to the literature of India,—and particularly in the vernacular,—an immense treasure of philosophic and poetical writings, the full value of which is even now not realised.

The Prakrit or the people's tongue in Aryan India seems to have been almost as old as the Vedic Sanskrit. We can, therefore, scarcely consider the Prakrit literature to be a whit less important than the Vedic and the classic Sanskrit.

In almost every one of these there is excellent literature developed in course of time, the oldest form of that literature being bardic poetry, dealing with the life and achievements of heroes. The epic tales in their poetic form must be of the utmost antiquity; though they must originally have been composed, in all probability, in the popular vernacular garb, convenient to the strolling minstrel. The great Brahmanic venture in this field,—the finished, classic, Sanskrit epics of the *Ramayana* and the *Mahabharata*,—were, no doubt, originally in the popular dialect: "I believe," says Barth, (*Ind. Ant.* (1895) p. 71.) "that the Hindu epic is ancient, as ancient in its origin as the earliest traditions of the nation."

Their present form and clothing is dated by scholars to somewhere between 300 B. C. and 100 A. D.—a large margin, unavoidable when we think of the immense interpolations in these works. We need not, in this chapter, go over the story of the classic Sanskrit Epics. We need not even concern ourselves, here, with the glimpses of philosophic thought inspiring the poems, nor with the picture of social structure unfolded therein. Judged only as works of art, as masterpieces of the classic poetic genius, these creations of Valmiki, the father of Indian poetry, and of Vyasa, are instinct with dramatic feeling that never flags throughout the interminable narrative; and are tense with emotion that defies the art of the subtlest analyst. Scenes like the Denudation of Draupadi in the full Court of the Kauravas, with her mighty husbands defeated in gambling looking on helplessly, the elders perplexed, the wise and the thoughtful shuddering, the Kaurava princes mad with the joy of this public humiliation of their rivals; and Draupadi herself, the heroine and the centre of the scene, in wild disorder of her hair and clothes, now appealing in infinite pathos, now struggling with her ravisher with all the force of outraged womanhood, now arguing like the subtlest casuist, now praying the prayer of her life to the Almighty and the Omnipresent to save her from shame, and at last confounding her insulters by the miraculous way in which her prayers are heard and answered by the Lord Krishna—scenes like these, recurring in endless succession, make an inexhaustible feast for the eye and the ear when recited by the bards, who themselves live again every incident they describe. The beauty of the language, the variety of the incident, and withal the unity of the story, the simplicity of the theme,—at least in one of them, and yet the touching appeal,— are all merits of the great Indian Epics, which stand unchallenged in their own sphere. As a means of rich and varied expression of the finest shades of meaning, Sanskrit was decidedly superior to the vernacular; and must, therefore, have been used for purposes of secular literature as well, quite as early as the Prakrit. The practice, moreover, of the Sanskrit drama, dating from the first century A. C., if not earlier, makes it clear that the two forms of speech,—the refined, rigid, well-regulated Sanskrit, and the later, easier, more popular Prakrit,—existed, and were used as vehicles of literary expression, side by side from time immemorial. Hence we cannot fairly use the available evidence to argue that as a literary tongue of a secular nature either Sanskrit or Prakrit had precedence over the other.

The folk-tale in its epic form must be held to be the direct, immediate ancestor of the *Kavya* (Poetry), which the Sanskrit critics are agreed in regarding as the highest form of literature. Panini does not mention the epic; but that is not conclusive to say that epic or poetry was unknown in his day. As well might it be said that because the epics ignore several of Panini's rules in their subtler nuances, therefore the great grammarian himself did not exist. Still it is probably in accordance with historical development to say that the classic Sanskrit language, as we now have it, was born of the epic. She is a lady of a noble house, whom it would not do to take liberties with. Patanjali, Panini's follower two hundred years later, is perfectly familiar with almost all the forms and peculiarities of the classic Sanskrit literature, as well as with the rules of prosody and kinds of metre patronised in the later *Kavya*. With the Prakrit tongues of old becoming stereotyped and frozen, to be used, under set rules, for dramatic purposes only, Sanskrit came to be more and more the ordinary medium of polite intercourse.

Next to the *Ramayana* and the *Mahabharata*, though less known to fame, the best epic work in classic Sanskrit is that of Ashwaghosha, the Abbot-president of the great Buddhist University in Magadha and Scholar Laureate of Kanishka. His

Buddha-charita is a poetic account of the life and mission of the Sakya Sage, originally in 28 cantoes, of which now only 13 are available. The poem is a product of consummate art, if only because of its rhythmic regularity in precise poetic form. Ashwaghosha seems to have been the model for that Prince of Poets and Poet of Princes,—Kalidasa,—in more than one place of this great Epic, the *Raghuvamsa. Sundarananda*, another creation of the Buddhist Bard, is still more definitely poetic, in its wonderful tribute to the power of human life, (VIII) and the eloquent homage to the charms of woman (X). The author is a master of metre and the *Alamkara* (figures of speech), and can write the most delicious, the most fanciful lyrics, like the *Gandistotra Gatha*, which remind one of the *Bells of Castille*, by the most musical of English poetesses. Ashwaghosha in this poem describes the religious message conveyed by the sounds arising when a long piece of wood is beaten by a club.

The greatest, however, of the Epics in classic Sanskrit, as the chastest and the most beautiful poetry in the whole range of Sanskrit literature, belongs to Kalidasa. This master-poet,—*Kavi-kul-Guru* as he has been styled by one of the most famous of his successors,—has others besides epic poems to his credit. We shall speak of these in another connection. Let us here mention his two Epics: the *Birth of the War-God* (*Kumara-Sambhava*) and the *House of Raghu* (*Raghuvamsha*). It is impossible to say which of their many charms is the most arresting, which of their thousand beauties the most fascinating. Being, however, largely descriptive, the palm must be assigned to those numerous passages giving the most exquisite delineation of scenes of nature's glories and man's emotions, in which his favourite figure of speech,—Simile,—had the fullest play. The stanzas giving the sorrows of Aja are unequalled for their pathos in the entire Sanskrit literature. Simple and unaffected, and yet refined to daintiness, Kalidasa is, nevertheless, a master of words, who can combine sounds so skilfully that their mere utterance conjures up the scene, as by a touch of the magician's wand, before the mind's eye of the reader. The subject matter of these his poems may not have been new even in his day (4th Century A. D.); but the treatment is decidedly original and the master's own. No translation, however erudite and exact, can render the subtle spell of the original in sound, in style, in meaning.

Other metrical compositions of an epic character after Kalidasa only serve to emphasise the greatness of the Master and of his inimitable style. Vatsabhatti's *Prasashti* or panegyric in praise of the Temple of the Sun at Mandasor, written in about 472-3 A. C. can scarcely be called an epic at all, and, with difficulty, even a poem, though it is rich in illustrations of the rule of poetics, and a certain attempt at conforming sound to sense. The *Kiratarjuniya* of Bharavi, describing the struggle of Arjun with the God Shiva in the form of a huntsman; and the *Bhattikavya* of Bhartrihari appear to be tricks in comparison; the one illustrating the author's genius in verbal sleights; and the other illustrating the forms of the Sanskrit grammar. Bharavi's work, however, is not without a degree of poetic fancy, particularly in its descriptive portions. Magha has a greater reputation, popular

PLATE XXXVII

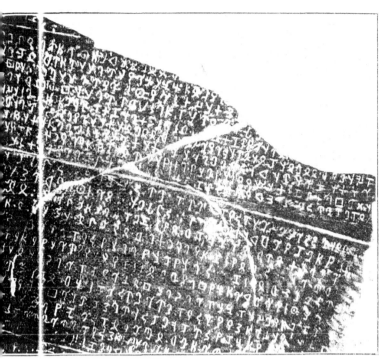

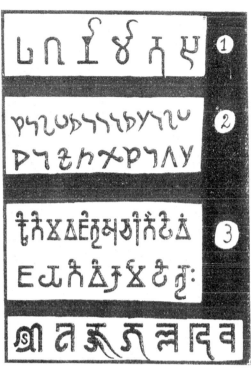

INSCRIPTION OF ASHOKA ON THE GIRNAR ROCK

COINS OF INDIA—ANCIENT INDIAN SCRIPTS

1. Brahmini 2. Kharoshti 3. Gupta 4. Nāgāri

DENUDATION OF DRAUPADI

(Painting by S. L. Haldankar)

tradition making him an honoured rival of the Laureate of all ages. But his *Sishupaula-Vadha* is a museum of metrical *tour de force*, in which at least two stanzas (XIX 33 and 34) are so arranged that the succeeding, read backwards, spells exactly the same as the preceding read in the ordinary way. The *Janakiharana* of Kumaradasa is mentioned by a tenth century poet critic, Rajasekhara, to be of a level with Kalidasa's *Raghuvamsha,* and modern critics do not quite deny him this high praise. He seems to have been a Ceylonese king (517-26 A. D.) whose mastery of Sanskrit seems to be wonderful. This trickiness is carried to its highest in the *Raghavapandaviya* (800 B. C.) of Kaviraja, who narrates the story of *Ramayana* and *Mahabharata* in one work by the use of ambiguous words and phrases. Finally, we may mention the *Nalodaya,*—a versified episode of the *Mahabharata,*—whose author aims pre-eminently at exhibiting his skill in manipulating artificial metres and elaborate tricks of style. This poem is also remarkable in the history of Sanskrit literature, inasmuch as it is in this that the *Rhyme* in verse first makes its appearance. Rhyme, however, does not seem to have become very popular in Sanskrit poetry; though the greatest lyric poet after Kalidasa, Jayadeva, in his *Gita Govind;* and the most philosophic,—Shankaracharya, in his *Moha-Mudgara* (8th century A. C.),—use rhyme with the most delightful mastery.

The place of the rhyme seems, however, to be more fittingly in the Lyrics. The classical Sanskrit is, like her daughters,—the leading vernaculars of modern India,— rich in this most appealing form of poetry. They occur, most commonly, as isolated stanzas in the classic drama, which may, therefore, be regarded as really lyrical, the more so because the characteristic feature of what we would nowadays call drama,— action and movement,—is lacking in the Sanskrit drama generally. Lyrics by themselves are, also, not unknown. Kalidasa is here, as in other departments of poetic art, the sublime master. His *Cloud Messenger,—Meghaduta,—*is the most exquisite piece of the kind, so full of a simple, touching appeal, that Göethe declared: if one had to send a messenger to one's heart's beloved, who would not send the *Cloud Messenger?* The story is quite simple. A Yaksha,—a kind of a demigod,—was remiss in his duties, which offended his Lord, the God Kubera. The latter sentenced him to an exile on a peak in the Vindhya Hills, from whence, one evening in the rainy season, he saw a cloud floating on to his northern home in Mount Kailasa, where his beloved is forced to reside without him. The Yaksha sends his message of love and longing, with a thousand wonderful endearments, to the darling of his heart, by this most original of all messengers,—the Cloud in the monsoon current. The description of the journey northwards, and of the towns and hills and rivers on the way, displays not only the poet's wonderful knowledge of geography, but his marvellous love of nature. A man of cultured ease and travelled tastes, he has something choice and yet characteristic of each place to say, in his own inimitable grace of manner and charm of words. And when the journey is done, when the Messenger has reached the destination, the message, with its touch of pathos, its depth of love and reverence for the beloved, leaves a haunting spell on every reader that has ever read its magic strains. "Tell my beloved," says the Yaksha through the *Cloud Messenger*:—

> "Goddess, beloved! how vainly I explore
> The world, to trace the semblance I adore:
> Thy graceful form the flexible tendril shows,
> And like thy locks the peacock's plumage glows;
> Mild as thy checks the moon's new beams appear,
> And those soft eyes adorn the timid deer;
> In rippling brooks thy curling brows I see,
> But only view combined those charms in thee." [1]

Could the most ardent lover say,—could the most exacting mistress ask,—more?

The other lyric of the Laureate of Sanskrit literature *Ritusamhara*, or the description of the six seasons of the Sanskrit year, is not quite so great a favourite with the critics. Perhaps it is a product of his yet immature genius. The work is, however, on a different plane from the English poet Thompson's *Seasons;* for the erotic is a dominant sentiment in this lyric of the Sanskrit Virgil. Taken individually, the seasons may each be said to be better described, objectively, in other works than in the *Ritusamhara* of the Master. His own description of Spring is much better in *Kumara-Sambhava*, while Bharavi's *Kiratarjuniya* gives a much more delightful description of Autumn (IV), as Shudraka's *Mrichha-Katika* has a more excellent picture of the rainy season,—the most beautiful of all.

Another praiseworthy piece of this class is the *Shringara Shataka*—the *Centaine Erotique*—of the Poet-prince Bhartrihari. Exactly when he lived and died is a mystery, like the lives of almost all the Sanskrit poets. Even of the master, Kalidasa, little is known, and that by uncorroborated tradition, except that he was a rather wild young man, whom suddenly the Goddess Kali favoured so much that he was raised to be the brightest star in that galaxy of scholars and savants that surrounded the legendary King Vikramaditya. Sober history believes him to have been a Poet-Laureate at the court of Chandra-Gupta II, somewhere about the close of the fourth century of the Christian era. We get this rough approximation by placing the Mandasor inscription, with its reproduction of the *Ritusamhara* verses, at the upper limit, and the filtration of the knowledge of Greek astronomy into India, as evidenced by Kalidasa's work, as the lower limit (300 A. C.). Popular tradition makes Bhartrihari an elder brother of the far-famed Vikramaditya; and therefore a contemporary,—even though slightly senior,—of Kalidasa. Bhartrihari was jilted by the woman he had loved more than everything else in life; and so, in disgust, he left his Court and Queen to become a Sannyasi, writing, in his retirement, those famous 3 centaines: known as the *Shringara Shataka*, or the Centaine

---

[1] श्यामास्वङ्गं चकितहरिणीप्रेक्षणे दृष्टिपातान्
वक्त्रच्छायां शशिनि शिखिनां बर्हभारेषु केशान् ।
उत्पश्यामि प्रतनुषु नदीवीचिषु भ्रूविलासान्
हन्तैकस्मिन् क्वचिदपि न ते चण्डि साहृश्यमस्ति ॥

Erotique, the *Niti Shataka*, or the Ethical Centaine; and the *Vairagya Shataka*, or the Centaine of Renunciation. These are great favourites among the Indian people with any pretention to education. Their chaste simplicity and elegant appropriateness make them oft repeated platitudes to point a moral or adorn a tale.

Other examples of Sanskrit lyrics might be found in the *Chaura-panchashika* and the *Gata-karpana*, which are, however, not quite so well known as those already mentioned. On a totally different footing of popularity stands, the *Centaine* of Amaru, dealing with the endless and eternal theme of Love. He is a master of the class of Kalidasa in the universal art of painting lovers in all their varying moods of joy and grief. To the puritan, the descriptions sound a trifle too sensual; and to the wicked and the depraved everything will appear debased. The magnificent love-song of Radha and Krishna, sung by the immortal Jayadeva of Bengal in the twelfth century, may also incur the censure, on this score, of hyperpuritanical critics. Those, however, who can enjoy the untranslatable charm of the original in its mellifluous stream of easy alliteration and unlaboured rhyme; the unparalleled imagery, and unequalled wealth of emotion, cannot but overlook—if ever they give a thought to it—the sensual side of the love scenes.

*   *   *   *   *   *

Even more important than poetry in all its forms, the most prolific form of classic Sanskrit literature, and the one most prized, is the **Drama.** We have barely a dozen good specimens of the best Sanskrit effort in this branch now surviving. The paucity of the extant Sanskrit drama has led some critics, more ingenious than honest, to suggest that the entire Indian drama is exotic,—of Grecian origin. Their only real argument is that the curtain is called *Yavanika*—amongst several other names; and that by Yavana the ancient Indians meant the Greeks ever since the days of the Alexandrine invasion. They forget, in their zeal to deny India any contribution to the world's treasures of creative art, that even the oldest known works in any language now known in the world,—the hymns of the Rig-Veda;—are instinct with dramatic feeling; that many of the sacrifices of the Vedic times must have involved considerable scenic and recitative effort; that even where the hymns are unconnected with ritual, they embody dialogues in the course of the narrative; that from the earliest times the rhapsodes,—the progenitors of the Indian epic, which is the source of most dramatical works in India,—have been an integral feature of Indian society; and that, given all these elements, the creation of the drama from an utterly unaided indigenous impulse was inevitable.

> "The most likely explanation is that the Indian drama derives its origin from scenes of a historical and a popular character, which are initiated in the Vedic ritual; as when a Brahmin buys Soma from a Shudra, who is then driven out with sticks. Such scenes of horseplay would be accompanied by dance, song and music, which are designated as the most important elements of the dramatic art (*Natya*). It is also noteworthy that the ordinary words for "actor", "play", and "dramatic art" are . . . . . derived from the vernacular root *nat* to "dance". The mimic dance becomes the drama as soon as the words are added."[1]

---

1) A. A. Macdonnell. *India's Past.* p. 99.

This and the remarkable peculiarities of the Indian drama, such as the introductory dialogue, the use of different dialects of different classes of personages, the mixture of prose and verse, and of dance and music, must all go to prove the entirely indigenous character of the Indian drama.

As to when the drama first emerged from the rude village show to be the finished product of an elaborate art, we have no means of knowing. The science of dramaturgy of Bharat was complete and effective, long before the Christian era; but the extant specimens of the Art come from a much later date.

The earliest Sanskrit drama, as now known, is that of Ashwaghosha of epic fame. By many the play *Mrichha-Katika* (The *Little Clay-Cart*) of King Shudraka is dated much earlier—from about the 2nd century B.C. If the wealth of social information, combined with high poetic excellence and considerable movement or action,—a quality in which the best Indian drama is comparatively deficient,—could entitle a play to take high rank, the *Little Clay-Cart* certainly deserves to be called the first of the Indian dramas. The one play, so far known, of Ashwaghosha,— *Sariputra-prakarna*—and found in Turfan, deals with the conversion of the two chief disciples of the Enlightened One. Bhasha,—whom Kalidasa mentions in the Introduction to his own *Malavika-Agnimitra* with obvious praise,—is the next great dramatist, in point of time. He has no less than 13 plays credited to him; but the question of their authenticity,—and, therefore, of the real work of this poet,—is still undecided.

The two greatest of the classic Sanskrit dramatists are Kalidasa and Bhavabhuti, the Shakespeare and Milton of India. Kalidasa is, by universal consent, the greatest of the Indian Sanskrit playwrights, as he is the acknowledged master of all forms of the poetic art. A wild unruly youth, like Shakespeare, his works reveal the most perfect mastery of all the highest learning of his time. Take the famous test scene in *Malavika-Agnimitra*, where the King and the Recluse are judging the relative excellence in dancing. None but a past-master in the technique of dancing could have hit off—as Kalidasa does—all the marks of perfect dancing shown by Malavika. None but a connoisseur of beauty could have summed up the fleeting charm of the dancer's pose in a single stanza. Or take, again, Canto VIII of the *Kumara-Sambhava*. None but a perfect adept in the science of erotics,—Kamasutra,— could give in such detail the love passages between the Divine Couple. In the IX Canto of the *Raghu-vamsha* the poet exhibits a mastery of the poetic composition, rarely equalled and never excelled, by using as many as 14 different metres (thirteen of them in less than 20 stanzas); and by employing *Yamakas*—or paronomasias—in which the same syllable repeated in changing form and meaning makes for the most admirable effect when sense comes to correspond to sound. In *Vikramorvashiyam* Act IV, he displays his familiarity with the music of his day with an ease and eloquence that bespeaks the master in excelsis. Altogether, he is no untutored genius or a freak of Nature, but, like Tennyson, a poet *par excellence* of the cultured and comfortable classes.

Kalidasa's plays are far too famous all the world over to need a repetition, even in outline, of any one of them. The moment it was published in the West, Göethe remarked of *Shakuntala*: —

> "Would thou the young year's blossoms and the fruits of its decline,
> And all by which the soul is charmed, enraptured, feasted, fed?
> Would thou the earth and heaven itself in one sole name combine,
> I name thee, O Shakuntala, and all at once is said."

This and all his other plays would perhaps in modern eyes be defective in point of action, and so unsuitable for the stage purposes of to-day. Their glory, however, is the glory of the true classic; the eternal character of their theme; the unspeakable charm of their language. The Vaidarbhi style, in which the Master wrote, lays emphasis on "simplicity, clearness, richness in sentiment; variety, attractiveness and elevation through the use of poetic terminology". Kalidasa is throughout free from affectation. He is a master of simile and metaphor, which, despite the difference in poetical conventions between the East and the West, has claimed unstinting admiration from all his critics. Simple, chaste, and yet exquisitely adorned, Kalidasa's works, — particularly the dramas, — are most easily readable even by beginners in Sanskrit literature; while the homeliness of his sentiment makes him for ever the poet of the people, even though in his own day the mightiest monarch strove to do him the utmost honour in his court.

The *Abhignāna-Shākuntalam*, to give the master-piece its full title, is the true *Nātaka*, according to Sanskrit dramaturgy. It does not deal with every day life but gives an idealised picture of God-like and heroic characters. So, too, does his other classic, *Vikramorvashiyam*. The only one of his plays dealing at all with life as it really must have been about his time is the *Mālavikā-Agnimitram*, woven round the historical name of King Agnimitra, whose father as well as son were great warriors and ambitious conquerors, but who himself seems to have been a master of dalliance. Certainly, Kalidasa portrays him as such, not by direct description, but indirectly, by inevitable contrast with the other characters mentioned in the play. Orthodox critics do not give the same place to this comedy, as they give to the two others mentioned already. Yet those who have an eye to realism, those who wish to obtain from the Master's works a mirror of his days, will find the copious descriptions of men and events most interesting.

*　　　　*　　　　*　　　　*

Bhavabhuti, frankly, does not write for the masses. Tradition makes him a contemporary and a disciple of the Master; but there is nothing in the extant work of this author to suggest any similarity in style or sentiment. Reliable history is, as usual, unavailable about the date of this master-singer; but what data we so far have point to his having lived somewhere about the beginning of the 8th century of the Christian era. He does not, indeed, banish the erotic entirely from his works; but, in the presence of the awful grandeur of his theme generally, the mere by-play of lovers stands awed and rebuked into a subdued second place, even though the lovers are Rama and

Sita—in separation. "How little do they know," he has himself written in the Introduction to *Malati-Madhava*, "who speak of us with censure. The entertainment is not for them. Possibly some one exists or will exist, of similar tastes with myself; for time is boundless, and the world is wide". To this may be added, as pendant, this judgment of Grierson: "I do not believe that there ever was even a Pandit in India who could have understood, say, the more difficult passages of Bhavabhuti at first hearing, without previous study."[1]

Of his 3 plays, the *Uttara-Rama-Charita* is remarkable in the whole range of Sanskrit literature for its intense pathos. The classic Indian drama knows no tragedy; and, therefore, this play is made to end happily. But if there is anywhere a real approach to the tragic in the Sanskrit drama, it is surely in this eloquent expression of the grandeur of love in separation. As in the heroic plays of Kalidasa, the personages are here also semi-divine, and the incidents of a marvellous kind, bordering on the miraculous. Only in the *Malati-Madhava* is there any hint of a realistic sketch. This play would, in modern times, be the very acme of perfection for the film-maker. Malati, a daughter of a minister in Ujjain, has been brought up by a Buddhist nun, as any high class demoiselle in mediaeval Europe. She is in love with Madhava, son of the Berari Prime Minister, who had been sent to Ujjain to finish his education. The prince of Ujjain demands Malati of her father for one of his own favourites, and therewith commences the real interest of the drama. The high-priest of the Goddess Chamunda has sworn to sacrifice to her a chaste virgin; and his choice falls on our heroine, who is led to the dread temple by sorcery. The play is most valuable, thus, by its full, though gruesome, picture of the unholy rites connected with Tantric worship. The temple is situated near a burning-ground, where the arch-priestess, Kapala-kundala, intones the awful sacrificial hymn to Shakti—Divine Energy. Madhava, too, who has resolved to seek the aid of magic spells to win his lady-love, enters upon the scene. He is, however, unaware that his beloved lies bound a captive in the temple which he enters with the dread offering in his hands; slays the high-priestess who is dancing the Tantric dance while invoking the Goddess, and rescues Malati. The whole scene is grand and awful,—more even than the witches' scene in *Macbeth*. The Indian dramatist shows a more thorough appreciation of the mysteries of black magic, which is, in the end, foiled by the greater glory of the Buddhist nun, who has mastered all the charms and counter-charms enough to frustrate the practices of the Shakti-worshippers.

Two plays ascribed to the Imperial Bard,—Shri Harsha of Kanouj—*Ratnavli* and *Priyadarshika*, are of the drawing-room type, giving a fairly faithful picture of the life and manners in an Imperial Court. These are just the plays most accurately to illustrate the rules of the *Natyashastra*, or the Science of Dramaturgy. In their plot and general get-up they resemble Kalidasa's *Malavika-Agnimitra*, with passages of real poetic charm, not at all inferior to the verses of the Master. A third play ascribed, apocryphally, to Shri Harsha, deals with another theme,—the

---

1) *A Literary History of India.* p. 288, by Frazer.

life of a Bodhisatva. The subject matter of the *Nāgānanda* could not be unfamiliar to the Buddhist Emperor; but the style is remarkably different from that of his authentic works already mentioned.

The political drama *Mudra-Rakshasa* is a most singular piece by the poet Vishakhadatta. It is the only great poetic work in the Sanskrit language utterly free from even a mention of Love. It is an account, in the most highly dramatic form, worthy of a Sardou or an Augier, of the Revolution in Bihar in the fourth century B. C., by which the throne of Magadha passed from the proud Nandas to the low-born—but well advised—Chandragupta. The main revolution is really over when the play opens; but its interest is most cleverly sustained by the efforts of the Nanda Minister Rākshasa for a counter-revolution, and the counter moves of that arch-politician Chānakya, who had aided Chandragupta in his success. It is a subtle and wonderful tribute to the loyalty of the great Minister; as well as a marvellous picture of the great Brahman sage, who is prone to take affront, as the nobles of the court of Francis I, but who is equally indifferent to wordly wealth and grandeur. For a realistic painting of historical personages, there is probably no other piece in the Sanskrit literature to surpass this.

The works of Bhatta-Narayana, (C. 800 A.C.) and of Rajasekhara (C. 900 A.D.), can only be barely mentioned here. The *Veni-Samhar, The Binding of the Braid,* of the former deals with a well-known episode in the *Mahabharata;* while the *Bāl-Rāmāyana* and the *Bāl-Bhārata* of the latter are amongst the richest of the juvenile poetry in India. His *Karpura-Manjari* is a master-piece of the Prakrit tongue, in which he was as good a master as in Sanskrit. Indeed, all his works, though perhaps not first-class poetry, make excellent reading because of the correctness of his diction, and the wealth of idiomatic phrases strewn all over the plays. The *Prabodha-Chandrodaya* of Krishnamishra (Circa 1100 A. C.) is another work, remarkable for its allegorical characters, comparable to the *Pilgrim's Progress.*

On the whole, however, the modern criticism is not utterly unfounded that the Sanskrit drama suffers from a degree of monotony. The inventiveness of the Indian artists is by no means amazing in plot and purpose, in theme and motive, in characterisation and sentiment. Perhaps the rigid rules of the Indian *Natyashastra,* followed by the Masters a shade too slavishly, explain this flaw. But in so far as the accusation touches the literary artistry of India as a whole, it can be easily rebutted by a reference to the prose works in Sanskrit. The story as a story must have been the favourite recreation of our fathers five thousand years ago as it is to-day; and it would have been naturally much more easy to recite or recount in the freer, easier speech of the people than in the rigorously regulated language of the learned. But even in the Sanskrit tongue there is surviving a sufficient number of specimens to mark the appreciation of the learned for this form of literary creation. The distinction between the fable and the parable,—between the tale and the novel or romance,—is, necessarily, not rigidly observed. The *Pancha Tantra,* a veritable store-house of the beast-and-bird fable, is one of the most ancient creations of the Indian genius, whose origin is lost in the mists of extreme antiquity. Imitations of it are found in every tongue from the Chinese and the Arabic to the Greek and the French. Originating most probably in Prakrit in prose form, the Sanskrit version has taken a poetic garb, without affecting the smoothness and simplicity of its origin.

If this marvellous collection of fables may not be classed as a prose work proper, the *Great Collection of Stories* presented by various authors under various titles, is undisputed prose,—a faithful, reliable, genuine portraiture of the life and manners of the peoples of ancient India. The prose works, however, which embody beauties of style as well as of narrative, are relatively of recent creation. Dandin and Subandhu, Bana and Kshemendra, are classic examples of first-class sanskrit prose of the latter day ornateness. The two first-named are of uncertain date. But neither the *Story of the Ten Princes (Dasha-Kumara-Charita)*, nor the *Tale of Vāsavadattā* suffer on account of the uncertainties attaching to the history of their authors. The former displays many a flaw in style, which its author has himself inveigled against in his standard treatise on *Poetics (Kāvyā-darsha.)* But what of that? The story is complex, involved, often depending on the marvellous and the miraculous to work out its mechanism. But what of that, either? Dandin's art is still unquestionable, and reminds one of the prose creations of a Victor Hugo or a Eugene Sue. Indeed, all the classic Sanskrit prose works now extant display a minuteness and elaboration of description, which would be the envy of the modern psycho-analysts. Dandin is admittedly a master of style,—cultured, correct and dignified. Subandhu, the author of *Vāsavadattā,* is, on the other hand, a kind of cyclopoedist of his day. In his long compounds, in his tremendous piling of adjectives, and immense love of resonant phrases, he reminds a modern reader of the interminable prefaces of Bernard Shaw. His love of pun brings him nearest to his more famous confrére Bana, the biographer of Harsha (606-648). Bana's much more famous Romance,—*Kadambari,*— is at once the admiration and despair of the modern Sanskrit student. The author's infinite love of far-fetched allusions, puns and *double-entendres;* and his interminable sentences, which would eclipse Mark Twain's parody of the German language, place him in a class by himself. Even his son, who continued and completed the unfinished Romance, does not come near him in this regard. Dhanapala in his *Tilakmanjari* shows a certain imitation of this curious style, as also the Jain writer Somadeva in his *Yasastilaka.*

The tale as a tale is further illustrated by such works as the *Vaitalapanchavinshika*, the *Shuka-Saptati*, or the *Simhāsana-Dvātrimshikā*, wherein all the elements of the modern story-writing,—problems, riddles, detective tales, sex-novels, psycho-analytical and historical romance—are discernible in the making. The original *Brihat-Kathā* of Gunādhya was in a vernacular,—the Paishachi dialect; and the Sanskrit versions of Kshemendra and of Somadeva are adaptations in the cutlured language of the learned,—the original being lost.

* * * * * *

PLATE XXXVIII

APSARA DANCING

From N. C. Mehta's book "Studies in Indian Painting".

The literary treasures of India, however, are not contained solely in the rigid, sonorous, highly cultivated Sanskrit language, or in the dead and gone Prakrits. The South Indian,—Dravidian,—languages, the speech of the great Andhra Desha, of the Chola and the Pandya Kingdoms, have preserved their own wonderful creations from long before the Aryans came into this country. Perhaps the entire land was once Dravidian, and the Dravid languages were the languages of the people of India. Even after the Aryan conquest, the mountain and the forest made for the South an impenetrable barrier, shutting up the people there as in a walled fort with a goodly garrison. The South, has, indeed, been Brahmanised; and Sanskrit, as a learned and sacred language, has come to be adopted there as much as in any other part of India. Without mentioning, at this stage, the glories of such scholars and philosophers as Sayanacharya and Madhavacharya; Shankaracharya (a prodigy, if there ever was one) and Ramanujacharya; we may mention that not an inconsiderable portion of the classic Sanskrit literature, and some of its best, is of southern creation. The choicest and the most elegant style was Vaidarbhi, or Berari. The dialect most favoured for songs in the classic drama was the Maharashtri,—may we call it the Deccani, now?—whose sweetness and elegance easily made it popular throughout the land. Apart from this tribute to the conquering race, the South has maintained its own monuments of literary genius, in Telegu, Tamil, Kanarese and Malayalam, and in innumerable dialects. For one not personally familiar with any of these languages it would naturally be difficult to give a just appreciation of their literature. But the relative paucity of our remarks on the Dravidian treasures of prose and verse must not be held to imply any poverty of that literature.

Says Caldwell in his *Grammar of Dravidian Languages:*

> "There is no proof of Dravidian literature, such as we now have it, having originated much before Kumarila's time (700 A. D.); and its earliest cultivators appear to be Jainas."

> "It was through the fostering care of the Jainas," says Mr. Frazer in his *Literary History of India*, "that the South first seems to have been inspired with new ideals, and its literature enriched with new forms of expression."

Brahmanical influences may have penetrated to the southern countries in pre-historic antiquity, when Agastya first broke through the mountain barrier. But the Jain and the Buddhist missionaries seem to have followed close on the heels of the Brahmans. The last two have now fallen very much in the background; but the literary historian of the land must admit their contribution to the southern vernacular literature,—particularly of the Jains,—to be the most substantial. In the true spirit of protestantism, these Jains and Buddhists always preferred the speech of the people to the language of the learned to convey their message; and hence their influence on language-building and literature for the masses. One of the greatest of these Jain masterpieces in the South is the *Natadiar* in Tamil, traditionally reputed to be composed in a miraculous manner by the 8000 Jain monks. They had fled the ravages of a 12 years' drought in the Empire of

23

Chandragupta Maurya to the court of the Pandya king in the Deccan. When the famine was over, the monks wanted to return; but the king would not let them. So they departed secretly, leaving each a stanza as a souvenir of their stay, and of His Majesty's courtesy. The King was angry when he discovered their departure, and ordered their mementoes to be thrown in the river. To the surprise of all beholders, four hundred of these quatrains floated, and make up the most wonderful reminder of the Jain genius in the vernacular. The judgment of the English scholar and translator, Dr. Pope, is summed up in the sentence.

> "There seems to be a strange sense of moral obligation, an earnest aspiration after righteousness, a fervent and unselfish charity, and generally a loftiness of aim that are very impressive."

The poem deals with virtue, wealth and pleasure, in a strain of acute worldly wisdom, a quaint fancy and a homely imagery, pointed wit and elegant satire, that seem most surprising when one remembers that the authors were so many, and all of them ascetics. Take this picture as a sample.

> "She, of enticing beauty, adorned with choice jewels, said forsooth, "I will leap with you down the precipice". Because I had no money, she, weeping, and pointing to her aching feet, withdrew and left me alone."

Could even the Camel-driver of Baghdad have bettered this in sentiment? It is not cynicism, but merely knowledge of the world.

The same theme of wealth and virtue inspired the pariah-poet,—Tiruvalluvar,—a thousand years after the authors of the *Natadiyar* had left the southern shores. The wonderful mastery of the poet over his language, as seen in his successful handling of the *Vempa*, the most difficult metre in his language with "some of the most perfect combinations of sound set to the most delicate play of fancy," establishes his indisputable claim to have been a veritable genius wondrously inspired. His verses on love are perfect, pregnant with meaning, proverbial in setting. Dr. Pope's metrical translation of the poet's *Kurral* embodies a faint aroma of the warm fragrance of the original.

> "The pangs that evening brings I never knew,
>   Till he, my wedded spouse, from me withdrew (1226).
>
>   *   *   *
>
> "My grief at morn a bud, all day an opening flower,
>   Full-blown expands in evening hour (1227).
>
>   *   *   *
>
> "Or bid thy love, or bid thy shame depart,
>   For me, I cannot bear them both, my worthy heart (1247).
>
>   *   *   *
>
> "In lover quarrels, 'tis the one that first gives way,
>   That in reunion's joy is seen to win the day (1327).

Another great Tamil poet was Manika Vachagar, a fierce opponent of the dominant Jainism of his day, an ardent devotee of the dread God Shiva. Dr. Pope, his learned and sympathetic translator, assigns him to the 11th century Christian era, and considers him to be a mixture of St. Paul and St. Francis of Assisi. But perhaps the poet dates from much earlier,—the 4th century A. C. Born at Madura of a Brahman courtier of that place, he is said by tradition to have acquired all the learning of his day by the time he was 16, when the king appointed him Prime Minister. The laurels of even a Richelieu or a Pitt must pale before this prodigy, who wanted to re-establish an old Church. The poet is, of course, still most popular in the country he converted, his verses being even now sung with rapture by the high caste and the low caste, by the aged and the youthful, who all delight in committing them to memory. Two centuries later was born Tirunana Sambandha, another Tamil poet-saint and Shaivite of lyric fame.

These were the immediate predecessors of Shankaracharya. He was their true descendant in spirit, as their compatriot in space. The greatest revivalist, the greatest commentator the *Upanishads* have ever known, he reminds one of the fiery zeal of a Loyola, combined with the vast learning and profound thoughtfulness of an Aquinas. An ascetic and a scholar, a poet and a Yogi, he compressed the most varied and bewildering activities in the short space of barely 32 years. In the intellectual sphere, he was the sovereign master in his day (788 A. C. to 820 A. C.) from Dwarka to Puri, from Badrinath to Shringeri. The fading glories of Aryan cult and culture find in him a most brilliant luminary. His life, or rather an account of his *Digvijaya*,—or the Great Conquest,—has been preserved for posterity by another great Vedic commentator of the South, Madhavacharya of Vijaya-nagar. But little or nothing is known about his personal life. Born in Malabar about 788 A. C., he died at Kedarnath in the Himalayas about 820 A.C., after having enriched the Indian sacred literature by the most terse and profound commentaries on all the later Scriptures. His teaching, summed up, emphasises the delusive nature of the outer world and its phenomenon, and the unreality of sense perceptions. The most popular and yet the most poetic of his creations is a song in Sanskrit of some 31 verses, which embodies, as it were in a nutshell, the philosophy of the most learned and yet the most musical of philosophers. The versification of the *Moha-Mudgara* is exquisite; its rhyme unequalled; its alliteration unsurpassed.

*   *   *   *   *   *

With the establishment of the Muhammadan Empire in India, a subtle transformation comes over the native genius. The real creative impulse seems to be killed, at least for a while. The country was staggered by the rude hammering of Mahmud's sacrilegious axe on the idol of the great, far-famed temple of Somnath on the shores of the Arabian Ocean. And while it gathered itself together again, the heavy cavalry of the Pathan and the Mughal had thundered through the land from Peshawar to Kanyakumari, defiling where they could not destroy. The ranks of the invaders were replenished by fresh hordes of savage fanatics. Natives of India, however, gradually accepted Islam, if not in fear of the sword, then out of consideration of worldly good. With the growing force of Muslim dominion, and the rising tide of conversion, the old cultivation of the Sanskrit tongue declined. In

Kashmir and in Bengal there were, indeed, stray writers in Sanskrit, even after the advent of Muhammadanism. The lyric genius of Jayadeva of the *Gita-Govinda* fame is second to none in all the annals of Indian literature. That wonderful poem, picturing the love of Krishna and Radha, deals with an old and yet ageless theme. The combination, however, of the most exquisitely musical phrases, in some of the strangest and boldest metres ever handled by a Sanskrit bard, with a wealth of alliteration and imagery bewildering in its riotous luxuriance, stamps the author as the peer and equal of the brightest stars in our literary firmament. Apart, however, from such sporadic outbursts of a stray genius, the Sanskrit language languished in the Muhammadan era, until the cultured Muslims came, of their own accord, to appreciate the charms of this noble tongue. We may take the Sanskrit scholarship of Akbar's Mughal courtiers; and the Sanskrit education of Dara, Shah Jahan's eldest and the most favourite son, and translator of the *Upanishads*, as indexes of the changed viewpoint. In spite, however, of this revival; and the undying lustre of the old language of scholars, singers and seers of India, Sanskrit became, in the Muhammadan era, a dead language; and so, from about the 12th century A.C., the laurels of literary creation go to the vernacular languages of the people.

*   *   *   *   *   *

The present day vernaculars are not, however, the creation exclusively of Muslim dominion. They are all rich beyond words in literary creations that sway the heart of the simple souls making up the mass in any country. It is impossible to select for special mention the literature of any of these, or even the outstanding names in them all. All that we can or might do in this place is to mention some of the towering personalities, who, without regard to provincial or linguistic boundaries, make the collective literary consciousness of India.

It is, curiously enough, in Bengal that we find the first re-appearance of the light after it has been extinguished by the crash of steel in the war of faiths. Jayadeva is a Bengali from the Birbhum district, preaching, through the haunting strains of his unforgettable verses, the doctrine of *Bhakti*,—faith absolute and unquestioning,—which had first been taught by Krishna himself to his chosen devotee Arjuna. Born, perhaps, for popular consumption, from the system of Yoga which aimed at the absorption of the Soul into the Essence of the Deity, the doctrine of *Bhakti* has been transmuted by such great alchemists as Shankaracharya and Ramanujam, Jayadeva and the Sikh Gurus, the Tamil Tiruvalluvar and the Gujarati Narasimha Mehta or Mira Bai, the poet-queen of Mewar; so that for myriads of Indians to-day, it is the only road to salvation. Bengal, as already remarked, leads the way, with Jayadeva the Poet, and Chaitanya the philosopher,—a second Buddha. The labours of the great jurists, beginning with Medhatithi and Jimutavahana of *Dāyabhāga* fame, might be thought to consort ill with the lyrics of the poet, or the longings of the philosopher. And yet the soil was the same. Ramanand sang his songs of devotion round about Agra, where his followers still form a goodly number. But his fame has been increased a hundred-fold by his more famous disciple, Kabir, a simple weaver of Benares, even as in modern times, the fame of

Shri Ramakrishna Paramahamsa has been increased by his more celebrated follower, Swami Vivekananda. Kabir, his followers believe, was born of an immaculate conception. His trite little sayings, with homely imagery and every day application, are the first manifestation of the Hindu reaction on contact with Islam, breaking through the suffocating hold of Hindu ritual to a glimpse of natural theology so easy of acceptance in the days of warring creeds. The Vedantic conception of a single supreme Deity is insisted upon in place of these; and the warring legions of Allah (or Ali)-worshippers and Rama-worshippers are sought to be reconciled in that common adoration of the one Omnipotent. The way to know Him might be shown by a Guru, a spiritual preceptor,—a principle, which Kabir's contemporary, Nanak, used with the utmost felicity. The *Shahbdavli*,—A Thousand Gems from Kabir,—and the *Sukha-Nidhan*, combine the Vedantic doctrine of unreality, with the Jain universal conception, the Buddhist notion of *Nirvana*, and the Islamic idea of a personal God, into a common cult. "Behold but one in all things," cries the poet. "It is the second that leads you astray. Every man and woman that has ever been born is of the same nature as yourself."

Bidyapati Thakur,—an archaic namesake, if not a previous Avatar, of Tagore—in northern Bihar, and Chandidas in Bengal, carried on the torch kindled by Kabir; while the royal Mira of Mewar reproduced the ecstasies of St. Teresa a century in advance of that Spanish Saint.

The change from this mystic devotion to realistic sensuousness followed soon after, when the curb of spiritualism was relaxed by the growing breeze of agnosticism. Vallabhacharya built his epicurean mansion on this new form of the sentiment of devotion, though Chaitanya, his contemporary, had taken the spiritual line. Born at Nadiya in Bengal (1485-1527 A. C.), Chaitanya's wonderful eloquence and magnetic personality was endowed with an almost mesmeric force. Devotion, utter and absolute, to Krishna is the key-note of this passionate preacher of Muhammadan India.

The line of Hindu poets is next continued by the simple, pathetic figure of Surdas, and the towering genius of Tulsidas. The blind Bard of Agra, Surdas, sang, in his *Sur-Sagar* of sixty thousand verses, innumerable songs for the worship of Krishna, even as Milton composed his masterpieces. Of Tulsidas (died 1624 A.C.) an English critic writes:

> "Pandits may talk of the Vedas and the Upanishads, and a few may even study them; others may say they pin their faith on the Puranas; but to the vast majority of people of Hindustan, learned and unlearned alike, the norm of conduct is the so-called *Tulsikrit-Ramayana*."

The basis of this far-famed work of the greatest poet during the Muhammadan age is Valmiki's *Ramayana;* but the genius of Tulsidas has made it all his own, even as the cantoes in Kalidasa's *Raghuvamsha* are all his own. The work of Tulsidas spread far and wide the doctrines of Ramananda and the faith in Vishnu, in the chaste, refined garb of Rama and Sita that would not offend the most exacting moralist. In mystic words of ever abiding charm and unfading fragrance, Tulsi exhorts the reader to ponder on the name of Rama, the symbol of the good, the perfect, the eternal, and all-pervading.

"Perish property, house, fortune, friends, parents and kinsmen, and all that does not help to bring one to Rama . . . Even a dog-keeper, the savage hillsmen, the stupid foreigners, the outcaste, become purified and renowned by repeating the name of Rama."

＊　　　＊　　　＊　　　＊　　　＊　　　＊

While these great seers and singers flourished in the North and the West; while Chaitanya preached his new faith, and the Rajputs and Marathas fought and bled for their old,—poets and preachers in the South and the West were by no means idle. Narasimha Mehta in Gujarat was propagating the same cult of devotion to Vishnu that Mira Bai had sung before him in Hindustan. In the South, in the country of the Marathas, Tukaram, a Shudra Saint and poet of Poona, was singing his 5000 hymns on the same theme. Schooled in adversity and persecution, his piety, devotion, simplicity, and unblemished life won him the worship of the greatest soldier and statesman of his age, Shivaji Maharaj. When however Shivaji begged him to pay a visit to the court, the Shudra poet wrote back:

"What pleasure is there in paying a visit? The days of life are fleeting past. Having known one or two duties which are the real Essence, I shall now live in my own delusion. The meaning of the whole which will do thee good is this—God is the all-pervading soul in every created object. Live with thy mind unforgetful of the all-pervading soul, and witness thyself in Ramdasa." (Frazer p. 301.)

Against the names of these heroes of the song and the sermon amongst the Hindus, the Muslims in India have but few names to offer from amongst native-born Indian Musalmans. Amir Khusru in the Tughluq days is claimed to be Indian. But the bulk of the Muhammadan creations was by foreigners and in non-Indian languages, until the days of the Mughals. Perhaps we do not yet know all the contributions of the pre-Mughal Musalmans to the Splendour of India in the world of art and literature. Perhaps the memories of untutored fanatics and irresponsible autocrats have obscured unduly the longings of the soul among the devout and the thougtful of the Muslims, like a Nizamuddin, or a Shaikh Salim Chisti, or even a Faizi.

In any event, with the advent of the Mughals, the scene changes at once. They are polished, cultured, aristocrats,—in the best sense of the word. Babur was himself a writer of no mean ability, and his son and daughter were as refined specimens of their age and culture as the best. Akbar was unlettered, and yet the most educated of the Emperors, who appreciated scholars and thinkers so much that he sought them in every way, in every place. His Court was a replica of the glorious days of the great Guptas and Mauryas centuries before him. His son was a literateur, and his grandson the most magnificent patron of the gorgeous art India has ever known. The children of Shah Jahan were all the most finished ladies and gentlemen of their day,—with Dara Shukoh, the eldest, the most erudite, the most refined, and the most tragic, leading in the way which promised his reign would become that of

PLATE XXXIX

106   KABIR   107   GURU NANAK

(From Coomaraswamy's "Rajput Painting")

108   BAJ BAHADUR AND RUPMATI

PLATE XL.

109 SHIVA
(Ceylon)

110 BUDDHA STATUE FROM TAXILLA
(From M. Hurlimann's "Picturesque India")

111 RUINS OF ANCIENT UNIVERSITY OF TAXILLA

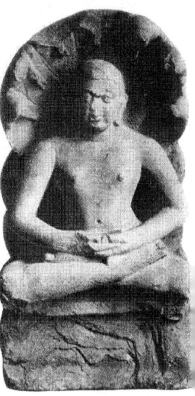

112 PARASWANATH, XXII JAIN SAINT
OR TIRATHAKAR (MATHURA)

a second Akbar,—a promise of the Golden Age which, if it bloomed at all, faded all too soon!

With the fanatical and puritanical Aurangzeb, these splendours began to pale. But the impulse the Imperial patronage had given was too great to flicker out at once. The century of darkness following upon the fall of the Mughal Empire was, perhaps, the dreariest and gloomiest period India has ever experienced; but the new impulse born the moment a settled government was formed and even now pulsating through the land, is evidence enough of the yet surviving genius of the people. We are, however, yet much too near a Tagore or a Toru Dutt, an Iqbal or a Sarojini Naidu to be able to form a just appreciation of their contributions to the Splendour That Was 'Ind.

CHAPTER VI

RELIGION AND PHILOSOPHY

We have been looking so far at the splendours of Indian literary genius, mainly as creations of the poet's art. But a yet more voluminous literature is to be found in the Scriptures of the various religions that took their root on this soil, and in the marvellous flights of philosophy that accompany the more dogmatic parts of the sacred writings. Scholarship as such, and passionate pursuit of science, also distinguish the early Indian genius. No picture of the *Splendour That Was 'Ind*, could claim to be complete, which does not cast a glance at these, our still most popular treasures; and so, this chapter is devoted to a brief survey of the wonders of Indian Science and Philosophy.

The philosophy of the Vedas is a little difficult to describe. The words are simple, but their meaning not always clear, precise, certain. The striking sensuous nature-worship of the earliest of the hymns to the World God (Varuna), the Fire-God, the Wind-Gods, the Sun-God, is tinged with a feeling of oneness of the natural phenomena, which later on came to be recognised as the unity of the Divine immanence in the forces of nature and the myriad forms of life. Says the Rig-Veda: (R. V. I. 164, 46):—

> "They recall him Indra, Mitra, Varuna, Agni, and He is the heavenly winged Garutman."

The question is ever asked in one form or another:

> "What pathway leadeth to the Gods? Who knoweth this of a truth, and who will now declare it? (R. V. III, 54-5.)

And the answer rises strident from the stanza of the early Hymns.

> "One All is Lord of what is fixed, and moving, that walk, that flies, this multiform creation." (Wallis, *Cosmology of the Vedas*, p. 51.)

The soul of the Seer is, indeed, not always satisfied by this simple answer; and the *cri de coeur* rises again, "*Kasmai Devaya-Havisha Vidhema*" (To what God shall we sacrifice?). But this cry of despair goes hand in hand with growing sophistication,—widening as well as deepening human knowledge; and so the question meets with varied answers in the systems of philosophy built largely on the Vedas themselves, discovering in them meaning which it may fairly be doubted if the Vedic Seers themselves were aware of. The *Brahmanas* and *Aranyakas*,—a later development of the *Brahmanas*,—are a kind of prose commentaries on the Vedas, which also constitute in themselves philosophic treatises. It is from the Age of these *Brahmanas* that the four-classed organisation of the Indian society may be said definitely to date, though in the *Purusha-Sukta* of the Rig-Veda there is a reference to the same. The sacrificial ritual, elaborate as it was complex was made the rigid monopoly of that class, and so ensured its unchallenged supremacy.

The "Forest Treatises" (*Aranyakas*), compiled as a kind of theosophic pendant to the *Brahmanas*, make an easy transition to the *Upanishads*, which are considered to be the basis and storehouse of the systematic philosophy of the Hindus. Composed in the Vedic tongue, they must necessarily have preceded the date assigned by scholars to the origin and perfection of the classic Sanskrit tongue— circa 500 B. C. About a dozen of these esoteric treatises stand out as pre-eminently clear, thoughtful, suggestive, works, marking the zenith of the literary production of the Vedic period. They carry on the speculative side of the *Brahmanas*, putting forth,—under the guise of exposition, elucidation, and comment,—their own distinct philosophy, independent of the ritualistic religion of the *Brahmanas*. The *Upanishads*

> "do not aim at securing earthly and afterwards heavenly bliss in the abode of Yama by sacrificing correctly to the gods, but at obtaining deliverance from mundane existence by absorption of the individual soul in the world-soul through correct knowledge. The Upanishad conception of the world-soul (Ātman) is the final development of the personal creator Prajāpati, who has become the impersonal source of all being, Brahmā."[1]

The illusiveness (Māyā) of the outside material world is first formulated in *Shvetashwatara Upanishad;* but the idea is implicit in the oldest. The identity of the individual with the world-soul is enunciated by the *Chhandogya Upanishad* which, with the *Brihadāranyaka Upanishad*, is regarded as the finest outcome of Vedic philosophy. The development of philosophic calm is furthered by the rise of the theory of Transmigration, which appears first in the *Shatapatha* (Hundred Paths) *Brahmana;* and the working mechanism is supplied by the doctrine of *Karma.*

The Brahman canonical literature,—apart from the *Vedas*, the *Brahmanas*, and the *Upanishads*,—is of course, in classic Sanskrit. It is in the form of concise treatises or aphorisms, called *Sutras*, and is divided into three main groups. The *Shrauta Sutras* deal with the sacrificial ritual. The *Grihya Sutras* deal with the domestic life of the Hindu from birth to death, and furnish data of unparalleled importance for the history and ethnology of the people. Finally, the *Dharma Sutras* are legal treatises concerned with the relations of man to his neighbours in society.

*   *   *   *   *   *

The *Sutras* of the Jains, and the Buddhist canonical works, when finally settled, were, on the other hand, in the every day language of the ordinary people. Before, however, we have a hurried survey of these Scriptures, let us cast a brief glance at the life and teachings of these great masters on the Indian soil. Scholars are now generally agreed that Jainism is an older religion than Buddhism,—though the surface similarity of the two had led the first European scholars to consider the former to

---

1) cp. Macdonell *India's Past*, p. 46.

be only an offshoot of the latter. Siddhartha Gautama,—the Buddha,—and Vardhamana Mahavira, are now considered to have been contemporaries, though Jain tradition, and stray remarks in the Buddhist Scripture, suggest the founder of modern Jainism to have preceded the author of Buddhism by about 50 years. Even if we hold, with modern European scholars, Vardhamana Mahavira to have died a few years after the Buddha, there is no doubt now that the religion and dogma Mahavira preached constituted only a new edition of the doctrine of Parshwa, his predecessor in the Jain pantheon, had preached. It seems not unlikely that Parshwa lived a couple of centuries before Mahavira; and preached a doctrine, a philosophy of life, which was even then not utterly unfamiliar. Mahavira was, according to Jain tradition, born about 600 B. C., at Vaisali in the country of the Lichhavis, who were a warrior tribe governing themselves like the ancient Athenians or the medieval Venitians. Siddhartha was a prince or noble of this clan, allied through his wife with the chief of his race; and, through him, with the powerful monarch of Magadha. Vardhamana Mahavira was his second son, and lived in his father's dominion till he was 30. He was married and had a daughter; but in the fullness of time he renounced his princely heritage, and retired to practise severe austerities. For 12 years he strove in unheard of penance to cut through the bonds that held him to life and its vanities. At last he reached the final and complete stage of knowledge. The French say: "*Tout comprendre c'est tout pardonner;*" the Jains suggest rather that "to know and understand all is to transcend all". For 30 years after reaching the stage of all-knowledge, Mahavira preached the doctrine of *Ahimsa*, love and fellow-feeling with all living beings. The Hindu practice of animal sacrifice became an abomination to the Jains and the Buddhists alike; but the Jains went beyond the Buddhists in holding life to be in existence in wind and water, in earth and fire, as much as in the smallest worm and the strongest, highest, best of men. Modern Science seems to confirm,—very strangely, indeed,—the belief of the Jains. But it also seems to show how utterly impracticable the Jain dogma would be in daily life, if practised in its absolute rigour. Historians, however, agree that if the Jains unlike the Buddhists, though relatively few in number, still survive the field, it is because they have had the minority's intense instinct of self-preservation shown in conservative tactics. The Jain doctrine is cognate to the Buddhist in its rejection of a personal, creative, omnipotent Divinity; but it is not on that account, without its own code of ethics, both individual and social. The abhorrence of untruth and unchastity among men and women ranks almost on a par with the canon of *Ahimsa* for the lay as well the clerical Orders. The Jain *Samgha* or Society is made up of the monks and nuns,—or those who have renounced utterly all worldy riches and relationships; and of the *Shravaks* and *Shravikas*, the laity male and female, who, without renouncing the householders' responsibilities, are required to conform their life and conduct and dealings to the main canon of their religion. The Jain canon seems to have been codified in the time of the Emperor Chandragupta Maurya about 300 B. C., by the pontiff Bhadrabahu; though schism seems to have made its appearance in the life-time of Mahavira himself. The

PLATE XLI

113

A JAIN NUN

(Painting by Rao Bahadur M. V. Dhurandhar)

distinction between the Swetambaris and Digambaris dates from the days of Mahavira; but the internal differences of to-day seem to have gone on somewhat minute points, the most considerable relating to the worship of idols. It is to the idolatrous, however, the student of art and architecture in India must feel thankful for those superb creations, such as the Temples of Mount Abu or the statue at Shravan Belgola, which relieve in part the otherwise ascetic puritanism of the Jains.

The bulk of the Jain Scripture now extant is certainly not all as the founder himself uttered it. Such as it is, it is contained in 32 Sutras, made up of the eleven *Angas*, the 12 *Upangas*, the 4 *Mul Sutras*, 4 *Chheda Granthas*, and 1 *Avshak Sutra*. Its rigour is obviously inconsistent with the demands of organised Society and its government; though in Western India the Empire of Gujarat had at one time Kings and Ministers of State professing the Jain faith. From the innocuous character of their practices, however, and from the unambitious nature of their faith, they seem, generally speaking, to have disarmed any active hostility from the days of the Maurya to those of the Mughal.

The Buddha was a contemporary of Mahavira. Born of a Sakya Prince at Shravathi, or Kapilavastu, in the foot-hills of the Himalayas, the founder of Buddhism was also a Kshatriya by birth. King Suddhodana was a King probably in the same sense as many a modern princelet in Kathiawar is styled "His Highness". The story of his wife Mayadevi having wonderful dreams at the time of the conception of her great son may be taken to be some of those postmortem embroideries, which hang like aureoles round the birth story of every great man. Siddhartha was born in a garden,—the far-famed Lumbini Grove,—where the Queen his mother had halted on her way to her father's home. Prince Siddhartha was a strange child,—even in his childhood, exceedingly sensitive to any spectacle of sorrow and suffering in the entire living world; and so, by the orders of the King, his father, he was spared every such scene, lest the great pity of his heart might make him do some unusual act. His mother, Queen Mayadevi, was spared the sight of his great Renunciation by death soon after the wondrous child was born. The young Prince, however, continued to grow as any other young man of his rank and day, going through all the exercises and enjoyments his position entailed. He was, by nature, disinclined to marry; but was lured into it by the wiles of his father's Court, as much as by the bewitching eyes of the noble Yashodhara. Soon after the birth of his first child, the Call came to him; and Buddha left, at dead of night, his sleeping wife and babe, his father's Court and all its treasures, to solve the riddle of the universe, and find an unfailing antidote to suffering and sadness.

For years he journeyed to and fro; for years he meditated and practised the most rigorous austerities. The saints and sages he met were all unsatisfying in their answers to the queries of the Sakyan inquirer. The Gods of the Vedas were only the magnified images of the type of man, held in awe and reverence amongst his fellows. To the searching queries of the Sakyan's heart they made no reply, even in the more rarefied atmosphere of the *Upanishads*. The endless cycle of birth and death seemed, perhaps, the perfection of hopelessness, which dismayed, if it did not revolt, the inquirer.

After years of patient suffering in incredible austerities and meditation, Light at last came to the Sakyan sage under the sacred Bo-tree at Buddha Gaya. He rose, and proclaimed aloud his message.

> Many a House of Life
> Hath held me seeking ever Him who wrought
> These Prisons of the Senses, sorrow-fraught.
> Sore was my ceaseless strife.

But now he was free, and his message of hope was carried by Him in His own life-time throughout the length and breadth of the land from Bengal to the Punjab. From the day he first preached in the Deer-park at Benares to the five ascetics who had for a while accompanied him in his researches, he insisted on the one truth, the Middle Path, that gave freedom from the bondage of *Karma*. His message consisted of the Eightfold Precept, *i. e.* Right Views, Right Aspirations, Right Speech, Right Conduct, Right Living, Right Effort, Right Thought and Right Self-Concentration.

Buddhism, in spite of its seeming emphasis on the utter emptiness of things mundane, was not a mere freak in the evolution of Indian thought. The Buddhist Scriptures, like the Jain, are in the Magadhi or Pali language,—very likely the language spoken by the Venerable One Himself; though that does not mean that he was unfamiliar with the vast philosophical lore of the Hindu *Upanishads*. In fact, the body of doctrine that was later on systematised as the Buddhist philosophy may well be taken to be considerably influenced by the systems preceding. When however, the wisdom of the Venerable One came out of His mouth, it seemed to be a direct outcome of the conditions under which men's minds were then agitating.

> "A congeries of conflicting theories and guesses," says Prof. Radhakrishnan, "accepted by some and denied by others, changing with men, reflecting the individual characters, emotions and wishes of their authors, filled the air. There were no admitted facts or principles which all recognised, but only dissolving views and intuitions. In actual life, ritualism reigned supreme, with its cruel accompaniments of meaningless sacrifices and puproseless incantations, in which people had ceased to believe."

It was against this the Buddha raised his voice in passionate protest, and proclaimed the superiority of the natural law over such meaningless supernaturalism. His doctrine permitted each man to work out his own salvation for himself, irrespective of caste or birth, independent of the ministration of priests or the interposition of the gods. "It is a foolish idea to suppose that another can cause us happiness or misery; He declared. If ethics is made to rest on the shifting sands of methaphysics or theology, it has an uncertain tenure. Buddha wished to build it on the rock of facts". (Radhakrishnan.) So he went about, discarding priest and dogma, eschewing sacrament and sacrifice, insisting only on the perfection of character and the inner self as the only way to salvation.

We need not go into the particulars of the Buddhist philosophy beyond just mentioning the four cardinal points,—the central truths,—which comprise it, viz., "that there is suffering, that it has a cause, that it can be suppressed, and that there is a way to accomplish it". Suffering, like the world, is endless, and without beginning; but the Buddhist is inclined, perhaps, to over-emphasize it. The cause of suffering is the craving for the gratification of the senses. All that is transient is painful; and if only the permanent deserve to be called Atman or the soul, then the Buddhist would have nothing to do with the Soul. The Second Sermon of the Buddha himself was delivered to his first five disciples on the non-existence of the soul. When the wandering mendicant Vachhaghatta asked the Master, " Is there the Ego ?" He remained silent; and when the persistent inquirer asked again: " Is there not the Ego "? He remained silent. He is clear, indeed, about what the soul is not,—neither body, nor sense-perception, nor the constituents of the individual. But as to what it is,—He has nothing to say; for He felt it would be transcending experience to assert the existence of the soul by going behind phenomena. *Karma* He believes in, and regards as an explanation of suffering; and when one is freed from it, one reaches *Nirvana*,—the actionless state of do-nothingness,—in this life, and *parinirvāna*, when the body—purged of all *Karma*—falls into decay. The way to reach this consummation is by the Eight-fold Path already mentioned. "Still persisting, still achieving" in the Eightfold Path, the Buddhist becomes free from all bodily passion and worldly desires of life and its longings; and when *Nirvana* is attained, he becomes finally, absolutely, completely free from any longing whether of earth or of heaven, of pride and passion and ill-feeling, self-righteousness and ignorance.

The doctrine of Personal Responsibility, implicit in the theory of *Karma*, was the greatest recommendation of Buddhism to the non-Indian Princes who came to establish an Empire in India. To the Hindu the idea of a non-caste or Shudra sovereign would be anathema; but to the Buddhist the slave-girl's son Chandra-gupta was as acceptable as Kanishka the non-Indian. The pride of birth and caste being dispensed with and denied, manhood was left to assert itself free of all restrictions. India, however, seemed not to be ready yet to assimilate this message of the Master; and so when the bewitching influence of his wonderful eloquence was removed, the purity, simplicity, and withal the daring, of his doctrines was gradually lost sight of. Soon after his death in 478 B. C., 500 of His most chosen disciples met together in the Satapanni Cave near Rajagriha,—the ancient capital of Magadha,—to collect together, in an authorised version, the Master's sayings. In the three Baskets or *Pitakas*, the Pali books contain, according to the strict orthodox belief, all the doctrines of the Master Himself, given out in his 44 years of Enlightened preaching. But the purity and simplicity of these was modified in the Second Æcumenical Council held at Vaisali in 377 B. C., where the first great schism commenced over the attempt of the northern followers to introduce the Ten Indulgences, *e. g.*, the permission to the Buddhist monk to receive and accept gold and silver. The two great divisions of the Higher Vehicle,—*Mahāyāna*,—and the

Lower Vehicle,—*Hinayāna*,—commencing here were eventually split up into sects. Buddhism flourished in India, though divided into sects, and in a gradually more and more Hinduised form, for over a thousand years after the founder's death. Meanwhile, the more ancient Vedic philosophy and religion had never died out. More than one effort was made for its revival during this period; but universal success was unattainable till the great Shankaracharya came on the scene.

The philosophy of Vedantism, with which Shankaracharya's name is associated, is, perhaps, a shade too refined for the ordinary mortal. By his insistence on the idealistic non-duality, and yet of non-reality of the sense-perceptions, Shankara supplied a charm to hold the faith of the religious mystic, and of the rarefied idealist who is repelled by crude materialism. Ramanuja, also a Vedic commentator, and born about the beginning of the eleventh century A. C., was a preacher of qualified Adwaitism—or non-duality,—in which the Supreme Spirit, the Universal Soul, becomes at once the cause of the outside world and the material of all creation. In the God Vishnu he finds this Supreme Soul particularly and pre-eminently embodied; and hence his insistence on the adoration of Vishnu as the only means of gaining freedom from rebirth. Madhavacharya (14th century) also took the same view. While, however, philosophers debated on Adwaitism, the countless masses of the Indian villagers were content with the worship of the village godlings, with here and there an awful variety provided by some foul Tantric rite, for which the temples of the great Hindu Gods were resorted to only by stealth, and in a perverted form.

Philosophy in India has, however, never been able to divorce itself completely from Theology and religious ritual, thanks to its origin in the study of the Vedas. The classic Six Systems,—the *Shad-Dharshana*,—though each an independent development, have all this common origin, as reflected in the Six Systems being really only three pairs. Even if we do not reckon Jainism and Buddhism as philosophically parts of these Six Systems; and even if we include all the minor divisions as independent systems,—following the *Sarva-Darshana-Samgraha* of the famous Madhavacharya,—there would be in all sixteen different schools of thought hailing from the most ancient times. The Muslim contribution of Suffism is really a variant of Vedantism, though it did not take its origin in this country; while the practical rejoinder to the iconoclastic zeal of the early Muslims in India, as made by Kabir and Nanak, and as now embodied in the doctrines of the Sikhs, can hardly be described as independent systems. We shall, therefore, confine ourselves in this review to the principal Six Schools—the famous, classic *Shad-Darshana*.

In the Six Systems are comprised; the *Purva* and *Uttara Mimāmsā*, the *Sānkhya* and *Yoga;* the *Nyāya* and *Vaisheshika*. Each system has a body of aphorisms (Sutras) as its basis, and a varying host of commentaries, both critical and explanatory. A brief review of the most salient feature of each would reveal the relationship *inter se*, and its place in the story of philosophic thought in this country.

PLATE XLII

115   CEILING PAINTINGS IN JAIN TEMPLE
(CONJEEVRAM)

114   ABU: SIDE CHAPEL IN THE NEMNATH
TEMPLE

116   DILWARA TEMPLE: ADINATH TEMPLE HALL

117 BUDDHA STATUE (SANCHI)

PLATE XLIII

118   TEMPTATION OF BUDDHA
(Photo: Archaeological Survey, Hyderabad)

119   SIDDHARTA
(Boston Museum)

120   BUDDHA'S PARNIRVANA
(Boston Museum)

121   DIVISION OF BUDDHA'S BONES
(Government Museum, Madras)

1 and 2. THE MIMAMSAS.

These are the immediate offsprings of the Vedas; the *Uttara Mimamsa* being more commonly and compendiously known as the Vedanta System. The first, or *Purva Mimamsa* deals with the practical or ritualistic aspect of the Vedas, while the *Uttara Mimamsa,*—the theoretical or philosophical side,—is concerned with the World-Soul. Jaimini, author of the *Purva Mimamsa Sutra,* emphasizes the importance of the sacrifices and ceremonies prescribed by the Vedas as the only way to Salvation. A great commentator Shabara-Swamin is made greater by his more famous annotator Kumarila Bhatta, who wrote about 700 A. C., in Southern India. Madhavacharya followed in his footsteps in the fourteenth century. The basic Sutra of the *Uttara Mimamsa* is the *Vedanta Sutra* of Badarayana, composed, very likely, contemporaneously with Jaimini's great work in the sister school. The most famous and now the oldest extant commentary on his work is that of Shri Shankaracharya of immortal memory. The chief exponent of Adwaitism or Monism, he developed the doctrine of Maya, which regards the outside world of sense perceptions and phenomena to be an appearance. His extensive, learned, scientific treatises,—on the fundamental *Vedanta-Sutra,* the *Upanishads,* and the *Bhagvad-Gita,*—make a complete system, religio-philosophic in its nature, which even now claims the largest proportion of the keenest intellect of modern India. Ramanuja of Conjevaram, another South Indian (1175 to 1250 A. C.), modified Shankara's note of Adwaitism by a greater emphasis on Devotion or *Bhakti,* and by disputing the latter's views on the relation between *Karma and Jnana,* on the nature of true knowledge, and on the relation between Brahman and the world. On the whole, however, it would be true to say that the disputations of philosophers for two thousand years and more have succeeded in abolishing the difference, or at least in minimising it, as between the Path of Action *(Karma-Marga)* and the Path of Knowledge *(Jnana-Marga);* while the difference between these and the Path of Devotion *(Bhakti-Marga)* remains still undiminished.

3. THE SANKHYA SYSTEM.

This is a Dualistic school of thought, which is so-called Enumerative, because the classification and numbering of principles is an important feature. As opposed to the idealistic schools of the Vedas and Upanishads, this is a philosophy of Realism. It was founded by Kapila, of whom only the name survives. The ultimate authority here is not the *Vedas,* but the experience of each one by himself. The founder and his followers reject the doctrine of the World-Soul; consider matter and the phenomenal world to be real; and admit as per experience a multiplicity of individual souls. The First Cause of the world is *Prakriti,*—Nature,—or primeval matter. The origin of suffering is the non-distinction between soul and matter; and its end, the true knowledge. Though independent of, and even in opposition to, the Vedas, the Sankhya doctrine soon made its way in the Brahmanic literature, and came to permeate the *Mahabharata* and the *Puranas.* Certainly, at the time of the Buddha, and even of Mahavira or Parshwa, it must have been an important body of thought; for these great founders of non-Vedic religions in India taught doctrines which were essentially Sankhyic. The oldest extant Sankhya treatise is the *Sankhya-Karika* of Ishwara-Krishna, dating from about 300 A. C. Barth, the great French scholar, considered it to be the pearl of the whole scholastic literature of India; and the Arabian Alberuni in the 11th century bases his description of the Sankhya-System on this concise exposition of the Doctrine.

4. THE YOGA.

This is another non-Vedic school of thought in India, dating even from the days before the Vedic ideas took shape in philosophical systems.

> "The primary meaning is the 'Yoking' of the mind with a view to concentrate thought on a single point; for these exercises aim at the regulation of breathing, sitting, and restraining the senses, for the purposes of exclusive concentration on a single supernatural object, in order to obtain as a result supernatural knowledge as supernatural powers."

These exercises play a great part in the Brahmanic, Buddhist and Jain religions, owing, partly at least, to the value of the doctrine in teaching a rigorous restraint of the senses from the point of morality. In pure philosophy, Yoga is akin to the Sankhya, except that it accepts theism, and emphasizes asceticism as the way to salvation from life and its suffering. This has elicited the high praise given to it by Shri Krishna in the *Gita*, which is otherwise a poem of praise for the One God. The Yogic God, however, is not the same as the personal, creative, Lord and Judge of men, as imagined by the theistic systems generally. The basic Sutra of this system is ascribed to a Patanjali, (not the celebrated grammarian,) dealing, in four sections, with the nature, means, results, and end of concentration. There are a number of commentaries, as usual; but the handbooks now commonly used seem to be so utterly divorced from the essence of the old system, that they only invite, more often than not, the ridicule of the sceptic and the critical. This ridicule,—or at least scepticism,—cannot but be intensified by the histrionics of the modern pushing salesmen from the European shopkeepers.

5. THE NYAYA SYSTEM AND 6. VAISHESHIKA.

This is, essentially, Indian Logic, the two schools, once separate, having at last coalesced. They are wholly independent of religious belief, and may thus be rightly styled the systems of Scientific Logic and Theory of Knowledge. The *Nyaya Sutra* of Gautama is in five books, the first two dealing with Logic and Theory of Knowledge, the third with Psychology, the next with Transmigration and final salvation, and the last a final supplement to the whole. In its latest form it is supposed to date from 300 A. C., but must have originated centuries earlier. The Buddhists and the Jains, at the height of their prestige, encouraged and cultivated this science of dialectics, which even now forms an integral part of any scheme of liberal education in India.

Mention may also be made of the system of Charvaka, the Indian Materialist, who frankly preached the doctrine of making the most of this world as we find it. The oldest Buddhist canonical work—*Vinaya Pitaka*—mentioning it, the doctrine must be taken to be very old indeed, though all that we now have of it is the distorted version of its successful opponents. It regarded soul as nothing but an attribute of the body, and pleasure and pain as being caused by earthly causes to the mortal coil. Frankly opposed to anything supernatural, it was the perfect *rationalism* of antiquity, and as such opposed to the vested interests of the Sacerdotal order.

OTHER SCIENCES

The literary achievements of ancient and medieval India do not, however, exhaust themselves in the magnificent monuments of philosophical and canonical writings, nor even in the very remarkable treasures of poetic or dramatic creations. Secular sciences were also cultivated both in their abstract and practical forms. Of the sciences which have translated themselves in the yet enduring creations of Indian art and craftsmanship, we shall speak incidentally in the chapters dealing with the Arts and Crafts of India. Here let us speak only of those other sciences which are unconnected with religious and philosophic literature on the one hand, and with their practical application in the form of concrete arts on the other, e.g. the *Kama Shastra* (Erotics), or the *Artha Shastra* (Political Economy).

The earliest to be cultivated of these sciences was in all probability the Science of Language, or Grammar. Indians have considered this from the earliest antiquity to be the most important science, indispensable in any system of education calling itself liberal. Beginning with the linguistic investigation of the Vedic hymns, the Science was well termed by its early professors *Vyakarana* or analysis; and the works on phonetics must be considered to be among the earliest of our grammatical treatises. Yaska's Vedic *Nirukta* shows a very considerable grammatical advance, even in the age of the *Brahmanas* and the *Upanishads* and the later *Samhitas*. Panini's celebrated classic, *Shabdanushasana* or the Doctrine of Words, has been the standard classic on Sanskrit grammar since at least the 5th century B. C.; and he mentions ten of his predecessors in the science by name. A native of the Indus Valley near the town of Attock, Panini is an ideal writer, laying down his rules with algebraic terseness. Katyayana, a century or so after Panini, and Patanjali, another like period after Katyayana, make the most brilliant links in the long series of master-grammarians of ancient India. Those who followed them added nothing of their own to the work of these masters, though a later day Katyayana did try to make Pali an independent language by itself, not a derivative from Sanskrit. Thus the *Kashika Vritti* (Commentary of Benares) by Vaman and Jayaditya in the 7th century A. C., or the *Sidhhant-Kaumudi* of Bhattoji Dikshita in the 17th century (1625 A. C.), are mere handbooks on the standard treatises. The grammarian Bhartrihari wrote about 631 A. C., however, from a slightly different point of view. He considers the science of language, and not merely of words, their roots and forms, their combination in sentences. The *Katantra*, again, of Sharvavarman dating from 300 A. C., is another attempt at emancipation from the domination of the old masters. The Jain saint and scholar, Hemachandra of Gujarat, (12th century A. C.) writing mainly for the Jains, has little interest, except as a philologist, in the Vedic roots and accent of the classic Sanskrit words. He also wrote a comprehensive Prakrit grammar. Vararuchi, on the other hand, broke away completely from the older tradition by composing a grammar of the four Prakrit languages prevailing in his time; the *Maharashtri*, the *Paishachi*, the *Magadhi*, and the *Shaurseni*.

Closely allied with the work of the grammarians, are the labours of the Lexicographers. The Vedic *Nighantus* are the beginning of the Indian Lexicography; but the lexicons now most famous date rather from classic than from Vedic times. The *Dhatu-Pathas* (List of Roots) and the *Gana Pathas* (List of word-groups) from the Vedas make an easy transition from the *Nighantu* to the classic *Kosha* or Dictionary. Like the Treatises on Poetics, these are indispensable for the dramatist and the poet. The standard lexicon of the Sanskrit language now known is *Amar-Kosha*, ascribed to a learned scholar Amar Simha, a contemporary of Kalidasa at the court of Vikramaditya. The dictionaries of Halayudha (950 A. C.), and of Yadavprakasha, are the creations of South-Indian scholarship; while the works of Dhananjaya (1123-1140 A. C.) and of Hemachandraacharya, — a veritable mine of learning, — are Jain contributions from the South and the West to the same branch of learning.

Next in importance in cultivation, perhaps, but second to none in their significance to the daily life of the people, are the innumerable Legal Treatises dating from the earliest antiquities. The *Dharmashastras*, — (The Science of Duties or Obligations), — take their origin in the Vedas, and are, in their early form, more religious treatises than works on law and jurisprudence. Their remarks, however, on religious or sacrificial ritual and penances, the duties of priests and kings, make an excellent foundation for their later development into complete treatises on social, personal and public law and morality amongst the Aryans. The *Apastambiya Dharma-Sutra* is regarded by some modern scholars to be the best and oldest of these, dating from about 400 B. C. This is a product of the Black Yajur Veda school in South-India, like the still later work of Baudhayana. But older, most probably, than these is the *Dharma-Shastra* of Gautama, which follows the *Sama-Veda*. The work now regarded as the standard, authoritative treatise in this branch is the celebrated *Manava-Dharma Shastra*, or the "Code of Manu," which even now rules the life at every important stage of the largest section of the Hindus. The widest difference of opinion prevails as to the date of the author, Manu. Dates as varied as the 13th century B. C. and the 2nd century A. C. have been suggested by modern scholars. Even the *Mahabharata* quotes this *Manu-Smriti* with approval. Yagnavalkya, another legist, has been rendered famous by his commentator Vijnaneshwara, whose *Mitakshara* dates from the later half of the 11th century. It was adopted as a standard soon after its publication both in Benares and in Maharashtra, becoming, through the latter, a part of the modern law in British

PLATE XLIV

122   BUDDHA-GAYA, NAVAGRAHA
TEMPLE, ORISSA

123   KHAJURAO—SHRINE OF THE
SURYA TEMPLE

124   AIHOLE TEMPLE, BIJAPUR, EARLY CHALUKYAN STYLE
BIJAPUR DISTRICT

(Photo: Archaeological Survey of India)

125   KONARAK—WHEEL OF THE
SUN CHARIOT

PLATE XLV

126 JAI SING'S ASTRONOMICAL
OBSERVATORY, DELHI

127 JAIPUR—INSTRUMENTS IN JAY SINGH'S
ASTRONOMICAL OBSERVATORY

128 GENERAL VIEW OF AJUNTA—ANCIENT
UNIVERSITY
(Photo: Indian State Railways)

129 GENERAL VIEW OF ELLORA—ANCIENT
UNIVERSITY

India. We can do little more, in this place, than a bare mention of other such works, attributed to Narada and to Brihaspati, or the more mortal creator of the *Dayabhaga* (Jimutavahana), whose work forms the basis of the modern law of inheritance in Bengal.

POLITICS AND POLITICAL ECONOMY

In modern India, the great centres of learning, the Universities, fight shy of a regular, official, authoritative treatment of the sciences relating to public life. Politics and Civics; Economics and Sociology, have not met,—except in isolated cases and in very recent times,—with the recognition that is their due. In ancient India, on the other hand, the most powerful intellect was enlisted in the service of these most important sciences. Apart from the juristic works already noticed, the sciences of Politics and of Economics, in all their numerous departments, were most intensely cultivated. No less a personage than the Prime Minister of the first historical Emperor of all India, Chandragupta Maurya, is the reputed author of the standard classic on the subject, giving, in unrivalled detail, a wealth of information on the social, political, and economic conditions of his time, which would do credit to a Richelieu, or a Roseher. Kautilya, Chanakaya, Vishnugupta—the author is variously named; but there is no doubt as to his identity. There is not a nook or corner of the public life and activities of his day, which escapes his eagle eye, or baffles his colossal genius. His work assumes a structure of society mainly Brahmanical in its grouping and ideals of life; and proceeds to lay down rules for the governance of each class or section, each rank and department, each authority and officer in a community. Even if we leave aside politics and economics proper, he is a mine of information on architecture and mining and military science, not to mention law and jurisprudence, engineering and chemistry. The other classic works on this compendious science are either offshoots or commentaries upon this masterly treatise, like Kamandaka's *Nitisara;* or they lack practical insight, like the Somadevasuri's *Nitivakyamrita* of the 10th century.

The *Kama-Shastras,*—or the Science of Enjoyment,—may, however, be mentioned here, if only because its subject matter is closely connected with what the classic philosophers called the achievement of the purpose of life. In form, however, the most well-known treatises on this branch of learning,—like Vatsayana's *Kama-Sutra*, dating from before the Christian era,—are manuals of erotics, whose minute details and frank descriptions of some of the most vital phenomena of life have hitherto combined to place them outside the pale of "polite society." The modern revival of public interest in the Sex problem may, perhaps, succeed in reviving the vogue of a genius, in no way inferior to a Freud or even a Marie Stopes. To the Sanskrit poet, these treatises were as indispensable as those on poetics proper. A knowledge of the Science of Erotics and of the Art of Dalliance was amongst the indispensable requirements of good poetry. There is only one Ovid in Latin to describe the *Ars Amatoria;* but in Sanskrit almost every classic poet and dramatist is a master in this Art.

MATHEMATICS—PURE AND APPLIED

At the other end of the scale, we way mention the abstract science of Mathematics, both pure and applied, which in all its important branches was, long before the Christian era, very highly developed in this country. Geometry arose from the need to measure out most carefully and accurately the sacrificial ground in the Vedic times; and the *Shilpa-Sutras*, forming part of the Vedic *Kalpa-Sutras* systematise and sanctify all the then attained knowledge of measurement. The placing of the altar on this carefully measured ground was another integral and indispensable detail of the sacrifice, which had to be most meticulously adjusted with reference to the presiding deity of the sacrifice. The need for exact planning and lay out thus arising compelled the Vedic Aryans to learn the construction of right angles, squares, circles, as well as the mutation of one set of figures into others e. g. a circle from a square. Trigonometry was, similarly, known to these early Indians, if only as an aid in their very advanced astronomical calculations. Algebra is a science with an Arabic name, but of indisputably Indian origin. The great mathematicians Brahmagupta and Bhaskaracharya were adepts in their subject, handled simple and quadratic equations, and had even arrived at their own solution of indeterminate equations of the second degree, which Hankel declares to be the most delicate operation in the theory of numbers achieved by the ancients.

In Arithmetic, Aryabhatta, Brahmagupta, Bhaskaracharya,—not to mention the famous and fascinating name of the only great woman mathematician of this or any other country, Lilavati, daughter of the last named,—have between them, exhausted all the branches of their science. It is they who have given to the world the decimal system; it is they who first penetrated through the mystery of the square and the cube root; it is they who first realised the magnitude of squaring and cubing a number.

In the succeeding centuries, the practical manifestation of these high attainments, took the form of ever increasing excellence in such arts as building and architecture. The *Shilpa-Shastra*, and particularly the *Manasara*,—(Essence of Measurement),—enabled the Indian builder from the Mauryan to the Mughal days to create those wonderful master-pieces of poise and massive grandeur, embodying exquisite grace and harmony in the vast proportions of a Palace or a Chapter-House, as much as in the smallest Stupa, to which we shall have to invite attention more fully in another section of this work.

The science of Astronomy may justly be taken as a branch of applied mathematics, though to the vulgar or the superstitious it symbolises the elusive mystery of Astrology. The origin of astronomy in India, like that of all other sciences, must be found in the Vedas, in those hymns dealing with the cosmic forms, forces, or fancies, which later philosophy has sought, with doubtful success, to rationalise. Already in the *Brahmanas* the real meaning of the phenomenon of day and night,—sunrise and sunset,—is understood as a mere phase of the diurnal revolution. The sacrifices enjoined by the Vedas demanded the most meticulous calculations as to time, which in turn involved a careful study of the phases of the moon, the course of the sun and the stars, and of the cycle of seasons. The *Jyotish-Vedanga* is a brief treatise of a somewhat later epoch dealing with these calculations. The *Garga-Samhita* of the age of the *Brahmanas* is a frankly astrological work; while the *Suryapannati*, or Instruction regarding the Sun, is a Jain contribution of a more scientific character. In the Epics and the Puranas, in the Smritis and the Manava-Dharma-Shastras, there are astronomical (or astrological) references, which suggest a very high state of knowledge in this department. In the post-Christian era, the science seems to have been affected by the knowledge derived from the Greeks; and the standard treatise,—the *Surya Siddhanta*,—is even supposed to have been first composed or revealed in the city of Rome. Varaha-Mihira, the most famous astronomer of the early sixth century,—the Astronomer Royal of Vikramaditya,—mentions this in his *Pancha-Siddhantika*, though the other four *Siddhantas* have been lost. His *Ramaka Siddhanta*, is evidently of foreign (Greek) origin, especially as shown by the length of the year, and the calculation of a Yuga or age. On this point Prof. Macdonell observes :—

> " But though the doctrines of the *Ramaka-Siddhanta* are Greek, it nevertheless diverges in essential points from Greek astronomy. It further differs quite considerably from the Surya Siddhanta, which also shows Greek influence. These two Siddhantas must therefore go back to different sources. But since the Surya-Siddhanta, though agreeing generally with the astronomy of Ptolemy (140 A. D.), yet also differs from him, it is impossible to answer with certainty the question when and through what works Greek astronomy influenced that of India."[1]

But is there really any urgent need to postulate any such influence? Aryabhatta, who is anterior to Varaha-Mihira, and who was the first to systematise the teaching of the Siddhantas, was original enough to maintain that the rotation of the celestial vault was only apparent, the real rotation being that of the earth on its own axis. If thinkers could be found, even amongst the fraction of scientific literature now extant, with so much daring, originality and research, might it not quite possibly be the fact that the science of astronomy, like the cognate science of mathematics, was borrowed by the Greeks from India? Aryabhatta was, indeed, assailed by his contemporaries, but so was Copernicus. Brahmagupta wrote in 628 A. C., while the last most famous astronomer of pre-Muslim India, Bhaskaracharya, was born in 1114 A. C. and wrote his simple, systematic treatise,—*Siddhanta Shiromani*,—in 1150 A. C. Two sections of this—the *Lilavati*, and the *Bijaganita*—deal respectively with Arithmetic and Algebra; while the two remaining, styled the *Planetary Calculus*, and the Spherical section, deal with astronomy proper.

In the Muhammadan times, too, the science continued to be cultivated, both as astrology and as astronomy proper. The Arabs had imbibed through the Greeks a great love for these abstract natural sciences; and what was Arabic the Indian Muslims had no objection to copy or cultivate. The most famous name in the Science in this later age is that of the Royal Astronomer, Maharaja Jaysingh of the 17th century,

---

1) *India's Past*. p. 184.

whose Observatory even now endures to testify to his love of the science, and his researches therein.

India, it may be mentioned in conclusion, is rather poor in the science of History — at least in the pre-Muhammadan age. If we eliminate the apocryphal histories of the Puranas, and if we except Bana's *Harsha Charitra* or Kalhana's *Raja Tarangini*, there is hardly a single work on history or biography, in the entire range of Sanskrit or older vernacular literature. The life of the Buddha or Mahavira is more a record of marvels for the devout than a sober narrative of fact. The rock inscriptions of Asoka and his successors make the first beginnings of historical writings in India, and constitute to-day the best data in regard to the history of ancient India.

Of the more material sciences, Chemistry, — organic as well as inorganic, — came to be studied as part of the Vedic ritual, and continued to be attended to as ministering to the enjoyment of the elite and the wealthy. In its aspect of Medicine, it came to be most intensively cultivated all through the centuries succeeding the vedic era; while one of the Vedas themselves, — the *Yajur Veda*, — is made the foundation of the science of Surgery. The vedic sacrifices necessarily involved an amount of vivi-section, which did not fail to be utilised for ministering to the health of men. The real work of Shushruta and Charaka is lost — or known to us by legend worse than utter loss; but the science of indigenous Medicine and Surgery, continuing through all the intervening centuries to the present day, indicates even now a degree of intrinsic worth and vitality, which would, in my opinion, well repay a closer study and research than it is now fashionable to accord this science.

UNIVERSITIES IN INDIA

All these sciences, and the arts arising from them, were taught in the great centres of learning famous all over the world, which would now be called Universities. Almost every famous capital city, — Kapilvastu and Rajagriha, Pataliputra and Benares, Ujjain and Takshila; and almost every great monastery or place of pilgrimage, like Nalanda or Benares, were natural centres of learning. For there congregated the most famous scholars of the world, seeking adversaries worthy of their intelligence and attainments; or expounding truths, — like a Buddha or a Mahavira, an Ashwaghosha or a Bharata, — which never failed to appeal to the thirst for knowledge that characterised the ancient Indian society. Secular as well as spiritual lore was disseminated in these places, under fairly well known regulations, and with definite gradations of pupils according to their varying stages of advancement, somewhat like our modern classification of undergraduates, graduates, postgraduates, and professors. According to the famous Chinese traveller, there was not in the seventh century in the whole world a seat of learning which might compare with the splendid establishment at Nalanda. It had been magnificently endowed by a succession of monarchs, and still enjoyed the royal favour as much as ever. There were open courts and secluded gardens; splendid

PLATE XLVI

SCENES FROM NALANDA—AN ANCIENT UNIVERSITY

130   VARIOUS CARVINGS

131   MONOLITH AND BAUDDHA SCRIPTURES

(Blocks from J. Burgess "Mediaeval Monuments of India")

PLATE XLVI A

131 A   LADY MUSICIAN
(From H. L. Parekh's Collection, Bombay)

131 B   HINDU ASCETICS

PLATE XLVI B

131 C   **PORTRAIT OF JEHANGIR**
Mughal line drawing
(From N. C. Mehta's book "Studies in Indian Painting)

trees, casting grateful shade, under which the monks and novices might meditate; cool fountains of fresh water that gurgled delightfully in the hot season. Ten thousand inmates dwelt in six blocks of buildings four stories high, which looked out on large courts. There were a hundred rooms set apart for lectures on religion, and on all the science and literature of the time. There were halls wherein socratic discussions frequently took place. Says Hiuen-Tsang: "From morning to night, young and old help each other in discussion, for which they find the day too short." The study of medicine and natural history, and of the useful and useless branches of mundane research, was by no means cast aside for speculation. The latter was of so sutble a character that, while ten hundred might be found capable of expounding twenty books of the Shastras and Sutras, only five hundred could deal with thirty books, and only ten with fifty. Students were not admitted until they had proved themselves men of parts and well-read in books, old and new, by hard public discussion; and of ten candidates for admission, seven or eight were rejected. Altogether, Hiuen-Tsang spent five years in study here; and he became one of the ten who could expound fifty sacred books. But Silabhadra, the Father Superior, who was his tutor, had left no sacred book unstudied.

The Indian Universities of the Mauryan and the Gupta eras, and even in the still later age of Shri Harsha, had a most catholic, comprehensive curriculum. They were necessary, not only to the professional scholar, the monk or the sannyasi; but also to all the artists in the plastic, pictorial, literary, or social arts. Says Mr. Havell, in his *Ideals of Indian Art.* (p. 40-41):

> "It is hardly possible for a western artist to appreciate the psychology and practice of oriental art, without knowing that the practice of Yoga was combined with a most elaborate and scientific mnemonic system, by means of which the whole of Sanskrit literature was handed down from one generation to another, from the Vedic period until medieval times, without being committed to writing in any form. Probably the severely mechanical kind of mental exercise which this entailed was considered a necessary intellectual complement to the psychic training of Yoga. However this may be, the whole practice of the Indian, Chinese, and the Japanese schools of painting were based upon methods derived from this mnemonic and psychic training, and given in the Universities of northern India; and here the West has much to learn from the East, for the essential faculties of the artist—imagination and memory,—are those which are least considered in the curriculum of modern European academies, where the paraphernalia of the studio are used to make up for the deficiencies in the mental equipment of the student.

> *   *   *   *   *

> It is not only as centres for the propaganda of the Buddhist faith, but much more as schools of Hindu philosophy, that the influence of the Indian Universities was felt in China and Japan.

What wonder, then, that the ancient Indian Universities became the prolific breeding-ground of the Seer and the Sage, the Statesman and the Sculptor, the Poet and the Painter, as much as of accomplished ladies and gentlemen.

CHAPTER VII

MUSIC AND DANCING: PAINTING AND SCULPTURE

The complete curriculum of an ancient Indian gentleman's education,—or of a lady, for the matter of that, either—included a number of arts, some of them now almost lost, others strange to the degree of bizarre; others, again, requiring for proficiency a length of training, which it is all but impossible to imagine as being actually devoted. Tradition speaks of 72 Arts or *Kalas* for gentlemen claiming to have had a proper education; and 64 for ladies of a like degree. These included, besides the ordinary learning and training in the arts of self-defence and preservation, (e. g. swimming), the art of stealing, and of dalliance. The *Little Clay-Cart* of Shudraka is an eloquent testimony to the Indian's love of reducing even the art of the thief to a system; and the numerous works on the *Kama-Shastra* provide a wonderful reading on professional coquetry and sex-attraction, as a deliberate exercise. Singing and playing musical instruments in all their infinite variety; dancing in ballet or merely to keep time; painting and modelling in clay and in stone,—these were arts and graces, ranking in importance for a gentleman of the Maurya or the Gupta times, along with the art of horse-judging or chariot-driving, or wielding martial weapons of all sorts.

It is impossible to say what infinite trouble and pains they must have taken to arrive at anything like a passable mastery of these arts. Judging, however, from the folk-lore of the past, no mean standards of excellence must have been expected. A master artist in *Tabla*-playing could detect the presence of an artificial thumb of ivory of another master-player, in spite of a perfect execution of the performance to all appearance. A supreme dancer, tradition says, could trace a pattern of a peacock, for example, blind-fold on the dancing floor, simply by the rhythmic placing of her toe-marks; and if packets of colour were placed on the floor with appropriate tints at the required distance, she could even give all the glowing hues of this prince of birds. This seems incredible; and, certainly, the modern Indian professional dancer shows little of the mastery in execution, report speaks her ancestors to have possessed. But there is nothing inherently impossible in it. It is a matter of patient study and long practice, as the mastery of the art by a Pavlova can easily testify even to-day.

There must, however, have been a difference, from the very earliest times, between the professional and the amateur. The excellence of the amateur,—like that of the great Gupta Emperor in the arts of poetry and music, or of Shri Harsha in drama, or of the scholar and the sage Ashwagosha in epic poetry, was by no means insignificant. Nevertheless, there must have been a difference between the master and the pupil. The history of Art in India is, according to the greatest living exponent of the spirit and ideal of Indian artistic creation, Dr. A. K. Koomara

MUSIC PARTY

Prince of Baba Museum, Benares

133

DANCE OF SHIVA

(From Coomaraswamy's book "Rajput Painting")

132

PLATE XLVIII

A MUSIC PARTY (BAGH FRESCOES)
(From N. C. Mehta's book "Studies in Indian Painting")

Swamy, a history of pupillary succession. Speaking of the Art of Music in India he says:—

> "The art of music of the present day is a direct descendant of those ancient schools, whose traditions have been handed with comment and expansion in the gilds of the hereditary musicians.

> *   *   *   *   *

> The civilisations of Asia do not afford to the inefficient amateurs those opportunities of self expression which are so highly appreciated in Europe and America. The arts are nowhere taught as a social accomplishment. On the one hand there is the professional, proficient in a traditional art, and on the other the lay public. The musical cultivation of the public does not consist in everybody doing it, but in appreciation and reverence."

This does not, indeed, mean that the appreciation, or even reverence, for the artist, is to result without any understanding of the nature or technique of the effort. For a proper appreciation there must be knowledge and understanding and sympathy; but that need not, cannot, amount to the proficiency of the master.

Let us select a few leading ones as specimens of India's artistic splendour and cultural glories in her deathless past.

According to Indian tradition, all art takes its origin from the Vedas. This is, indeed, somewhat unjust to the Dravid races, who had peopled and civilised India long before the Vedic Aryans. But history is, as yet, relatively silent about their attainments in regard to the spiritual arts of music and poetry, of drama and dancing; and tradition has been swamped or smothered by the assertive egoism,— or was it the superior artistry,?—of the invading Aryans. The ancient remains of the Dravidian civilisation, recently discovered, betoken an advance in the arts of architecture and ornamentation, which might, not inconceivably, have influenced the Aryans in their own similar efforts in that direction; but if so, the indomitable egotism of this fortunate race has prevented any record of that fact surviving for posterity. The arts, however, of which we have, in history or tradition, the longest record, and of which we possess in technique a most marvellous phenomenon, are all traced or traceable to Vedic inspiration or necessity. These are: Music, both vocal and instrumental; Dancing, symbolical as well as mechanical; Drama or dramatical Acting, which is considered inseparable from dancing; and arts of ornamentation, like Painting and Sculpture and carving in Architecture.

*   *   *   *   *

Beginning with Music, we find it the oldest amongst the oldest of Indian Arts. Its nature and object have seldom been fully understood by the surface observers of India's culture.

> "Indian music is essentially impersonal. It reflects an emotion and an experience, which are deeper and wider and older than the emotion or wisdom of any single individual. Its sorrow is without tears, its joy without exaltation, and it is passionate without any loss of serenity." (Koomaraswamy.)

Since the days of the Vedic Seers, the singer in this country was also the poet, and *vice versa*.

The language of the Rig-maker depended so much on accurate intonation, without the most microtonal variation, that the art of singing the hymn must have been inseparable from the art of composing it. Certainly, the hymns of the *Sama Veda*, which had to be chanted in their most precise intonation at the several sacrifices, had their own metrical system,—the *Sama Sutras* laying down their own canons of chant. These embody practically all the elements of Indian music, with a suitable notation, both modal and metrical. This is probably the oldest musical treatise in the world,—the *Sama Vedachhala* of seven sections, with the possible exception of the *Gandharva-Veda* whose origin is shrouded in mystery. The *Pingala Sutras* date from about 1000 B. C. or 800 B. C. If *Sangita* or music, and its accessory arts, suffered for a while during the puritanical re-action which gave birth to the Jain and Buddhist systems, the set-back was more than counterbalanced by the revival of the social arts and graces among the cultured and luxurious empire-builders of an ancient and medieval India. When Bharata composed his immortal treatise on Dramaturgy,—the *Natya* Shastra,—which dealt systematically with the three cognate arts of the Drama, including Acting, Dancing, and Music; when Kalidasa composed his immortal masterpieces; when the Emperor Samudra-Gupta played on the Vina, then music became once more a most honoured branch of the education of men as well as women, until another Puritan Emperor,—Aurangzeb,—discountenanced it in the seventeenth century. Of later works the *Rag-Tarangini* of Lochankavi, and the *Sangit Ratnakar* of Sarangdev, date from after the Muhammadan conquest, and form the standard musical treatises in vogue to-day.

A varied and vivid imagination has, however, associated the most fascinating myths with the earlier authors or founders of the musical systems, instruments, and even the tunes in India. Narada, the son of Brahma, the Creator, was the first musician in India, even as Shiva, the great God, was the first dancer! He,—Narada—is credited with the invention of the characteristic and the most difficult Indian musical instrument,—the Vina,—the favourite instrument of the Goddess of Learning, the divine Saraswati. Perhaps the Seer, Tambur, after whom another ancient and still popular instrument (the *Tambura*) is named, was even before Narada. The vice of vanity and its disastrous effects are most touchingly illustrated by a fable associated with the name of Narada. He fancied himself to be a master-singer, when he was yet unable to intone each and every note in a mode precisely. Vishnu took compassion on him, and showed him, in a vision, the havoc he had made by his faulty singing. For, in that vision, Narada saw in a spacious hall men and women weeping over their mutilated limbs. He turned to Vishnu and asked who the maimed and the weeping were. Vishnu asked the sufferers, and they replied, "We are the unfortunate *Ragas* and *Raginis* whom Narada has sung in his ignorance out of tune." The sage was humbled, and knelt before the God to be taught the art and mystery of correct, tuneful singing.

Leaving the region of mythology, and descending to the sober facts of relatively recent history, we find that the one art which the advent of the Muslims in India

PLATE XLIX

135 TODI RAGINI

136 HINDOL RAG

137 MEGH RAG

138 SORATH RAG

139 **VASANT RAGINI**
(Prince of Wales Museum, Bombay)

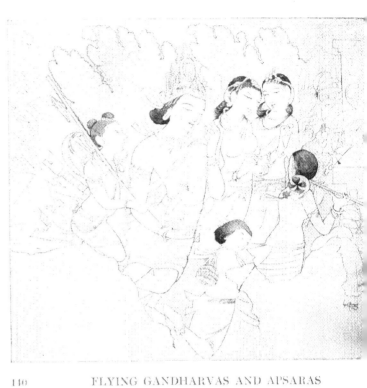

140 **FLYING GANDHARVAS AND APSARAS**
(Ajanta Caves)
(139—141 Photo: Archaeological Dept., Hyderabad Dn.)

141 **SHIVA'S TANDAVA DANCE**
(Ellora Cave)

142 **SHIVA DANCING AS NATARAJ**
(Government Museum, Madras)

did not destroy was music and its accessories. The early Muslims were, indeed, intolerant puritans. But they derived their culture and civilisation, their arts and graces, from a race, which was highly poetic, even before it became fanatically puritanical. The Arabs were a most emotional people, keenly alive to all the joys of living, richly sensitive to every contact with the refined and the beautiful. They had borrowed and assimilated not a little of the art treasures of ancient India, mainly through the Greeks and the Persians; but often through their own direct intercourse in commerce with the Indian peoples. The Arab courts of Baghdad, Cairo, or Cordova were, in the middle Ages, the most munificent as well as discerning patrons of all the arts that ministered to their amusement or delectation. The first Musalman conquerors of India had imbibed and brought with them these Arab traditions. The Sufis particularly, with their philosophic leanings of a distinctly Vedantic complexion, were the first to appreciate the real genius and greatness of the Hindu Music; and so they helped to make the latter popular with the new invaders. The most famous name, perhaps, or at least the earliest, among the Muhammadan musicians of India, is that of Amir Khusru, poet and courtier of the early fourteenth century, who invented the now popular *Kavali* style of singing, and the three stringed *Sihtar* which is no less beloved of the people. His contemporary was Naik Gopal, whom Alauddin or his general Kafur had imported from the Deccan. Alauddin Khilji himself, like Ravana, was no mean lover of music.

The greatest name, however, in the history of Indian music, in all the Muhammadan age, if not in all history, is that of Tan Sen, the musical gem of the court of the greatest of the Mughals. Originally a Hindu, like the other great names in the artistic firmament of his age, there has, perhaps, been no greater master in all the world of vocal harmony, of modal perfection, than Tan Sen. The complex emotions which a Wagner could render by the aid of the most elaborate orchestration, Tan Sen could achieve with the unaided mastery of his own voice. True, however, to the spirit of India, tradition speaks of a master or *Guru* of even the master himself,—Hardas Swami, a sannyasi of Mathura. It is said that when the Emperor Akbar desired to see, at his court, this marvel, the master and teacher of his matchless singer, Tan Sen replied: "He is greater, Sire, than all the Emperors of the world. If your Majesty wishes to see him, you must even go to him". The Emperor went to the cave of the Sannyasi, and was treated there after many entreaties, to marvels of music such as mortal ears have never sensed! Asked as to the reason of this superhuman excellence, Tan Sen replied, in all humility, "Sire, when I sing at the command of the Emperor, I sing to please Your Majesty; but my Guruji sings to please God only!" Can there be a greater tribute to Art for its own sake?

This is not the place, even if the writer were competent to undertake the task, to enter into the details of the technique of Indian Music. Suffice it to say that, the Indian masters of music seem to have thoroughly understood the nature of sound and the technique of voice production. Their ear was so perfectly trained, that they could discover even an infinitesimal variation from the true note. They had learnt to adapt their music to the season of the year, the hour of the day, the mood of the performer. According to the fabled lore of ancient India, there were once as many as 16,000 tunes and three hundred and sixty *Talas*, when music was the most cherished amusement of the gods. These were divided *inter se* in the four main *maths*, or schools of music, named respectively after Someshwar or Shiva; Kali Math, after Krishna's subjugation of the great serpent Kali; Hanuman Math, after the monkey-prince and messenger of Rama; and Bharata Math, after the last human founder of the science and art of music, dancing, and drama including acting. Each of these schools had its own system of playing the various tunes, though the difference was not very great. If one school classed and played a given tune as a *Ragini*, another made of the same tune a *Putra* by adding one or two *Tivra* (Sharp) or *Komal* (flat) notes. Tan Sen made a thorough study of the science, determined the distinctive marks of each melody, and consolidated the four schools into one, at the same time reducing the *Talas* to twelve, without in any way marring the beauty of subtlety of any tune.

This applies, of course, to the music in northern India, the dominions of Tan Sen's master. It constitutes even now the school known as Hindustani music. In the South, a different school has always held the field, and is known to this day as Karnataki Music, where the instruments also differ. Instead of the elaborate classification of the tunes and their wives and sons, —*Ragas, Raginis* and *Putras*,— of the North, the South recognises only 72 main tunes, Ragas or scales, each such scale having a name signifying the note on which it is built. Speaking of the Hindustani and the Karnatic music schools now in vogue in India, Mr. Clements, in his *Introduction to the Study of Indian Music*, observes:—

> "Many scales are common to both, but the general spirit of the two systems is apparent from the scales which are first taught to beginners; in the West the scale is the same as the just major scale of Europe, in the South it is a chromatic scale (known in Hindustani music as the scale of the Rag Bhairav), with semitones between the first and the second, third and fourth, fifth and sixth, seventh and eighth degrees. There are grounds for believing that the remote precursors of these two scales were pentatonic, one, the scale which has been found amongst all nations, and which may be roughly indicated thus— C. D. G. A. C.;—and the other the old Greek scale of Olympos."[1]

Music, as a science, in India has 7 parts, viz: *Sur* or Musical note; *Tal* or Rhythm; *Raga* or Tunes and melodies, *Astadhyaya* or Instruments, *Nritia* or gesticulation accompanying music; *Bhava* or Sentiment, and *Artha* or meaning. The

---

1) Apart from the keyed instruments of modern Europe, there is scarcely a fixed scale; at any rate in India, the thing fixed is a group of intervals, and the precise vibration depends on its position in a progression, not on its relation to a tonic. The scale of 22 notes is simply the sum of all the notes used in all the songs.

* * * * * *

The quarter-note or a *Shruti* is the micro-tonal interval between two successive scale notes; but as the theme rarely employs two, and never three-scale notes in succession, the micro-tonal interval is not generally conspicuous except in ornament." (A. K. Koomaraswamy. Essay on Music.)

PLATE LI

DANCING TO-DAY ILLUSTRATIVE OF GESTURES

MUSIC LESSONS

146

HINDU MUSIC

144

PLATE LIII

A PROFESSIONAL SITAR PLAYER

145

Surs or notes are 7 in number, according to the region of the body from which each note takes its origin. These are *Kharaj* or *Shadja* produced from the navel; *Risabha* from the chest; *Gandhara* from the throat; *Madhyama* from the palate; *Panchama* from the nose; *Dhaivata* from the teeth; and *Nishadha* from the lips. From the initial letter of each of these principal notes is made up the common Indian scale of seven notes called the *Saragam*, for short. All these various notes were personified, and horoscoped, with their nature and characteristic neatly marked. Thus, *Kharaj* or *Shadja* is neither sharp nor flat, but permanent, under the protection of Agni the God of Fire, has a happy temperament, is cold and moist, has pink complexion, and the most beautiful white garments and ornaments. Every other note has a similar genealogy and horoscope.

Next in importance to the *Sur* or *Swaras*, is the time and rhythm, an indispensable element in the beauty of Indian music, regulating the relative duration of musical sounds in singing and playing, and the movements of the limbs in dancing. For the exact rendering of the rhythm, the Indian science of music depends on the drum, *Pakhwaz, Tabla,*—or the like instrument. These drums are tuned to the key-note of the singer, the drum-player denoting rhythm by his fingers, palms, and even elbows.

The third division of the Indian science of Music deals with *Ragas* or melodies. The Hanuman Math classifies them into six *Ragas* or principal melodies, each with five *Raginis* (female tunes), eight *putras*, and their eight *Bharyas* (wives), or a total of 132 tunes. The principal ones are, of course, the 6 *Ragas* and their 30 female companions. Heavy and melodious, a rich vein marks them all, and touch our profoundest emotional chords. In execution, they are extremely difficult, master singers alone being able to render them with perfect exactness. *Inter se* they vary according to the numbers of notes they possess in octaves to form their scales, in some all the seven notes occurring, in others a few only. There are again various methods for singing a given melody, e. g. the *Dhrupad* style, which requires that each note be dwelt upon for some moments in masterful control. *Hori*, another famous style of singing, is peculiarly appropriate to the most popular love-songs of Krishna and Radha.

Says Dr. A. K. Koomaraswamy :—

> "Indian music is a purely melodic art, devoid of any harmonised accompaniment other than a drone. In modern European art, the meaning of each note of the theme is mainly brought out by the notes of the chord which are near with it; and even in unaccompanied melody, the musician heaves an implied melody. Unaccompanied folk-song does not satisfy the concert-goer's ears; as pure melody, it is the province only of the peasant and the specialist. This is partly because the folk air played on the piano, or written in staff, is actually falsified; but much more because under the conditions of European art, melody no longer exists in its own right; and music is a compromise between melodic freedom and harmonic necessity. To hear the music of India as Indians hear it, one must recover the sense of a pure intonation, and must forget all implied harmonies."

This is, certainly, a great peculiarity of vocal music in India, where exact intonation or pure melody is prized much more than harmony. The hair-breadth (*Kaishiki*) differentiation between successive notes in the Indian scale,—the quarter-tones,—are not merely artificial and capricious embellishments of an over-refined people, but a natural distinction, which, however, will not be perceived without the aid of great proficiency in the science.

This chapter on Tunes *(Ragas)* is ever more rich in imagery than that dealing with Instruments. "Psychologically," says Koomaraswamy, "the word Raga, meaning colour or passion, suggests to Indian ears the idea of mood; that is to say that precisely as in ancient Greece, the musical mode has definite ethos." Mr. Clements describes the Raga in English thus:

> "The name of the Raga connotes a scale, bearing fixed relationship to the drone, with its harmonic structure determined by a *Vadi* and *Samvadi*, a chief note occurring more frequently than others, a lower limit described in terms of the *murchhana*; occasionally an upper limit also, certain characteristic turns of melody recurring with frequency, certain rules regarding the employment of embellishments, and a stated time of the day for its performance."[1]

Of the remaining parts of the Science of Music, particularly *Nrita* and *Bhava*, we shall speak more appropriately while discussing the histrionic art in India.

Let us round up this subject by a brief reference to the attempts, now being made, for introduction of some definite system of Notation for keeping a written record. Indian music, however, has never lent itself to a systematic notation. It was peculiarly the artist's own art, handed down from professor to pupil by oral tradition. As a means of popularising musical knowledge, or preserving existing melodies in concrete form, as also for the benefit of the non-Indian student, such attempts are welcomed, and even encouraged. But the system of oral transmission is still the best for preserving the real music, as well as the true genius of the artist.

Nevertheless, Instrumentation of a very high and complex kind has likewise been a most distinguishing feature of music in India. Of the Musical Instruments in use from the earliest times, it is impossible to speak in this review with anything like completeness. Mr. Koomaraswamy holds, indeed, that there was no public concert in India, Indian music being mainly either chamber-music for the delectation of the most aristocratic and trained ears; or temple-music for the worship of the gods. In neither of these was the musician obliged to cease to be a musical artist, and become a musical tradesman. But, even if we leave out the *Naubat*, where nine performers concerted together, the scope for musical instruments is very considerable. These are divided into four classes, viz. (1) Stringed ones, strung with brass or steel wires, or silken cords, and tuned by a piece of wood, or ivory, or finger-nails, like the Vina, Sarode, Tambura etc.; (2) those which are played with a bow, like a Sarangi, Mayuri, Dilruba; (3) drum-like instruments struck by the hand or a wooden stick, like the Pakhwaz, Tabla, Nakara; and (4) wind instruments, pipe-like, blown by the mouth with full or half-breaths, such as Senai, or Bansri. Each of these instruments has, in Indian tradition, a divine progenitor or god-parent, e. g. Mahadev of Vina

---

1) "The Raga" says Koomaraswamy, "like the old Greek and ecclesiastical mode, is a selection of five, six or seven notes, distributed along the scale; but the Raga is more particularised than the mode, for it has certain characteristic progressions, and a chief note to which the singer constantly returns. The Raga may best be defined as a melody-mould, or the ground-plan of a song."

PLATE LIII

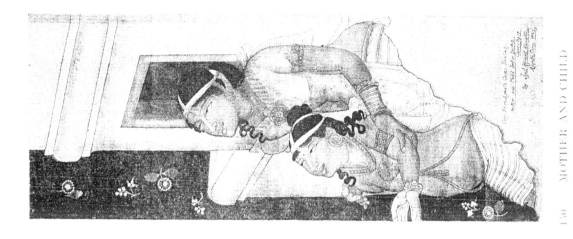

150   MOTHER AND CHILD

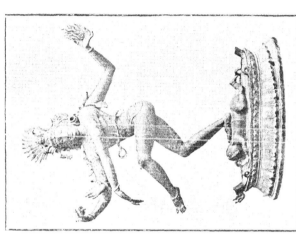

149 SHIVA, THE PRINCE OF DANCERS

(Photograph at Mueseum, Madras)

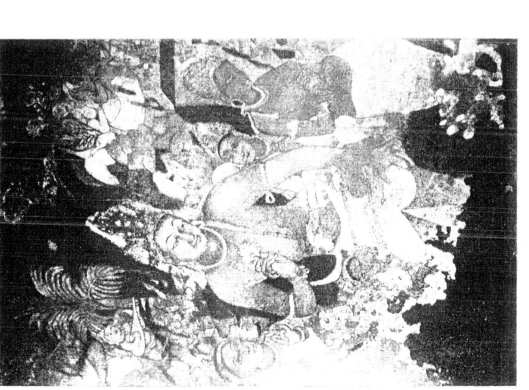

148   PADMA PANI

(148 and 150 Ajanta Frescoes Photo. Archæological Dept., Hyderabad 1905)

PLATE LIV

RASA-MANDALA
(From N. C. Mehta's book "Studies in Indian Painting")

and Dumru ; Ganesh of Mrudung or Pakhwaz ; Krishna of Bansri. Each one of these instruments requires a life-time of practice for mastery ; but the opinion is generally held that if you have grasped the mystery of playing on the Vina, Sarangi, Senai, Dilrubah and the Mrudung,—each the most difficult representative of a class,—you will find it not very difficult to manage the other instruments of that class.

ACTING AND DANCING

The art of acting,—Histrionics,—which in India as elsewhere, is closely connected with drama and music, with dancing and singing, is equally ancient, though to-day we see very little of the old Indian type of acting. Tradition ascribes the creation of the Art of the Drama and Acting to Brahma himself, the God of creation in the Hindu Trinity. At the request, says Bharata, of Indra and the other gods, Brahma created the fifth or *Natya-Veda*, taking from each of the existing four Vedas certain elements, *e. g.*, from the Rig-Veda, the words; from Sama Veda, the singing; from Yajur-Veda, the gesture; and from Atharva-Veda the flavour. Writers on Indian poetics have all been agreed since creation that the beauty of poetry lies in the *Rasa* or flavour. Kavyam, they say sententiously, is *Rasatmakam Vacham:* Poetry is speech which has flavour for its soul. Drama is, again, a part of poetry ; and therefore, the task of those who give a representation of the drama is to depict in their actions, expressions and movements, the varying flavour, sentiment or emotion, of their role to the best of their ability.

The study of the Indian theatre, hitherto made by Western scholars, has been based much too exclusively on the literary aspect of the drama to be really helpful in technical artistic study. Judging, however, from the stage directions, given in the text of the classic plays still surviving, it seems very likely that the stage in the days of the ancient Hindu dramatists was by no means the elaborate arrangement, with a wearisome wealth of every conceivable accessory, that we are now familiar with. Perhaps a slight curtain, made of cloth, very likely divided the stage proper from the tiring room of the actors not on the stage; while the audience sat roped off from the stage at no great distance from the actors. It is not even unlikely that the really popular performance was in the open, in some vast central square, as they do more and more in Bolshevist Russia; and that only the very choice classic dramas,—whose beauty it required considerable cultivation in the audience itself to appreciate,—were represented indoors. The fact, however, is explained by the belief that the true appreciation of dramatic and histrionic beauty can only come from the educated intelligence and imagination of a cultured audience. Bharat, the father of Indian Histrionics, observes :

"All the activities of the Gods, whether in house or garden, spring from a natural disposition of the mind; but all the activities of men result from the conscious working of the will; therefore it is that the details of actions to be done by men are to be carefully prescribed."

Hence it is that the Indians held that every action of the artist in every department must be the result of long, careful, patient, minute study, according to the definite, detailed, elaborate, rules of science in that regard. Nothing must be left to chance, or the impulse and inspiration of the moment, or even to the 'genius' of the artist.

> " Precisely as the text of the play remains the same, whoever the actor may be; precisely as the score of a musical composition is not varied by whom-so-ever it may be performed, so there is no reason why an accepted gesture language (*Angikabhinaya*) should be varied with a view to set off advantageously the actor's personality." (Koomaraswamy. *Mirror of Gesture.*)

This *Abhinaya* language has been most minutely elaborated in standard ancient classics, which every actor must rigorously follow, and which the audience expect him to follow. That does not, of course, imply that there are no degrees of excellence among Indian actors, that there is no such thing as personal factor. Only, the superior actor would have a more perfect command over his limbs and muscles, over his pose and expression, than the inferior one, though both will generically be following and be judged by the same standard. The convention is absolute and universal in the Indian critical world that the actor's business is to act, simply to act, only to act. He must not only keep his own personality in the background; he must positively suppress it, at least for the time being. Real good acting must be perfectly spontaneous, and exclusively objective. The Indian theatre-manager, following his classic guide, sought to achieve the same result by training his actors in the conventional or symbolic language of gestures, so as to convey without fail, even if the actual actor was a mediocrity, the real emotion or sentiment *(Rasa)* of the piece to a cultured, sensitive, appreciative audience.

> " The more deeply we penetrate the technique of any typically oriental art, the more we find that what happens to be individual, impulsive, and 'natural' is actually long-inherited, well-considered, and well-bred." (Koomaraswamy. Ibid.)

This classic, symbolic, expressive language of the gestures is, as has already been observed, highly elaborated in standard works like the *Natya-Shastra* of Bharata, or the *Abhinaya-Darpana* of Nandikeshwara. A learned Indian commentator on the flower of Indian drama, Raghava Bhatta, in his commentary called *Arthadyo-tanika*, gives very explicit and exhaustive instruction to the actors as to carrying out the several stage directions of the dramatist. When, in the course of the play, Shakuntala is required to act "watering the plants", the commentator advises the following course:

> " First show *Nalini-Padma-Kosha* hands, (which is a position of folding of the hands in the form of a parrot-beak, with the palms joined but not touching, and pointing downwards; to give them the Padma-Kosha turn, they must be drawn a little backwards), incline the head, bend the body slightly, and then make as if pouring out water; *i. e.* move the hands so folded, in that pose of the body, downwards."

The actor or actress has simply to follow these. Directions of this nature abound in every song, recitation, or representation; they become with the professional actor almost second nature. Hence that wealth of gesticulation even in present-day acting, which may appear to the uninitiated as unmitigated nonsense, which the actor and

PLATE LV
PAINTINGS IN AJANTA FRESCOES

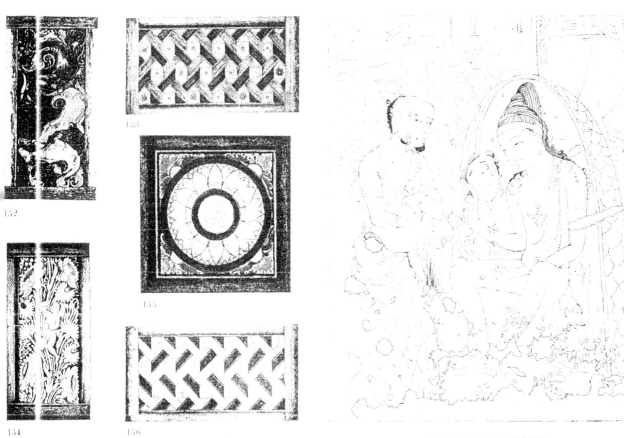

152-156 PANEL DECORATIONS

157   BRAHMANA BEGGING

158   CHHADDANTA JATAK

PLATE LVI

PAINTINGS IN AJANTA FRESCOES

160   A LOVE SCENE
(Prince of Wales Museum, Bombay)

159   QUEEN'S TOILET

161   ANOTHER AJANTA PAINTING, CAVE XVII
(159 and 161 Photo: Archaeological Dept., Hyderabad Dn.)

the singer of to-day themselves hardly understand; but which, to those who have any idea of the science of acting as practised in the days of the Old Masters in India, have each its own exact place in the general scheme of gesticulation.

*   *   *   *   *   *

These observations apply even more rigorously to classic Dancing in India. The reader must never forget, while engaged on this theme, the traditional origin of dancing. It is a divine art, with the greatest gods in the Hindu pantheon as the fathers of the several styles of dancing. Each of these divine dances is symbolical, pregnant with meaning that only the adept can know. Of the Gods who originated the several styles of dancing, the most prolific is the great Shiva; the most popular, the Eternal Lover and the universally beloved Krishna. The famous Nadanta dance of Shiva has a cosmic significance. Says Woodroffe, in his translation of the *Tantra-Tattva*.

> "In this drama of the world, He is both the chief Actor, and the Chief Actress. This drama commenced in the beginning with the union of the Actor and Actress, and will conclude, according to His unfailing will, on that night which is the end of time. In the images of Shaivite sculptors, dating from the earliest times, and representing the Great God in this Dance, He is shown as a four-armed Deity, with braided, jewelled hair, stray locks from the lower masses of which whirl in mad abandon with the rhythm of the dance. The mermaid form of the sacred Ganges peeps out, with a hooded cobra and a human skull, from the hair of this ancient Yogi. The crescent moon is at the top, surmounted by the crowning wreath of cassia leaves. From the right ear hang a man's ear-ring; from the left a woman's; while other ornaments include necklaces, armlets, anklets and bracelets, finger, and toe-rings and jewelled belt. Of dress he has a pair of tight-fitting breeches, a fluttering scarf. and the sacred thread of the twice-born. In one right hand is a drum, and the other is lifted in *Abhaya-Mudra*, or the sign of peace and goodwill and perfect assurance to all the mortals. In one left hand burns the sacred fire, while the other points down to the demon Mayalaka, whom the heretic rishis had discharged as their last weapon at the Great God, and whom the latter crushed to the earth with just the tip of his right toe. The left is poised most gracefully in the air. The images also provide a lotus pedestal from which spring an aureole, fringed with flame and touched from within by the hands holding the drum and fire.

What is the meaning of this wonderful dance of the Prince of Dancers, (Nataraja)? In the ornaments, dress, and pose of the different limbs, they have traced symbolic significance, which makes of this dance a cosmic drama. Many of the ornaments have puranic stories and meaning attached to them, like the celestial stream falling from heaven and being lost in the matted hair of the ancient Yogi. Others, like the man's and woman's ear-rings in the right and the left ear, are suggestive of the God's dual nature, man and woman in one. For the rest the dance

> "represents His five activities *(Panchakritya)* viz. *Shristi* (overlooking, creation, evolution); *Sthiti* (preservation, support); *Samhara* (destruction, evolution); *Tirobhava* (veiling, embodiment, illusion, and also rest); *Anugraha* (release, salvation, grace). These, separately considered, are the activities of the deities, Brahma, Vishnu, Rudra, Maheshwara and Sadashiva."   *   *   *   *
>
> "Creation arises from the drum, protection proceeds from the hand of hope; from fire proceeds destruction; the foot held aloft gives release." (Koomaraswamy.)

The *Tandava* Dance, another favourite terpischorean feat of the Great God, is a manifestation of the *Bhairava,*—Terrible—aspect of Shiva. It is danced in the burning ground, where the Mahadeva dances on black nights in wild abandon, with troops of goblins in attendance, with Devi, the Goddess, his other self, also in the company. Representations of this Dance are to be found in the cave temples and ancient sculptures of Ellora or Elephanta. It is however, so awful, so wild, and terrible, that mortal hand rarely dare touch this subject, just as the first divine dance of Shiva, danced on an evening in Kailasa, with the Gods and Gandharvas in chorus, Saraswati playing the Vina, and Indra the flute, Vishnu playing the drum and Brahma the cymbals of eternity, and Lakshmi giving the tune in words, is impossible of human imitation.

Classic Dancing in India is an attempt to reproduce the various aspects or phases of the cosmic mysteries. Every Hindu temple has, even to-day, its ritual of dancing, with its troops of attendant *Deva-Dasis,*—women dedicated to the service of the God, even as in heaven the Nymphs are supposed to discharge that office. Every Hindu ceremonial of any importance and significance, like marriage, has its festival of dancing, with the professional dancing-girls in attendance. The institution of Deva-Dasis has now-a-days fallen into disgrace, thanks to some unsavoury associations entwined with it, even as the ordinary 'nautch' at the social gatherings has attained an evil flavour. It is impossible to deny that there is much in these institutions that would disgust the puritanical conscience. Nor is it only to-day that the evil has attracted public notice. Manu, the author of the Indian legal system, forbade the respectable gentleman to dance or sing or play on musical instruments; and classes actors and dancers amongst those unworthy men, who could not be invited to the ceremonies of offerings to the dead. Chanakya ranks dancers with courtesans. The association of the prostitute with the arts of music and dancing has been fatal to the latter, so far, at any rate, as it concerns the regular cultivation of them by more leisured, more devoted, people. This does not mean, however, that dancing and music are not among the finest of the fine arts; or that the arts, as even now practised, have not much in them that is exalting to the utmost.

If the mighty, terrible, celestial dancing of the Divine Dancer and his Consort is all but impossible of human imitation, that of Krishna is much more popular. The dance occasioned by his subjugation of the great Jamna serpent,—Kaliya,—when he jumped from one head to another of this hundred-headed monster, is a rhythm too delicate to be translated by mortals; but his *Rasamandala,* or the general dance with the cow-herdesses of Mathura, is even now daily reproduced in all parts of India, in all classes of society. If Shiva is the Lord of Dance, Vishnu is the Prince of Poets, and Sovereign of Song. His immortal flute enticed the Gopis from their homes and husbands; and the joy of the dance, its simple yet beautiful rhythm, are too stirring not to move the most stony-hearted of mortals.

Dancing in India is thus a symbolical art. It is of two kinds, one consisting in simple movements to keep time with the music; the other a theme in itself. The

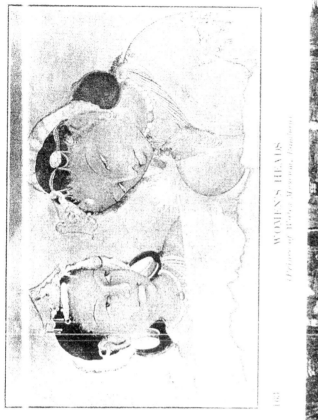

WOMEN'S HEADS

Fresco at Bagh, Gwalior, Gwalior State

163

A PRINCELY COUPLE

By the Photo Archaeological Dept., Hyderabad State

164

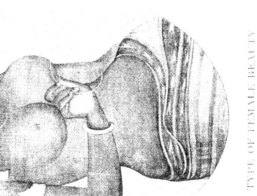

TYPE OF FEMALE BEAUTY

162

165 THE MONTH OF MARGASHIRSHA
(165-166 Prince of Wales Museum, Bombay)

166 A RAJPUT LADY

167 KRISHNA AND RADHA

168 LADIES BATHING

(From Coomaraswamy's book "Rajput Painting")

dance of professional dancers—the nautch-girls of to-day—is of the second type generally, though the crass ignorance of the theme in the average modern audience makes for very little encouragement to the artist. It may also be that the very elaborate and exact language of conventions in such dancing is absolutely unintelligible to the modern spectator. Almost every conceivable movement and pose of the arms, the hands and the fingers, the legs, the feet and the toes, has a significance, all their own. The hieratic meaning being lost on the spectator, the dance as a whole proves a failure. But because the spectator has ceased to be a connoisseur, the artist cannot in justice be said to have lost his art.

The ultimate origin of the classic as well as popular dances in India seems to lie in the worship and ritual of some far off deity of a vanished race and a lost religion. Even the divine dances of the Great God are ascribed to some such source. Certainly, the dances of the aboriginal hill-tribes, like the Todas,—who still maintain their own ancient rude ways,—seem to be incapable of any other meaning. That this ancient aboriginal dancing has influenced the folk-dance of our country-side in India to-day,—like the *Garbas* of Gujarat,—is not unlikely; though, of course, the superior varnish in these dances of the later Vaishnavite cult ought also not to be forgotten.

The influence of religions other than Hinduism seems to have been scarcely friendly to these arts with a sensuous appeal. Both the Jain and the Buddhist faith were in open war with these delights of the flesh. Buddhism did, later in its career, come under the permeating influence of Hinduism so far as to transmute the art of dancing from the debased, mortal, sinful recreation into an act of divine worship. The later reformers within the fold of Hinduism itself were either too busy fighting the rival cults, or working out metaphysical refinements, to be worried much about the place of arts in the scheme of life. The temple, wherever it became rooted, transplanted so much at least of the corner of Hindu elysium as to include, in its offices, some kind of dancing. In the polite social world the art never could lose all its charm. The Muhammadans, when they came, were by no means disinclined towards these langorous diversions of a luxurious people. Luckily, their fanatical or puritanical zeal was not roused in this case, as they never understood the inner significance of the dance-poses in their association with the Hindu mythology. Hence, at the Muslim courts in India, the art of dancing became an integral part of the pomp of royalty,—descending, unavoidably perhaps, in the scale of respectability, because the patrons perceived only the bodily movements displaying the physical charms, the mortal beauty of the dancer, and knew nothing of the inner meaning of her art. The art nevertheless continued to be preserved in a form, which has not even now lost all its ancient grandeur, grace, beauty, or significance.

PAINTING

Artistic creation from the earliest times in India presents a bewildering variety of form and a riotous wealth of fancy, which make it impossible to have anything like a complete survey, however brief and sketchy, of the still surviving remnants of that creation. All those arts, which we class as Fine Arts seem to have flourished from long before recorded history. Judging from the frequent allusions in classic Sanskrit literature to the high degree of excellence the Painter's Art had reached, it is evident the elements of drawing and painting must have formed an integral and important part of liberal education among the richer classes of ancient India. The description of foreign contemporaries of the Royal Palaces in historic times indicate a high level of decorative art, which is amply borne out by the remains so far discovered elsewhere. Those grand cathedral caves, containing the masterpieces of eight or ten centuries of painters, and locked away in mountain secrecy to conceal and protect and preserve the Masters' efforts from the vandal hordes of the fanatic Muslim, amply confirm the literary evidence. But, even the most ancient coins indicate, in their effigies, a considerable mastery of the lines and proportions of human and animal forms.

The more important and abiding contribution of the Vedic times, in the progress and perfection of the Painter's Art, is the inspiration they supplied to the Painter throughout the ages of Indian history.

Like most other features of cultural life and manifestation, the Painter's Art in India also took its origin in the symbolic representation of the Vedic ritual. In the Vedic age proper, the gods and goddesses of the pantheon were perhaps not translated in pictorial groups round a sacrificial fire; but the paraphernalia used at these rites of daily worship first suggested in all probability the need for decoration and adornment in the loving devotee's mind. In this sense the early Aryan Art may well be called 'Decorative,' or more accurately, "Abstract and Symbolical." The ornamented sacrificial vessel was probably the direct ancestor of the mural painting, consisting at first of floral design enclosed in a framed space. The essential in these decorations was rather the pattern than any clear notion of exact representation. Landscape of this kind can be easily recognised in the early Buddhist paintings, though the ideal and symbolism used by the old Masters is Vedic, framed and presented in a Buddhist environment. Dravidian civilisation in Southern India had advanced, even before the impact of the ancient Aryans upon the Peninsular people, sufficiently far to develop its own conventions of the Painter's Art in the Deccan, as is but too clearly shown by the ghostly remains in that region. In fact, the Southerners so far conquered their conquerors as to impose their own peculiar worship of the phallic symbol and of the Mother Goddess on the simpler nature-worship of the early Aryans. The transition from "Abstract Symbolism" to "anthropomorphic iconography" must be ascribed entirely to the Southern or Dravidian influence, though when that took place, or how it came about, it is impossible to say. The process must have been five or even ten centuries.

Certain it is, however, that by the time we come upon the more material remains of the ancient Painter's Art in the Cave Temples of Ajunta, embracing a period of well nigh a thousand years, we find ample evidence to hold that Indian Art and Culture are clearly the product of Dravidian and the Aryan genius

PLATE LIX
MUGHAL PAINTING

169 CAMELS FIGHTING
16942 Prince of Wales Museum, Bombay

171   A HIMALAYAN CHEER PHEASANT
By Ustad Mansūr
(Victoria and Albert Museum, London)

170 A BLACK BUCK AND HIS MATE

PLATE LX

MUGHAL PAINTINGS

173 EMPEROR BABUR DICTATING
HIS MEMOIRS (Painting by Hashim)

172 AKBAR HUNTING
Outline by Basawan, Painting by Dharm Das

coalesced into one distinct school of Indian painting,—a welding together of the symbolic and the representative, of the abstract and the explicit, which mutually benefitted both the combining traditions. Their initially distinct origin is naturally lost sight of in this complete merger and fusion, influencing not merely the technique of the Art, but also the ideal of the artist, dictating his subjects, and prescribing conventions. It seems to be something more than a mere accident of history that the still surviving relics of the most ancient Indian painters are to be found in the Cave Temples of Ajunta,—(Does the word really mean *Adi-Anta*, the Beginning and the End?) at the junction of the Aryan North and the Dravid South.

Leaving aside, however, these dim vistas of a still unknown history, and turning to the more authentic records and relics of the days after the Maurya Empire, we find a growing wealth of pictorial art. The earliest Buddhist Stupas may have been plain and unvarnished. But soon after the culmination of the Maurya glories, these holy shrines began to be adorned and beautified, with sculptured forms and symbols of the Buddha's life in the ages past. Next, the flat walls of the temples and palaces came to be decorated within and without, with pictured scenes, or painted "wreaths and creepers". No Art Galleries of the ancient Royal Palaces have survived. But take this as an illustration. An entire Act is devoted in Bhavabhuti's masterpiece of the *Uttara-Rama-Charita* to a lovely description of the Picture Gallery in Rama's palace at Ayodhya; and though Bhavabhuti is now believed to have lived somewhere about the time when the Gupta Empire was at its zenith, the realistic description cannot have been altogether imaginary even for such a master-poet. Painting appears prominently in every list of the traditional *64 Kalas*, or the accomplishments of a finished gentleman and lady of the classic days; while standard treatises, like the *Vishnudharmottaram*(?) or *Shilpa-Ratnam*, bestow a great deal of learning on the effort to distinguish between the paintings appropriate for the Temples of the Gods, the Palaces of the Kings, and the houses of private gentlemen.

The pristine spirituality of the Vedic days was, of course, gradually obscured and abandoned in these days of growing wealth and Imperial splendours. But the teaching of the Buddha gives the next great refining impulse to the development of Indian Art, widening the intellectual outlook, and correcting the abstract ideas and spiritual vision of the Vedic age with common conduct and the reaction of life. In the classic age of Indian culture (300 A. C. to 1100 A. C.), the various kinds of paintings were classified as *Satya*, *Vainika*, *Nagara*, and *Misra*, which Kumaraswamy would render as True, Lyrical, Secular, and Mixed, and which may also be styled, perhaps more closely, as Realistic, Idealistic, Social, and Mixed. How far these distinctions of the Treatise-writers were observed in practice is, of course, impossible to say. But every kind of painting must certainly have endeavoured to embody the portrayal of type, and maintain a sense of proportion. Indian painting has been criticised because of its alleged failure to understand perspective; but the directions of the standard authors give no room for such an assumption, any more than the extant specimens can quite warrant such a criticism.

32

The admission of *Rasa* and *Bhava*—the sentiment or mood—is, of course, a peculiarly Indian contribution ; while the Indian master's emphasis on Realism (*Sadrasyam*) is rarely perceived by European critics.

The earliest known paintings now in existence are the frescoes of Ajunta and Bagh, estimated by historians to have been executed between 50 A. C. to 640 A. C. The Ajunta masterpieces were re-discovered in 1819. It is a marvel how fresh they have remained in those parts at least that have not fallen a prey to the insensate vandal, in spite of the centuries that have rolled upon them. The problem of light alone seems to add to the marvel of these wonderful paintings, spread on a vast canvas fit for the tremendous subjects the painters set themselves to delineate. Unless one has seen the most modern method,—which probably was also the method when the painters were actually at work,—by means of which the sun is reflected into the inmost recesses of the caves, one fails to understand how the draughtsman could have maintained his sketch in proportion and perspective, as he has so wonderfully succeeded in achieving; how the painter could have maintained his subtle harmony of colour that is throughout such a peculiar feature of these frescoes. The subject matter is almost entirely Buddhist religious lore; but the objects embodying the painter's art are wonderfully realistic even to the minutest detail. Says Lady Herringham:—

> "The outline is in its final state firm, but modulated and realistic, and not often like the calligraphic sweeping curves of the Chinese and Japanese. The drawing is on the whole like medieval Indian drawing. * * * The artists had a complete command of posture. Their knowledge of the types and positions, gestures and beauties of hands is amazing. Many racial types are rendered; the features are often elaborately studied and of high breeding. * * * Some of the schemes of colour composition are most remarkable and interesting. * * * There is no other really fine portrayal of a dark race by themselves."

Speaking of the technique of the Ajunta Cave painters, a modern scholar and critic writes:—

> "The surface of the hard porous rock was spread over with a layer of clay, cowdung and powdered rock, sometimes mixed with rice-husks, to a thickness of from three to twenty millimetres. Over this was laid a coat of fine white lime-plaster, which was kept moist while the colours were applied, and afterwards lightly burnished. * * * The under-drawing is in red on the white plaster surface, then comes a thinnish terraverde monochrome showing some of the red through it, then the local colour, followed by a renewed outline in brown or black, with some shading, the latter employed rather to give some impression of roundness or relief, than to indicate any effect of light and shade. The bold freedom of the brush strokes seems to show that all the work was freehand, or if any use was made of stencils, freely re-drawn."

Mr. Griffiths, the most painstaking reproducer of these paintings, writes:—

> "After years of careful study on the spot, I may be forgiven if I seem inclined to esteem the Ajunta Pictures too highly as Art. In spite of its obvious limitations, I find the work so accomplished in execution, so consistent in convention, so vivacious and varied in design, and full of such evident delight in beautiful form and colour, that I cannot help ranking it with some of that Art, which the world has agreed to praise in Italy."

Fergusson objects to "the flatness and want of shadow" in these frescoes; but even he had to recognise that "the perspective, grouping and details are better, and the story better told, than in any painting anterior to Orcagna and Fiesole." "Flatness," however, is scarcely a flaw in wall paintings; while "want of shadow"

PLATE LXI

MUGHAL PAINTINGS

EMPEROR SHAH JEHAN

EMPRESS NUR JEHAN
(Copied by Prince of Wales Museum, Bombay)

EMPEROR AURANGZEB IN OLD AGE

177 SARASWATI PLAYING ON THE VINA
(British Museum)

178   GAUTAMA BUDDHA
(Sarnath)

179 TORSO REPRESENTING PRINCE SIDDHARTHA 180   BESNAGAR YAKSHI
(From the Sanchi Tope)

shows an effort of imagination on the part of this standard author on Oriental Architecture for which there is little warrant in sober fact. On the whole the paintings display a perfect fidelity to the type the artist was portraying, which, by its very strangeness to the European critic, has led the latter wholly astray. The ordinary Hindu type of manhood has always been characterised by a slenderness, softness, suppleness, which the painters throughout the centuries have done their best to reproduce. But the European, accustomed to his massive muscular type, naturally misses perhaps the chief beauty of the Indian artist. As Mr. Kumaraswamy has pointed out again and again, the master artist in India had to be a finished, disciplined scholar, versed in the canons of his art, more than anywhere else in the world. "A more conscious, or, indeed, more sophisticated art could scarcely be imagined." The paintings relate mostly, indeed, to court scenes, depicting a voluptuous, luxurious, but withal cultured and refined aristocracy, whose extreme sensitiveness to all forms of outward beauty made them regard a flaw in colouring or a fault in grouping as a blow on the pupil of the eye. The praise bestowed by Lady Herringham on the Indian artist's marvellous skill with the hands he delineated is well deserved. But the wonderful pose and eloquence of the hands are not the result of happy, accidental spontaneity; but rather the creation of an infinite scholarship. The painter-scholar has yet to be born in India, who could make alive again to us the language of the gesture. But even to-day, those who have made a study of the wonderful play of the Indian's palm and wrist and joined finger will realise the infinitive suggestiveness of these most expressive gestures in beseeching and caressing, explaining and deprecating. The female figure, again, popular with the Indian artist of the Caves, has given offence to the European critic by the large almond-shaped, languishing eye, the luscious lips, the full breasts, the swaying hips; but such a critic only displays his ignorance of the life and society for whose delectation the pictures were first painted. It was a highly sensuous, sophisticated aristocracy, which prescribed the model to the painter. To them the women, drawn with all the alluring grace and subtle charm of Indian womanhood, in an endless variety of position, infinite diversity of dress and ornament, and sometimes even nude, had a suggestion of beauty, which the European Art-critic naturally fails to realise. The artist revels in the most effective draping of the most sensuous, langorous forms of female beauty, dispensing, like the originals, with all those tawdry aids of pin and clasp and button, which might serve to keep a garment in position, but which must fail irretrievably in setting off the wonderful lines and contours of the female form divine. Kalidasa's ideal type of female beauty laid down in the *Meghaduta*:—

तन्वी श्यामा शिखरिदशना पक्वबिम्बाधरोष्ठी
मध्ये क्षामा चकितहरिणीप्रेक्षणा निम्ननाभिः ।
श्रोणीभारादलसगमना स्तोकनम्रा स्तनाभ्याम्
या तत्रस्यायुवति विषये सृष्टिराद्येव धातुः॥

was throughout maintained by the Indian artist.

The height of fashion in ancient India, according to the painter's evidence, seems to have lain in the manifold ways of hair-dressing. The cave-paintings are the most vivid and inexhaustible treasury of fashion-plates in this regard. Sometimes friezed and fronted with coquettish ringlets; sometimes tied in chignon, with a coronel of flowers peeping out from behind heavy folds; sometimes framed in knots with side-loops adorned as ever with flowers; and sometimes caged in wire strands or jewelled strings—these are amongst a few of the fashions of hair-dressing affected by these *Grandes dames* of a vanished society. To quote a competent modern critic (Capt. G. Solomon of the Bombay School of Art).

> "The Ajunta Masters use Woman as their best decorative asset with brilliant zest and extraordinary knowledge. Woman is the finest achievement of their art, and obviously its most admired theme. * * * They use woman like flowers, garlands of girls surround their Rajas and their Princes, embellish their palaces, dominate their street scenes, crowd the windows of their cities, and are often painted, as in the delicious panel in the First Cave of the Queen and her maids giving alms to a mendicant, for the sheer joy of painting them, and with no perceivable literary or religious intention. * * * As *Apsaras* or radiant Peris they float across the porches; as Sirens they lure the sailor to his doom; but chiefly they shine for us as mortals, and as mortals these artists depicted them best and most often. They painted them at the toilette, in repose, gossiping, sitting, standing, always with a sort of wonder akin to awe. They did not pose women; they simply copied their poses."

       *   *   *   *

It is impossible to give a sketch of the great series of paintings in these Caves. Their subject matter is, chiefly, scenes in the previous lives of the Buddha; and they were intended to inspire the Buddhist pilgrim by the pictured story of those that had attained *Nirvana*. They are the earliest surviving illustrations of the rooted ideal of the Indian artist, viz. that beauty is spiritual, not of the matter. When these artists began to reconcile themselves to the idea of representing in visible form the spiritual conception of their Gods, they instinctively avoided the Hellenic ideal, which sought to fashion god-like beauty from a faithful copy of human loveliness. They were familiar, of course, with the outlines and the anatomical details of the human form, on which they obviously modelled their gods or heroes; and in this sense it is perfectly correct to say they did not altogether dispense with the copying of the real human beings as they saw them. But in that which makes a painting really a creation of the artist's own,—in the pose and expression of the figure,—they introduced an element of studied elaborate idealism, which marks the works of the Indian artist as being totally apart from his contemporary in Greece. The type of divine manliness they loved to portray suggested the majesty of the lion and the grace of the deer in the face and waist and legs of the subject; and so we find a certain recurrence of the type, in form and features and expression, even among artists separated by centuries, when they came to deal with the same subject. If Mark Twain had visited the remains of the Indian picture galleries, he would have certainly expressed his astonishment at the identity of the Buddha painted and sculptured by artists as wide apart as Michael Angelo and Gustave Dore. The artist in India is throughout no mere craftsman, or technician; he is an inspired

PLATE LXIII

181 CAURI-BEARER

182 BIMARAN CASKET

183 PIPRAWA INSCRIBED VASE
(Containing relics of Buddha)

184 RELIQUARY CASKET, PESHAWAR
(Containing Buddha's Ashes)

PLATE LXIV

185 LOWER PART OF ASOKA'S PILLAR
Lauriya Nandangarh

186   ASOKA'S PILLAR
Lauriya Nandangarh

187   SEALS FROM MAHENJO DARO

188   RAILINGS ROUND THE BUDDHA TEMPLE, GAYA

seer, who makes an absolute surrender of his self in the product of his art. It is his form of worship, his manner of adoration. Shri Krishna has taught on the Battle-field of Panipat the supreme cult of perfect surrender; and ever since the artist in India has held; "Whatever I do is of Thee, and for Thee, and as impelled by Thee."

Perhaps, however, the frescoes of the Ajunta Caves, or even of Bagh, do not represent the first efforts of Indian Painters. They are much too mature; too finished, too perfect in technique, in design, and execution, to be the creation of the earliest artists. The absence of any relics earlier than at Bagh or Ajunta is very likely accounted for by the fact that the earliest medium for the painter's expression was the wooden floor and ceiling of Royal Palaces, and not the stone walls of rock temples as they subsequently came to be. As wood is more easily destroyed, there is little wonder that the most ancient specimens of the Indian Painter's art have been lost.

It is difficult, likewise, to say whether it was the Vedic-Aryan, with all his sensuous relish of ritual, or the dry puritanical Buddhist Indian, who first began to indulge in pictorial representation. Our extant specimens indicate, however, the almost exclusive sway of the Buddhist in the domain of painting; though, of course, the basic conventions,—the root ideals,—of the Art, must have been of much more ancient origin. To the idealisation of the actual, so instinctively characteristic of the Indian Artist, the Buddhist painter added a dash of realism, which made him render the most faithful likeness of life in all its myriad phases in his day. The idealistic,—the transcendental religious,—conception of Art is present all over Ajunta, no doubt; but the undercurrent of fidelity to fact adds a charming variety of pose and mood and expression, that make the Ajunta paintings, once seen, unforgetable.

Like remains are also to be found in Gwalior, and perhaps more abundantly in Ceylon. We must, however, await the fuller excavations now in progress at such famous centres of Art and Culture in ancient India, as Taxila, the world-famous University, or Pataliputra, the classic capital, for the yet more early,—and perhaps, who knows,—more exquisite, more delicate, more perfect creations of the Master Painters of the Mauryas and their predecessors. For the present, however, we must perforce content ourselves with these fresco remains, and judge of the splendours and triumphs of the Indian Artist from these.

The story of Indian sculpture is yet more wondrous, more rich, more continuous, probably because the object it is written upon is more lasting. We shall tell it in another place. We mention it here to illustrate, by a parallel, the rooted idea of the Indian Artist's mind that true salvation could only be had by acts, not intentions,—by deeds, not by words. The artist made a religious duty of his craft; and so to him no labour was too great to express his worship. If the results of his labours came to have a more abiding form,—why, so much more to the good. The poet's creations were ethereal, and could endure only in so far as the reader's soul comes to be in tune with the spirit of the Seer. The painter's work is more material, no doubt; but still, as compared to the carver in metal or the sculptor in stone, it is delicate, fragile, perishable. The labour, however, is the greatest and most toilsome in Sculpture and her twin-sister, Architecture; and as the artist was convinced that the greater his toil the higher his merit, he applied himself more and more to the exacting task of writing poems in stone, and making pictures from rocks.

This universal *motif* of religious zeal succeeded to perfection in achieving the object of the artist's work. The primary intention of Art in India has always been, at least among the Hindus, to convey most effectively the central ideas of the Hindu religion and philosophy to every class of society. Hence the use of symbols, which make the most universal appeal; and so convey to the simplest soul the inner meaning of things that no amount of learned lecturing to them would ever achieve. In the use of these symbols and the adoption of these conventions of his art, however, the Indian artist never offended in the least against the universal laws of æsthetic design and rhythm; and so succeeded in maintaining his high level of excellence, which has seldom been equalled since.

Of the pre-Mughal vestiges of the genuine Indian pictorial Art, we have so far discovered few other remains besides those of Ajunta. Probably, they were all destroyed in the sweeping tide of iconoclastic zeal that characterised, the early Muhammadans. The Ellora traces of fresco painting are, indeed, of the same *genre* as the Ajunta masterpieces; and, being in the same neighbourhood, they were probably executed by the same school of Artists. While the iconoclast Muslim utilised for his own purpose the native Indian genius for architecture, and built his mosques on ideals that had governed temple-sculpture and palaces, no whit different from those of the decaying Hindu principalities, and so continued the ancient tradition in that art, there was distinctly an interlude of a Dark Age in the history of Indian Painting while the first Muslims overran the land. For 500 years and more, the Painter was neglected, despised, ostracised. But at last he comes into his own when once again the Imperial and luxurious Mughals held sway in Hindustan. They had out-grown the idol-breaker's narrow viewpoint, which considered the Painter's glories to be directly against the laws of the Quran. Abul Fazl has a highly sophisticated argument in praise of the Painter and his Art. The love of that Art was carried so far in Akbar's age that, his son and successor Jahangir could, on his accession, truthfully boast in his memoirs such a perfection of his connoisseur's skill that, if he had only once seen a Master Painter's single specimen, he could always thereafter most easily and readily identify that Artist's work.

The first Mughal painters derived their tradition and convention from Persia, then the centre and acme of Islamic culture. This differed materially from the native Indian artist's work, as enshrined in the caves of the Ajunta Hills. The Hindu had learnt, by centuries of practice and high standard of artistry, the secret of combining the art of line and form; and at the same time he had learnt to endow his creation with that vein of idealism, which reveals the introspective bent of his mind. With the Muhammadan painters of the Persian School, and in Mughal miniatures, the brush outline is often of one artist, and colouring by another. The contrast of this new style with the ancient Indian School of painters lay in the fact that, while the Hindu painter dealt almost wholly with religious subjects inspired by a deep idealism, the Muhammadan painting was definitely an aristocratic,—a courtier's,—accomplishment. It was, therefore, realistic in a sense in which the old Hindu artist never tried to be realistic. Its subjects were the living personages of the Court and the every day pomp of the Camp and the pageantry of the Palace. The illustrations to the highly mystic strains of the *sufi* poet afforded the only occasion to the Mughal painter to introduce a strain of religious idealism in his artistic creations.

It may be an open question whether the undercurrent of the vein of spiritual idealism in the old Hindu creations really tended to enrich the work of those artists. The Mughal painter, however, at the height of his glory in the seventeenth century, could rightly lay claim to the creed of worshipping his Art for Art's own sake. The puritan Muslim sentiment steadfastly refused to concede to the noblest productions of Art the living glory of creation. Art, to the orthodox Muslim, was merely material, and, had, therefore, an exclusively secular scope. For a liberal patron like Akbar, the artist instinctively recalled the ancient conception of his Hindu fore-runner that no artistic production could be perfect or praiseworthy without the painter identifying himself, in spirit at least, with the object of his creation. The painter in old India was wont and content to efface himself so utterly and completely; he sought so little of the worldly fame for himself; that we know not the name of a single one of the generations of master painters who must have been at work in Ajunta alone. Bar those who were attracted directly from abroad, the Muslim court painter of the Mughal Emperors was a Hindu in descent and in the profoundest recesses of his soul and being. While he let alone his traditional ancestral work, he could ignore the canons of the art, and confound its apparent heresy or sacrilege. But when once he returned to the work of his progenitors, the call of his blood was irresistible. In his delineation of themes of universal and eternal human interest, or pageants of State, he found ample scope to steer clear of the ancient religious themes and their entrancing idealism. But when he once took to themes like the mystic notes of the Sufi poet, or the portrayal of musical melodies personified, he could not go against the instincts of his heredity.

For reasons already given, we must refrain from any particular description of the Mughal Painters and their works. The wealth of material is, once again, so great that there is no hope of doing any justice to the artists and their masterpieces, were we to attempt even a bare summary of the productions. When after an eclipse of five hundred years or more, they come once again into prominence, under the greatest of the Mughals, the Painters begin as innovators, some of them being probably Persians. The innovators were, however, soon overwhelmed by native talent; for the indigenous genius for pictorial representation was by no means dead.

Persian Painting declined in its homeland, however, after the sixteenth century, to be reborn in India with wonderful life and pulsation under the fostering care of the Mughals. The Mughal painters, were, as already remarked, pupils of the

Persian Masters; but they were no soulless imitators, without a genius of their own to immortalise, or a message of their own to deliver. An independent characteristic style was developed by the Court Painters of Akbar, and kept up under his two immediate successors. Throughout the short but glorious history of the Mughal Painting, the Hindu influence is visible; but at no time was the latter so strong as under the inspiring influence of the Imperial connoisseur, who first dared to invite the latitudinarian Persian to his court. He himself disdained not to take lessons from the great masters; and was enthusiastic enough to found and endow a State School of Art, worked under his own personal direction and control. The Persian fore-runners and inspirers of the new Art soon coalesced under the influence with the native Indian talent; and so was reborn the Indian Mughal School proper, which continued down almost to our own days. As the might and the means of the Emperor advanced, his vision of Imperial Palaces began to take shape; and the need was soon felt to decorate them with pictures unequalled even as the magnificent architecture of the Palace-Town as a whole. Remains of the mural decorations of the Fatehpur-Sikri Palace are still visible. Persian subjects were not absent in these early efforts; but much of even that was characteristically Indian, and in all probability, is the work of Hindu artists collaborating.

From mural decoration, the Mughal painter soon passed on to exquisite portraiture, which seems to have attained its zenith under Jahangir and Shah Jahan. The bulk of the Mughal Painter's commissions consisted of portrait painting of grandees, and of Court scenes. As paper of the right texture had just begun to make its appearance, the artist became independent of the large surface offered for his work by the Palace walls. The palace of Fatehpur-Sikri, so lavishly embellished, was also about this time suddenly abandoned; and the artist began to work in a milieu and on material peculiarly adapted to the new task he had imposed upon himself. Even in portrait painting, though the Indian and the Persian schools went on working side by side throughout the reign of Akbar, they rapidly developed an individuality of their own. Jahangir, than whom no keener or more discerning, more munificent or more critical, patron has ever been found by the Painter in all history, gave a fresh impetus to the School of his father's creation. His patronage and appreciation carried the Indian Painter's art to the highest point it ever reached under the Mughals. The Persian and Hindu traditions were fused into one, each enriching and improving the other, each demanding a minuteness of attention to detail, which has made the creations of that age the wonder of all succeeding generations and the despair of all would-be imitators. Mansur, that Prince of Painters, whom Jahangir officially styled the "Wonder of his Age," was a master in animal portraiture; and his pictures of birds and beasts are yet the marvels of the painter's brush. The master painter in portraiture was Bishandas, an obvious Hindu. Every grandee of the Court has been immortalised by his undying brush; and every noteworthy incident at Court or in the Camp, where the Emperor was present, or in which he was interested, has been recorded and preserved by the labours of these immortals.

PLATE LXV

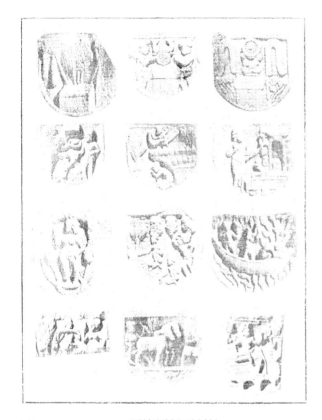

189   BUDDHA-GAYA
Medallion from the Rail Pillars

190   LION CAPITAL
Sarnath Pillar

191   CATHEDRAL CAVE, KARLE

192   GENERAL VIEW, SANCHI STUPA
(Photo: Indian State Railways)

PLATE LXVI

193   INTERIOR OF A CHAITYA SHOWING STUPA, (AJANTA)

(Photo: Archaeological Dept., Hyderabad Dn.)

194   CARVINGS ON NORTH GATE, SANCHI TOPE

(Photo: Indian State Railways)

With the death of this Prince of artists, Jahangir, the soul of Indian painting departed. The outward form remained for a while after, but the spirit inhabiting had flown away. From portrait painting and scenic display, the painter had learnt the value of light and shade; and so the figures of the later Mughals acquired a new roundness, and a background or landscape, which had been lacking in the works of their predecessors. This last development, together with the revival of the perspective, is nowadays claimed to have occurred not until European influences had been decisively at work. Akbar himself was the first to be interested in European painting, and had even sent an agent to the Court of Goa for European curiosities and craftsmen to work under the Imperial eye. Through the Jesuit Missionaries at his Court in 1580, Akbar made his first direct acquaintance with European painting, already very rich with the labours of the great Cinquecentists. Secular as well as religious masterpieces of Europe found some imitators in miniature at the Court of Akbar and his son; but for the major part of their productions were wholly Indian in conception, design, and finish. Jahangir, while appreciating at their true value the efforts of European artists, was definitely opposed to any deliberate adulteration of Eastern and Western methods, technique, or ideals. And so, while he suffered some of the characteristics of European painting to creep into the work of his Court artists, he insisted upon their maintaining an individuality of their own. The European features imported into Indian art were thus wholly Indianised, even before the magnificent Shah Jahan gave a fresh impulse to the ornate court painting of his time. Portrait painting becomes, under the successor of Jahangir, the most fashionable; and the most wonderful profiles were drawn by the lightest of light touches. The Imperial patronage was now no longer the monopoly of the poet or the painter; but every kind of artist was recognised and encouraged; giving us, in consequence, those wonderful creations, which, like the Taj and Delhi palace and the several mosques, must for ever immortalise the name of the Imperial patron.

Under Shah Jahan, miniature-painting underwent a further elaboration. Miniature artists were not unknown in the days of Akbar; but the classification of their works under their respective sign-manual is all but impossible, since more than one artist laboured on one and the same piece. One painted the border and outline, while another did the colouring in the main body of the picture. In Shah Jahan's time, miniature-painting came to be considered as utterly incomplete, unless a most elaborate and ornamental border of bright-hued flowers, birds and butterflies was deftly woven into the main theme. The Mughal miniature-painter, despite these flourishes and embellishments, was the lineal descendant of the ancient Hindu Court and cave-painter, and not of the Persian artist, though first resurrected by Persian influence. Between the Mughal court miniaturist of Agra and his Hindu progenitor there was only this difference; that the former lacked wholly the latter's subtle idealism. As introduced first by the grateful Humayun after his return from Persia, the new phase of the Painter's art seemed distinct in its realism, its peculiar personal appeal to the living and the powerful. But the Indian pupils of the Persian

34

innovators soon assimilated the mysteries of this novel cult; and enriched it by a certain something of their own inspiration from unconscious heredity. The excessive richness, however, that came in course of time to be associated with miniature-painting, marks, in Shah Jahan's time, the beginning of decline from the very high level the Painter's art had attained to in India.

The accidents of history also played their part in this consummation. The Fratricidal War of Shah Jahan's sons resulted in the defeat and death of that noble Prince, Dara Shukoh, than whom the entire line of the cultured, liberal, highly refined Mughal Imperial family can boast of no greater in erudition, enlightenment, or artistic appreciation. In the place of Dara came the iconoclastic and fanatical Aurangzeb Alamgir. He, too, was a true scion of his glorious race in general culture; but his mind was the mind of a puritan, his outlook on life that of an ascetic. His pleasures were not of the Prince, as understood by his father and grandfather, at any rate. And so he set his stern warrior's face against the lighter arts and lovelier graces, that had made so much of the beauty and grandeur and splendour of his ancestors' Court. The Fine Arts did not die at once the death that the Emperor is said to have wished to the body of Indian music. The painter still continued to ply the brush; and Alamgir's edicts did not touch him, in spite of the obvious sacrilege of his art in the eyes of the convinced Musalman. For, the Emperor himself delighted in the pictorial records of his own grand doings. But he sought to discriminate invidiously between artists of his own creed and those of others; and so sowed the seeds of decline that ultimately brought about all but a total decay of the Fine Arts in India.

This brief survey of the painter's art in India must suffice to give the reader a taste of the pristine splendours of artistic achievement in this country. After Aurangzeb, the painter, like the musician and the architect, continued to eke out a miserable existence at the court of minor princes. After Nadir Shah's invasion and inroad upon the magnificent library of portraits and miniatures, the artist lost that living communion with the soul of the departed masters of the past, which looked out from their works in the Imperial Art collection. The decline once set in went headlong on the downward course till, by the end of the eighteenth century, little of the true artist's genius remained in India.

At this stage the question may well be asked: What was the mission of Art in India? And what has been the sum total of its contribution? There is, indeed, a striking difference in the ideals that inspired the Indian artist, and those of his confrere of the Near and Far West. While in ancient India, Art was more or less an expression of the Ideal,—itself a creature of a rich and ardent imagination, glowing with religious zeal and fervour,—in the West the artist has even now not been able to discard the crutches of the model, and emancipate himself from the restraint of reproducing the real. Art indeed is ever young, and ever old. It is catholic without being apostolic, universal without being enigmatic. But, while the artist in India was evolving and executing his conception of the Ideal, his prototype in countries now leading the vanguard of civilisation had hardly emerged from his rude cave-dwelling and ruder charcoal sketching. Even when the Greek copyist of Egyptian dexterity in craftsmanship came upon the scene, all that he contributed was a Cult of Beauty, which went no further than what the eye could see. If the poet's eye in a fine frenzy rolling was not quite absent in the finest of the Athenian sculptor, the painter of imaginative perfection did not make very great headway in Greece, especially in comparison with sculpture. We have no specimens of the best Greek painting now surviving. The greatest of the Greek philosophers have no doubt assigned a high place to the art of painting; but until their testimony is corroborated by more tangible evidence, it is not quite free from question whether the art of painting had attained in Greece the same height as sculpture. The point, therefore, still remains: What is Art? The Athenian answered the query by making it a handmaid of beauty. It was not the Goddess herself, not even a pale reflection of her divine effulgence; but only a poor, humble, servitor, whose claim to a niche in the pantheon was conceded begrudgingly. The Greek artist was a copyist, not a creator, and contented himself with a mere translation of the beauty of man and things into permanent forms of bronze and marble. Beauty of this kind is necessarily transient; and the artist tries, by incorporating it into more durable forms, to invest it with a sort of immortality,—a property of the Divine into the human or the mortal. La Gioconde or Holbein's Duchess of Milan, for example, would never have been remembered, except for an immortalisation of this kind. But this is far from that creative effort, which seeks to catch and embody the fleeting message of the age by a flourish of the brush, so that generations to come may read and reflect and profit by the message thus conveyed. The spirit of the age remains unenchained in such endeavours to embody the beauty of form and expression as seen in the earthly models. Hence, Grecian art, even at its best, falls far short of that excellence of creative genius which distinguishes the earliest Indian art. Even the later European painter has hardly ever transcended the limitation imposed from the infancy of art in Europe by the traditions of Greece. For though he had his Christs and Madonnas, his saints and angels, they were all, as Mark Twain remarks somewhere, Italians in Italy, and French in France, and dull, slow, heavy in Holland,—with rarely a hint of the original Judaism in the curve of the nose, or the swell of the cheek, peculiar to the Semitic physiognomy. Not so the inspired artist of India, seeking to visualise the perfection of his ideal. That ideal— born of the spirit, not of matter—gave him a pattern, a model, which was made universal from Madura to Peshawar, by the elaborate, exhaustive, and withal, rigid, canons of the master-artists.

SCULPTURE

The plastic arts, particularly sculpture, seem at first sight more difficult of execution and perfection than the pictorial. The manual labour is obviously greater, and the knowledge of anatomy has to be unavoidably higher, owing to the need to show the third dimension. The creative excellence and uniqueness is, however, distinctly superior in painting, which knows no limits. Because of the nature of sculpture, we might be inclined to believe, from the still surviving examples of that art, that it was cultivated long before painting. As a matter of history, however, the two seem to advance together hand in hand, and intimately influence the best creations in either. The art of the painter, however, has left very few concrete survivals due to want of durability in the medium through which the painter had to express himself. The frailness of the medium is, however, in no way responsible for the paucity of plastic remains of our ancient artistic creations. But even in their case the earliest material for carving selected by the Indian artist seems to have been wood; and wood in India is peculiarly liable to decay and destruction. The Aryans of the Vedic age seem to have mastered the mysteries of carpentry and metal work, particularly of *Ayas*, (copper, if not iron), for all household and ritual purposes. They seem to have been also very fond of gold jewellery, and were adepts at weaving, sewing including embroidery, leather work, and pottery. But the pure nature-worship of the early Vedic religion, coupled with the lively imagination of the early Aryans, seems to have put a ban on image-making, though decoration of the products of some of the crafts mentioned could not have been quite unknown. For sculpture and iconography on the Indian soil, we are, according to the evidence of history now available, indebted to the Dravidian strain.

> "Amongst the elements of Dravidian origin," says the historian of *Indian and Indonesian Art*, A. Koomaraswamy, "are probably the cults of the phallus and of mother-goddesses, Nagas, Yaksas, and other nature spirits; and many of the arts. Indeed, if we recognise in the Dravidian a southern race, and in the Aryans a northern, it may well be argued that the victory of kingly over tribal organisations, the gradual reception into orthodox religion of the phallus cult and the mother-Goddesses, and the shift from abstract symbolism to anthropomorphic iconography in the period of theistic and *Bhakti* development, mark a final victory of the conquered over the conquerors."

But, recognising the full value of the Dravidian contribution, the historian is still bound to conclude:—(*Ibid.* 8-9).

> "Indian art and culture, in any case, are a joint creation of the Dravidian and Aryan genius, a welding together of symbolic and representative, abstract and explicit, language and thought. Already at Bharhut and Sanci the Aryan symbol is yielding to its environment and passing into decoration; Kusana art, with the facts of imagery and its root in *Bhakti*, is essentially Dravidian. Already, however, the Indra-Santi figure at Bodhgaya shows Aryan affecting Dravidian modes of expression, anticipating the essential qualities of all later *Sattvik* images. * * There is an originally realistic intention, but accommodated to the terms of pure design. * * This is in a real sense was a marriage—marriage of the East and the West, or North and South, consummated, as the donors of an image would say, "for the good of all sentient beings"; a result not of a superficial blending of Hellenistic and Indian technique, but of the crossing of spiritual tendencies, racial *Samskaras* (pre-occupations), that may well have been determined before the use of metals was known."

However this may have been, by the time the Indian artist had begun to work in more durable materials, he had attained a degree of excellence, and a mastery of outline and design, which give a character all their own to the sculptured glories of India. The artist consciously placed before him an ideal, which, though it did not

PLATE LXVII

195   SANCHI STUPA, NORTH GATEWAY   196   SANCHI STUPA, EAST GATE

(By the Photo: Indian State Railways)

197   A TREE NYMPH, SANCHI   198   ASOKA'S PILLAR, LUMBINI GROVE
Birthplace of Buddha

PLATE LXVIII

340 CHAITYA SLAB, AMRAVATI STUPA
(Reproduced at Bezwada, British)

398 THE GODDESS KALI—SCULPTURES FROM KAILAS (ELLORA)
(Photo: Archaeological Dept., Hyderabad Dn.)

make him completely independent of the aid of mortal models for realising his conception of Divine Beauty, grace, matchless and perfect serenity, made him ever strive for the super-human. To realise this goal he submitted himself to a training and discipline, which is seldom paralleled in other parts of the world.

> "Let the imager," wrote Sukracharya, the classic guide of the Indian Sculptor, "establish images in temples by meditations on deities who are the objects of his devotion. * * * * * * In no other way, not even by direct and immediate vision of an actual object, is it possible to be so absorbed in contemplation as thus in the making of images".[1]

The Indian artist was, in other words, working not for a mortal patron, but for the immortal gods. He is styled in Sanskrit variously,—and significantly,—the Achiever *(Sadhaka)*, the Wizard *(Mantrin)*, or the *Yogin*. The sculptor or painter has his human preceptors and guides; but not the most proficient pupil ventured to create his master-piece without first undergoing in its entirety that wonderful ritual which the classic writers of India called "the Seven-fold Offices". When the artist-devotee of the gods had offered up his prayers,

> "He must meditate on the emptiness of *(Shunyatwa)* or non-existence of all things, for, by the fire of the idea of the abyss, it is said there are destroyed beyond recovery the five factors of ego consciousness. Then only should he invoke the desired divinity by the utterance of the appropriate seed-word *(Bija)*, and should identify himself completely with the divinity to be represented. Then, finally, on pronouncing the *Dhyana Mantram*, in which the attributes are defined, the divinity appears visibly 'like a reflection' or 'as in a dream' and this brilliant image is the artist's model."[2]

The artist was enjoined to become one with the Divinity. *"Devam Bhootwa Dewam Yajet"*, was the motto of his whole school. Because, however, the Indian artist dispensed more or less with mortal models, his creations show no flaw in figure or defect in proportions. Because he evolved his own type of beauty in divine personality, he never failed to suit the pose and expression of every figure to the varying shades of emotion which had each such figure in its grip.

The earliest monuments of sculptural achievements in India, so far discovered, are the burial mounds of Lauriya Nandgarh in Bihar. Constructed from alternate layers of clay and straw with leaves, two of these have a salwood post standing erect in the centre of each, with a deposit of human bones and charcoal accompanied by a small gold leaf. On this is impressed a primitive outline of a female figure, supposed by many to represent the Goddess of Earth. Other remains of a period authentically going beyond the Mauryan age are embodied in the decayed walls of the great pre-Mauryan Metropolis of Rajagriha, built of rough cyclopean masonry. Archæologists in India seem to be agreed, however, that in Vedic India buildings of material other than wood must have been rather the exception than the rule. Climatic reasons alone must have rendered brickwork insecure as well as expensive in the earlier homes of the Vedic Aryans. Wood must have been cheaper, as well as more admissive of rich surface decoration by the master-pieces of the pictorial

---

1) Sukracharya quoted in A. Kumaraswamy—*Essay on Hindu Ideal of Art.*
2) Foucher: *Iconographie Buddhique.* 11, 8-11.

art that seem to have vanished for ever from the ken of mankind. The finds in the Bhir mound at Taxila must, however, be mentioned even in this bare sketch, as examples of pre-Mauryan, if not Vedic, remains, particularly because of the *Terra Cotta* reliefs some of which resemble the Earth Goddess of Lauriya. [1] Says Kumaraswamy, in his *History of Indian and Indonesian Art.* (p. 10):

> "The antiquities found here and elsewhere prove that *glass-making* had attained a high level before the Maurya period, and that the cutting and polishing of hard stone in the fourth and fifth centuies B. C. had reached a level of technical accomplishment which was sustained in the Maurya period, but never afterwards surpassed."

The dominant *motif* and the chief characteristics of the art of this period in India seem in no way to be different from the more authentic examples coming from the Mauryan age. Strange animals, peculiar figures, striking symbols, like the *Swastika* or the spiral, seem to be common in Aryan India as in the countries to the north and the west of India right up to the shores of the Mediterranean. The bell-shaped capitals in the Mauryan remains have been exampled by many students of the artistic heritage of India as indicating a borrowing from Persia. But more likely is the suggestion that India in those days formed an integral part of that cultural unit which stretched from the eastern shores of the Mediterranean to the mouth of the Ganges, in which all artists worked on the same lines, with the same ideals.

From the days of the Mauryas begins a continuous history of India's artistic master-pieces. Fergusson has said that the history of Indian art is written in decay. Sir J. Marshall will have none of it, regarding that history to be "one of continuous forward progress." Apart altogether from the giant pillars and magnificent stupas being the official and authentic mementos of the court art under the Mauryas, the colossal stone-figures from Besnagar and Parkham may justly be taken to be splendid specimens of the non-official, popular and wholly indigenous art of the period. Wonderfully designed, these free-standing figures of a Yaksha and a Yakshi,- defaced and of archaic appearance as they are,—give a magnificent impression of mere volume and massiveness. The sense of dignity is greater, if anything, in the Chauri-bearing female figure recently found at Patna, giving a most wonderfully realistic picture of the female form divine. It is from such beginnings that the triumphs of the Buddhist age, inspired with rare spiritual exaltation, were finally achieved in the centuries that followed.

There is, in these specimens of purely popular art, no trace of imitation of foreign art-creations, sometimes urged against the surviving remnants of the court artists of Asoka and his successors. The monuments of these first historic Emperors of India comprise a number of pillars erected in his dominions by Asoka to commemorate his triumphs in the field, or to preach imperial sermons to his people; a pillared hall at Patna, the seat of his Government, alleged by some to have been modelled on the Royal Palaces of the Persian Kings; a group of rock-temples in Bihar, a monolithic rail at Sarnath; a throne in the temple at Buddha Gaya; and parts of

1) Kumaraswamy's *History of Indian and Indonesian Art.* p. 10.

Stupa umbrellas at Sanchi and Sarnath.[1] All these remains are alike remarkable in the marvellous chiselling of their surface, and its dazzling polish. Let us take, for illustration, the famous Sarnath pillar as typical of the class. It was here the Blessed One first turned the Wheel of the Law; and so, to mark the sacred site, his Imperial disciple erected, two hundred years later, a circular shaft of plain sandstone, brilliantly polished, and slightly tapering towards the top.

> "The capital consists of four addorsed lions, which originally supported a *Dhamma Cakka* or Wheel of the Law, resting on an abacus bearing in relief an elephant, horse, bull and lion, separated by four small *Dhamma Cakkas*, below which is the inverted lotus forming the "bell."[2]

It is these so-called "bell-shaped" capitals of the Asokan pillars, which have led many European students of the Indian art-forms to trace in them a borrowed *motif*. The "bell," as a matter of fact, is nothing but the lotus, so common a feature and emblem in India in the days long before the Mauryas. As Mr. Havell has justly shown, the "bell" of the European critics is only an adaptation to structural purposes of the common, popular, well-known lotus-and-vase *motif*, which, in the case of these Asokan pillars, served to present a symbol of Buddha's nativity.

> "The vase," says Mr. Havell in his *Ideals of Indian Art*, (p. 43) "forming the base of the pillar stood for the cosmic waters—the all-Brahman; the shaft was the stalk of the mystic flower, the unreality upon which the world-life was supported; the bell shaped capital was the world itself enfolded by the petals of the sky; the fruit was *Moksha*."

At Bharut and at Sanchi the flower is carved with marvellous precision in all its petals and stamen ; while the body of the pillar is rooted at the base in water-base, as is the case even more prominently at Karle. Perhaps, too, the entire structure of the pillar had a deeper spiritual significance in the hands of Asoka and his artists. It symbolised the *pragna-parmita*, the Supreme Wisdom. The *Tantra Tattva* says :—"In the root she is all-Brahman; in stem she is all maya; in the flower she is all-world; and in the fruit all-liberation." If the flower at the top of the Asokan pillar is "all-world", may it not signify, also, the universal sovereignty of the Emperor? In any case, it is inadmissible to call these capitals "Persepolitan," and so to deny the Indian artist of the Mauryan monuments the credit that is his due for his marvellous imagery and perfect symbolism manifested in the most exact fidelity in every detail of his creations.

Sir John Marshall is inclined to regard, in the *Cambridge History of Ancient India*, the Sarnath pillar as being of Perso-Hellenic creation. In praise of its artistic beauty he is warmer than the most sympathetic students of Indian art, both native and foregin :

> "The Sarnath capital, on the other hand, though by no means a masterpiece, is the product of the most developed art of which the world was cognisant in the third century B. C.—the handiwork of one who had generations of artistic effort and experience behind him. In the masterful strength of the crowning lions, with their swelling veins and tense muscular development, and in the spirited realism of the reliefs

---

1) cp. Marshall in *Cambridge History of India.* p. 618-9.
2) Kumaraswamy *History of Indian and Indonesian Art.* p. 17.

> below, there is no trace whatever of the limitations of primitive art. So far as naturalism was his aim, the sculptor has modelled his figures direct from nature, and has delineated their forms with bold, faithful touch; but he has done more than this: he has consciously and of set purpose infused a tectonic conventional spirit into the four lions, so as to bring them into harmony with the architectural character of the monument, and in the case of the horse on the abacus he has availed himself of a type well-known and approved in western art. Equally mature is the technique of his relief work. In early Indian, as in early Greek sculpture, it was the practice, as we shall presently see, to compress the relief between two fixed planes, the original front plane of the slab, and the plane of the background. In the reliefs of the Sarnath capital there is no trace whatever of this process; each and every part of the animal is modelled according to its actual depth without reference to any ideal front plane, with the result that it presents the appearance almost of a figure in the round which has been cut in half and then applied to the background of the abacus."

From the point of view of the sculptor's art, the Sarnath rail and the Buddha Gaya throne are relatively uninteresting, wanting as they do in any conspicuous ornamentation. Each of these is cut out of a single block of stone with perfect exactness; and though the umbrellas are very plain, the simplicity is beautified unspeakably by the exquisite clearness of the ribs of the umbrellas.

Cognate, however, to the sculptured figures on the pillars of Asokan type, or the gate-ways at Sanchi in a slightly later era, may be mentioned the examples of Maurya terra-cotta figurines found at the lowest levels from Pataliputra, the capital, to Taxila, the chief university.

> "These moulded plaques and modelled heads and busts represent in most cases a standing female divinity, with very elaborate coiffure, dressed in a tunic or nude to the waist, and with a *dhoti* or skirt of diaphanous muslin. Despite the garment, especial care is taken to reveal the mount of Venus in apparent nudity. * * * These types may have behind them a long history; they may have been votive tablets or auspicious representations of mother-goddesses and bestowers of fertility, and prototypes of Mayadevi and Lakshmi."[1]

In the age following the Mauryas' there seems to have been a slight decline. The Stupa at Bharhut in Central India is ascribed to the middle of the 2nd century B. C., and is lavishly sculptured, both in the massive stone railing going round the base of the stupa, and the gateway of colossal dimensions leading to the shrine proper. Series of scenes from the previous lives of the Buddha,—the *Jatakas*,—first begin in these sculptures to challenge the artist's imagination and embody his skill. The *Naga Jataka*, the dream of Maya Devi, the famous Jetavana in all its leafy glory, and covered with the concrete evidence of the devotion and munificence of Anathapindika, here begin to oust the old severe simplicity of the first Buddhists, whose monuments up to the days when Asoka reigned are chaste, their virgin beauty undefiled by any superstructure suggestive of the remotest approach to idolatry. Single images also add to the richness and variety of these decorations, and make a subtle connection with the Vedic pantheon. Technically and artistically, however, the work seems to be inferior. Marshall finds these

---

1) Kumaraswamy. *History of Indian and Indonesian Art,*

PLATE LXIX

263　　　　　　　　　　　　TRIMURTI, ELEPHANTA

264　INSCRIBED FIGURE OF BUDDHA, MONGHIR

figures "portrayed as silhouettes sharply detached from their background, " thus giving a rather crude idea of space and primitiveness in modelling or general composition. The railing of the famous temple at Buddha-Gaya, with its wealth of flower and animal decorations, lotus medallions, or upstanding figures in high relief, evidences again a distinctive advance in artistic technique in conception, design and execution. Even for the Bharhut reliefs, such a keen critic as Fergusson remarks:—

> "Some animals such as elephants, deer and monkeys are better represented there than in any sculpture known in any part of the world; so too are some trees * * * The human figures, too, though very different from our standard of beauty and grace, are truthful to nature, and, where grouped together, combine to express the action intended with singular felicity. For an honest purpose like pre-Raphaelite kind of art, there is probably nothing much better to be found elsewhere."[1]

Marshall, comparing the Bharhut sculptures with those of Buddha-Gaya, in favour of the latter, says:—

> "Taken as a whole, their style is considerably more developed than that of the Bharhut reliefs, and, at the same time, more pronouncedly affected by the influence of western art. Witness, for instance, in the matter of technical treatment, the freer movement of planes leading to more convincing spatial effect, the more organic modelling of the figures, the relative freedom of their pose and composition, and the effort to bring them into closer relationship one with the other; and witness, again, in the matter of *motifs*, centaurs, winged monsters, and tritons, the schematic treatment of the animal friezes, and the scene of Surya in his four-horse chariot copied directly from a Hellenistic prototype (Pl. XIX, 51)."

Let us here note the origin and form of the *Stupa.* Though now identified with Buddhist symbolism, the true origin of the Stupa is traced by the historians of Indian art to the exigencies of Vedic ritual. Perhaps it represented, in the millennia before the Buddha came, the funeral mound of the Vedic hero, even as it did in the Buddhist age. Perhaps it began as a special sacrificial pavilion of the Aryan chieftain, made of bamboo with its curved top, and rounded form. When the early Aryan king performed the sacrifices enjoined by the Vedas, he acted as the son of Surya, the Mithra or Sun-God. His tent or chariot, and later on his special hut or palace, where the sacrifice was performed, must necessarily have been kept apart from the "impure," and must have been marked by some symbol or emblem indicative of the purpose of the place and the rank of its occupant. The very name *Vimana,* given technically to the temple shrine, marks this ancient origin of the Indian temple. When the followers of the Buddha first adopted it as their symbol, the Stupa became the funeral monument *par excellence* of the princely sage and prophet. Havell would even urge that "the metaphor of the Eight-fold Path was borrowed from the processional path of the Aryan fortified settlement, which generally had eight gates " *(Handbook of Indian Art);* for " Buddha only changed

---

1) Fergusson. Vol. II. p. 36.

the Aryan concept of the law from a law of sacrifice to a law of spiritual evolution." (*Ibid.* p. 15.)[1]

All these features are evident in the Buddhist Stupas in the centuries that followed the adoption of that creed as the State Religion in India. Originally made in the Aryan days of wood or bambu, the royal craftsmen of Asoka and his successors soon began to make enduring structures of stone or brick, solid instead of hollow as they once were, and with a steadily increasing wealth of inside and outside decoration and inscription. The brilliantly polished surface served admirably to record in rock-cut letters the deeds of the heroes; while the elimination by Buddha of the distinction between the "pure" and the "impure,"—so essential to Vedic sacrifice,—opened a far wider field of choice for the craftsmen of the Buddhist princes. But even the Buddhist Stupa continued to carry that unfailing symbol of royalty,—the Umbrella; though in many of the monuments now surviving it is missing. The relic-casket, or *Harmika*, was also there serving as a pedestal; and one of these has now been found at Taxila almost intact.

The most glorious example of the Stupa now in existence is that at Sanchi in the Central Indian State of Bhopal. The gateways here are famous all over the world for their unparalleled marvels of story-telling in stone. The Stupa itself, as now seen, is 54 feet high without the railing and the umbrella at the top, and is in form an almost hemispherical dome reposing on a high plinth. Its four principal gateways, facing the four cardinal points, came successively in the following order; the Southern, the Northern, the Eastern and the Western, the order being evidenced by the styles of their carving. Each gateway is made up by two square pillars, with a cross beam of capitals supporting a superstructure of three architraves with voluté ends, ranged one above the other at intervals of slightly more than their own height. On the capitals are standing dwarfs or lions or elephants addorsed. Other figures of men and women and animals of all kinds occur between and above the architraves. The pillars and superstructures are richly ornamented by bas-reliefs, while surmounting and dominating all is the Sacred Wheel, flanked by attendants and *Trishula* emblems on either side.

It is impossible to give even a bare outline of this tremendous monument of Indian artistic history. Those who have seen it with the living eye will never find in the most glowing word-picture anything more than a tepid reflection. The single example of the *Chhandanta Jataka,* carved both on the Southern as well as the Western gateways, would suffice to show the vast scope of the Indian artist's work. The technique of the artist seems to have improved in the interval between the

---

1) Mr. A. K. Kumaraswamy thus sums up the form and purpose of the Stupa in his *History of Indian Art.* (p. 30.)

"A Stupa usually rests on a basement of one or more square terraces *(Medhi)*, or is at least surrounded by a paved square or circle for circumambulation, the terraces being approached by stairs *(Sopana)*; it consists of a solid dome *(anda or garbha)* with a triple circular base, and above the dome a cubical "Mansion" or "God's house" *(Harmika)*, from which rises a metal mast *(Yasti)*, the base of which penetrates far into the *anda;* and this mast bears a range of symbolical parasols *(chatra)*, and at the top a rain-vase *(Varshasthala,)* corresponding to the *Kalasha* of a Hindu shrine."

carving on these two gateways. Spatial effect, perspective, contrasts of light and shade are attempted with greater success in the later than in the earlier sculptures; but the earlier indicates a creative genius, whose flaws of technique in no way mar the pleasure at the sight of his work to a lay observer. Of only one figure,—that of the wood-nymph hanging from the boughs of a tree,—Havell says:

> "The robust young damsel with arms and legs over-weighted with ornaments, who appears on the Sanchi gateways as a wood-nymph hanging on to the boughs of a mango-tree, may seem less graceful and refined than the dryad of pure Greek art, though the primeval forest might know this rustic beauty better than the elegant town-bred maid of Athens * . * . * . But few artists would assert that the sculptor who created this vigorously drawn and admirably modelled figure had anything to learn from the academic technique of the Gandhara School." (*Ibid.* p. 36.)

The School of Sanchi sculptors was, as evidenced by their creations, in marked contrast with the latter day Indian workers. Their treatment is wholly secular. Though the theme is Buddhist, and the purpose to edify, the figures themselves are not religious. They are true to nature and sensuous, and have no affinity with the later creations of the Mahayana Buddhist under the Kushan Emperors and their successors. The High Priests of Buddhism raved against these creations as impious, for they had not yet come to regard art as a means to embody the spiritual ideas in concrete forms. "A theory of Beauty as perfect Experience (*Rasasvadana=Brahmasvadana*) had not yet been imagined," explains Kumaraswamy. Hence the Historian's conclusion that: "The Art of Sanchi is not, as art, created or inspired by Buddhism, but is early Indian art adapted to edifying ends, and therewith retaining its own intrinsic qualities."(Kumaraswamy, *History of Indian Art.* p. 36.)

The transition from the predominantly secular and sensuous, even if edifying, art of the Maurya days to the religious and idealistic creations of the Kushan and Gupta period must have been accomplished gradually. Perhaps the first sign of the change was the personification of the Blessed One in the concrete. While previously the artist had contented himself with indicating the Master's presence by unmistakable symbols, like the foot-steps of the Teacher, now the seated and standing Buddha, with the varying but well known poses stereotyped in the several definitely indicated *Mudras* of the canonists, begins to invite the chisel as well as the brush. It is impossible to say if the form and features now familiar to us in the innumerable *Chaityas* and *Viharas* of a thousand years represent faithfully the real Siddhartha as he lived and worked amongst his contemporaries. The Indian artist has, indeed, never followed a definite model; and so it is by no means unlikely that the Master, as we know him in innumerable cave-sculptures or paintings, was only the idealised,—and afterwards standardised,—vision of some gifted genius. It has been well observed:—

> "To the Greek, man, man's beauty, man's intellect were everything, and it was the apotheosis of this beauty and this intellect which still remained the key-note of Hellenistic art even in the Orient. But these ideals awakened no response in the Indian mind. The vision of the Indian was bounded by the immortal rather than the mortal, by the

infinite rather than finite. Where Greek thought was ethical, his was spiritual; where Greek was rational, his was emotional. And to these higher aspirations, these more spiritual instincts, he sought, at a later date, to give articulate expression by translating them into terms of form and colour." (*Cambridge History of India* p. 649. Sir J. Marshall.)

It is impossible to review the innumerable specimens of this period discovered in the region round about Peshawar. Taxila, the most famous Indian University even in the days long before Alexander of Macedon, had continued to be a favourite home of Indian culture, radiating its influence, its ideals, and its conventions of art and æsthetics to all corners of the Buddhist world, and so bringing about a similarity of type or standard, which is surprising in all its myriad manifestations all over Asia. If we are to judge from what has been called the greatest monument of the Emperor Kanishka's reign,—a magnificent Stupa of stone and wood in 18 stories, surmounted by an iron column of a total height of 638 feet, which claimed the unstinting wonder of the Chinese sage and traveller six hundred years later,— or from the relics stored in the Mathura Museum, the artistic activities of the period must have been immense. The chief characteristics of the Buddhas of this age still display the sculpture in round or high relief. But the conventions with regard to dress and pose and appearance, which were afterwards standardised, now manifest themselves as in the making.

"The head is shaven, never covered with curls; the *usnisa*, wherever preserved, is spiral; there is no moustache; the right hand is raised in *Abhaya Mudra*, the left is often clenched, and rests on the thigh in seated figures, or in standing figures supports the folds of the robe the elbow being always at some distance from the body; the breasts are curiously prominent, though the type is absolutely masculine, and the shoulders very broad; the robe leaves the right shoulder bare; the drapery moulds the flesh very closely, and is arranged in schematic folds; the seat is never a lotus, but always a lion throne (*Simhasana*), without miniature figures, there is often a seated lion between the feet; the gesture and features are expressive of enormous energy, rather than of repose or sweetness, nor is there any suggestion of intended grace. The nimbus is plain or scalloped at the edge in low relief."[1]

Contrast with this spiritual type, the magnificent martial statue of the great Emperor Kanishka. Headless as it is, the inscription on it makes the identity unmistakable. The impression of tremendous physical force is eloquent in the wide shoulders, deep chest, long arms, all encased in a stiff long *jama* clearly suggestive of the armour of the period. The great straight sword could have been wielded only by a man of gigantic stature and strength; while the full square stance, with feet encased in plate-armour shoes, shows an attitude of rock-like firmness, that is alone enough to convey the firmly established renown of the Emperor.

But the same artist who could create figures of such awesome martial grandeur could also make those fine, delicate, sylph-like forms of an utterly elusive charm that many have mistaken to be the Indian dancing girls; but which are, more accurately, the embodiments of wood-fairies or sylvan sprites, suggestive of vegetative fecundity in frank outline.

---

1) Kumaraswamy. op. cit. p. 57.

Before, however, we conclude this section, let us take note of a very strange criticism urged against Indian Art creations in some quarters. Says the late Mr. V. A. Smith, in his article on the subject in the *Imperial Gazetteer*, Vol. II:—

> "After 300 A. D. Indian sculpture, properly so called, hardly deserves to be reckoned as art. The figures both of men and animals became stiff and formal, and the idea of power is clumsily expressed by the multiplication of members. The many-headed, many-armed gods and goddesses, whose images crowd the walls and roofs of medieval temples, have no pretensions to beauty, and are frequently hideous and grotesque."

Because the shapes of these deities are unfamiliar to them, these historians and critics of the artistic products of India have been overwhelmed by their innate contempt for things with which their own imagination is unfamiliar; and so they are ready to condemn what they are unable to understand. But, as a matter of sober historical fact, many-armed and many-headed images,—or even those with peculiar shapes,—are by no means the exclusive creations of the Indian artist. In Greece as well as in Egypt such sculpture is by no means unknown. The critics, however, who are prone to condemn such unusual creations, are basing their criticism, unknown to themselves, perhaps, not so much on the true canons of art, but rather on their own personal prejudices. According to the immortal Leonardo da Vinci, "That figure is most worthy of praise, which by its action best expresses the passion that animates it." Judged in this light, the Indian figures of an elephant-headed Ganesha; or a four-armed Nataraja; or a ten-armed Mahisha-Mardini, are most expressive of the passion, the real sentiment that pervades and animates them; and the critic that does not perceive their beauty only exposes his own unfamiliarity with the canons of art and of artistic criticism. There is such a thing as synthetic— or explanatory—art, which may differ from purely representative art; but which is none the less deserving of the highest glories of artistic creation. The artist in India, it must further be remembered, did not evolve these images entirely from his own imagination. Advances in mythology, or elaboration of Puranic legends, were stereotyping the description of particular gods and goddesses, giving them a form and accompaniments,—e. g. the particular conveyance of each of the gods of the Trinity, and the symbol of their consorts,—which they were not at liberty to ignore. The problem before the artist, representing a legend,—like that of the Man-Lion *Avatar* of Krishna undertaken for the destruction of the demon Hiranya-Kashipu,—was rather to see that the peculiar shape of the principal figure required as per legend harmonised best with the balance of the sculpture as a whole. In these essential attributes of Unity and Vitality, which no true work of art should lack the Indian artist was at his highest from the days of the Guptas, if not earlier still, right down to the eclipse and neglect of the art of the sculptor beginning with the iconoclastic days of the Musalman emperors of Delhi.

From and after the days of the Guptas, however, the sculptural creations become more and more intertwined with the architectural. The two arts had, indeed, marched hand in hand from the earliest times; but it is under the Guptas that the image first becomes an integral part of the general architectural scheme. It is by no means unnecessary or superfluous in the centuries that followed. Its technique is steadily more perfected, and it becomes a veritable and accepted "medium of conscious and explicit statement of spiritual conceptions." (Kumaraswamy.) Along with painting, sculpture has still a thousand years of glorious history, till the iconoclastic Muhammadan came to banish it from the public buildings of the country, and often even to destroy it wantonly, its only resting place being the great public edifices of the country. As, however, architecture flourished as much under the Muhammadans as under the Hindus and the Buddhists, it would perhaps be as well to see the subsequent triumphs of that art in the architect's contribution of over two thousand years to the Splendour that was 'Ind.

CHAPTER VIII

TEMPLES AND TOMBS: PALACES AND PLEASANCES

In spite of the ravages of time, the extant architectural glories of ancient and medieval India make a most wondrous chapter in the *Splendour that was 'Ind*. Buddhists and Jains, Shaivites and Vaishnavites, have all contributed their marvels of temple-building, rich in mystic symbolism, amazing in the ever-growing wealth of ornamentation, perfect in plan, proportion and finish, the like of which few other countries in the world can show in a similar stretch of time. The artists and their patrons—both alike devotees—were ever anxious to build more firmly and finely the House of God than ever they thought of the homes of man. Hence it is that among the most ancient Hindu buildings, we seldom find a palace or a villa planned with care, decorated with enthusiasm, built with a view to last for ages. The Temples on the other hand, dedicated to each of the great cults, occupy the choicest beauty spots in cool, hilly retreats, well-wooded and well-watered, and exhibit the most lavish display of artistic creation. Secular building in the days before the Muslim invasion obtained attention only in so far as it had some connection with religious worship; and so the only mention we find of remarkable architecture in structures devoted to temporal uses is in the Universities,—Taxila for the country round Pushkalavaty, Nalanda for Magadha, Sanchi for Vidisha or Malwa, Ajunta for the lands below the Vindhyas,—which were universally revered as the haunts of the Goddess of Learning.

When the Muhammadan came upon the scene, the temple-glories began to wane. The Musalman had, indeed, his own religious architecture in the mosque; and though the early Muslim architecture in India was Hindu for all the purposes of the builder's art, he introduced in mosque-building a tone of severe simplicity free from ornamentation, which could not but make it an effective contrast with the Temples of later day Hindus. When the Musalman had learnt to temper his religious zeal with a perception of the beauty and goodness in art, he used it in his palaces and mausoleums, his gardens and pleasances, which are a unique contribution of this new line of rulers to the artistic glories of India.

To understand better the true meaning and real beauty of the design and finish of these several classes of the architectural monuments in India, let us first consider if there is any common origin and general purpose underlying them all. The only specimens of the ancient Indian builder's art that have come down to us are the rock-temples of the Buddhist worship,—save the recent discoveries in the Indus Valley near Mahenjo-Daro,—which take back the builder's art some three thousand years before Christ. The glories of the Imperial Palace at Pataliputra or Pushkalavati are unknown; the great halls of learning at Nalanda or Taxila, which for centuries upon centuries rang with the echo of holy communion and scholarly debate, are no more; even the garden of sacred Lumbini, where the Blessed One was born, is lost, its very site a problem for the groping archæologist. They were built in stone in remote mountains girded by forests, impenetrable except to the zeal of the devotee, to last for ages, even though the first Buddhist temples were built for three generations only. The earliest Aryan shrine, or sacred spot for holy sacrifice, was built of bambu, so admirably suited to give a curvilinear roof, and intended to serve the Aryan chieftain as his tent in peace, and his chariot in war. In one temple at least, that of Surya—the sun God—at Konarak, the wheels of the warrior's chariot are to be seen carved one side of the *Vimana* or Temple shrine. The insignia of the royalty presiding, and the emblem of the Divinity specially sacrificed to, soon came to be integrally embodied into the main structure of the temple. The *Shikhara*, the Hindu spire, the most distinctive feature of this class, emanated from the old bambu pole—or umbrella—which marked the first sacrificial hut of the early Vedic chieftain. The other symbols came gradually to be evolved and adopted as the mysteries of an elaborate cult began to develop. The treatment of the lotus and the *kalasha*—the water-pot—has its own mystic symbolic significance, thus summed up by Havell *(Indian Architecture)*.

> "The shining lotus flowers floating on the still dark surface of the lake, their manifold petals opening as the sun's rays touched them at break of day, and closing again at sunset, the roots hidden in the mud beneath, seemed perfect symbols of creation, of divine purity and beauty, of the cosmos evolved from the dark void of chaos and sustained in equilibrium by the cosmic ether, *Akasha*. Their colours red, white, and blue, were emblems of the Trimurti, the three aspects of the One: red for Brahma, the Creator; white for Shiva, the Divine spirit; and blue for Vishnu, the Preserver and Upholder of the Universe. The bell-shaped fruit was the mystic *Hiranyagarbha*, the womb of the Universe, holding the germ of the worlds innumerable still unborn. The Lotus was the seat and footstool of the gods, the symbol of the material Universe, and of the heavenly spheres above it. It was the symbol for all Hinduism, as the *mihrab* was for all Islam. Closely connected with the symbolism of the lotus was that of the water-pot,—the *Kalasha* or *Kumbha*,—which held the creative element or the nectar of immortality churned by gods and demons from the cosmic ocean."

Of the evolution of the Lotus as a universal mystic symbol, the same writer says, in his work on *Indian Sculpture and Painting:*—(p. 29.)

> "Perfect knowledge, or abstract thought, regarded as the male principle and imaged in Indian art in the figure of the Divine Yogi, though it contains within it the germ of all things, remains inert without the will and power to create, which imply a cosmic energy or *Shakti*. An equilateral triangle is the geometric symbol of the three co-ordinated cosmic powers:—Will *(Ichha)*, knowledge *(Jnana)*, and Action *(Kriya)*, or the three aspects of the One embodied in Divine form. When standing on its base the triangle symbolises the male principle; on its apex the female principle. The two triangles, intersecting each other, make the six-petalled lotus, symbol of the mystic Divine Embrace, which completed the first act of creation."

We have already noticed the origin of the Stupa, its form and purpose, its symbolism and ornamentation, as it came to be evolved under the fostering care of the great Buddhist Empire. It is the ancient funeral mound of an Aryan chieftain,

PLATE LXX

206 GENERAL VIEW OF THE CAVE TEMPLES
AJANTA
Photo: Indian State Railways

208 SARNATH STUPA

205 TAJ MAHAL, AGRA
Photo: Indian State Railways

207 ELLORA: VISHWAKARMA CAVE CHAITYA HALL
Photo: Archaeological Deptt. Hyderabad Dn.

PLATE LXXI
CHAITYA SPECIMENS

209   CHAITYA CAVE X
HORSE SHOE WINDOW, AJANTA

210   CHAITYA CAVE, BEDSA (BOMBAY)

211   CHAITYA CAVE, NASIK

212   CHAITYA CAVE, KARLI

preserving his ashes for sacrificial purposes. As the Buddha was a Sakya prince, his ashes were preserved in specially built Stupas, by 8 different Indo-Aryan tribes. Before the days of the Buddhist Emperors, no remains of these ancient graves are to be found, probably because the ancient Aryan stupas were temporary wooden buildings, the ancestral sacrifice being ordained to last only up to three generations. But the names given to the various parts of the Stupa are too clearly reminiscent of the Vedic sacrificial terminology for us to doubt for a moment the origin and ancient purpose of the Buddhist Stupa. The railing round the sacred relics was the *Vedika*, which signified in Vedic ritual the sacrificial ground generally; the cross-bar of the railing is styled *Shuchi*, suggesting the shoots of the sacred *Kusha* grass which lay strewn on the holy ground; the Pilgrims' Path round the altar was the *Medhi*, implying the ritual of the *Pradakshina* (circumambulation). The Buddha changed the Vedic injunction of sacrifices to the law of spiritual evolution via the *Karma-Marga* and the *Jnana-Marga*. So, when Asoka adopted Buddhism as the State Religion of his Empire, he had no difficulty in adopting and converting this Vedic practice and ideology to his own purpose. He alone is reputed to have built 80,000 stupas. Though the earliest Buddhists were inclined to be puritanically protestant so far as to banish from the Tabernacle the sculptor and the painter as worldly snares unbecoming to the devout, the later *Samgha* gradually permitted a varied and rich ornamentation of the Buddhist shrine.

Connected with the Stupa, was the Cathedral or *Chaitya* of the Buddhist, which, first began to afford scope to the most lavish display of the Indian architect's genius. The primitive Buddhist cathedral was built in the form of an apse, as the pilgrims followed the shape of the Stupa in their circumambulation. A double row of posts,— or pillars of stone in later creations,—divided the nave from the aisles, and supported a huge barrel-shaped roof. Three doors,—the central one facing the Stupa larger than the two on the sides,—admitted the throng of the devout to the body of the church. Over the main door was the famous horse-shoe window, from which shone the sun upon the ancient Vedic altar, The lay pilgrims entered the church through the smaller side-doorway on the left into the wing to follow the procession path, and left by the doorway on the right, the main entrance being reserved for the monks.

The Karle caves near Lonavla on the Western Ghauts contain perhaps as complete and beautiful a specimen as any in the rest of India. Dating as a primitive cave tabernacle from the days before Asoka, the structure is believed to have been completed by the first century B. C., though some ornaments of a later period are not excluded. The grand Assembly-Hall, compared by Fergusson to Norwich Cathedral, and described by him as "the finest of all," is the largest now known, and the one most complete in all details. Built at a time when this particular style of architecture was at the zenith of its purity, the cave is 124 ft. 3 in. from the entrance to the wall at the back of the Stupa, while in width it is 45 ft. 6 in. from aisle-wall to aisle-wall. The wings are only 10 ft. each, so that the nave is broad and majestic in proportion, supporting 15 octagonal pillars on either side.

"Each pillar has a tall base, an octagonal shaft, and richly ornamented capital, on the inner front of which kneel two elephants, each bearing two figures, generally a man and a woman, but sometimes two females, all very much better executed than such ornaments usually are; behind are horses and tigers, each bearing a single figure. The seven pillars behind the altar are plain octagonal piers, without either base or capital, and the four under the entrance gallery differ considerably from those at the sides. The sculptures on the capital supply the place usually occupied by frieze and cornice in Grecian architecture" (Fergusson. I. p. 145).

As the total height is only 45 ft. from floor to roof, the impression of the grandeur of the nave is very much deepened. A gigantic sun-window, rounding in sympathy with the vaulted roof, and filled in part "by a massive timber framework resembling the *torana* of a palace gateway," lights the nave. A spacious, lofty, ornamented porch in front of the *chaitya*-hall adds to the dignity of the edifice, and leads into the body of the church by the usual three doors. In front is a screen of two plain eight-sided pillars, supporting, once upon a time very probably, a music gallery, where in the words of the Monk-Emperor the noise of the Drum of Religion was to be heard instead of the Drum of War. Ahead of this screen is a lion column,—a plain shaft of sixteen facets,—with a capital crowned with four lions originally supporting in their turn the Wheel of the Law. A companion to this column must have stood on the opposite side in ancient times; but its place is now taken by a Hindu shrine of the Durga. The place of the altar is taken in this case by the *Dagaba* exactly under the semidome of the apse, a plain dome crowned by the reliquary and umbrella on a two-storeyed circular drum, carved in the upper margin with the usual rail ornaments. The surface is throughout brilliantly polished, as also the pillars.

What were these noble halls used for?

"The imagination" says Havell, "must fill in what is now wanting in this noble deserted assembly hall of the *Samgha*—the painted banners hung across the nave; the flickering light from the lamps reflected upon the glittering surface of the Stupa, and losing itself in the vaulted roof above ; the bowed figures of the yellow-robed monks, solemnly pacing round the relic shrine and chanting the sacred texts, or seated on the floor in meditation or grave debate; the pious laymen looking on from between the close-set pillars of the nave, and following the sacramental path along the outer ambulatory."

Close by the grand cathedral was constructed the Monastery, or *Vihara*, where the monks lived useful, pious lives. At Nasik, Kanheri and Ajunta, even as at Nalanda of yore, the monastic hall appears as an open centre-court, flanked by cubicles for the monks on three sides, with a growing number of pillars to support the roof. Cave No. 12 or No. 17 in the Ajunta group may be cited as a most wonderful example, the latter not only because of its typical construction and plan as a monastic habitation, but also because of the marvellous paintings on the walls and ceiling that lend a unique distinction and charm to these rock-temples.

There was, however, another type of more popular *Vihara*. The *Sangharama*— the monastery proper was, Fergusson suggests, of pyramidal shape. The great

PLATE LXXII

213. SCULPTURES FROM THE INTERIOR SCREEN AT THE BUDDHIST CAVE, KARLI

214. DAGHOBA AT CAVE XXVI AJANTA

PLATE LXXIII

215   CATHEDRAL CAVE, BADAMI
(Verandah of Cave III from the West End)

216   CATHEDRAL AT KANHERI (BOMBAY)
(Verandah, Left End)

(215—216 Photo: Archaeological Survey of India)

217   "VIHARA" INTERIOR
Castellated Pyramid, Railing, and "Chaitya" Arch Motives, Ajanta

Magadhian University and Monastery of Nalanda, dating certainly from the first century of the Christian era, and described in enthusiastic language by a foreign eye-witness in the seventeenth century, seems to have been in this form. Situated between two ancient capitals of the homeland of Buddhist empires, south-west of Patna and north of Rajagriha, it was surrounded by a high wall 1600 ft. lengthwise and 400 ft. breadthwise, containing eight separate courts within its fold. Outside the wall were a number of town-like *Viharas*. According to the Chinese pilgrim:

> "In the different courts, the houses of the monks were each four storeys in height. The pavilions had pillars ornamented with dragons, and had beams resplendent with all the colours of the rainbow—rafters richly carved, columns ornamented with jade, painted red and richly chiselled, and balustrades of carved open work. The lintels of the doors were decorated with elegance, and the roof covered with glazed tiles of brilliant colours, which multiplied themselves by reflection, and varied the effect at every moment in a thousand manners. The *Sangharamas* of India are counted by thousands, but there are none equal to this in majesty or richness, or the height of their construction." (Hiuen-Tsang quoted in Fergusson. p. 174.)

Well might the old Chinaman get enthusiastic over this famous centre of learning—the Cluny and Clairvaux of Indian Buddhism. Only Taxila could excel it in scenic grandeur, Benares of Hindu fame remaining for ever the incomparable in learning as in sanctity.

THE HINDU TEMPLE

If the Buddhist *Stupa, Chaitya* or *Vihara* is distinctly traceable to the needs and formulas of the ancient Vedic sacrifices, far more so must be regarded the exclusively Hindu Temples dedicated to Surya or Vishnu,—to Shiva the Great God, or the Lord of Death. The most peculiar feature of the temple architecture throughout India,—the curvilinear spire,—was considered to be indigenous in India by Fergusson. As to its origin, however, this great authority on Indian architecture is by no means clear.

> "Neither the pyramid nor the tumulus affords," he says, "any suggestion as to the origin of the form, nor the tower, either square or circular; nor does any form of civil or domestic architecture."

Prof. Macdonell is of the view that the *Shikhara* is a natural evolution of the Buddhist Stupa. Later critics of India's art treasures are inclined, however, to hold that the *Shikhara*, with all the symbolism of which it was the concrete and complex expression, was introduced in India by the Vedic Aryans. As it developed on the Indian soil, in the centuries after Buddhism had become an Established Church, it indicated clearly its origin from the primitive bamboo and thatch structure over the sacred place where the Aryan chieftain performed his daily sacrifice to the Sun-God. In a utilitarian sense, it was a kind of chimney over the temporary tabernacle of the Vedic cult to permit the smoke from the sacred fire to escape. The early Buddhists had, in their revolutionary zeal, no use for this already mystic structure of the ritualist Aryan. They reverenced the Blessed One as a great *Yogin*, the perfect *Sanyasin*, to whom the wordly symbols men set their hearts upon had no significance. The conception of the Buddha as a Messiah, as a spiritual Prince, was of later day creation, when the pristine simplicity of his preaching was elaborated by his *Mahayanist* followers. Hence emerges the idea of a *Bodhisatva*, a sort of celestial ruler, whose worship demands a more elaborate shrine. The curvilinear steeple or spire is thus added to the Mahayanist shrine to denote the heavenly crown, not unlike the high-peaked *Mukuta* of the Bodhisatva himself. The purer, or at least the more puritanical, Buddhists of the *Hinayana* school,—content to adore the Buddha as a Yogin, Sanyasin, or a Guru,—thenceforward adopted the simple, chaste Stupa house as their distinctive form of tabernacle.

To the Hindus, as their ancient cult began to revive under the imperial patronage of the Guptas, the spired shrine was no novelty. The symbolism of the nectar and lotus is with them an ancient heritage; and "the shrine crowned by the *Shikhara* and by Vishnu's lotus emblem was a symbol of the holy mountain Mandara, or the mystic Meru, round which the sun and the moon revolved." In the course of time the *Shikhhara* shrine came to be the place of worship reserved for the Sun-God or Vishnu. The *Amalaka*, the fruit of his blue-lotus, became the symbol of the world-ruler; and hence came to figure on the Imperial standards of Asoka. The Shaivites, on the other hand, adopted the dome as *their* peculiarity. The form of the *Shikhara*, however, lent itself easily to the structural and symbolic requirements of a Vaishnava Shrine. The God—as Upholder of the Universe—stood rigidly erect, personifying by his body the holy Mount Meru, round which the solar world revolved. His weapons are those of an Aryan Prince, his gems emblematic of the three stages in the daily life of the sun. The temple usually faced east, through which the morning sunbeams streamed to light up the image, even like the Goddess Lakshmi rising from the cosmic ocean to greet her Lord.

Two main forms of the *Shikhara* are now in evidence,—one may even say two main types of temples: One, mostly in the south, of the Dravidian style, consists of a square base ornamented externally with pilasters, and containing the real shrine holding the image. Over this rises the *Shikhara*, a pyramidal structure, divided into storeys, and crowned with a circular or octagonal dome. Perhaps the oldest, if not also the best, example of this style is the one at Mahabalipur, the Seven Pagodas, some 35 miles south of Madras. The Gopura, or a towered gateway opposite the shrine, becomes a regular feature of this type from the eleventh century.

The other, the Indo-Aryan style, found mostly north of the Vindhya, has a rectangular cell, containing the symbol or the image of the God, with a curvilinear *Shikhara* surmounted by vertical ribs, with often a porch in front of the gateway.

Of this kind of Temple architecture there are a number of remains, the oldest being that of Bodh Gaya, where Buddha first had enlightened, and where, therefore, Asoka built a commemorative shrine. The present shrine on this spot is a restoration of the Huvishka structures, while the original temple of Asoka represented the Mystic Tree, which in Asoka's time was taken to symbolise the Holy One. This is interesting, however, more for its historical associations than for

PLATE LXXV

AJANTA CAVES

HORSE SHOE WINDOW

"CHAITYA" FACADE

PLATE LXXV

MUKTESHWAR TEMPLE, BHUBHANESHWAR, ORISSA

221

KAILAS TEMPLE, GALLERY, SOUTH SIDE, ELLORA

THE GREAT TEMPLE, BUDDHA GAYA

220

the architectural or symbolic peculiarities. For this we must turn to the temple at Bhuvaneshwar, the capital of Kalinga, the modern Orissa. In other parts of India, where the unreasoning fury of moslem fanaticism raged unchecked, the great monuments of the classic age of temple-building—the Gupta Empire—have been wantonly destroyed, or unrecognisably converted. But in this far away corner of the country, locked in mountain fastnesses, a group of temples of varying dates still survives to hold up proudly the conspicuous Vaishnava emblem of the *Shikhara*. In the centre rises a mighty, lofty, curving mass, the *Shikhara* of the Linga Raj temple, towering to a height of 180 feet, a masterpiece of exquisite masonry, perfectly jointed without mortar or cement. " For purity of outline and dignity of its rich but unobtrusive decoration, as well as for its superb technique, the Linga-Raj *Shikhara* must rank as one of the greatest works of the Indian builder." (Havell p. 64.) The central fane dates, according to tradition, from the seventh century of the Christian era. A King of the ninth century of the Christian era, who, according to archæological research built the present Linga-Raj temple, enclosed within the royal spired fane a yet more ancient temple, where his predecessors had worshipped the Jain or Buddha emblem, or even the Shiva *Linga*.

To understand better the details or dimensions of the classic temples of India, let us here note certain peculiarities of Hindu rites of worship. These rites are essentially individual, not congregational. Hence in building temples, the architect, who was not infrequently a priest as well, had only to think of a main shrine, and a surrounding porch or courtyard of varying dimensions, chiefly meant for the chaplain in charge. When, however, a mighty cathedral was undertaken by royal orders on some specially sacred spot; and when the attraction to vast hordes of pilgrims was particularly likely to be heavy, the architect had also to add a verandah for the accommodation of these devotees. From time immemorial, again, the temple porch had served the Aryan philosopher as a lecture-hall. Hence in more ambitious structures, taken in hand by royal mandate or by wealthy communities, a series of vast assembly-halls were added to provide an ever-ready lecture-theatre, on which the master-builders were wont to lavish the choicest creations of their skill and imagination.

We cannot even glance at the most classic examples of these types, within the space at our command. One exception, however, must be permitted in favour of the marvel of marvels—the Kailasa temple at Ellora. In wealth of sculptured ornamentation and exuberant detail, others may be superior,—like the unfinished temple at Halebid, whose single band of frieze has a procession of 2000 elephants, no two of which are exactly alike in all details! In majesty of dimensions, in antiquity of associations, in the beauty of environment, others again may excel the wonder of Ellora. But, taken all in all, the enormous monolith of Kailasa, with its bewildering variety of carving, its majestic proportions and impressiveness, is unrivalled. The temple is dug, as it were, into a pit in the solid rock, with a floor area of 280 feet by 160 ft., and a depth of 106 feet at the inmost side, addorsed to the rock. In the centre stands the temple, its *Vimana* 96 ft. in height, preceded by a large square

39

porch supported on 16 magnificent columns of living granite. A detached porch in front accommodates a wonderfully modelled bull,—Nandi,—to represent Shiva, while in front of all is a huge *Gopuram* connected with the temple and the porch by a bridge. On each side of the detached porch stand gigantic trident-crowned flag staffs of solid stone, guarded by life-size elephants, perfect in contours and chiselling. A cloister runs round three sides of this vast structure, over which are halls of assembly and cells for individual priests. Over the central shrine rises an elaborately carved pyramidal spire, or *Shikhara,* distinctly of the Dravidian type.

This stupendous mass makes, in its entirety, a picture, which, once seen, can never be forgotten. It is supposed to have taken some 250 years to complete! It involved, during its construction, labour, whose single aspect,—cutting and removing 100,000 cubic yards of granite,—gives some idea of the mastery of the builder's and the sculptor's art embodied for ever in this shrine of shrines! Says Havell:—

> "The design of the Kailasa at Ellora remained, for all time, the perfect model of a *Shivalaya,*—the temple craftsman's vision of Shiva's wondrous palace in his Himalayan glacier, where in his Yogi's cell the Lord of the Universe, the great magician, controls the cosmic forces by the power of thought; the holy rivers, creating life in the world below, enshrined in His matted locks; Parvati, His other Self, the Universal Mother, watching by His side."

The peculiarly *Shaiva* shrine does not make its appearance till about the 7th or the 8th century of the Christian era; and even then and thereafter it is confined largely to the southern plateau. Northern India was Buddhist, almost wholly, since the Mauryan days, and remained loyal to its faith practically till the beginning of the Muslim invasion. Thereafter, the mild and merciful religion of the Sakya Prince was of little avail to a people, who for the next six centuries had to keep incessantly in arms against a relentless foe—enemy to all that they held in love, esteem and veneration. Perhaps, also the south was beginning to be resurgent, and paying off to the north its debt of civilisation in the latter's own coin, by the revival of the Hindu cult, and particularly Shiva worship. Hence the fierce warrior, Lord of Death and master of all carnal weapons,—who was also the Eternal Yogi in the snow-clad Kailasa,—became more and more popular with the Rajputs of northern India, as He already was with the resurgent Hinduism of the South.

If the Princes of the latter day Hindustan built any great *Shivalayas* in any of the several provinces they ruled, their remains are very scanty, probably because the destruction of the temple was enormous in the first centuries of Muslim invasion. The great shrine of Somanath,—the Lord of the Moon,—on the shores of the Arabian Ocean, was typical of the hundreds and thousands that the successors of Mahmud of Gazni so fanatically destroyed. The more discerning of them, or the more astute, converted the more ambitious fanes into their own cathedral mosques. We must, however, postpone consideration of these re-formed mosques until we come to the Muhammadan era. Here let us observe that the central emblem of Shiva-worship,—the *Linga* or *phallus*,—could be easily adapted out of the Buddhist

PLATE LXXVI

ELLORA CAVES

224   THE KAILAS TEMPLE, GENERAL VIEW, ELLORA

225   KAILAS TEMPLE, CENTRAL SHRINE AND LAMP-POST
(Photo: Archæological Dept., Hyderabad Dn.)

PLATE LXXVII

226   RUINS OF SOMNATH TEMPLE

227   CEILING OF JAIN TEMPLE, ABU

228   MOUNT ABU—JAIN TEMPLE
(Interior Carvings)

229   DILWARA TEMPLE, CARVED PI
(MOUNT ABU)

or Jain Stupa, and so link up the *Shivalaya*, historically as well as structurally and symbolically, with the ancient religions of India. In the temple dome or tower, the difference between the Hindu *Shivalaya* and the Buddhist *Stupa*, is: that while in the former the finial is the *Kalasha*, the jar of immortality, in the latter it is the reliquary, or the royal umbrella, of the Sakya Prince. A slight extension or structural modification of this *Kalasha* led to the mighty pyramidal domes of the great temples of southern India, the pyramid being taken by the Shaiva devout to symbolise Shiva's home in the eternal snows of Mount Kailasa. The Kailasa at Ellora, or the shrine at Tanjore, may be cited as perfect types of the Shivalaya, built as architectural units on a definite, preconceived plan.

In passing, it would be interesting to note here some of the established canons of the Hindu symbolic builders and scientific town-planners. In the ancient Indian town the King's Palace and the Council-hall stood at the centre, the intersection of the *Raja-marga* or King's Road, and *Vamana-marga*—People's path or South Street.

> "(The palace) was to be placed in the midst of the council buildings, to have sides of equal length, "be well adorned with spacious tanks, wells and water-pumps," and surrounded by fortified walls with four beautiful gates at the cardinal points. The dining-rooms, chapels, baths, kitchens and wash-houses were to be on the *eastern* side. Reception rooms and sleeping apartments, "those for drinking and weeping," servants' rooms, rooms for keeping and grinding corn, and latrines were to be on the *southern* side. The armoury, guard-house, gymnasium, store-room and study were to be on the *north*. The court house and record-room on the north, and the stables on the South." (Havell p. 97-8.)

The temple shrine is a replica in miniature of this ancient town-plan. The *Gopuras*, courtyards, assembly-halls of these mighty cathedrals of the south, represent the plan, in accordance with Shastric injunctions, of the bazaars and gardens, baths and the forum, of a great capital city in a vast empire.

The temple architecture was, indeed, affected by the revivals of Shankaracharya and Ramanuja, the last one's preachings being concretised by the so-called Chalukyan or the mixed style of some of the later Temples. In this style the *Shikhara* and the Stupa are combined in a common tower, built in the Dravidian style, and carved with the lotus-fruit cup distinctive of the pure *Shikhara*; while the tower as a whole is like the lotus with turned down petals. "It seems that the builders of the temple would make the temple stones declare that Shiva is Vishnu and Vishnu is Shiva" (Havell).

JAIN TEMPLES

Side by side with Buddhism in the North as well as the South; side by side with the Shaiva and Vaishnava revivals of later centuries, the Jains continued their peaceful existence, and made their quiet, unobtrusive contributions to the monumental history of ancient as well as modern India. The historian of Indian architecture is puzzled as to the early history of the Jain temples, their style and ornament.

"This style, always singularly chaste and elegant, was essentially Hindu, and was doubtless largely common to all Hindu sects in Western India; but in its evolution it became modified by Jain taste and requirements. And, the Brahmans in turn, through the influence of the workmen, gradually accepted most of the stylistic improvements of their rivals." Fergusson, Vol. II, p. 5.

The peculiarity of the Jain style of temple-building, and particularly of the Jain iconography, arises from the social position of the Jains as much as their religious tenets. Though the two doctrines,—Jain and Buddhist,—are philosophically closely similar, the former were rarely the favourites of the Buddhist Emperors of Northern India. In the South—the Deccan—they had a great influence in reclaiming the people; and, not unlikely, Jainism formed the State religion at the Cholan and Pandyan, the Pallava and Chalukyan courts of the Peninsula. With the revival of Hinduism, however, the Jains,—more abstemious, puritanical and peaceful than even the Buddhists, particularly of the Mahayana school,—lost countenance at court. The monuments, if any, of their previous prosperity were destroyed or converted to the creed and ritual of their more successful rivals; and in sheer response to their instinct of self-preservation, they sought increasingly to concentrate their holy shrines in remote hill fastnesses, or in those centres of civilisation, where their wealth and influence,—never altogether inconsiderable,— procured them a measure of immunity to pursue their own scheme of life. The surviving monuments, therefore, of the Jains are to be found on certain hills in Western and Eastern India, particularly sacred according to Jain tradition to one or the other of their *Tirthakaras*. These are veritable cities of Gods,—not in the sense of a single vast Dravidian temple, a number of enclosures,—but as containing a number of independent shrines devoted to a corresponding number of saints or godlike men. The Jain temple-building, moreover, differs from similar activity amongst the Buddhists and the Hindus, inasmuch as, while the more classic cathedrals of the latter are the creations of royal fervour and imperial munificence, the Jain temple is more often than not the outcome of an individual's religiosity, and correspondingly modest in dimensions. While both Hindus and Musalmans rarely touched a house of worship once discarded, the Jains, with their more limited resources, made restoration as highly meritorious an act as building a new temple. Restoration, however, may not infrequently mar an old temple's pristine purity of design or ornamentation. On the other hand, these same characteristics may also account for the fact that the Jain temples are more ornately finished, more exquisitely decorated, than the corresponding places of other religions.

A cognate reason why the Jain monuments now surviving are relatively so few may be found in the fact that in the earlier centuries the Buddhist and the Jain shrines had little to distinguish the one from the other. For the Jain *Tirthakara* is represented almost in the same style as the Buddha,—the same pose of cross-legged meditation, the same features instinct with infinite compassion, the same characteristics of curly hair, large eyes, long arms, and hands raised in *abhaya mudra*, that marked the sainted hero with both. Later, however, specific emblems,—

FAMOUS FORTRESS OF DAULATABAD

UDAIPUR: MARBLE GHAT, RAJNAGAR

UDAIPUR: ROYAL PALACE AND LAKE

FORT OF JHANSI
Photo: Johnston & Co., Lucknow

PLATE LXXVIII

230   GENERAL VIEW OF JAIN TEMPLES, PALITANA

231   CHITORGARH (TOWER OF VICTORY)
Details of Lower Portion

232   CHITORGARH, VIEW OF FORT WALLS AND PALACE
(From Martin Hurlimann's book "Picturesque India")

the birthmarks, if we may say so,—of the several *Tirthakaras* began to give a distinctive appearance to the Jain shrine. In the temple-plan itself, the distinctive Jain feature is the *Samosaran,* the seating space for the divine congregation that gathered to hear the Jina preach his Sermon of Pity, and Lesson of Love, among all living beings.

The Jains have their rock temples hewn out of mountain sides as much as the other Indian sects. At Udayagiri, Badami, Ellora they figure along with the Buddhist and the Hindu places of worship. In the capital cities, too, in the great cathedral mosques of Ajmer, Delhi, Kanauj, Dhar or Ahmadabad, the pre-mosque Jain temple is clearly noticeable. Of the hill-temples even now surviving, those of Girnar and Palitana in the ancient Saurashtra; of Mount Abu on the southern scarp of Rajputana; of Parashnath in Bengal, are the most famous. Space would not permit even a passing notice of all these last-named even. Suffice it to remark that they are all cities of Temples, founded at points whose importance may be gathered from the single instance of Girnar. Here on the living rock, Asoka has carved one of his Imperial edicts; here Rudradaman had *his* inscription carved four hundred years after Asoka, and boasting of his martial triumphs over Satkarni of the Deccan; here Skanda-Gupta, last of the great Guptas, had his inscription carved three centuries after the Kshatrapa King of the modern Kathiawad. We cannot, however, spare space to notice the marvels of Palitana or the treausures of Girnar, which, strange to say, seem to have escaped altogether the iconoclastic crusade from Mahmud of Ghazni to Alamgir of Delhi. But we must notice the marble miracles of Abu, which exemplify all that is richest and noblest in the Jain temple architecture.

The two more famous temples at Dilwara,—Abu,—date from about 1030 and 1230 A. C., and were built by the great Jain Ministers—or bankers—of the Solanki or Chalukya kings of Gujarat. The later fane,—Vastupala's Temple,—is considered by Fergusson to be unrivalled all through this land of patient, lavish, devotional labour "for minute delicacy of carving and beauty of detail". The earlier or Vimala Shah's Temple is one of the oldest known examples, and yet most perfect, of the Jain style. Built on a rectangular ground-plan, it is approached by a domed portico, leading into a square open hall supported on six columns, and containing ten elaborately carved elephant figures, perfect in every detail down to the tiny links in the chains round the feet of the majestic animal. In the floorway is an equestrian statue of the founder of a much later date, behind which is the usual *Samosaran* rising in three tiers. Right in front of the door is a cell containing the holy of holies, a seated cross-legged figure of the first *Tirthakara,* Adinath. The shrine is covered by a low pyramidal roof, which does duty for the usual *Shikhara.* A *Mandapa* or a closed assembly-hall, lies in front of the cell, and is covered by a dome resting on eight pillars. The portico has 48 pillars making a graceful, dazzling colonnade, which is repeated with smaller pillars—making new porticos—to the range of 52 cells, each with a cross-legged figure of its own.

Except the central shrine, the entire structure is marble. The adjoining temple of Vastupala, situated on the North-east of Vimala Shah's, is another oblong

40

measuring over all 175 ft. It is entered from a court on the South-west between it and the older structure, and has nearly the same features of a pillared porch, a procession of worshippers, a carved dome, a central shrine with a pyramidal *Shikhara*, as in the former. A pierced screen of open tracery, separating the corridor behind the shrine from the court, is its distinctive feature, as also the elaborately carved *Chaumukh*, with five processional elephants, lavishly carved and fully accoutred, on either side. The columns of the porch are somewhat taller and of eight different types; while the dome, slightly smaller than in the other temple, in no way yields in respect of its chaste carving and exquisite craftsmanship. Resting on the octagon formed by the massive architraves across the capitals of the pillars, it has, over the second row of ornaments, sixteen bracket pedestals to support beautifully modelled sylph-like statues of goddesses, *Vidya-Devis*, with a central pendant that knows no peer in the entire range of Indian architecture, Hindu or Muhammadan.

The temples make a veritable poem in marble. As Cousens observes:—

> "The amount of beautiful ornamental detail spread over these temples, in the minutely carved decoration of ceilings, pillars, doorways, panels and niches, is simply marvellous; the crisp, thin, translucent, shell-like treatment of the marble surpasses anything seen elsewhere, and some of the designs are dreams of beauty. The work is so delicate that ordinary chiselling would have been disastrous."

And Kumaraswamy adds:—

> "It will be understood, of course, that all the figured sculpture is necessarily in the same key, each individual figure being but a note in the whole scheme, not a profound invention to be separately studied. The same applies even to the images of the Jinas in this period; each is severely simple, but all are alike in representing nothing more than the skilled realisation of a fixed formula" (op. cit. 111-12).

SECULAR ARCHITECTURE OF ARYAN AND DRAVIDIAN INDIA

We have already made a reference to the principles of town-planning and palace-building in classic India. It is regrettable that no considerable examples of the civil and military architecture of ancient Indians now remain, visibly to testify to the splendour and security of their achievements. Asoka's lofty halls and terraced sky-scrapers, rivalling the glories of Susa and Ecbatana, are gone. Hastinapur, Dwarka and Ayodhya, Anhil Pattan or Kanauj, are but names, or sorry shadows of their pristine glories. It is only in the South that the creations of royal splendour even now survive in places from the days before the Musalman. A solitary specimen as it is of the military architecture of those times, Daulatabad vividly recalls, under its Persian name, the impregnable strength and massive grandeur of the ancient Hindu fort of Deogiri, which stood a siege in almost every generation from time immemorial. Placed by nature on a solitary rock, rising in sheer perpendicular a thousand feet over the surrounding plain, and girt by a deep broad moat, the fort has a series of thick concentric ramparts, pierced with heavily piked and plated gateways, that could easily defy the onrush of the most powerful rams or the most

PLATE LXXX

FORT OF GWALIOR

GENERAL VIEW OF BHARATPUR

PLATE LXXXI

239   BHARATPUR FORT

240   RUINS OF COUNCIL HALL AT VIJAYANAGAR   241 THE ARHAI-DIN-KA-JHONPRA, AJM

maddened, goaded elephants. Within, the fort has a tortuous, under-ground, secret, Stairway, leading to the highest point on the rock, on which is perched a Muhammadan palace several centuries old. Magazines and mosques, storehouses and courtyards, minars and even prisons, occur at various stages in the ascent, each recalling perhaps an entire century. With the exception of the classic Rajput capital of Mewar, Chitor; and with the possible exception of Kalanjar, and Ranthambhor, there is hardly a fort of pre-Muslim days in India which could tell so many tales of heroism in long sieges, or of wonderful strategy, bravery and generalship among the besiegers, not to mention the tales of romance inseparable from every such place all over the world.

Of civil architecture proper, the only remains from ancient India are in the south. The golden palace of Vijayanagar is in ruins, its very outline a matter of conjecture. But the palace at Madura has its great range of state apartments round a courtyard 160 feet in length and 100 ft. in breadth, surrounded on all sides by arcades with the pointed arch of the Moorish style. The pillars supporting the arches are of stone 40 ft. in height, with a cornice and entablature that add another 20 ft. to the height. They "are joined by foliated brick arcades of great elegance of design." A Celestial Pavilion stands on the west, 235 ft. by 105 ft., now serving as a High Court of Justice. There are three domes, the central one rising to a height of 75 ft. from the floor, supported by 12 columns enclosing a square 64 ft. in length and breadth.

Other specimens from Tanjore or Chandragiri are of much later date. The pure Indo-Dravidian scheme of palace-architecture is noticeable only in the ruins of Imperial Vijaynagar, though even that was built after the Muhammadan impact had been felt in the south. The Muslim monuments are as rich in secular majesty as in religious solemnity; and so we shall now turn to the Muhammadan period in the North as well as the South.

MUHAMMADAN ARCHITECTURE IN INDIA

Authorities on Indian architectural monuments seem to have generally assumed that with the advent of the Musalman in India there commences a wholly new style,—or several new styles,—of building in this country. As a matter of fact, there are several good reasons why it could not be so. For one thing, the Hindus of the days when the Pathans and the Turks first began to make their inroads were far more advanced in these arts of peace than the very fountain-head of all Islamic culture had ever been. Arab civilisation was a marvel of its kind; and it was to the Arab heritage on which all Islamic peoples looked for inspiration and model. But, at its very best, Arab civilisation was, particularly in regard to these arts of peace, imitative rather than creative. It had borrowed sometimes from Greece; more often from India; and though the assimilation may have been so thoroughly complete that at times it may be impossible to distinguish the borrowed elements apart, comparative scrutiny and chronological co-relation cannot but reveal the fact of the borrowing. The best of the Arabs were, indeed, themselves aware of the immense superiority of Indian cultural and artistic achievements over their own. Al Beruni, the famous philosopher and contemporary of Mahmud of Ghazni, familiar with the splendours of Baghdad at its best, was amazed at the excellence of Indian architectural monuments. "Our people", he says "when they see them wonder at them, and are unable to describe them, much less construct anything like them." Even the iconoclastic fanatic, Mahmud of Ghazni himself, could not restrain his wonder at the triumphs of Indian art he discovered at Mathura. Farishta records a letter of the raider to his lieutenant at Ghazni, in which he says:—

> "There are here a thousand edifices as firm as the faith of the faithful; nor is it likely that this city has attained its present condition but at the expense of many millions of dinars, nor could such another be constructed under a period of two centuries"

The first Musalman conquerors, in India just as much as in Persia and the provinces of the Eastern Roman Empire, adapted to their own use the structures of the conquered. The continuation of the tradition thus involved led easily to the perpetuation of all the builder's conventions,—himself a fresh convert, if not a persisting alien in faith,—in the architecture that came into vogue after the Muslims had been established in the countries of their conquest. Those peculiar features, indeed, which did not square with the fanatic prejudices of the new faith, were removed. Iconographic ornamentation, or sculptured splendours of the converted Hindu temples, were thus excluded from the mosque, architecturally designed on the same principles as the temple it had replaced. But in the spirit and the essence, in conception and design, the building remained the same, even if it came to be called by another name.

There is, indeed, nothing surprising in this consummation. The Muslims who came with the conquerors were soldiers, not artists. When, therefore, they had to plan works of art, like a Jami Masjid or Cathedral Mosque, they had of necessity to employ the local artists; and the latter unavoidably took as their model the achievements they were themselves most familiar with. Besides, in the countries across the north-western frontiers of India, from which the first Muslim invaders came, Buddhist or Hindu influence had penetrated long ages before, thanks to the missionary zeal of the Buddhists. Now these people, accustomed for centuries to those conventions of building which had satisfied their urge for a thousand years, could not discard their cultural skin merely because they had adopted a new creed. Hence we find the conquerors themselves imperceptibly adopting the Indian rules and conventions of building, in their most solemn and stately structures of public worship or royal habitation. Even those features of the Muhammadan monuments of architecture in India, which have been considered to be peculiarly Saracenic, seem to be, when closely studied, Indian—Hindu—in origin, conception, and execution. The ornamentation by arabesques was no doubt a Muslim contribution in public buildings, as also the intricate geometric patterns, or the ogee curve. But the pointed or trefoiled arch, and the ribbed or spherical dome,—commonly considered to be distinctive features in Muslim architecture,—were in reality of Indian—Hindu—origin.

PLATE LXXXII

24   COLONNADE OF HINDU PILLARS NEAR Q'UTB MINAR, DELHI

24   THE PILLAR OF ASOKA, FIROZABAD, DELHI

PLATE LXXXIII

244   A STREET SCENE IN JAIPUR
showing the Palace of Winds and the Great Square

245   MOSQUE IN THE PRECINCTS OF THE MAUSOLEUM OF SHAH ALAM, AHMEDABAD

The pointed arch, was originally the temple niche of the Buddhists and Hindus. The sculptured figures of religious significance were removed by the Muslim iconoclastic; and the niche, bare and simple, came to serve as the *Mihrab* in the converted or the new mosque. The foliated arch was, even more than the pointed, peculiarly associated with the Buddhist sacred architecture, since the trefoil was a plastic representation of the *aureole* that was supposed to hang round a semi-divine personage. In its simplest form the *aura* was shown by a lotus-leaf carving, itself saturated with symbolic associations even before the advent of the Buddhists; and the outer curve of the lotus-leaf had only to be drawn to indicate the shape of the pipal leaf, under which the Buddha became enlightened.

According to Havell:—

> "The trefoil arch was a compound aureole, or nimbus, made up of a combination of the lotus and pipal or banyan leaf. * * * * * The pipal leaf stood for the glory round the head of the Buddha, while the lotus leaf remained as before to indicate the shape of the aura which surrounded the body. The intersection of the two formed the trefoil arch. A very common variety of this was made by the *chakra*, or Wheel of the Law, which was also the emblem of the sun-gods,—Vishnu, Surya and Mitra—taking place of the pipal leaf, making the crown of the arch round instead of pointed." (p. 85.)

The dome, that other supposed peculiarity of the Muhammadan architecture, was also known and used in Indian building long before Islam was born in India, and with a wealth of ornamentation abhorrent to the followers of the Prophet of Arabia. The Stupa was the origin of all such rounded construction; and this, and the different forms of the temple *Shikhara*, exemplify to the highest the excellence achieved by Indian builders in this department. The cannonical works of Indian master-builders also gave the fullest possible directions for the construction and symbolism of domical buildings. When the Stupa was a solid hemispherical mass, the technique of dome construction could not be noticed; but when images came to be placed under the head of the Stupa, the dome had to be raised high and supported on columns, giving ocular evidence of the art and craft of the Indian builder. The principles of dome construction being familiar to the Hindus in the so-called ribbed or bulbous dome or the bell-shaped dome, the mosque or tomb only modified or adapted them when Islam ruled India. While the finial of the pure Arab dome in Egypt or elsewhere is a mere spike, that of the Indian Musalman's dome was the ancient Hindu and Buddhist symbolism of the *Kalasha*, or water-jar, and the *amalaka*, or the lotus-flower. Only, in the dome the lotus is found twice over, once with open petals at the base of the dome where it springs from the columns, and again with the petals hanging down from the top.

But while all these most prominent characteristics of Muhammadan architecture in India were Hindu or Buddhist in origin, the simplicity,—almost the severity,— they acquired in the Muslim buildings was as peculiarly of Islamic inspiration. In the mosque as well as the tomb, the builder in India had necessarily to discard those established conventions, which made clear the nature and purpose of the Hindu builder's handiwork at first sight. He need no longer remember in the shaping of the pillars that a square shaft would mean Brahma worship, an octagonal that of Vishnu, a sixteen-sided one, Shiva. Nor was it any use to pay special heed to the planning of the gateways. God is one and only one, said the Prophet of Arabia; and provided the faithful turned, in India, to the West, at the time of the prayers, the mosque architect had nothing more to worry about in regard to the symbollic significance of the general plan of the structure.

The architectural monuments of the Musalman rule in India are too many, and too widely scattered to be mentioned in detail in these pages devoted to the *Splendour That Was 'Ind*, in every department of civilised life. Let us rather take one specimen of each class or period :—a mosque in the north and the south, in the east and the west; a mausoleum in each of these; a palace and pleasance; a fortress or city, saturated with the Islamic spirit,—and we shall have had a fair glimpse of these architectural splendours.

*

The oldest Mosque in India, Qutbuddin's Mosque, was originally a Jain temple, which the first Turkish conquerors of Delhi converted to their own use. The mosque itself was 135 feet in length and 32 ft. deep; but with its grand colonnaded courtyards it makes a far more imposing figure even in its ruins. The main gateway is on the east under a small dome some 20 feet in diameter, with a corridor of 4 rows of pillars running all along the eastern side, terminating on the northern and southern sides into storeyed pavilions. The west side of the court is occupied by a screen 8 ft. thick, with magnificent arches leading into the mosque itself. The screen was really the only Muhammadan contribution to the ancient Jain temple and its colonnaded courts. Built or converted into a mosque first about 1196 A. C., it was extended considerably by the third Slave Emperor, particularly the screen, which was lengthened by 119 ft. with five arched gateways in each section. Very little of these extensions remain. Alauddin Khilji made still further extensions, making the entire court 385 ft. from east to west, with the great Alai Darwaza as a kind of terminus or entrance. He also planned doubling the old court on the north, and another Minar to be a fellow to the Qutb; but death deprived him of his intended additions. While, thus, the sides and the court and entrances were Musalman, the pillars were ancient Jain, as also the roof, domes, and other inner ornamentation, where they did not offend the zeal of the true believer. A still greater glory is in the series of magnificent arches on the screen wall on the west, which were indisputably of Muhammadan addition, though the builders were Hindus.

As a kind of pendant to this ancient monument now in ruins, let us also mention the peerless shaft of red sandstone and marble, known as the Qutb Minar. It is in a far better state than the old mosque, at the south-east corner of which it stands. Over 240 ft. in height, it is a cylindrical structure. The flutes,—24 in number in the lower storey,—are alternately angular and circular, in the second only circular; in the third only angular. Arabic inscriptions from the Muslim Holy Writ,—the names of the

PLATE LXXXIV

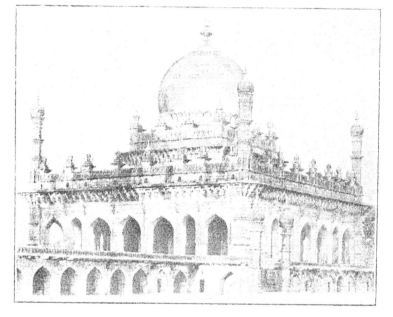

16   CHITORGARH
(Tower of Victory, Chitor)

17   Q'UTB MINAR
(Photo, Indian State Railways)

18   IBRAHIM RAUZA, BIJAPUR

19   GOL GUMBAZ, BIJAPUR

PLATE LXXXV

JUMMA MASJID, AHMEDABAD

251

TOMB OF SHER SHAH, SASARAM

250

Almighty as well as the titles of the Emperor,—are its only ornament. It is the "most beautiful example of its class in the world," says Fergusson, though he is not unaware of the famous Hindu Towers of Victory, which were lineally descended from the Asokan pillars of a thousand and more years before. The Chitor Tower of Victory was built by Maharana Kumbha of Mewar, and is a nine-storey structure 122 ft. in height. It is about 250 years later than the Delhi Minar; but its ornamentation cannot but claim to rival the splendour of the Minar.

At the foot of the Taragadh Hill, Ajmer, is another ancient mosque,—popularly known as the two-and-a-half-days' cottage. The columns and the roof are here, as in the Imperial Mosque at Delhi, of Hindu or Jain build; but the basic plan and the general scheme has been altered by the Muslims, and the screen of seven arches is a contribution from the same source. It is differentiated from the Delhi mosque, probably, by the addition of the minarets,—themselves, apparently, an after-thought,—which, in the centuries to come, were to form such distinctive features in mosque-building and mausoleums.

The Jami Masjid of Jaunpur dates from the middle of the fifteenth century. Based on a plinth raised some 20 ft. from the ground level, the structure is practically a square (214⅓ ft. by 211½ ft.) courtyard, with the mosque building proper on its western side. The main entrance is a pyramidal gateway rising to some 86 ft. in height, supplying the place of a minar. The centre of the mosque building is covered by a dome nearly 40 ft. in diameter; and on each side of the dome are two-storeyed colonnaded compartments, beyond which are other compartments, crowned by a vaulted roof. The Atala Masjid in the same place, with its fivefold colonnades and flat, slabbed roof, is far more ornate than the Jami Masjid, though the latter is one of the grandest ruins of that extinct race of rulers in the eastern provinces.

In Gujarat on the west, conquered by the Musalmans early in the fourteenth century, the bulk of the people, their religion and culture never admitted the domination of the foreigner. The Ahmad Shahi rulers, beginning as independent sovereigns in 1396, were a race of renegade Rajputs, who were themselves too saturated with the ideals and conventions of the people they sprang from to depart from them in their public buildings or monumental achievements. The old capital of the Solankis and Vaghelas at Anhilwar, with all its magnificence of the Sahasraling Temple and the Siddha Sagar Tank, ramparts and palaces, is too utterly in ruins to demand a special mention of its ancient splendours. The memories, however, stored up in this city, adorned and exalted by centuries of Hindu rulers, were perhaps too great and living a reproach to these renegades. Hence they took their capital to a place without memory or associations, the old Karnavati, renamed the modern Ahmadabad. But even here the spirit and heritage of their origin clung to them. Their new creations were for all essential purposes Hindu in conception, design, decoration, and finish. The Jumma Masjid of Ahmadabad "is one of the most beautiful mosques in the east". Laid out on very nearly the same lines as a great Jain temple building contemporaneously at Ranpur in the Mewar dominion, the mosque proper covers an area 210 ft. by 95, though the total dimensions of the edifice including the courtyard are 382 by 258 feet. Within the mosque, a veritable forest of pillars, 260 in number, support fifteen domes, of which the three in the middle are much larger and higher than their fellows. The Ranpur temple is more delicate and graceful than its contemporary mosque, and therefore more pleasing in its effect. But for the domes, the mosque would be monotonous, even though its mass of pillars is of the same model and ornamentation as the Hindu scheme. The light and graceful minarets, which once crowned the sides of the mosque, have been destroyed by an earthquake of about a hundred years ago. But the pillars,—the chief glory of the building,—remain. Those supporting the main dome are twice as high as those on which the side domes rest, while two rows of smaller columns on the roof make up for the height. Inside is a solid balustrade exquisitely carved, over which comes the light and air for the worshippers within. "The sun's rays can never fall on the floor, or even so low as the head of any one standing there. The light is reflected from the external roof into the dome, and perfect ventilation is obtained, with the most pleasing effect of illumination without glare."

The wealth of Gujarat in the Muslim era is fully evidenced, not only in these sacred edifices, but also in the group of royal pavilions, tombs and gardens at Sarkhej, five miles from the city. The pavilion stands on a raised platform with sixteen square pillars—not arched—supporting a roof of nine small domes. The mosque is "the perfection of elegant simplicity", with five small domes in a line. The side niches are used by the mosque architects for an exhibition of the most delicate carving, in which, as years went by, the Muslim artist attained to a perfection that can safely challenge comparison with the best of that kind from any age or in any country in the world.

We may mention here, in passing, the so-called step-wells,—deep, long, staired, and adorned reservoirs of water, fed by underground springs, which also abound in this part of the country. These wells either served royal or noble orchards, or even common agricultural purposes. The Asarwa well near Ahmadabad is the most magnificent example of its kind, built by a Hindu lady in the time of Mahmud Shah (1501).

"A fine domed pavilion covers the approach to the shaft of the reservoir, the descent to which is made by flights of steps, $18\frac{1}{2}$ ft. in width, connected with a series of pillared platforms, the roofs of which serve to strengthen the stone-faced sides of the excavation. The central shaft of the reservoir, which is 24 ft. square, has two spiral staircases on the sides of it, to make access easier. Here there are four tiers of pillared galleries supporting the sides of the shaft, and providing cool resting places for the people using the well * * * . To the Indian craftsman the construction of a well was as much a religious work as the building of a mosque or temple. What a treasure-house of fine culture for the people who come daily to draw water from this well! What profanity and impertinence for Europeans to transport their modern secular vulgarity to India, under the pretence of teaching principles of design to a school of craftsmanship inheriting such traditions"! (Havell's *Indian Architecture*, p. 148-9 Edn. 2.)

PLATE LXXXVI

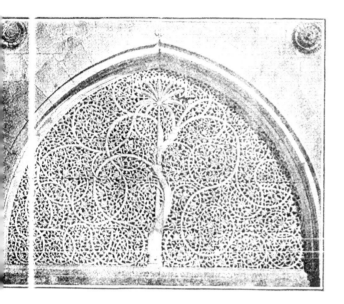

PERFORATED STONE WINDOW
Sidi Sayid Mosque, Ahmedabad

255 STEP-WELL, AHMEDABAD
(From Havell, "Indian Architecture")

256 THE JUMMA MASJID, DELHI
(255—257 Photo: Indian State Railways)

257 SHAH JEHAN'S MOSQUE, AGRA FORT

PLATE LXXXVII

TOMB OF HUMAYUN, DELHI

250

INTERIOR OF PEARL MOSQUE, AGRA

258

The Moti Masjid at Agra, built by that king of builders, the magnificent, splendour-loving Emperor Shah Jahan, may be taken as the last and the finest,—the culminating example of Muhammadan architecture in India. The Cathedral Mosque of Delhi, with its tall, slender minarets visible from a great distance, and pleasing from outside beyond compare with any other similar structure, is an edifice on a more imperial scale. But the perfection of architectural art is much greater in the smaller Agra specimen. Built between 1646 and 1653, it occupies an area, over all of 234 feet by 187. Entering from the eastern gateway, we see in the courtyard of dazzling white marble a black-marble inscription inlaid in the freeze of the mosque itself. On three sides is a low colonnade, and on the fourth—the west—the mosque proper 159 by 56 feet. Seven arches of surpassing beauty debouch the mosque on to the court, while three domes of the Taj style crown it in indescribable splendour. Fergusson knows of no building "so perfectly pure or elegant" anywhere in the world.

TOMBS

In the tombs and mausoleums the same peculiarities of style and construction are evident in the different provinces, and in the successive centuries, of Muhammadan India, except that the tomb architecture is more simple, chaste, and severe than that of the mosque or the palace.

The finest example of tomb-building, before the lavish outburst of Mughal æstheticism, is to be found in the South, and notably in Bijapur. The Gujarat tombs,—at Ahmadabad and Sarkhej,—are distinctly of Hindu conception, though the Musalman ideal of utter simplicity obtains in these structures more than anywhere else perhaps. In Bijapur, however, during the last hundred years of the kingdom before its merger in the Moghul Empire, public buildings were created

> "as remarkable as those of any of the Muhammadan capitals of India, hardly excepting even Agra and Delhi, and showing a wonderful originality of design not surpassed by those of such capitals as Jaunpur or Ahmadabad, though differing from those in a most marked degree." (Fergusson p. 269.)

The Jami Masjid of Ali Adil Shah,—not quite completed even after a century of building,—is amongst the finest dozen mosques in India, notable for its wonderful domes. But the splendour and majesty of this great Shia cathedral pale before the architectural masterpiece of the tomb of Muhammad Shah. The Rauza of Ibrahim Shah, blessed with a long and prosperous reign, is built on a small scale, but so enriched with the carvings of texts from the Holy Writ that tradition holds the whole Quran is carved into the walls of this mausoleum. The aggrandisement of the tomb by a mosque followed as a matter of course, while its embellishment with fountains and kiosks inside and colonnades and caravanserais outside are among the ordinary features of Muslim buildings of this kind. The wonderful contrast afforded by the tomb of Muhammad Shah is noted in the world of architecture by a number of peculiarities. Its dome, until recently, was the second largest in the world; while the principles of the engineering science involve veritable feats of architecture, which by themselves would suffice to earn for Indian builders immortality. We cannot improve upon Fergusson in the description of this triumph of architectural design and finish. Says he:—

> "As will be seen from the plan, it is internally a square apartment, 135 ft. 5 in. each way; its area consequently is 18,337 sq. ft., while that of the Pantheon at Rome is, within the walls, only 15,833 sq. ft.; and even taking into account all the recesses in the walls of both buildings, this is still the larger of the two." *   *   *   *   *

> "At a height of 57 ft. from the floor line, the hall begins to contract, by a series of pendentives as ingenious as they are beautiful, to a circular opening 97 ft. in diameter. On the platform of these pendentives, at a height of 109 ft. 6 in., the dome is erected 124 ft. 5 in. in diameter, thus leaving a gallery more than 12 ft. wide all round the interior. Internally, the dome is 178 ft. above the floor, and externally 198 ft. from the outside platform; its thickness at the springing is about 10 feet, and at the crown 9 feet."

> "The most ingenious and novel part of this dome is the mode in which the lateral or outward thrust is counteracted. This was accomplished by forming the pendentives so that they not only cut off the angles, but that, as shown in the plan, their arches intersect each other, and form a very considerable mass of masonry perfectly stable in itself; and by its weight acting inwards, counteracting any thrust that can possibly be brought to bear upon it by the pressure of the dome. If the whole edifice, thus balanced, has any tendency to move, it is to fall inwards, which from its circular form is impossible; while the action of the weight of the pendentives being in the opposite direction to that of the dome, it acts like a tie, and keeps the whole in equilibrium, without interfering at all with the outline of the dome. *   *   *   *   *   *

> "The external ordinance of this building is as beautiful as that of the interior. At each angle stands an octagonal tower eight storeys high, simple and bold in its proportions and crowned by a dome of great elegance. The lower part of the building is plain and solid, pierced only with such openings as are requisite to admit light and air; at the height of 83 ft. a cornice projects to the extent of 12 ft. from the wall, or nearly twice as much as the boldest European architect ever attempted. Above this an open gallery gives lightness and finish to the whole, each face being further relieved by two small minarets."

Bijapur, at the height of its glory, was a veritable city of palaces; and its builders carried out the same ideas of daring construction in the civil buildings as they had done in the more sacred structures. The Audience Hall of 1561, with its magnificent arch; the Asar Mahal and the *Sat Manzila*, not to mention the palaces of courtiers and nobles, must have given the city, in their prime, an imposing appearance that might well rival the glories of any other capital in India.

The tomb of Sher Shah at Sahsaram in Bengal is one of the last and the finest examples of the earlier type of buildings of this kind. Situated on a platform about 30 feet high and 300 feet square, the tomb, in the middle of a large tank, makes a most picturesque appearance. Rising on an octagonal base, with 36 ft. on each side, the main apartment is surrounded by a gallery of 10 ft. 2 in. in width, and crowned by a vast dome, the second largest in India, 71 ft. in diameter, and purely Hindu in style. Right underneath the dome is the sanctuary of the great warrior and general, who had matched himself successfully with the rising might of the Mughals. Round this central pavilion, the terrace is ornamented in each angle by smaller octagonal

PLATE LXXXVIII

THE TOMB OF EMPEROR JEHANGIR, NEAR LAHORE

THE TAJ MAHAL, AGRA

(The Tomb of Mumtaz Mahal, wife of the Emperor Shah Jehan)

PLATE LXXXIX

264   GATEWAY OF THE TAJ MAHAL, AGRA
A magnificent structure of red sandstone inlaid with marble

265   MARBLE SCREEN IN THE TAJ MAHAL, AGRA
(Photo: Indian State Railways)

pavilions in perfect harmony with the central majesty; while between them are little bracketed kiosks pleasantly filling up the outline. Similar kiosks cluster round the central dome itself, and round the drum from which it springs, relieving "the monotony of the composition without detracting from its solidity or apparent solemnity". "The stateliest of funeral monuments," as Havell calls it, this tomb reveals the character of the man whose last resting place it is,—solid, solemn, severe.

*　　　*　　　　*　　　*

By this time the accessories of a funeral edifice had become standardised. Situated almost always in the centre of a walled garden, often with a magnificent gateway, the sanctuary building proper was a square or octagonal structure, in which the dead grandee and his family or friends rested. Lilies bloomed on the sheet of water running at right angles to the sarcophagus on either side, and roses on the banks; while breezes from tall cypresses were supposed to fan the dead while they awaited the call of the Last Trumpet. Once used as a place of interment, sounds of revelry cease to echo through its vaulted roof for evermore; and one after another the mortal remains of those intended by the founder to rest there are brought and interred around him. Perfect silence reigns in this house of Death; and, coupled with the quiet beauty of the place, it makes a most solemn and yet graceful symbol of life and death.

*　　　*　　　　*　　　*

The tomb of Humayun,—the first of the Imperial Mughals to be buried in India,—was commenced by his wife and completed by his renowned son. Standing, like his rival's mausoleum, on a large terrace, with arching piers inlaid with marble, it is an octagonal apartment crowned by a graceful dome of dazzling white marble. On four of the eight sides are gateways, while the other four are occupied by smaller octagonal apartments, richly marbled, and projecting from the facades of the central bays on each face. The tombs of the Haji Begum and nine other relatives take up the corner rooms. Lacking in any profuse ornamentation of the kind that made the Mughal buildings of the next century famous all over the world, the mausoleum of Humayun is remarkable for the exceeding purity and simplicity of its design, the main plan of which was afterwards followed in the Taj.

The other buildings of Akbar either at Agra or at Fatehpur-Sikri we have no space to describe. His Red Palace of Agra Fort, now called Jahangiri Mahal; the Diwan-i-khas in the Mahal-i-khas of Fatehpur-Sikri, with a throne in the shape of a flower supported on a single richly carved pillar; his Record Room and Assembly Hall; his magnificent Mosque with its classic *Buland Durwaza* in the fullest bloom of the ancient Hindu style, 130 ft. by 88 ft., its appearance "noble beyond that of any portal attached to any mosque in India, perhaps in the whole world"; his hall of forty pillars in the palace at Allahabad; above all, his tomb at Sikandra, "quite unlike any other tomb built in India either before or since," and built exclusively on a Hindu or Buddhist design in pyramidal structure, richly ornamented with kiosks, arches, mosaics,—these, and a whole host of other minor buildings in all parts of the vast Empire, write Akbar's romance in stone and marble unforgettable for all time.

Jahangir suffers, like Humayun, on account of coming between a great father and a great son. The architectural monuments of his reign, in comparison to those of his father and his son, are very few, unless we reckon the wonderful mausoleum at Sikandra, and the Royal Palace at Agra called after him, to be among his creations. The magnificent mausoleum of Itimad-ud-Daula,—the Prime Minister and Chief Noble of Jahangir's court,—erected by his daughter the Empress Nur Jahan,—is in white marble, in two storeys, in a square walled garden 540 ft. on each side. The tomb proper is on a raised platform 60 ft. square, with an octagonal tower or minar at each angle, crowned by an open pavilion,—all in dazzling white marble, but for which the structure would probably not evoke the enthusiasm it now does.

It was thus left to Shah Jahan to rival the achievements of his grandfather in the domain of public architecture. By his time the canons of architecture in public buildings were gradually altering. As bamboo had yielded to brick, and brick to stone, so stone was now yielding place to the rich marble peculiar to north India. The severe chastity of the early Muhammadan buildings had already yielded before the quiet persistence of their Hindu or converted craftsmen, long before the Mughals came on the scene. Subtle ornamentation in pillar and cornice, in arch and dome and ceiling, was gradually altering the style and appearance of Muhammadan buildings in the north and the south. This ornamentation came side by side with the arabesque carving which the first Musalmans had themselves introduced; and it was followed by inlay work, to be succeeded in its turn, or improved upon, by mosaics. Shah Jahan's buildings represent the zenith of this style. They lack the warrior vigour of the earlier structures even to the day of his grandfather; but they introduce an element of loveliness,—a sensuousness,—which is all their own. This is why historians of Indian architecture are inclined to describe his works as of the lyric age of Indian architecture, while those of his grandfather and predecessor those of an epic style.

Let us take the Taj Mahal—the supreme example of this new style in architecture, *chef d'ocuvre* of Shah Jahan. A veritable poem in marble, Havel calls it the Venus de Milo of India—an apotheosis of Indian womanhood. Stripped however, of all the hallowed, romantic associations clinging to this lovely monument of an Emperor to the Queen of his heart and the crown of his harem, the Taj still remains a peerless beauty in form and finish. To those who have not seen that masterpiece of Mughal building, it is impossible to convey in words,—mere words,—any idea of its surpassing loveliness, in all the delicacy of its creation, in all the complexity of its design. But to those who have seen it in all its unspeakable charm, clad in the soft moonlight of some autumnal evening, the following attempt at a verbal picture will not be quite in vain.

The Taj stands on a terrace 18 feet high, and 313 ft. square, entirely faced with marble. The corners are all adorned with slender marble minars, 133 ft. in height cast in the most exquisite proportions in perfect harmony with the main structure. Right in the middle of the platform is the mausoleum—a square of 18 ft. with th

BULAND DARWAZA, FATEHPUR SIKRI
Gateway of Victory

CARVED PILLARS IN PANCH MAHAL, FATEHPUR SIKRI

ET-MUD-DAULA'S TOMB, AGRA

PANCH MAHAL, FATEHPUR SIKRI

PLATE XCI

270   LOTUS SHAPED THRONE PILLAR
(FATEHPUR SIKRI)

271   HIRAN MINAR (ELEPHANT TOWER)
FATEHPUR SIKRI

272   OLD PALACE, DATIA

273   CARVINGS IN LOKENDRANATH PALACE, DATIA

(Photo: Indian State Railways)

angles cut away 33 ft. 9 in., and the facade rising 92 ft. 3 in. from the platform. The central apartment is crowned by a fine dome, 58 feet in diameter and 74 feet above the roof, or 191 ft. from the platform. Under the dome, a beautiful screen of matchless trellis-work of white marble,—itself a masterpiece of elegance,—makes the sacred enclosure, in which lie the tombs of Arjumand Bano Begam in the centre, and of the Emperor on one side,—the bodies of this pair of princely lovers lying in a vault exactly underneath the ornamental tombs.

In each corner of this main building is a small domed apartment of two storeys, $26\frac{2}{3}$ ft. in diameter, connected one with the other by several halls and passages. The main apartment is lighted by a double screen of white marble trellis-work, superbly carved, one on the outer and one on the inner side of the wall. The soft shaded light reaching through this screen is in tune with the solemn atmosphere of the place.

> "This building, too, is an exquisite example of that system of inlaying with precious stones, which became the great characteristic of the style of the Mughals after the death of Akbar. All the spandrils of the Taj, all the angles and more important architectural details, are heightened by being inlaid with precious stones, such as agates, blood-stones, jaspers, and the like. These are combined in wreaths, scrolls, and frets, as exquisite in design as beautiful in colour; and, relieved by the pure white marble in which they are inlaid, they form the most beautiful and precious style of ornament ever adopted in architecture."

Fergusson, however, questions if the author of this unrivalled monument or his children realised the full beauty of the long rows of cypresses lining the marble pathways of the vast garden, and of the canals studded with marble fountains running alongside? Shah Jahan is said to have died, gazing to the very last upon that beloved place, housing a yet more beloved form, whose place remained for ever vacant for over thirty years even in an oriental harem. Could this have been without the author and worshipper at this Shrine of Love having realised to the full the charm of his devoted creation?

The style of this exquisite monument of matrimonial felicity has also been criticised as being too feminine. To them Havell's reply is sufficient.

> "Those critics who have objected to the effeminacy of the architecture unconsciously pay the highest tribute to the genius of the builders. The Taj was meant to be feminine. The whole conception and every line and detail of it express the intention of the designers. It is Mumtaz Mahal herself, radiant in her youthful beauty, who still lingers on the banks of the shining Jumna, at early morn, in the glowing midday sun, or in the silver moonlight. Or rather, we should say, it conveys a more abstract thought: it is India's noble tribute to the grace of Indian womanhood,—the Venus de Milo of the East."

Needless to add that the Taj is entirely Indian in conception and execution, from the platform to the dome, with its lotus crown.

* * * * * *

Shah Jahan's palaces exhibit the same tendency to extreme ornamentation, which merits more fully the charge of effeminacy, than the structure of the Taj. The need for strength and security against battering rams and charging elephants no longer dictated the architecture of the Mughal palace from his time; and so we do not find at Delhi or Agra or Lahore the mighty pile, the fortress palace, which still abounded and even now endure in the capitals of Rajputana. The fortress palace at Jodhpur of the fifteenth or sixteenth century is in marked contrast, even in that historic home of Indian chivalry, with the lovely grace and sensuous charm of the lake palace at Udaypur. The battled might of Bikaner dates in its castellated strength from a yet earlier age. The palace of Bir Sing Deo of Dattia, Jahangir's associate or instrument in the murder of his father's trusted minister, is the best specimen of Hindu architecture in the Mughal days. A massive granite pile, some 300 ft. square, and raised on a vaulted basement 40 ft. high, the palace is built in four storeys, the two lower ones of which run round an inner court of royal dimensions. The private apartments of the prince are in the centre,—four-storeys 140 ft. high,— standing in the midst of the council halls, Durbar Hall, offices and apartments for the retinue, the public reception rooms, corresponding to the *Diwan-i-Am*, and the *Diwan-i-Khas* of the Muhammadan palaces, are in the two lower storeys of the main building; while the larger apartments in the upper storeys, placed at the corners and in the middle of each side of the main quadrangle, are crowned with domes, and supported by four kiosks with cupolas in the usual Hindu symbolic style.

*　　　*　　　*　　　*　　　*　　　*

But, of course, the habitations of these minor princes could not compare in splendour and magnificence to those of the Emperor of all India. The Palaces at Delhi and at Agra, enlarged and embellished by three generations of the most wealthy and powerful emperors, were in their day the most magnificent palaces in the East, if not in the world. Both these palaces stand on the banks of the Jumna. Let us take the more classic pile of Delhi. It makes a more or less regular parallelogram, 1600 ft. by 3200 ft. A high battlemented wall of red sandstone girds it, broken by kiosk-crowned bastions at regular intervals. A noble gateway deeply recessed; a vaulted hall-way 375 ft. long, and two storeys in height;—make a most imposing portal to the imperial abode. The hall-way opens into a court 350 feet square. From the centre of it run, on either side, a noble bazaar,—a kind of Rue Royale and Bond Street combined in Delhi; while at the palace-end of the court was the celebrated *naubat-khana*, where, at stated hours, the mighty kettle-drums,—those jealously guarded emblems of Mughal royalty,—proclaimed the presence and the various activities of the Prince, the change of his Rajput guard, and other such incidents of the palace day. Beyond the *naubat-khana* is the inner court of the palace, a noble rectangle of 500 ft. by 385, in the centre of which stood the court-room, the *Diwan-i-Am* or the Audience Hall for the people, 200 ft. long by 100 broad, with noble rows of richly jewelled pillars supporting a magnificent ceiling. The hall had in the centre a lavishly decorated niche with a marble platform inlaid with precious stones, on which stood once the peerless Peacock-Throne. The beauty and splendour of that magnificent seat have been described in awe-struck tones by European travellers of the age, whose estimates vary in particulars, but

PLATE XCII

254 THE INTERIOR OF DIWAN-I-KHAS OR HALL OF PRIVATE AUDIENCE IN THE FORT, DELHI

255 THE LAHORE GATE OF THE FORT, DELHI

PLATE XCIII

276   SHAH JEHAN'S SERAGLIO, DELHI

277   DIWAN-I-AM, DELHI

(Photo: Indian State Railways)

278   SHAH JEHAN'S PAVILIONS, AJMER

agree in the general statement that it cost a vast amount of treasure running into tens of crores. Says Tavernier :—

> " The principal throne, which is placed in the hall of the first court, is nearly of the form and size of our campbeds; that is to say, it is about 6 feet long and 4 wide. Upon the four feet, which are very massive, and from 20 to 25 inches high, are fixed the four bars, which support the base of the throne; and upon these bars are ranged twelve columns, which sustain the canopy on three sides, there not being any on that which faces the court. Both the feet and the bars, which are more than 18 inches long, are covered with gold inlaid and enriched with numerous diamonds, rubies, and emeralds. In the middle of each bar there is a large balass (balet in origin) ruby, but *en cabuchon*, with four emeralds round it, which form a square cross. Next in succession, from one side to the other along the length of the bars, there are similar crosses, arranged so that in one the ruby is in the middle of four emeralds, and in another the emerald is in the middle and four balass rubies surround it. The emeralds are table-cut, and the intervals between the rubies and emeralds are covered with diamonds, the largest of which do not exceed 10 to 12 carats in weight, all being showy stones, but very flat. There are also in some parts pearls set in gold, and upon one of the longer sides of these there are 4 steps to ascend it. Of cushions or pillows which are upon the throne, that which is placed behind the King's back is large and round like one of our bolsters, and the two others that are placed at his sides are flat. There is to be seen, moreover, a sword suspended from this throne, a mace, a round shield, a bow and quiver with arrows; and all these weapons, as also the cushions and steps, both of this throne and the other six, are covered over with stones which match those with which each of the thrones is respectively enriched.

> The underside of the canopy is covered with diamonds and pearls, with a fringe of pearls all round, and above the canopy, which is quadrangular-shaped dome, there is to be seen a peacock with elevated tail made of blue sapphires and other coloured stones, the body being of gold inlaid with precious stones, having a large ruby in front of the breast, from whence hangs a pear-shaped pearl of 50 carats or thereabouts, and of a somewhat yellow water. On both sides of the peacock there is a large bouquet of the same height as the bird, and consisting of many kinds of flowers made of gold inlaid with precious stones. On the side of the throne which is opposite the court, there is to be seen a jewel consisting of a diamond of from 80 to 90 carats weight, with rubies and emeralds round it, and when the King is seated he has this jewel in full view. But that which in my opinion is the most costly thing about this magnificent throne is, that the twelve columns supporting the canopy are surrounded with beautiful rows of pearls, which are round and of fine water, and weigh from 6 to 10 carats each. At 4 feet distance from the throne there are fixed, on either side, two umbrellas, the sticks of which for 7 or 8 feet in height are covered with diamonds, rubies and pearls. The umbrellas are of red velvet, and are embroidered and fringed all round with pearls."

Behind the throne-room or Audience Hall in the Delhi palace of Shah Jahan was a garden court and the famous *Rang-Mahal*, recreation chambers for His Majesty, containing the most wonderful baths built in marble and adorned with precious stones, and fed by a canal brought direct from the Jumna. It may be of interest to note that the gorgeous marble bath of the Agra palace was torn up by the Marquis of Hastings who intended to present it to the prince of dandies, George IV; while the remains of the bath and marble flooring were torn up by Lord William Bentinck, and sold by auction, fetching probably 1 per cent of their original cost, but sufficient "to eke out the revenues of India in a manner most congenial to the spirit of its governors" (Fergusson. Vol. II. p. 398, note).

The range of buildings sketched so far ran right through the palace grounds, almost completely bisecting them. To the north of these was a series of small courts, in one of which was the still more famous *Diwan-i-Khas*, the Hall of Private Audience, "the most highly ornamented of Shah Jahan's buildings". Its Agra compeer may be more elegant; but the lavish inlay of precious stones in its walls and columns and ceilings make it a unique specimen of its kind, well worth the boastful inscription in Persian on the walls, saying: *Agar Firdaus Baru-e-Zamin ast, To Hamin ast! Hamin ast! Hamin ast?* "If there is a heaven on earth, it is here, it is here, it is here." In this was also that famous window,—*Zarokha-e-Darshan*,—from which the Emperor gave a sight of his person to his devoted, worshipping subjects. Below in the vast space stood ever ready pairs of fighting elephants for the delectation, whenever it suited him, of the Prince and his chosen courtiers.

On the south and east beyond the Bazaar were the Zenana apartments, with courts and gardens, fountains and kiosks, and all that art could devise and wealth could demand. Not a vestige of these now remains, and so we have no means of saying what they looked like in their prime.

The Agra palace,—enlarged or embellished in his own peculiar style by Shah Jahan,—was a fellow in all material particulars to that of Delhi. Volumes upon volumes might be written upon the still extant remains of these noble structures, looted and ravished by an unsympathetic soldiery of all nations. The Marathas and the Jats, the Sikhs and the English, have all had their share in the loot in the decadent days of the later Mughals, not to mention, of course, the savage hordes of a Nadir Shah or an Ahmad Shah. The notes to Fergusson's laborious tomes in this department are poignant with specific mentions of this cruel vandalism, which may be read and verified by those who feel incredulous when such stories are retailed to them.

Bootless, however, to bewail these wrongs of a departed past and a vanished glory. The garden palaces of the Mughals still endure in Kabul and Lahore, as in Kashmir and Agra, in wonderful preservation in some cases, giving a glimpse of the gay life and luxurious living in the days when the name of India was synonymous with wealth and splendour. The poetic soul of Babur ever delighted in gardens, and one of the gravest faults, in his eyes, of the land of his conquest was the lack of running water. His *Bagh-e-Wafa*, or the Nishat Bagh, or the Shalimar Bagh, are, however, careful creations of a most exacting and exquisite taste, a most luxurious and refined standard of life. A view of the garden palace at Deeg,—an edifice of the eighteenth century,—when the Jats of Bharatpur were rapidly fattening themselves upon the spoils of the Mughuls, or the leavings of the Marathas,— would perhaps supply a living example of those fairy creations of the pleasure-loving Mughals.

*   *   *   *   *

The foregoing is the barest of all brief sketches. The achievements of the Indian architect, even in the ruins, are too numerous, too varied, too scattered, to be done justice to in such a superficial survey. Volumes could be written upon the artistic achievements of almost each style, each province, each capital, if not each structure like the Taj, or the Domes of Bijapur. We are here attempting only a sketch of the Splendour That Was 'Ind; and so it is not too much to hope that these stray specimens will suffice to give some slight idea of that splendour, which, to be fully appreciated, must demand a veritable pilgrimage to these empty and deserted, or neglected, shrines of the past.

CHAPTER IX

INDUSTRY AND COMMERCE

Whenever it comes to be properly studied and written, the history of the trade of India will prove as fascinating as it is bound to be an instructive chapter in the annals of mankind. Popular tradition in India carries the story of Indian commerce right back into the earliest dawn of human history; and there are passages which amply support such a tradition. The economic phenomenon of exchange as such may be taken to be coeval with civilisation; and, in India, it may be antedated even the advent of the Aryans. The dispute, if any, concerns the origin of the overseas trade. The compilers of the *Cambridge History of India* seem to be strangely oblivious of the significance of these passages, when they say of the Vedic Age:—

> "But there is still no hint of sea-borne commerce, or of more than river navigation."

They had, indeed, no knowledge of the recent discoveries in the Indus Valley, which seem to carry further back the history of Indian civilisation of a commercial kind 3000 years. But even without the knowledge of those discoveries, the story of the sea-borne commerce can be carried far, far back into the dawn of history. Without having recourse to the specific mentions in the Vedas of sea-going vessels, we may point out that the list of occupations given on the very page from which the above remark is quoted evidences the possibility of sea-borne commerce of India, since a good many of these crafts were destined to meet the needs principally of foreign commerce. Says Prof. Keith in the *Cambridge History of India* Ch. V.:—

> "We hear of hunters, of several classes of fishermen, of attendants on cattle, of fire rangers, of ploughers, of charioteers, of several classes of attendants, of makers of jewels, basket-makers, washermen, rope-makers, dyers, chariot-makers, barbers, weavers, slaughterers, workers in gold, cooks, sellers of dried fish, makers of bows, gatherers of wood, door-keepers, smelters, footmen, messengers, carvers and seasoners of food, potters, smiths and so forth. Professional acrobats are recorded and players on drums and flutes. Besides the *boatman* appear the *oarsman* and the *poleman*."

From the earliest available records of Indian foreign trade, the most frequently occurring articles of Indian export are cloth, dyes, precious stones, and metal-work and a list of occupations,—which includes jewel makers, dyers, weavers, smelters and smiths,—can never yield the conclusion that "there is still no hint of sea-borne commerce." The evolution of the boatman may have been occasioned by the needs of riverfishing. But if the oarsman and the polesman, taken along with the wood-gatherer and the boatman, are viewed in the proper perspective with the naval regulations of the Mauryan period, the existence of foreign sea-borne commerce even in the Vedic period of over 3000 or 4000 years ago, does not seem to be impossible.

In an interesting and erudite contribution to the *Journal* of the Royal Asiatic Society, on the " Early Commerce of Babylon with India," Mr. J. Kennedy, I. C. S. argued that the sea-borne trade of India with the Western Asiatic countries did not begin till about 700 B.C.; and so we may justly infer him to imply, in the above passage, that the transfrontier land-trade of India must have started much earlier. We have little data so far of the Dravidian commerce; but it certainly must have been much earlier still, if the recent finds at Mahenjo Daro are any guide at all.

Mr. Kennedy, as already remarked, has advanced the thesis that, at any rate, the trade of India with the countries beyond the Western Seas did not commence before 700 B. C. Even admitting that statement for the sake of argument for the moment, there is no need to conclude that the entire sea-borne trade of India is of no greater antiquity. It is a common place of Indian history that the Aryan invaders, coming into the Punjab through the snow-clad passes of the Hindu Kush, spread principally in a south-easterly direction along the plains watered by the Ganges. The natural course of their further progress would take them, by land or by sea, eastwards; and there is nothing in our still surviving records to gainsay the possibility of a good seaward trade on the eastern side. The trade with the Suvarna Bhumi, the Golden Chersonese of the classical writers, and thence to Java, Sumatra, China and Japan, would be possible by the purely Aryan agency, along and perhaps contemporaneously with, the Dravidian trade with countries across the Western seas.

Speaking of the Dravids, Mr. Kennedy is himself obliged to observe:—

> " But the Dravidians of Southern India were accustomed to the sea, and afterwards furnished a large proportion of the ships and sailors, not to say pirates, on the Indian Ocean. So that, although the coastline was long, perilous and uninviting, there is no obvious physical or ethnological reason why an early intercourse by sea should not have existed between India and the West. I can only say, that as a matter of fact, there is no valid proof of it." (J. R. A. S.—1897 pp. 241-288.)

But he is unjust in his assumptions, and unfair in his criticism of the available evidence. The story of the *Baveru Jataka* Mr. Kennedy regards as referring to a much later date, about the 5th century B. C.; and, as such, this distinct mention of trade with Babylon (Baveru) he considers as not disproving his main thesis. But the misfortune of an inexact or unavailable chronology of Indian peoples is pressed by him too far, when he tries to explain away the Biblical references to trade with India, and the Egyptian evidence for the same in periods much anterior to his assumed date. There are passages in the Bible distinctly referring to the Indo-Babylonian trade in the Mosaic period (1491-1450 B. C.), and much more frequently in the age of Solomon (1015 B. C.). The Hebrew words for cloth, ivory, apes, ginger, pepper, rice, peacock, sandalwood,—all products exclusively of India,—are distinctly of Tamil origin. Says Bishop Caldwell in his classic work, *A Comparative Grammar of the Dravidian Languages*:—

> " It seems probable that Aryan merchants from the mouth of the Indus must have accompanied the Phœnicians and Solomon's servants in their voyages down the Malabar

coast towards Ophir (wherever Ophir may have been), or at least have taken part in the trade. It appears certain from notices contained in the Vedas that the Aryans of the age of Solomon practised foreign trade in ocean going vessels."

*   *   *   *   *   *

"The Egyptians," says Lassen, "dyed cloth with indigo, and wrapped their mummies in Indian muslin."

Indigo is undisputably an Indian monopoly exported as a dye-stuff; and its presence in these early Egyptian tombs is conclusive of a much earlier origin of the foreign sea-borne trade of India than Mr. Kennedy allows.

If the fact of the trade between India and her neighbours across the sea on the West could be established as having commenced over at least 3 thousand years ago, the next question as to its organisation, and the relative share of the different maritime nations on the coasts of the Arabian Sea, would be of second rate importance. It is assumed that for a long time before the 9th century B. C., the Phœnicians were the sole masters of the eastern sea, and its only navigators. But even if it be granted for the sake of argument that the trade, if opened in times before the days of Darius, was conducted largely by the Phœnicians or their successors in the mastery of the Indo-African seas, it does not necessarily involve the corollary that Indians had no share in it; that they were content to remain merely passive importers or exporters, without being active carriers, at least in part, themselves. The folklore of India, as typified by stories like the *Baveru Jataka* or that of Bhujjyu in the Vedas, is definitely against such a conclusion. Common sense is also against it. For though the classical European writers like Herodotus or Strabo or Pliny believed, on the authority of the obscure compiler of the *Periplus* or *Navigation of the Erythrian Seas*, that the secret of the Monsoon,—the real trade-winds of the Indo-African seas,—was discovered by a pilot named Hippalus, about 47 A. D., it is impossible to believe that those who carried on this trade centuries before could have remained ignorant of such a regular, annual phenomenon as the south-west monsoon in the Indian Seas, and could thus have failed to make use of it. There is, in fact, positive evidence to show that Indian mariners, Tamils as well as Aryans, were familiar with this great annual natural phenomenon. Doctor Vincent holds, in his edition of the *Periplus*, that there was communication between India and Arabia before the days of Alexander; and it is impossible to believe that two such peoples, as the Indians and the Arabs, had to wait for centuries till a stranger should come and teach them the most obvious mystery of the seasonal changes in their own sea.

In McCrindle's translation of classical writers' notices on India, he reproduces a passage from Pliny which reads:—

"The same Nepos, when speaking of the northern circumnavigation, related that to Mettellus Coler, the colleague of Afrinius in consulship, but then a pro-consul of Gaul, a present was given by the king of the Suevi consisting of some Indians who, *sailing from India for the purpose of commerce, had been driven by storms into Germany.*"

And the following gloss upon this passage by the editor renders it still more interesting and significant:—

"Murphy, the translator of Tacitus, in one of his notes to Agricola, remarks thus upon the passage. 'The work of Cornelius Nepos has not come down to us; and Pliny, it seems,

SILVER AND COPPER SMITHS AT WORK
HAMMERING OUT SHAPES

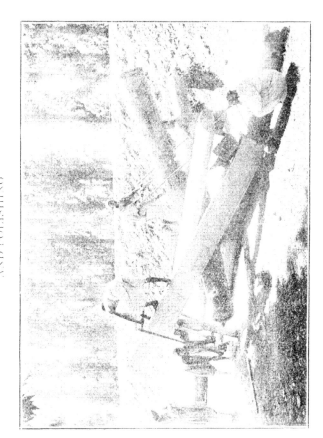

CARPET WEAVERS

SILVER AND COPPER SMITHS — CHASING, GILDING
AND POLISHING

WOOD SAWING IN INDIA

PLATE XCV

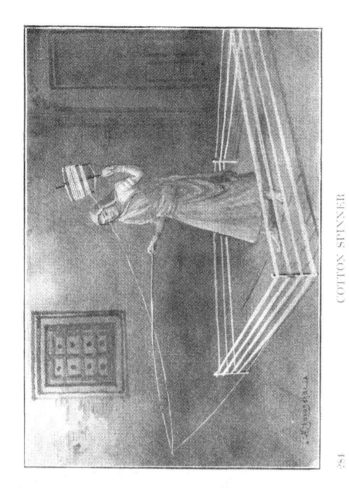

COTTON SPINNER

SHAWL EMBROIDERERS

has abridged too much. The whole tract would have furnished a considerable history for navigation. At present we are left to conjecture whether the Indian adventurers sailed round the Cape of Good Hope, through the Atlantic Ocean, and thence into the Northern Seas, or whether they made a voyage still more extraordinary, by passing the islands of Japan, the coast of Siberia, Kamaschatka, Zembla in the frozen ocean, and thence round Lapland and Norway, entered into the German Ocean.''

Without advancing, from such evidence, the perfectly agreeable hypothesis that the circumnavigation of the world was first accomplished by Indian navigators, including the discovery of the North Pole, we may at least hold that such a race of hardy sea-farers and adventurers could not have remained quite inactive in the foreign sea-borne trade of their own country.

CHARACTER OF THE ANCIENT INDIAN FOREIGN TRADE

Given, then, the fact that the phenomenon of international exchange had been familiar and practised by ancient Indians from times that certainly go back 3000 years,—the next point of some interest in this study is to inquire into the character and organisation of this trade of ancient India.

At the threshold of this inquiry we find that the main articles of trade are nearly the same as they are to-day, and have been for all these centuries. Speaking of this trade, Mr. Daniell, I. C. S., in his work on the *Industrial Competition of Asia*, has well observed that it consisted of an

> "Exchange of such of her productions as among the Indians were superfluities, but at the same time not only prized by the nations of Western Asia, Egypt and Europe, but were obtainable from no other quarter except India, or from the farther East by means of the Indian Trade."

It was thus a trade according to the true economic principle, *i. e.* in surplus of production or specialities. Speaking of Buddhist Indian trade, the *Cambridge History of Ancient India* observes (p. 213):—

> "The nature of the exports and imports is seldom specified. The gold, which was exported as early at least as the time of Darius Hystaspes, finds no explicit mention in the *Jatakas*. Gems of various kinds are named as the quest of special sea-farers anxious to discover a fortune."

And, quoting Rhys Davids on Buddhist India, the same authority adds:—

> "Silks, muslins, the finer sorts of cloth, cutlery and armour, brocade, embroideries and rugs, perfumes and drugs, ivory and ivory work, jewellery and gold (seldom silver) these were the main articles in which the merchant dealt."

This description may be taken to relate to the trade of the Mauryan Empire at its height. That, however, is not quite identical with the geographic unit India as we now reckon it. Imports and exports are, therefore, overlapping in a way, which would not occur if we considered the trade of India as the unit we now know it to be. A full and exhaustive list of the Imports and Exports of India from the port of Broach and Nelkunda is furnished by the writer of the *Periplus*, which makes little material variation from the known trade of the Middle Ages of Indian history, and even of modern times.

45

DIRECTION OF THE TRADE OF ANCIENT INDIA

If we examine these lists carefully, we find, however, one marked difference in general character between the trade of India to-day, and that about three thousand years ago. India was then principally an exporter of *manufactures*. Her imports, though diverse, and including some manufactured goods,—as for example silk and silk-goods from China, or pearls from Ceylon, or other precious stones from her western neighbours,—were mostly articles of raw produce or live animals like horses. Glassware (?), and again Porcelain, if imported, from China, must have been relatively of small importance. She need not have imported the raw material for her manufactures; for, with the possible exception of silk, which we may take to have been a Chinese monopoly, all the necessary raw material was found within her own frontiers. The most prominent example is, of course, that of cotton, the manufacture of which, from the indigenous material, had reached quite a high stage of excellence when Megasthenes wrote in the time of Chandragupta Maurya. India's ages old mastery of cotton manufacture has been vividly expressed by a European writer of the sixteenth century who remarks:—"Every one from the Cape of Good Hope to China is clothed from head to foot," in the products of the Indian looms; and though the authority reproducing this remark seeks to discount it by pointing out that the peoples who regarded clothing as a prime necessity were extremely limited in number, Mr. Moreland is obliged to concede:—

> "We may then restate Pyrard's picturesque and exaggerated account by saying that Indian looms had *a practical monopoly of the home market for clothes*, and, in addition had *three principal export markets*, Arabia and beyond, Burma, and the Eastern Islands."

This relates to the days of Akbar; but, from accounts no less trustworthy than those of the Portuguese and other European travellers of the sixteenth and seventeenth centuries, there is every reason to conclude that, in regard to cotton weaving, India's position was practically the same in the days of Asoka, and as far backward as history can take us. The same of course, must be said of the dye-stuff made out of Indigo, which was as much a natural monopoly of this country, as the art of making cloth from cotton. And these dyed cotton fabrics were the principal exports of India.

Of other textiles, the modern staple of jute was either unknown, or unused in any considerable quantity. The Indian protagonists of the medieval Christian monks did not wear sackcloth as a sign of penance; they preferred and used the skins of animals like deer, tigers, or lions. It is legitimate to assume from the frequent mention of tiger-skins being used as clothing by the ascetics of ancient India that the art of taxidermy must have been fairly well developed. We do not, however, meet with any record of skins or dressed hides as having formed an article of trade with India and so we may conclude that raw hides or leather manufactures, though quite well known, must have formed the subject matter of domestic or at most trans-frontier exchange only.

Of other animal products, Ivory was once a prominent article of export from India. Pearls and Coral are other instances of India's great export in olden time without a need of corresponding import. Musk is mentioned by Dr. Mukerji as amongst the exports of India from the earliest times; but he gives no authority for the statement. Perhaps it was included in the rich spices and unguents brought from India in the days of Solomon.

Among the animals forming part of the trade to and from India, Horses may have, on the balance, been imported; while Elephants are certain to have been exported, though chiefly by the trans-frontier land route. Historically, the most celebrated Indian animal exported is the Peacock, which was not only prized by the Greeks of the Alexandrian era, but apparently by the Jews of King Solomon's as well. Even the Hebrew word for Peacock,—Thuki,—is borrowed from Tamil, where this prince of birds is called Tokei.

Silk, which certainly formed a large part of the exports to the West from ancient Indian ports, and "which, under the Persian Empire is said to have been exchanged by weight with gold", cannot quite be regarded as a native industry of India. The art of silk-weaving may have been naturalised in this country for centuries before the rise of the first historical Indian Empire; and that the cocoon may have been developed here too is not improbable. But the evidence of Sanskrit literature, which identifies silk clothing with China, cannot quite be disregarded; and so we may take it that, however highly the art of silk-weaving may have developed in India, silk was an industry really native to China only. The undoubtedly considerable Indian trade was probably in the nature of the *entrepot* trade, in which the stuffs were, in the first instance, brought to India by the Indian merchants, or their Javanese and Malayan and Sinhalese cousins, from China; and thence re-exported to Arabia, Persia, Egypt, Greece, or Rome, via the Indian ports. The *entrepot* business, even now a considerable feature of our trade, was, perhaps, helped by the peculiarly Indian art of dyeing the stuff with fast natural colours, which increase their value in the minds of the Barbarians of the West. Porcelain is mentioned among Indian exports, in the *Periplus*; while pottery was an established Indian craft even in the Vedic Age. The former may have entered in our *entrepot* trade, as also pearls and other precious stones.

Apart from textiles, the most important category of manufactures exported from India was metalware, principally Iron and Steel goods. India must have reached a very high stage of manufacturing skill in iron at a very early date. Herodotus mentions that in the army of Xerxes, the Persian King, the Indian contingent was armed with cane bows and arrows, tipped with iron. Ironsmiths are quite an important class in the Mauryan Age. Speaking of the age of the Rigveda, at least seven centuries before the rise of the Mauryan Empire, the *Cambridge History of Ancient India* says:—

"Next in importance (to the wood worker) was the worker in metal, who smelted ore in the furnace, using the wing of a bird in place of bellows to fan the flame. Kettles and other domestic utensils were made of metal. It is, however, still uncertain what that metal which is called *Ayas* was. Copper, bronze, and iron alike may have been meant."

The same authority elsewhere gives 1000 B. C. as the probable date of the introduction of Iron in India. But whether or not iron and its manufactures were understood by the Vedic Indians, their descendants in the Mauryan Age had undeniably achieved great excellence; while another six hundred years later, in the hey-day of the Gupta Empire, their skill was equal to turning out such masterpieces, as the iron pillars of Delhi and of Dhar, of which a great geologist wrote :—

"It is not many years since the production of such a pillar would have been an impossibility in the largest foundries of the world, and even now there are comparatively few where a similar mass of metal could be turned out."

Describing the Delhi pillar, the late Dr. Vincent Smith wrote :—

"It is now established beyond the possibility of doubt that the material of the pillar is pure malleable iron of 7.66 specific gravity, and that the monument is a solid shaft of wrought iron welded together . . . . The total length of the pillar from the top of the capital to the bottom of the base is 23 feet 8 inches. Twenty-two feet are above ground, and one foot eight inches are below ground. The weight is estimated to exceed 6 tons."

Dr. Smith, we may observe in passing, does not seem to make sufficient allowance for the facts that the pillar stands in the midst of a Muhammadan mosque: that the iconoclastic zeal of the early Muslim may have lopped off a considerable portion, *c. g.* iconographic capital from the original pillar, if not through sheer iconoclasticism, at least on account of the exigencies of the mosque architecture: and that consequently, both the height and the weight of the original monument may have been much greater. Certainly, the three pieces of the Dhar pillar, aggregating 42 feet in height, must have weighed proportionally more, and involved greater skill and daring in forging and welding the same. The skill that made such pillars could not have grown in a day, nor be the property of a freak or genius. It must be the growth of centuries of silent development; and one does no harm to one's sense of history in assuming that iron manufactures,—like the implements and weapons of all sorts, armour etc.—must have been made in India centuries before the Christian era, primarily, of course, for domestic consumption, but quite appreciably for export as well.

As in the case of cotton goods so in the case of iron manufactures, the raw material being available in plenty at home, India needed no imports to offset the exports of her weapons, armour, and cutlery. In the case of other metals, gold was an exportable article in ancient India, supposed to be dug out by the so-called gold ants, which, however, though frequently mentioned by almost every classical writer, is now explained as representing the Tibetans and their crude methods of gold extraction. We are now so much habituated to regarding both gold and silver as articles of import largely; and even in the age of the Pandyas and the Cholas, gold was so frequently imported from Rome and her provinces to pay for the excess

MAKING AND POLISHING PAPER

TINSEL WORKERS

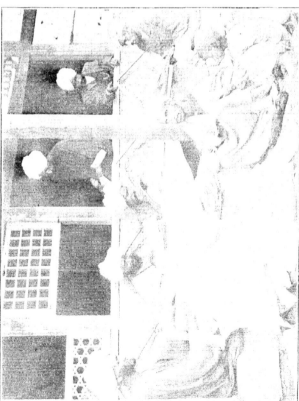

IRON PILLAR, DELHI

CARPET DESIGNERS

of Indian exports, that, at first sight, it becomes difficult to accept the view that gold could have been a native product of India. But even if we do not regard Tibetan gold as really native Indian gold, geological evidence suggests that alluvial deposits of gold must, at one time, have been very considerable in this country. On the other hand, the large stores of gold,—as ornaments and plate found in India at the time of the invasions of Mahmud of Ghazni and his successors,—were amassed, probably, as the result of the gold obtained in the balance of trade exclusively.

If metalware is heavy, and consequently difficult to introduce in trade during an age in which transport facilities were not very great, the trade in other minerals, like the precious stones, may have met with no such difficulty. Precious stones of all kinds, with pearls heading the list, formed the subject of trade between India and her neighbours from the earliest times. Indians had a surfeit of pearls, a monopoly of beryls, a surplus of onyx; and these, with others still more valuable, may have been exported after the domestic needs had been met. The precious stones, we may assume, must also have figured on both sides of the trade account. But, in view of the large imports of gold from Rome in the days when Pliny wrote, the guess may be hazarded, that the excess was,—at least from the stand-point of the value if not of quantity,—on the side of exports from India.

There are no other manufactures in the trade lists to consider, unless we consider *wood-work*, and particularly *Ships*, as having been articles of export from India. *Sandalwood* as a luxury, and *teakwood* as a necessity, were certainly in demand from the days of Darius Hyastaspes. But these must be treated as raw material mainly, no greater labour than that of collecting and carting being expended upon them prior to exportation. Of *ships*, it is difficult to say, though Indians were great shipbuilders and mariners in the days, when, on the most conservative estimate, the trans-marine trade of India had certainly begun. Dr. Mukerji's monograph on *Ancient Indian Shipping* nowhere quite states if the Indian ships were so far superior to the structures of their neighbours as to be in demand amongst the latter, and so bodily exported from India. Perhaps, the fact was, that, as with Britain in the later half of the nineteenth century, the Indian ships, two thousand years ago and more, formed items of the so-called "invisible exports," doing their work of transportation and charging for that service in the shape of increased prices. That shipbuilding was an industry essential to the national existence was quite well understood by the Mauryas, who held shipbuilding to be a state monopoly. Says Megasthenes: "But the armour-makers and shipbuilders receive wages and provisions from the King for whom alone they work."

Of raw material, the most important trade was in spices and drugs and unguents, including therein pepper, cinnamon, cardamom, cloves, nutmeg, assafœtida, betels, camphor, opium, musk and flower essences, oils etc. The last-mentioned may be classed as manufactures in so far as they were fragrant oils or flower essences *(attar)*, which were certainly very largely in demand among the Romans at the beginning of the Christian era, and quite probably in demand by the kindred peoples much

46

earlier. Opium is nowhere specifically mentioned in the lists of imports and exports; but it has so long been a practical monopoly of India, that it possibly escaped specific enumeration by Western traders or travellers, who were no great consumers of the drug. It is probably included in the drugs so frequently mentioned.

Of other food-stuffs, Rice has certainly formed part of Indian exports in the earliest times, as evidenced by the survival of the Tamil word for that article in the Greek tongue. But, as the *Periplus* says, in view of the difficulties of transporting such perishable commodities over large distances in ships of those days, the probability rather is that rice and other cereals like wheat were subject matter of trade only in so far as they were required for the victualling of ships. Wines figure in the list of imports, but not to a very large quantity.

* * * * * *

This brief review of the principal articles in the Indian Trade for the last three thousand years cannot be complete without mentioning one item, which deserves more than a passing notice. Slaves are mentioned in the *Periplus*, as imports from Kane, Obolesk, and Oman. But it is not clear where they came from. It is, however, perfectly certain that India never had a traffic in slaves.[1] Apart altogether from the religious sentiment of perfect equality of all living creatures, which, certainly from Buddhist times if not earlier, laid a positive embargo on this inhuman traffic, there is the known fact of history that traffic in human beings was never made the cold-blooded business in India of the Aryans, that it was made by the Christian Europeans after the discovery of the Americas. Megasthenes and his contemporaries may have exaggerated in completely denying the existence of slavery in India; though, in justice to these ancient observers, it must be pointed out that *their* class of domestic helps,—the *dasas*, common in India,—were not at all akin to the slaves as modern interpreters have sometimes imagined. The truth appears to be that *dasas* were a class of domestic servants, who, owing to the scarcity or unfamiliarity of coined money, were paid for their services almost wholly in kind; and they, being attached to the households where they served, did not leave them, perhaps were not able to leave them. But they had good opportunities to free themselves, if they so desired, usually their own earnings helping them to commute their services, as at a later date was the case with the serfs in England, and so gain their freedom.

CHARACTERISTICS OF OUR ANCIENT TRADE

On a general review, then, of the commerce of Ancient India from the earliest times to 1000 A. C., we find the chief character of that trade to be a heavy export of manufactured goods, qualitatively speaking. Raw material for further

---

1) Among trades five are ethically proscribed for the lay believer—daggers, slaves, flesh, strong drink, poisons. *Camb. Hist.* p. 135. See also *Manu.* VII. 96, which leaves out from the list of the conqueror's booty in victory the item of the vanquished soldiers as slaves. At a later age Akbar definitely forbade this inhuman practice.

manufacture abroad there certainly must have been; and food-stuffs, chiefly in the guise of edible spices, did also figure in our exports schedule. But, from the point of value, exports must have preponderated over imports, textile manufactures of all sorts forming the bulk of these. It was entirely on account of the preponderance of such valuable exports that India contrived, even in the days when Pliny was writing his *Natural History*[1] to drain the West of its supply of gold coin and bullion, even as she is reputed to do to-day, though in a quite different manner, and with radically different consequences to her own national welfare.

Another characteristic of the ancient Indian commerce was the presence of a large *entrepot* trade which still persists, though perhaps in slightly altered forms. Pearls from Ceylon; gold from Tibet, Burma and the Golden Chersonese (wherever that may be); precious stones and spices from the islands of the Indian archipelago; silk and porcelain from China; were all brought into the ports of this country, to be thence re-exported to the countries of the West, leaving us, presumably, a handsome commission as middle men.

The existence, however, of an *entrepot* trade could not have been possible in those days, without the necessary concomitant of a considerable fleet of merchant-men for transport by sea, and mighty caravans for similar office by land. And there is ample evidence to show that Indians of all ages since the earliest dawn of history have been great carriers by land as well as by water.

With the carrying business mainly in their own hands, and with a very considerable *entrepot* trade, it would not be surprising if we find the system of trade organisation carried to a very high level in ancient India. Whether or not the castes of modern India have developed from the trade guilds of ancient India, it is perfectly certain that, at least about the 5th century B. C. if not much earlier,

> "Crafts and commerce are flourishing, highly organised corporately, under conditions of individual and corporate competition, the leading men thereof the friends and counsellors of kings. We have found labour largely hereditary, yet, therewithal, a mobility and initiative anything but rigid revealed in the exercise of it. And we have discovered a thorough familiarity with money and credit ages before the 7th Century A. D. *(Camb. Hist. of India.*, p. 219.)

Partnerships in commerce were fairly well understood, though individual freedom of initiative and pluck were not restricted, as in a later-day joint stock enterprise, by merely travelling together in the same caravan, or bound on board the same vessel. For purposes of discipline, the *Sarthavaha*, or caravan-chief, may have been accorded a certain degree of prestige and authority among his fellow travellers and traders. But the latter by their acquiescence did not surrender their independence.

> "The act of exchange between producer and consumer, or between either and middle-man, was, both before and during the age when the *Jataka* book was compiled, a 'free' bargain and a transaction unregulated, with one notable exception, by the system of statute fixed prices." *(Camb. Hist. of India.* p. 216.)

---

1) According to Pliny's *Natural History* xii, 18, there was "no year in which India did not drain the Roman Empire of a hundred million sesterces". This would equal in English money a million sterling, or a crore and half of rupees at the normal rate of exchange.

The exception was the purchases of the King which were made by officially regulated prices;

Price determination was thus more in accordance with the conception of the normal price of modern economists, with the incidental result of the extraordinary profiteering, giving, in one recorded instance at least, a profit of 20,000 per cent. The intervention of money as the commonly accepted medium of exchange is perfectly well-known in India since the age of the *Jatakas* at least, and the chief coins were *Katiapana*, *Nishka* and *Suvarna*, all of gold. Subsidiary coinage of bronze and copper,—the *Kamsa*, the *Pada* and *Kaniska*,—were equally popular: while cowrie-shells were used for purposes of account-keeping in regard to small fractions of commonly used units of payment.

The late Dr. V. A. Smith was certainly mistaken as to the origin of currency in India, when he wrote:—

> "There is reason to believe that the necessities of commerce with foreign merchants were the immediate occasion for adoption by the Indian people of a metallic currency as well as of alphabetical writing. (*Imp. Gaz.* Vol. II. p. 135.)

We may take it as a commonplace of economic history that the evolution of domestic exchange precedes that of foreign commerce; and that the needs of domestic exchange, which even now is ten or twenty times more important than foreign commerce in the most advanced commercial nations, will at least be as insistent as those of foreign exchange to demand the creation of a commonly acceptable medium of exchange.

The coins, we may add, of ancient India, though crude and primitive, reveal a certain ambition to beauty in design, which seem to have disappeared in the subsequent ages.

In an age so accustomed to money valuations as the Buddhist age of India undoubtedly was, the evolution of substitutes for money, or credit instruments as we would now describe them, would be a matter of course. Says Mrs. Rhys Davids:—

> "Of substitutes for current coins (or what were used as such,) or instruments of credit, we read of signet rings used as deposits or securities, of wife or children pledged or sold for debt, and of *promissory notes* or debt sheets."

Even though the last would be in the form of mere registrations as between lender and borrower, their evolution and use must be held to mark a distinct advance in commercial civilisation. The *Shethis* of the Buddhist Literature apparently kept large cash amounts on hand, like the immense hoard of the devoted Anathapindika. These they either loaned, or, more probably, used in business of their own as merchant bankers. Certainly, the minute regulations as to loans of money and interest thereon, mentioned in both the Buddhist canonical works and in the Hindu *Dharmashastras*, like the standard code of Manu or Chanakya, could not have occurred, had not money-lending been a well-known business. The echo of the Aristotelian and Christian fulmination against interest on money loans is, indeed, found in the still earlier works of the Indian legists.

"The general tendency of this profession to evade any legal or customary rate of interest and become the type of profit-mongering finds condemnation in other law-books." *(Camb. Hist. p. 218.)*

But in the Buddhist period, and under the Buddhist influence, the

"Legal rate of interest probably between 400 B. C. and 200 B. C. was five *mashas* a month for twenty *Katiapanas*. This is a rate of $18\frac{3}{4}$ per cent per annum, if we take 16 *mashas* to the *Katiapana*, or 15 per cent per annum if, with Haridatta, who wrote only 400 years ago, 20 *mashas* are allowed to the *Katiapana*." *(Rhys Davids, J. R. A. S. 1901. p. 880-81)*

The importance of the mercantile calling, with its necessary adjunct of banking and credit, must have been particularly stressed under the Buddhist and Jain influences; since those two cognate bodies of religious doctrine would imply a general condemnation of many an industrial pursuit, that, according to their conception, would involve a harm or destruction of life. They consequently confine their faithful more and more to the relatively innocuous pursuit of commerce, and hence the growth of commerce under Buddhist rule.

COMMERCE AND THE STATE

With such a development of commerce, it would be strange, indeed, if the relation of the State towards trade were undefined or unknown. The conception of the King as embodying the entire state in his person is foreign to Indian history. Hence, the state activities which emanate from the King chiefly take the form of collection of taxes on merchandise, supervision of weights and measures, etc. The *Artha Shastra* of Chanakya, supposed to be composed in the days of the founder of the Mauryan Empire, gives minute details of such dues and taxes, those on commerce taking the shape of *octroi*, road and ferry tolls, ship-duties and a merchandise tax in kind, levied impartially upon exports and imports. Manu's list (VII 127-133) is strangely silent about cotton stuffs and silk goods, metal work and implements of war or chase, as well as aids in transport, like chariots, carts, horses or elephants, unless included in the general rule. It is a little surprising that such articles of manufacture and general trade do not come within the purview of specific taxation. As mentioned above, certain trades, like ship-building and munitions-manufacture, were either specially protected, or even made into a state monopoly from the days of the Mauryan Empire onwards. But, after a careful review of the evidence we can command, it seems unlikely that the Indian State had, in the period reviewed here, realised the duty of conscious promotion of indigenous enterprise and industry by means of active fiscal assistance of the type that now characterises the fiscal legislation of modern states. The explanation for such an absence of state interference may probably be found in the very high level to which Indian industry had no doubt attained, rendering it unnecessary as well as unwise to interfere in the natural development of commerce.

INDIAN TRADE IN THE MUHAMMADAN PERIOD

Coming next to consider the trade of India during the Muhammadan period,— roughly the period 1200-1700,—it may be remarked, by way of preface, that this

47

being a period relatively unsettled, trade development could not take place quite so effectively as would be the case under a more peaceful regime. The sway of the Delhi Emperors, until the advent of the Mughals, was never uniform throughout India, nor unbroken for even half a century or a generation. The Deccan was relatively free from the dynastic differences of the northern India, though even in the regions south of the Vindhyas, the clash of Hindus and Moslems was neither unknown nor without influence. The trade of Malabar with China and the West no doubt was flourishing all through this period in the principal articles which formed the staple of that trade in pre-Muhammadan and ancient India. Spices, including pepper, cloves, nutmeg, cardamom; precious stones, comprising pearls, diamonds, beryls, rubies from the mines of Golkonda; cotton goods of all description; woollen shawl, and carpets; Chinese porcelain and Venetian glass; Indian artware of all kinds; animals, principally horses,—these formed the bulk of imports and exports at the South Indian ports; and no doubt also figured in the overland trade from Agra via Lahore to Kabul, and thence to Central and Eastern Asia, and from Multan to Kandahar, and thence to Persia and Western Asia and Europe via the Ottoman Empire. Measured according to the standards common for this and other countries of this period, and after allowance is made for the admitted hindrances to trade, there is no reason to doubt that the volume as well as the value of the trade in this period must have been quite considerable.

INDUSTRY IN MUHAMMADAN INDIA

Premising in general that India was, during this age, very nearly self-supporting, Mr. Moreland in his *India at the death of Akbar* observes:—

> "The country produced all the food and food-adjuncts which ordinary people required, though not always in sufficient quantities to satisfy all needs; imports under this head were practically limited to fruits, spices and stimulants. In the same way, all ordinary clothes were made in India, but silks, velvets and broadcloths were imported from various parts of the world.

Foreign testimony, however, has been recorded to the effect that India herself manufactured large quantities of these last mentioned stuffs. Though conceding that all the metalware used within the country was made there, Moreland considers that much of the raw material was imported. But the remark can only be accepted, if the point is conceded that transport facilities in Muhammadan India were sufficiently developed to permit considerable trade in such cheap but bulky goods. Both Mr. Moreland and Dr. V. S. Smith incline to the view that roads in Muhammadan India were not very good. To speak of only one metal—iron; the great demand for it only for armament purposes, including artillery since the days of the Portuguese, not to mention the need for agricultural and other implements, could not possibly have been met out of raw material imported from abroad. As a matter of industry, India had excelled for ages past in iron and steel goods, particularly arms and armour of all kinds. It must have been the same with regard to copper, which loomed so largely in the currency system of the country throughout this period.

Salt was produced for local consumption from sources which probably have endured to this day,—Sambhar lake, the Punjab mines, and the sea-water on the coast. Internal trade in this article was very considerable, but it did not figure at all, either as import, like now, or as export in the foreign trade of the country. Diamonds, on the other hand, were easily producible almost on the surface; the famous mines of Golkonda, which are supposed to have yielded the Kohi-noor among other gems, were in full operation during the Muhammadan as during the earlier Hindu period. Tavernier, the French jeweller, travelling in India in the eighteenth century, estimated the diamond production as giving employment to 60,000 men on the Deccan mines, with another 8,000 in the Chhota Nagpur mines, while Moreland estimates the total yield at 20 lakhs of rupees in the currency of the period. Along with the precious stones may also be mentioned pearls, which continued to be the staple of Indian trade in either direction, all through this period, pearl-fishing giving employment to as many as 60,000 people. There cannot, of course, be any doubt that the Persian waters were productive of pearl-oysters; but quantitatively, all records seem to agree that in the Indian, including the Singhalese waters, trade was the most important. The consumption of pearls was very great in India itself, being used freely in dress materials and emblems of royalty. Leaving out such well-known uses of pearls as in the Peacock-Throne of Shah Jahan, we may quote here from a traveller, Abdur Razaak, of the XV century visiting Vijayanagar. Speaking of the King's dress he says:

"He was clothed in a robe of zaitun satin, and he had round his neck a collar composed of pure pearls, the value of which a jeweller would find it difficult to calculate."

As regards other precious stones, such as emeralds, saphires, rubies, topazes, beryls, onyx, which were mentioned in the earlier trade lists, they continued to be important in the trade of this period as well. The very minute regulations, concerning the classification and perforation of these stones and their values, given in the Ain-i-Akbari, ought alone to suffice to say that trade in these must have been as well known as the art of setting them up.

Turning from mineral to forest produce, we find wood-work of all sorts entering in the trade, though perhaps cabinet-making of modern type was not developed. But wood products most importantly occurring in trade must have been the Indian ships, which were built large enough to serve in their time as ocean carriers. [1] Says Moreland.

"The general attitude of authorities suggests to me that apart from the Portuguese trade to Europe, the great bulk of the commerce in the Indian seas was carried in ships built in India, and that most of these, and certainly all the large ones, were constructed on the west coast, not at any one centre, but at various points, or inlets within easy reach of the forests. It is practically certain that India also built all the small boats required for the coasting trade from Bengal as far as Sind, and the aggregate volume of shipping was therefore very great when measured by contemporary standard."

[1] "Writing in the fifteenth century, Conti had recorded the existence of ships of 1000 tons, much larger than any with which he was familiar in the Mediterranean, and the early English visitors to Western India described vessels of even greater size, second only to the huge carracs built by the Portuguese. These Indian ships were used only for the pilgrim voyage to the Red Sea, and all told there were not, I think, more than half-a-dozen of them in existence at one time." (Moreland. p. 171.)

Mr. Moreland is, however, more concerned to show that, if ship-building in India has declined since the Muhammadan period, compensating industries of road-carrying vehicles and railways have been built up; and that consequently there is a large balance in favour of the present regime. He, therefore, does scant justice to this obviously great, if not the greatest, industry of medieval India, contenting himself with the remark that the ordinary vessels were of small capacity; and that the larger ones were few in number. As usual, however, Mr. Moreland gives no authority for such a slighting judgment, beyond his rather exasperating "I think". One is therefore forced to adduce contrary evidence to show how completely an ingrained prejudice is apt to lead astray even a competent scholar.

The Sultans of Gujarat, the most advanced maritime power of India, second, if at all, in ship-building to Malabar, were in the habit of maintaining large fleets in the fourteenth and fifteenth centuries, and styled themselves Lords of the Sea. The European traveller, Nicolo Conti, says of the Indian merchants:—

> "They are very rich, so much so that some will carry on their business in forty of their own ships, each of which is valued at 15,000 gold pieces.

A ship costing 15,000 gold pieces of those days,—which in purchasing power would exceed a million of to-day,—can easily give us an idea of the size of such vessels. Given only a single such merchant in ports like Surat, Broach, Goa, Mangalore and half a dozen on the Eastern coast to Satgaon, we get a fleet of some 400 ships of the largest tonnage. There is nothing to show that shipping had declined from the days of the Sultans of Gujarat, the Bahmani Kings of the Deccan, and the Hindu Empire of Vijayanagar. Basing himself on the authority of the Englishman Fryer,—an English Doctor of the Cambridge University, who came to India in 1673 and published a *New Account of East India and Persia* in 1697,— Mr. Wheeler, in his *History of India*, says:

> "The Moghul shipping lay pretty close together in the Surat river. Some of the vessels were more than a thousand tons burden. Altogether there were more than a hundred good ships, besides smaller vessels.

Fleets, in Mughal wars in Sind and Bengal, of from 100 ships to several thousands, were not very rare on the Indian rivers. In the Indian ocean proper similar, though smaller, Indian fleets often engaged in battle the Turkish, Arab and European pirates from the fourteenth century downwards. We may then conclude that, ship-building was a most important industry in the Muhammadan and the Hindu period; that in point of value it is exceedingly difficult to estimate, but could hardly have been inferior even to the most well-known, as the best established, industry in India,—Cotton manufacture; and that its significance is probably obscured by the ships figuring only as 'invisible exports' of India in the Muhammadan period as they did in the Hindu period.

Next after forest produce, we may notice agricultural produce as a constituent in Indian commerce. As a rule, food-stuffs did not form any great proportion of the commerce of Muhammadan India,—food-grains being chiefly produced for local and immediate consumption. Some grain may have been the subject of commerce for

PLATE XCVIII

ANCIENT TRANSPORT

328

292 PERSIAN EMBASSY AT THE COURT OF SHAH JEHAN

PLATE XCIX

TRAVELLING EQUIPMENT OR VEHICLES IN MUGHAL INDIA

294   AMBARI—LADY'S LITTER ON ELEPHANT

295   CHANDOL—ROAD CONVEYANCE OF
ZENANA LADIES

296   PALKHI

297   A LITTER ON CAMEL BACK

provisioning travellers or ships, but the amount as well as the value must have been insignificant. A food material, however, which may have entered very considerably in the trade of Muhammadan India, is *salted* or *dried fish*, which, besides being an important item in the food of the people in the maritime and riverain provinces, should certainly have found purchasers in ship-masters and their fellow voyagers. Fish-oil was a by-product equally valued by ships as well as for local consumption, while the use of fish-manure was established in Gujarat when Thevenot visited Surat in 1666.

Coming next to the trade in animals, we find horses very largely imported from countries beyond the Indus, Arabia, Persia and Turkestan. This was not merely in the nature of a luxury trade, but one of national necessity in the South. Abul Fazl mentions several places, amongst them Cutch, as producing animals as good as the best Arabian horses. Akbar had 12,000 horses for his own personal use in his stables; and this fondness, coupled with the very wide-spread custom of including a horse in Durbar presents, required large imports even for northern India.

If the trans-frontier trade was thus brisk in northern India, which had its own breeding places, and which nevertheless imported several thousands every year, in the south the horse-trade was still more important, owing to the scarcity of local supply, and to the great, steady demand for purposes of war as well as of trade. We find notices of the horse-trade in the Deccan from the earliest writers. Thus Al Beruni, one of the earliest Arab writers on India, says:—

> "M'abar is, as it were, the Key of Hind. * * * There are no horses in M'abar, or rather those which are there are weak. It was agreed that every year Jamaluddin Ibrahim should send to the Dewar 1400 strong Arab horses obtained from the islands of His, and 10,000 horses from all the islands of Tars, such as Kalif, Lahsa, Bahrein, Hurmuz, Kailahat, etc. Each horse is reckoned worth 220 dinars of red gold current."

A dinar, it may be noted in passing, has been estimated to be equal in value, in Akbar's time, to Rs. 30; and at that rate the trade for this portion alone would amount to Rs. 7,52,40,000 per annum. The same story is told by Wasaf some three hundred years later, who adds that the sum total of the value of the horses imported

> "was paid out of the overflowing revenues of the estates and endowments belonging to the Hindu Temples, and from the tax upon courtezans attached to them, and no charge was incurred by the public treasury."

While horses figured chiefly on the import side, elephants may have been exported, but there is not much reference to that fact in the records we now have. Probably, the trade in elephants, in so far as it did exist, was by the land routes only; and may have amounted to a small fraction of the horse imports. Of other animals,—peacock, apes, parrots and other birds,—if exported or imported,—there is no specific mention. We may, therefore, conclude that the trade in them, if any, must have been insignificant.

Among other beasts, cattle,—counted with agricultural production, though used for purposes of conveyance all over India,—were more thoroughly used in agriculture

48

proper. Certain special breeds, like the Malnad cattle in the South and the Gujarat cattle on the West, may have figured in the inter-provincial commerce. But for foreign export, the prejudices and necessities of Indian people alike forbade them to export cattle. The only form in which cattle could be said to have formed part of the Indian trade during the Muhammadan period was, probably, in skins or raw hides.

Before discussing the most important group of Indian manufactures—the textile goods,—a word may be said about Sugar, which, certainly, even in Muhammadan India, occasioned some trade; and Oils, which have, as unguents and perfumes, always figured in the foreign trade. But in both instances, the locally produced raw material was made up into the finished article within the country itself. The trade in sugar was largely inter-provincial, Bengal, Lahore and Ahmadabad being the chief centres. The oil-trade was with foreign countries as well, though it is difficult to say precisely what proportion of the Indian produce was exported. Opium and Indigo with the dye-stuffs made out of the latter were practically Indian monopolies; and figured extensively by this time as exports from India. Paper, on the other hand, may have been imported.

Porcelain, also, and glassware must have been largely imported.

*   *   *   *   *   *

Historically, as well as commercially, the most important item in the trade of India, however, consisted of textile manufactures of all sorts. Mr. Moreland holds:—

> "Silk-weaving was a minor industry in the time of Akbar. * * * * Of the period about 1600, it may be affirmed that the export of manufactured goods was very small that the home market was limited in size, and that it was supplied largely by importation of foreign goods."

Other European writers, like Barbosa and Varthema, hold that silk goods were supplied from Gujarat to Africa and Burma; and the latter asserts that Gujarat supplied:—

> "All Persia, Tartary, Turkey, Syria, Barbary, Arabia, Ethiopia * * * with silk and cotton stuffs."

At Vijayanagar, Barbosa had noticed it a hundred years earlier; and Abul Fazl's detailed evidence in the Institutes of Akbar cannot pass for nought.[1] Mr. Moreland ignores the results of his own laborious research, for he has noted in the same work but in another place, that:—

> "Dress afforded similar opportunities for expenditure, both in the quantity of garment and in the costliness of the materials employed. If we may believe Abul Fazl, Akbar took much more interest in clothes than in food; * * * his wardrobe was sufficiently large to require an elaborate system of classification, but when we read that 1000 complete suits were made up for him every year, allowance must be made for the practice of conferring dresses as a reward of distinction upon persons appearing at court."
> (p. 258.)

---

1) "Through the attention of His Majesty, a variety of new manufactures are established in this country, and the clothes fabricated in Persia, Europe and China have become cheap and plenty." Gladwin. p. 91.

With such an etiquette prevailing, the domestic market, though small, must have been quite paying enough to stimulate the native manufacturer, encouraged by every device of royal, viceregal, and aristocratic patronage. With such centres for production as Burhanpur, Ahmadabad, Pattan, Benares and Lahore, besides the royal capitals, it is unreasonable to deny the existence of a good silk-manufacturing industry in India, serving for export as well as for domestic consumption. This does not, of course, mean that no silk goods were imported. Raw silk bulked largely in the Indian imports in this period; and silk goods also must have contributed an appreciable proportion. The Indian exports were a historical fact, though these exports may have consisted only in part of the stuffs manufactured in India.

Coming next to the woollen stuffs, we find that the Indian people did not consume any great quantities of woollens, and hence probably the relative indifference to that industry. The demand for woollen clothes from the Mughal nobles may have been met by foreign imports, India not producing wool at all worth speaking of. Exception, of course, must be made in connection with shawls,—pure wool and with silk mixture,—which were specially patronised by Akbar and manufactured largely in Kashmir; and with carpets, which were centred at Agra and Lahore in Akbar's time. But the latter were also imported largely from Persia during all this period.

*   *   *   *

It thus leaves us with cotton goods as the most important item in the trade of India. We have already referred to Pyrard's statement that,

> "Every one from the Cape of Good Hope to China, man and woman, is clothed from head to foot in the products of Indian looms."

and need now hardly repeat the same argument to establish India's unbroken mastery of the world commerce in this article.

VOLUME OF INDIAN COMMERCE

Dealing next with the volume of Indian trade, it is impossible to accept Mr. Moreland's estimate. The trading season in Indian waters must have been limited owing to monsoon currents. But the data he proceeds upon are either non-existent,— and therefore the inference is no better than an unsupported estimate; or relate only to isolated experiences of individual pirates, like Middleton in 1611-12, or travellers, like Jourdain. On the other hand, there is positive testimony to show that Indian trade must have been far more voluminous during this period. Until the rise of the Marathas introduced and popularised the mountain pony for cavalry use, the horse trade alone,—taking it only at 100,000 animals imported during the year on state as well as private account at all the ports beginning with Cambay southwards,—would have taken up a good proportion of the tonnage Mr. Moreland assigns to the Western trade. Then there is the evidence, already adduced, of considerable shipping in the best Indian harbours.

We can indicate the volume of this trade, and more particularly the value of that commerce, by another means. From the days of Pliny at least, there is a continuous story of India obtaining the annual balance of trade in her favour in the shape of gold and silver. The stores of gold accumulated by these means ought to give an idea of the volume of this commerce. Without going back to the time of Mahmud of Ghazni, whose plunder of India was reckoned in thousands of maunds, let us consider only the following well-authenticated historical facts. Ferishta, the Moghul historian of the time of Akbar, speaking of the first invasion and conquest of the Deccan by Malik Kafur under Alaud-din Khilji, says that the conqueror on his return from the Deccan presented his sovereign Alaud-din with

"312 elephants, 20,000 horses and 50,000 *mans* of gold, several boxes of jewels and pearls, and other precious effects."

The gold alone has been estimated by Mr. Sewell, in an appendix to his work on "*A Forgotten Empire*", at 15,672,000 lbs. equal, at 85 shillings per oz. to about £106,269,600 in value. A more stable account of the wealth of the Deccan alone may be had from the story of Vijayanagar, a hundred years and more after the invasion of Kafur. Abdur Razaak the Arab traveller already quoted, writing in 1442, says :—

"While the celebration of the Mahanawi was over, he (the king) sent for this humble individual (the writer) one evening at the time of prayer. On arriving at the palace, I saw four stages laid out about ten yards square. * * * *The whole roof and walls of the apartments were covered with plates of gold inlaid with jewels. Each of these plates was about the thickness of the back of a sword*, and was firmly fixed with nails of gold. On the first stage the King's royal seat was placed. This was formed of gold and was of large size."

Measuring this apartment at 900 square feet, the ceiling alone, without including the walls, must consume immense quantities of gold. Speaking of the princes of Vijayanagar defeated at Talikota by the allied Muslim kings of the Deccan, Mr. Sewell writes :—

"Within a few hours these craven chiefs hastily left the palace, carrying with them all the treasures on which they could lay their hands. *Five hundred and fifty elephants laden with treasure in gold, diamonds and precious stones, valued at more than a hundred million sterling*, and carrying the state insignia and the celebrated jewelled throne of the kings, left the city under convoy of bodies of soldiers who remained true to the crown."

This would mean 25,000 maunds of gold at least, giving only half the treasure as consisting of gold. Forty years later, Akbar's treasure was reckoned, in coined gold alone, at 40 million sterling in the six principal treasuries of his Empire. These instances would suffice to show that the gold which was so abundant in India as to be measured by the thousand maunds, could not have come to the country except as a result of favourable trade balance. This trade balance, be it noted in passing, was brought about, not by the complicated network of harassing regulations, which distinguished the Colbertiste regime in Europe of the XVI and XVII centuries but by the ingrained peculiarity of Indian industry. As far as the state was concerned, the Government taxed exports and imports impartially, the most enlightened of the rulers often remitting the more harassing forms of taxation.

PLATE C

FORMS OF WORSHIP AMONG THE HINDUS

TULSI PUJA

PHALLIC WORSHIP

WORSHIPPING THE GODDESS
OF WEALTH

PLATE CI

301   MARRIAGE OF SHIVA AND PARVATI (ELLORA CAVES)
(Photo: Archaeological Dept., Hyderabad Dn.)

302   DECORATING THE DOOR STEPS

Akbar had reduced the customs duties in his Empire to $2\frac{1}{2}\%$, and abolished all other taxes on trade, as well as reduced the excise duties on domestic manufactures to 5% from 10%. And Akbar was not alone in these wise measures. A hundred years and more before him, Abdur Razaak had recorded the Vijayanagar practice of charging the same low rate of duties on foreign imports at Calicut. Thus the wealth that was 'Ind in the days of the Hindu and Musalman emperors was the creation of a flourishing industry in all departments of human wants, a profitable foreign trade based on this industry, and a wise, far-sighted system of government which contented itself with the least possible interference with trade and its mysteries.

CHAPTER X

THE SOCIAL SYSTEM

The glimpses we have had of the Splendour That Was 'Ind are not easy to parallel, at least in the same degree of brilliance, in her social and political system, in her people's activities in peace and war. For thirty, forty, fifty centuries, perhaps, her people have wrought marvels of art and industry; of personal heroism and national achievement; of speculative thinking and social building, the like of which, even as seen in these glimpses, may be difficult to parallel elsewhere. We have drawn attention to several of them; but individually they do not reveal,—they cannot display to the fullest advantage,—the intrinsic grandeur of the whole. And yet, if we did not cast a glance at the marvel and the miracle of the whole; if we did not seek at all to know the disembodied spirit of the mass and its long, long history, our review would only make for despair,—all the keener because of an inevitable contrast with the present. We may not be able to separate and distinguish the specific contribution in the making of our history and our civilisation of each particular race that has now been indistinguishably absorbed in the common entity and the complex unity known as the Indian people. We may not be able to produce sufficient proofs for statements such as that the Dravid of the South excels in high abstraction and so contributes to metaphysics,—if the term may be used,—to the sum total of India's religions and her moral and spiritual philosophy; that the Aryan of the north provides the capacity to enjoy, and the conditions of enjoyment of life and all that we commonly imply in that complex conception; that the West brings the means of that enjoyment, even as the East contributes the disposition for it; that the Muhammadan introduces an appreciation of carnal, worldly delights, even as the Hindu achieves their refinement. But even if we cannot distinguish and ear-mark, as it were, the particular portion of each ingredient into this complex mass, we must, nevertheless, not fail to view the mass *en masse* if only to know its spirit, and to sense its significance.

THE CASTE SYSTEM

Viewing the mass as a whole, considering it as a social edifice, the most salient feature challenging our notice at the present day is the rigid stratification of society in India into castes. Has it always been so? To-day, indeed, caste is all-pervading. Even the Christian convert in Malabar or Madras acknowledges an aboriginal division that still separates from one another the children of the Cross, and makes them avoid indiscriminate marriage relations even among their brethren of the faith, if the original line of social circumvallation forbid it. The Musalmans, of course, have long since been acclimatised; they also are rigidly divided into Shias and Sunnis; Khojas, Memons and Borahs,—each again sub-divided into a hundred microscopic sub-communities separated, *inter se*, by geographic or occupational reasons; and so cannot claim that perfect democracy in their social structure which their creed implies and enjoins. Sister Nivedita has seen the *Web of Indian Life*, and realised for herself how in present day India each new race or community makes a new caste by themselves, at least in the Hindu's eye. His instinctive catholicism enjoins upon the Hindu to recognise and respect each such group and its peculiar forms of worship or social relations. But this does not tell us if, from the beginning of history, caste has been with us. The Vedic Aryans, very probably, made the first distinction,—the first ancestor of the modern caste,—which created a wide gulf between the aborigin,—the *Dasyu*,—and themselves, the proud conquerors swelling with the arrogance of their lighter complexion. Amongst themselves, however, the pristine Aryans had none of that perfectly water-tight compartmentalisation, which their descendants of a thousand years later came to enjoy. If there were any dividing line between the warrior and the priest, the line was a thin one and not impossible to cross, especially as both were alike the cultivators of land. It is difficult to say, on the evidence of history now before us, when the first absolutely water-tight compartments began to become manifest among the Aryans themselves. It is not unlikely that as they spread eastwards and southwards, there was an inevitable mixture of blood, before which, ideas of racial exclusiveness could not hold. For, the race must have become indistinguishably mixed long before the time of which we have any historical records. On the other hand, occupational differences, reinforced by regional exclusiveness, must have become more and more stable, and therefore respected amongst the people at large, since it made for a certain economy, which had only to be seen to be instantly accepted.

The spirit and purpose of the earliest social stratification in India is difficult exactly to understand or appreciate.

> "To describe the caste system" says Kumaraswamy in his Essay on *What Has India Contributed to Human Welfare, in the Atheneum* 1915, "as an idea in actual practice would require a whole volume. But we may notice a few of its characteristics. The nature of the difference between a Brahmana and a Shudra is indicated in the view that a Shudra can do no wrong, (cp. Manu X 126.)—a view that must make an immense demand upon the patience of the higher castes, and is the absolute converse of the Western doctrine that the King can do no wrong. These facts are well illustrated in the doctrine of legal punishment, that that of the Vaishya should be twice as heavy as that of the Shudra, that that of the Kshatriya twice as heavy again, that of the Brahmans twice or even four times as heavy again in respect of the same offence. *For, responsibility rises with intelligence and status.*"

Caste is thus, absolutely speaking, racial in origin, regional in tenacity, occupational in convenience. Soon after the emergence of these characteristics it must have become stereotyped. But if in its original form and condition it had

---

1) न शूद्रे पातकं किंचिन्न च संस्कारमर्हति ।
नास्याधिकारो धर्मेऽस्ति न धर्मात्प्रतिषेधनम् ॥

advantages, the present is not the only generation to perceive its disadvantages. Every law-book of the ancient Indians, while recognising its existence, testified to individual rebellion against its inevitable tyranny. Caste, once established, must have interfered necessarily with the personal,—and even the private,—life of men and women too much for the more daring or discerning among them not to have realised its inherent impertinence. To judge from the regulations in the ancient law-books,—e. g. *Anuloma* and *Pratiloma* marriages,—such cases of individual revolt must have been pretty frequent, even in matters which the present day caste conventions consider to be sacrosanct. The princely class must have from of old inevitably offended against caste regulations in this regard, not only by their matrimonial alliances with non-caste, non-Aryan India, but more particularly with marriages contracted for princes outside India.

They, the law-givers, did not, however, deny or seek to disestablish the caste system for this reason of a possible revolt against its unbearable tyranny. They only sought to regularise irregularities. A more thorough and wholesale opposition to the very principle of caste was attempted by Buddhist as well as Jain protestants, who provide monuments, alike to the spirit of revolt against the senseless tyranny of social stratification; and to the irony of history which has made the successors of those primeval protestants themselves becoming as utterly and irredeemably caste-ridden as the most orthodox Hindu. Caste,—without, of course, its stiffling rigidity and its suicidal tyranny; with its greater economy and convenience, its automatic mutual insurance and its unavoidable equality within its barriers; caste, with its catholic welcome to all,—old as well as new,—races and creeds, seems to be the only condition for this country to make of its people a nation. If only it could embody a degree of flexibility in consonance with the modern ideas of the freedom of the individual, the caste-system of India has in it yet sufficient vitality to have a long lease of life. Rebels, of course, there always will be, as well as protestants. Saints and Seers have, in the past,—from Mahavira and Buddha to Nanak, Kabir and Keshub Chunder Sen—more than once attempted to eradicate the very principle of caste; but, like some pliant bamboo grove in one of her own primeval forests, the caste-system of India has bent before the blast, and has re-asserted itself the moment the fury of reform had spent itself.

CASTE AND THE INDIVIDUAL

But, if the caste-system has such deep roots, how did the individual fare under its all-pervading influence ? What happened to those countless hundreds of successive generations, for whom it has everywhere been ordained :

> Theirs not to reason why.
> Theirs but to do and die !

For them, ordinarily, the caste provided a clear-cut life, a career, a series of definite, unexceptioned, unmistakable regulations, governing every event and activity from their conception to the final disposal of their ashes. Within its fold the caste-system provided a breadth and scope, an equality and an assurance, which

PLATE CII

303
BATHING
GHAT
BENARES

304
PILGRIMS
BATHING
IN THE
GODAVERI

305
VISHRAM
GHAT
MATHURA

(By Photo, Indian State Railways)

PLATE CIII

306 THE BURNING GHAT, BENARES

307 THE "JAUHAR"
Rajput Ladies' Self Immolation During the Siege of

to the vast majority spelt satisfaction, and even serenity. The injunctions of the original law-giver took on the more agreeable guise of ritual and ceremonial, socio-religious in form, and infinitely varied in aspect, providing, like some fairy landscape, a charm all its own, a scope wide enough not to be mortifying, and yet restricted enough not to be bewildering. Assuring a career, the caste, nevertheless, did not deny individuality altogether; enforcing a division of labour, the caste could not always deny scope for striking talent, and, of course, never confine absolute genius. Its native elasticity, or at least its recognition of exceptions; its temporary bending before a transitory fury of mass revolt, saved it from utter annihilation in the past; while, so long as its inherent advantages,—economic or biological,—could be demonstrable, it may feel itself assured against cataclysmic changes in the future.

The widening horizon of the individual is, however, an ever present contingency. Men as well as women have, on occasions, felt its suffocating effect, each time their mind rose above the appointed groove. For such, the only remedy was revolt. Transgression of caste meant penalties, of course; but seldom, if ever, a sentence of death. For such rare exceptions the experience must have been unique, as it could not but have been exhilerating.

All this presupposes, indeed, the caste-system to be universal and eternal in our history. As already remarked, its beginnings are uncertain, its scope in the earlier centuries limited; its tyranny for a thousand years and more in our history clearly in abeyance; its sovereignty ever liable to attack in the mass as well as by individuals. Few among its critics realise that it gained adventitious strength during the centuries of Muslim dominion, when the race's instinct for self-preservation combined with the individual's need for a guarantee of personal safety, to assure a fresh lease of life to the system. Fewer still among its friends remember that what has saved the system in the past was its adaptability and elasticity, which made it weather every storm practically unhurt. Its rigidity was more apparent than real, and was only a response to the call of the instinct of self-preservation. When such demands are no longer made upon its convenience, it would be suicidal to stress its rigidity, or deny the right of the exception to an exceptional treatment.

WOMAN IN INDIA

The lot of the Woman in ancient India was ordained, not by the caste-system, but by the still more anterior custom crystallising into law. The place of woman in the real framework of Indian society is thoroughly misunderstood by the alien missionary as much as the native visionary. Woman, is mainly viewed in the Indian social system with respect to marriage; and its consequence, motherhood. "Women," says Manu, "were ordained to be mothers, even as men were created to be fathers,"—a statement of the principal purpose, perhaps not quite in harmony with modern notions, but none the less significant of the hidden aim of human life. The reverence paid in India even now to motherhood is incapable of being understood by those nurtured in and accustomed to the modern western notions.

"Where women are adored, there Gods abide", says the classic Law-giver. The prevailing misconceptions of to-day in regard to woman's position do not change the corner-stone of the Indian social fabric. "A master exceedeth ten tutors in claim to honour," says the greatest of our law-givers, "the father a hundred masters; but the mother a thousand fathers in the right to reverence."

उपाध्यायान्दशाचार्य आचार्याणां शतं पिता
सहस्रतु पितृन्माता गौरवेणातिरिच्यते ॥ (मनुस्मृति २ २४९)

This injunction is even now being tacitly and universally obeyed, despite Manu's own *obiter dictum* that woman does not deserve freedom. The Cult of the Mother is one of the most ancient faiths, the Universal Mother being worshipped in symbols, often as soft and alluring as those of Mariatry,—sometimes awful and terrible,—but never oblivious of the essential functions of motherhood.

Motherhood is the one outstanding aim of the Indian marriage ideal. Marriage is not for the pleasures of the individual only; it must help to achieve the great social object of maintaining the race. Its links in the shape of the sacrifices to the manes of the ancestors stood hard and rigid throughout the centuries. All other considerations, even if present, are subordinate to this central dominant theme. The Wife is, of course, a *Sahadharmacharini*,—a colleague in religious rites, and a comrade in social responsibilities. But the wife has not realised the full purpose of her being, if she has missed motherhood. In the selection of the husband or the wife, again, the modern notions of a personal choice in such matters would find much that is bizarre, incongruous, even unnatural, in the Hindu practice of some thousands of years' standing. The history and tradition of India do not rule out altogether the element of personal election by the bride-to-be of her groom, in cases where a genuine election was possible. The early Aryan marriage was monogamic,—witness the *Ramayana*,—though polygamy for princes, or for particular reasons, may not have been unknown even in the earliest times. Though in course of time polygamy among princes may have come to be a common exhibition of royal license, multiplicity of wives could never have been more than a remote insurance against prolonged sterility for the vast majority of the people. But even granting that personal choice had very little scope in the Indian society, for woman particularly, it is a mating of perfect affinities which is sought in all the regulations laid down by the ancient Law-givers, and observed all through the centuries following by their followers as far as practicable. The modern world makes much of the freedom to choose on the basis of romantic love. Even assuming that there is real freedom of choice, what assurance does the present ideal provide for achieving the aim of a modern marriage—unity of spirit in identity of passion? The Indian marriage ideal as well as system is more truly social as well as sociological, in that its main purpose is so altruistic;—the preservation of the race, the continuation of the effort to penetrate through the mysteries of nature. Personal gratification for the parties marrying is a secondary incident of their union, and as both men as well as women were equally subordinated to the social end in marriage, it is untrue to consider India's regard for the dignity of womanhood, for the beauty of wifehood, for the reverence of motherhood, as being the outcome of a savage contempt for women.

The ideal underlying the Hindu marriage contract and ritual will be best illustrated by a brief description of the ceremonies most commonly accompanying the marriage even to-day. Every marriage assumes, and most marriages also assure, that the bridegroom is a fit and proper person carefully selected. The marriage is a *gift* of the bride by her father or guardian to the presumably most eligible suitor from within his caste. On his arrival at the bride's home, the groom is received and welcomed by the *Sampradana* ceremony, which is itself a gift, and is made up of a threefold offering of water and rice and sandal paste, to bathe, and perfume him, and make him fit to offer oblations to the gods of the hearth and the home. Each gift and its reception are made to the accompaniment of prescribed chants and prayers. The Bride is then presented, and her right hand placed in that of the Groom. Is it merely an accident that in the ancient classic sculptures, picturing the marriage of Shiva and Parvati, the Bride stands to the right of the Groom? Or is there a greater meaning than the eye can see? The Bride is *given*, no doubt, in marriage by her guardian; but the Hymn of Love recited at the moment is strangely significant of the purpose and nature of the performance: " Who gave her? To whom did he give her? Love gave her, and to Love he gave her. Love was the giver, Love the taker, Love that pervades the ocean. With Love I accept her; and, O Love, may this be thine." Other gifts follow; but they are only material accompaniments to emphasise the greatness and the beauty of the Gift of Gifts, the Wife. The skirts of the mantles of the pair are next tied together, symbolic of their joint and mutual obligation,—and not merely a ring from the husband to the wife, to mark the latter's life-long slavery to the former. The hand of the bride received in his own by the bridegroom, and *vice versa*, in the presence of the holy fire and the friends and relatives of either party, is evidence of the solemn and mutual sacrament, which is completed by the Seven Steps taken round the holy fire by the pair that mark the final completion of the ceremony. At the end of the seventh step, the Husband addresses his Wife and Companion,:—"Having completed seven steps, be my companion. May I become thy associate, and may none interrupt our association". And as the officiating priest pours water over the hands that are henceforth for ever united in health and in sickness, in sorrow and in happiness, the solemn prayer, voiced ever on these occasions from the Vedic days, is raised for the last time:—"May water and all the gods cleanse our hearts; may air do so, may the Creator do so. May the Divine Instructress unite our hearts."

In words strangely reminiscent of the orthodox marriage service in the Christian Church, the Queen of Heaven in the Hindu Pantheon describes her ideal of the duties of women in the *Mahabharata*:—

"The duties of woman are created in the rites of wedding, when in the presence of the nuptial fire, she becomes the associate of her lord, for the performance of all righteous deeds. She should be beautiful and gentle, considering her husband as her god, and serving him as such in fortune and misfortune, in health and sickness, obedient even if he *command* to unrighteous deeds, or acts that may lead to her own destruction. She should rise early, serving the gods, keeping her house clean, tending the sacred fire on the hearth, eating only after the needs of the *gods* and the guests and the servants have been satisfied."

This ideal may not find favour among the "girl-graduates" of the western universities in India growing up like mushrooms, but without any deep roots yet in the real culture of the peoples of India. The explanation, however, lies in the fact that the tendency of the modern civilisation,—itself a creature of capitalist industrialism, with its invariable concomitant of economic slavery for the masses,—is to stress rights and claims, rather than to face duties and responsibilities, to insist on personal freedom and overlook the need for social concert. Creature of our age and of its environment, it is, indeed, not at all surprising that the modern woman demands all over the world a recognition of her individuality, irrespective of its place in the frame-work of society; a concession of her rights regardless of the corresponding obligations inherent in or inseparable from those rights; a homage to her beauty, a deference to her judgment, a chivalry to her person, for which she has precious little to give in substantial return. In India the evil,—or at least the problem,—of the age is complicated by the transitional nature of the times. Woman in India, educated in our hybrid universities and tinctured by a desire to imitate her western sister, has begun to demand rights, without a thought to the obligations implied in those rights; and though the issue of the fight is a foregone conclusion, the result is not entirely a matter of supreme unconcern to those who can take at all a thought for the morrow.

That woman has, even in India, claimed an individuality for herself is evident from the Buddhist Nun's query to the Blessed One: "Why should our woman's nature hinder us?" India has never systematically and as of a set purpose closed her schools of law and divinity, of science and politics, to women, as the law-givers of Catholic Europe did in the Middle Ages. The claim of the individual exception to be treated as an exception has been admitted for the very sake of the rule. We have already seen in the earlier sections of this work, the glory and greatness of Indian women in art and letters, in sagacity and heroism, in learning and devotion. But the Gargis and Maitreyis, Lilavatis and Laxmibais, Nur Jahans and Ahalyabais, were exceptions, and so received an exceptional treatment. For the vast majority, however, there is no vocation outside marriage; and the profession of a *sannyasini* or of a *deminonde*, though not unknown, is seldom welcome even to the practitioner. The lot of the widow is, in all its rigour, by no means inviting; and though the institution of the *Suttee* is officially and legally abolished, the spirit which engendered it, the courage which accomplished it, if lost, would make India poor indeed.

For we have yet to devise an outlet for these exalted qualities, which are not yet extinct in India. It is foreign altogether to the genius of Indian culture to encourage mere dilettantes, only philandering with art or vocation in its manifold

JASMIN TOWER, AGRA

359

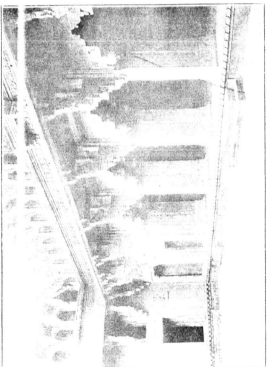

JEHANGIR'S PALACE, AGRA

358

INTERIOR OF SAMAN BURJ

361

SAMAN BURJ, AGRA

360

PLATE CV

312   MUGHAL ZENANA LADIES PLAYING POLO
(Prince of Wales Museum, Bombay)

313   DAMAYANTI'S SWAYAMWARA

314   SPORTS—AN ELEPHANT FIGHT
AND OTHER CONTESTS—AT BABAR'S DARBAR
(Victoria and Albert Museum, London)

aspects. India knows and reveres, as no other country, only the professional artist, devoting his or her whole life to the attainment of excellence in that art. She has, therefore, done little as yet to provide woman, whose primary and absorbing interest is supposed to be the home and all that it stands for, with other "interests", except for the professional doctor and teacher now slowly rising on our social horizon. These last, also, being creatures of blind imitation, still lack that sense of vocation which alone could securely root them into the soil.

For the rest, Indian womanhood, seen in its proper setting and true perspective, compares favourably with womanhood all over the civilised world. India suffers to-day from an economic blight, which affects her manhood as much as her womanhood. The calumnies, propagated of late intensively, against the Indian social system in general and the place of woman in it in particular, defeat their own purpose in wilfully forgetting the material handicap on India to-day. That however, is not the same thing as saying that the social ideals of India have not undergone, in course of history and under the force of circumstances, any changes for the worse, any enfeeblement, or perversion, or even abuse, in practice. But in so far as such perversion or abuse and enfeeblement is noticed; and remedies applied to stop the rot, the chances of a social resurrection, a cultural renaissance in India will be multiplied infinitely, if, in the efforts to remedy and recreate, the Indian reformer goes to the fountain spring of our ancient ideals, and avoids an easy, cheap, meretricious imitation of an uncongenial scheme.

＊　　　　　＊　　　　　＊　　　　　＊　　　　　＊　　　　　＊

SLAVES

If the place of woman in the scheme of Indian society has been often misunderstood, the position of the serving class is by no means always fully comprehended. The *Dasyus* of the Vedic age became, in a large measure, the *Dasas* of the ages following—with their definitely appointed scheme of duties as well as rights. It seems unreasonable to fasten on the mere accident of birth irretrievably to prescribe a man's station in life; and it cannot but appear inhuman, as it is indefensible to engraft on the sentence of eternal social degradation the penalty of untouchability. It is a social stigma which cannot but appear to be a heinous crime in its rigid, continued maintenance. In its origin this peculiar type of social exclusiveness was due to racial arrogance. When the race became mixed, the stigma still remained, even though its one possible explanation,—not justification,—was gone. The serving class in India was not altogether a mass of slaves, or even serfs. The Aryan born could not possibly be reduced to slavery. Seven classes of slaves—or occasions for enslavement—are mentioned by Manu (VII 415), e. g. capture, commuted death sentence, debt, self-degradation or judicial punishment; but the incidents of slavery in our classic times do not at all compare in hardship or ignominy with the slaves of the Greeks and the Romans, or of the Spaniards and the British in their colonies in the New World. Says the *Cambridge History of India,* on the authority of the *Jatakas:*—(p. 205).

> "The Slave or servant was an adjunct in all households able to command domestic service; but slaves do not appear to have been kept, as a rule, in great numbers, either in the house, or, as in the West, at mining or 'plantation' work. Their treatment differed, of course, according to the disposition and capacity of both master and slave. Thus we find, in the *Jataka*, the slave petted, permitted to learn writing and handicrafts, besides his ordinary duties as valet and footman. * * * But of actual ill-treatment there is scarcely any mention * * * We do not meet with runaway slaves."

Speaking of the historic days of the Mauryas, the same authority elsewhere observes:—(p. 482).

> "In all cases the slave may purchase his freedom by any earnings acquired irrespective of his master's service, and ransom from outside cannot be refused. The slave woman who is taken to her master's bed thereby acquired freedom, as also do her children."

This is slavery, no doubt; and unquestionably degrading. But, comparatively speaking, slavery in India was not quite so atrocious as in ancient Rome or modern America. The Muslim invader, accustomed to the harsher codes of a conquering fanatic, for a while intensified the horrors of slavery,—especially of the prisoners of war,—in India. But the inevitable touch of India's genius at last lighted upon the most gifted as well as the most merciful of the Mughals, who readily abolished this savage penalty of defeat. Ever afterwards, despite stray exceptions or local peculiarity of usage, slavery of the conquered as an institution has ceased to be on the Indian soil.

INDIAN POLITY

The social organisation thus developed is ruled by a political system in consonance with the ideals sketched above. Monarchy has been an ancient, immemorial institution on the Indian soil, even though the free, democratic village community, is not less ancient. For the Vedic rites, a chief, a *princeps*, a king, was indispensable. But was Vedic kingship elective? Or was it, from its very inception, hereditary, with a bias in favour of primogeniture? The Vedic references point to a hereditary monarchy; and in the epic times primogeniture seems to be too thoroughly established to be questioned. Scope was, however, not altogether denied to the aspiring and enterprising cadets of royal houses to carve out new kingdoms for themselves, even as the younger sons of great merchant princes had an equal opportunity to prove their mettle in the *Jataka* days.

But while kingship was hereditary; and royalty beginning to be hedged round with a halo of divinity, the obligations,—the duties,—the *Dharma*—of the King were no less onerous. If the King was exalted over all men, he was burdened beyond all men with duties for the good of the country and the people in his charge. A Chandragupta, a Kanishka, or an Akbar was easily the hardest worked man of his day in his whole empire. Rising, as we know Akbar did, like his great Maurya predecessors, while the day had not yet dawned, the sovereign of the Indies performed his ablutions, said his prayers, and got himself ready for the day's task, long before the meanest of his subjects had shaken off his slumbers. The daily public appearance of the Prince was as integral and important a part of the day's agenda as that semi-divine and unbroken custom for the King to preside in his own Court of

Justice, to dispense it, —free and impartial to all, —with his own royal hands. In the Mauryan age, we may rely on Megasthenes' authority to say that there was very little serious crime in the Empire of Chandragupta. The genius of the people and the living spirit of their social institutions must have prevented or minimised crime. By the time the Mughal Empire was being founded, the manners and customs of the people must have undergone a serious deterioration; but the kingly duty of dispensing justice was never relaxed all through the centuries preceding British rule.

This does not, of course, mean that the Sovereign was the only judge all throughout his dominions. There were lower courts, as well as separate tribunals of each city, each guild or caste, even each village. The village punch even now survives to bear witness to the deathless vitality of this ancient institution. But the supreme Sovereign remained the Chief Judge of his realm, the highest Court of Appeal, even as he might be the immediate arbiter in the first instance in any case that came directly before him.

In a vast Empire, there would naturally be a number of independent or over-lapping authorities. The Indian village was, until the other day, a republic in itself, autonomous for all the important purposes of its daily life, and acknowledging the sovereignty of the central government at periodic intervals by paying the village dues. But, besides the immemorial autonomy of the village, which no king could overthrow; besides the established orders of society, —the castes, and their own separate organisation which partook of divine ordination, —there were hardly any other checks to royal absolutism in the days of the Mauryas, and the Guptas, any more than under the Mughals or the Marathas. An aristocracy of birth, in continued possession of vast landed estates or liquid wealth, of the type that was evolved by force of circumstances in the great Rajput States of medieval India, was hardly anywhere of sufficient stability and importance to make a permanent, effective check on the royal power. And even when the purely feudal aristocracy of Rajput chivalry came on the scene, the traditions of personal loyalty to the sovereign were so ingrained and powerful, that their value as checks on royal authority in the framework of government was negligible. Among the Musalmans, even before Akbar had abolished the *Jagir* system of rewarding public service or personal merit, and had rendered every grandee of his court, Rajput as well as Mughal, a paid servant of the State, the peculiar law of inheritance never allowed families to be founded who could rival the splendours of their sovereign. All wealth, as all honour and distinction, came from the Sovereign, who resumed all the grants to each grandee and noble on the death of that individual. The latter's children had to depend on the royal bounty for their maintenance. While Emperors as generous as Akbar and as munificent as Shah Jahan were on the throne, the imperial bounty never failed; but there was no inherent, indefeasible right in the children of a Mughal grandee to succeed automatically to the wealth and dignities of their father. A Mir Jumla or an Itimad-ud-Daulah might, in his lifetime, rival the wealth and splendour of his sovereign; might even dazzle the Prince himself by gifts like that of the Koh-i-Noor, and leave wealth behind him computed in crores. But at his death, the entirety of his undisposed of possessions fell to the Sovereign as the universal heir in intestate succession.

But, while a feudal type of aristocracy was absent in the India of the Mughals; and so an inherent check of that type of polity on royal absolutism unavailable, freer institutions in the modern sense of the term were not unknown to the ancient Indians, even outside the village boundaries. The Lichchhavies,—of whom the Jain Saint Mahavir was a blood relation, and from whom came the Queen Consort of the first of the Gupta Emperors,—are an historic example of a number of tribes in ancient India living in a republic of their own, and governed by an oligarchy not materially dissimilar to that of Venice. These must have been, in their day, no insignificant contrast to the absolute monarchy of their neighbours. And, besides them, in every Indian Empire since the dawn of history, there have been Feudatories,—subordinate allies,—who in their own immediate charges must have been practically autonomous and independent. The relation of the suzerain and the feudatory is by no means new on Indian soil; but the light of historical research is so far much too meagre to tell us precisely the nature and conditions of that relationship in every day practice. The Gupta Emperors,—like their Maurya and Kushan predecessors in all likelihood,—subdued without annexing a number of local principalities, even as the Mughals did a thousand years later. But though the Rajput Princes, the allies as well as grandees of the Mughal Court, were amongst the greatest generals and viceroys of the Imperial provinces in all parts of the country, it is impossible to say where stopped the Emperor's authority in the domestic concerns of these grandees, who were also Princes and allies. The personal ascendancy and magnetism of an Emperor like Akbar apart; and apart also the influence of friendship, the claims of the Emperor for interference in the immediate jurisdiction of his allies were stoutly resisted in almost every instance of which history has record. We have already alluded to the case of that minor Maharaja of Jodhpur in the time of Aurangzeb, of whom the Emperor claimed guardianship; but though the claim cost him years of a most exhausting war, it had in the end to be abandoned. Akbar had stopped the *Satee;* but it is open to question if, where his allies demurred to such innovations, his imperious innovations could succeed.

While the regular, permanent, automatic check of a landed or feudal aristocracy was absent, the presence in every well-organised Empire in Indian history, of a highly developed Bureaucracy must have constituted, in practice, a material, effective check on the imperial autocracy, all the more effective because it was ordinarily unseen. This may sound strange to ears accustomed to the violent abuse of Bureaucracy as such in present day India; but the fact can no longer be concealed that Government to be good as well as efficient needs specially trained men with growing experience. The very vastness of the scale of administration in India demands the trained official; and if to the size of the country we add the growing complexity of the task of government, the case for a trained, experienced bureaucracy becomes irresistible. Chandragupta Maurya, or his minister Chanakya, seems to have realised this necessity as much as Akbar, the Great Mughal; and so

PLATE CV A

311A   COURTSHIP OF KRISHNA AND RADHA
(From N. C. Mehta's book "Studies in Indian Painting")

PLATE CVI

316 ELEPHANT FIGHT, SHAH JEHAN'S DURBAR

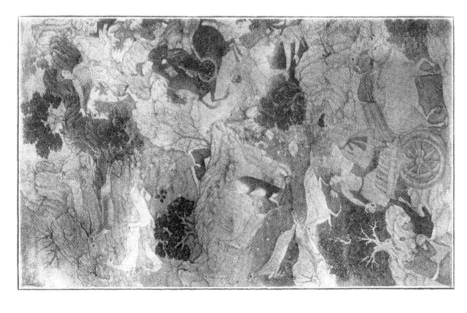

315 AKBAR HUNTING GAME, WITH TRAINED
LEOPARDS IN A ROCKY COUNTRY

From "Akbarnama"

we find in every strong empire in successive centuries, in every well governed province, a regular hierarchy of trained officials paid by and working for the State. No one was too high to avoid or despise this service. Asoka when Crown Prince, had served a regular apprenticeship, even as the great lords of the Moghul court, including the Princes of the Blood, were made to go through the routine of public service. This gave the ruler-to-be an insight and experience, which must have materially moderated his theoretical absolutism.

Whatever the exact nature and mechanism of the political structure in the successive empires in this country, the Imperial Court was, in every instance, the last word in magnificence and refinement, in stately courtesy and royal splendour. The ideal of an Emperor, always cherished in this country from time immemorial, was of a peaceful warrior, handsome and accomplished in person, grave and dignified in deportment, serene in his majesty, and supreme in magnificence. We have few authentic pictures of the earlier Emperors; but if the descriptions at their height of the court at Vijayanagar or Bijapur, Pataliputra or Delhi are at all a reliable guide, the splendour of the Imperial Court in India would have vied with the richest and grandest empires in any part of the world, and in any age of its history. On solemn days of national rejoicings, like the birthday of the Emperor or the new year's day, the Emperor held his court in some such hall of fairy splendour as the *Diwan-i-khas* at Delhi, whose walls and pillars and the very ceiling were studded with precious stones, making the most wonderful mosaics that imagination could conceive, and flashing and reflashing the brilliant forms of the princes and grandees and courtiers of every rank. The throne was a marvel of magnificence, and the figure upon it, the central personage in the assemblage, was, on State occasions, decked in ornaments that, in a case like that of Shah Jahan, cost crores upon crores. Princes of the Blood stood around the Emperor,—none but the Emperor being allowed to sit in that most exacting and punctilious of courts; while Grandees of the successive grades made an ever widening ring of the most brilliant kaleidoscope on a gradually lowering level. In the main courtyard stood those magnificent emblems of Indian sovereignty, the royal elephants, ready caparisoned to fight for the delectation of the court; while within the Hall of Audience stood, in some convenient corner, a troupe of singers and dancers, without whose songs and dances no court ceremonial in India could be considered to be complete. Armed guardians of royalty were not made painfully evident in the Durbar Hall on these occasions of stately courtesies, the Emperor being content with the immediate attendance of his pair of chowri-bearers to fan him through the heat of a sultry day. The Imperial Standards stood in the Hall as well as the courtyard fronting it; and mace-bearers, with gold and silver maces, cried out the titles and dignities of each noble or suppliant before the throne. Each new arrival at court was received in Durbar according to his rank, himself paying homage to the Emperor by salutations minutely regulated in every detail, and substantiated by presents of the most varied kind. An ambassador of Persia would present the most beautiful chargers from Iran and Turan, from Arabia and Turkey, each richly caparisoned, with cases of Persia's famous speciality of the *Attar* of Roses, and piles of velvet or carpets from Turkey, not to mention bejewelled arms and accoutrements of every kind. A returning Viceroy,—like Mir Jumla,—would offer the largest diamond and the richest emerald over and above horses and elephants without number; even a mere merchant,—like that famous Satya-vakta (Truth-teller) from Surat, who, when asked by the curious Emperor his name, gave the above; and earned it by declaring his ignorance when asked the name of his father,—would present a *pandan* or an *attardan* of gold richly chased and heavily bejewelled, at once a testimony of his wealth as well as his taste. To each such *Nazar*, which the Emperor would graciously accept after a public review of the same, he would make a fitting return in a *Sarpao* or Dress of Honour, and a grant in cash or kind. The *Nazar*, once an offering of spontaneous loyalty, has now become in Indian courts an instrument of exaction. But in the heyday of the Mughal Empire it made as wonderful an evidence of the Splendour That Was 'Ind, as any in the brilliant ensemble and ceremonial of the most splendour-loving court in history. Akbar, it is recorded, used to have made expressly for him a thousand complete suits every year, not because he himself needed all of them, but because he had to give away many by way of acknowledging the presents and homage of his subjects, servants, or allies. On the historic night of the Royal Birthday in the Mughal India, the person of the Emperor was weighed successively against gold and silver and baser metals of current coin to be distributed in largesse among the indigent and the unemployed. In the Durbar Hall, proper, the occasion would be marked by similar distribution among the courtiers of more precious, if less pretentious, articles; and the greatest noble would not disdain to swarm with the rest and struggle for a share of this yearly mark of imperial graciousness.

The Court of the earlier Indian Emperors consisted of soldiers and savants in almost equal proportion, with a fringe of varying width consisting of artists. Judging from the description of the Chinese traveller at the Court of Shri Harsha, imperial munificence on the most magnificent scale seems to have been a characteristic of Indian Durbars from time immemorial. But, though the early Hindu and Buddhist Emperors must have had their high Court Dignitaries,— Asoka himself had served his apprenticeship as a provincial viceroy,—the ordered *Noblesse* of the court of the Mughals seems to be a unique creation of Akbar's unrivalled genius for organisation. Dispensing almost entirely with a large standing army, Akbar distinguished the great *Umaras* of his court as commanders of five thousand, or seven thousand, or even ten thousand; and paid them from the imperial treasury regular salaries which reached up to as much as Rs. 30,000 per month in the money of those days. These Nobles vied with the Prince himself in maintaining a most imposing and impressive dignity for themselves. If, according to the ubiquitous gossip Manucci, the Imperial household cost for kitchen expenses alone rupees one lakh per day, a provincial viceroy, like that of Gujarat, spent as much as a crore per annum to maintain his viceregal court and its splendour.

PLATE CVII

36 A MOHAMEDAN DANCING GIRL.

Painting by Rao Bahadur M. V. Dhurandhar.

DRESS AND ORNAMENT IN INDIA

Dress in ancient and medieval India is another example of that vanished glory and Splendour That Was 'Ind. From the earliest times of which we have records, India has had no dearth of those arts and crafts of civilised life which are busied with supplying the need of clothing. Retaining her own individuality and compelling foreign influences to blend insensibly with her own, India still manifests, age after age in her deathless story, a steady development, as noticeable in her dress and ornament, as in the other departments of civilised life.

The basic idea of the truly Indian dress, as seen in the Cave Paintings and Statuary already mentioned, seems to be simplicity and lightness. The style and the get-up, the material and mode, all make for a remarkable degree of filmy simplicity, which may have been required by the extreme heat of the climate, but which could not have been attained to in the absence of a very high development of the particular crafts ministering to these needs. Says the *Indica* of Arrian, a Greek writer of the time of Chandragupta or about 300 B. C.:—

> "The dress worn by Indians is made of cotton, as Nearchus tells us. They wear an under-garment of cotton which reaches below the knee, halfway down the ankles, and also an upper garment which they throw partly over their shoulders, and partly twist in folds round their heads. The Indians also wear ear-rings of ivory, but only such of them do this as are wealthy, for all Indians do not wear them. Their beards, Nearchus tells us, they dye of one hue and another, according to taste. Such Indians, he also says, as are thought anything of, use parasols as a screen from the heat. They wear shoes made of white leather, and these are elaborately trimmed, while the soles are variegated, and made of great thickness, to make the wearer seem so much taller."

These two cotton garments, of a single piece each, were probably common to both sexes, though women seem to have further elaborated their toilette by supplementary clothing for such parts of the body as the prevailing notions of modesty required them to clothe. It is difficult to say if the twisting round the head of the upper garment, or part thereof, mentioned in the above passage, refers to the turban of the later period as worn by men. The common impression one gathers from a close study of ancient Indian pictures is that the head covering was either rare, or consisted of the *Jata-Mukuta* (the crown of hair), which seems to have been worn very long by both sexes, and which must have afforded infinite opportunity for additional adornment to the tasteful and the discerning. Perhaps the passage referred to concerns rather the ladies, or at least younger women or those in inferior social position, whom a sense of decorum compelled to cover their heads (and even faces) in the presence of their elders. The picture of a Queen's toilette in Cave XVII at Ajunta, and many other similar scenes, make it evident that the direct ancestor of the modern *Dhoti*, as worn by the Hindu male, was apparently quite common centuries ago even amongst women. The Queen, herself, it is true, appears to wear a kind of drawers, which may have been in addition to, and not substitution for the Dhoti, or the long *Sari*, which did duty both for the skirt or petticoat, and for a covering for the bust. Without going the length of saying that the art of the tailor was unknown in Ancient India, we may yet point out that the use of the thread and the needle, if any, was restricted to the minimum, the gorgeous borders and hems of the *Saris* and the *Dhotis* being woven bodily into the fabric by the art of the weaver.

As for the material, while Dushyanta speaks of Shakuntala as being clad in bark, cotton formed the basis for thousands of years for the majority of the people. Silk, even if known and used, must have been confined to royal and wealthy personages. The ornamentation of the basic fabric was by no means neglected. Says Megasthenes, —

> "In contrast to the general simplicity of their style, they love finery and ornament. Their robes are worked in gold and ornamented with precious stones, and they wear also flowered garments of the finest muslin. Attendants walking behind hold up umbrellas over them; for they have a high regard for beauty, and avail themselves of every device to improve their looks."

This is a noteworthy testimony, of the ancient Indian's love of beauty from one who came of a nation of beauty worshippers *par excellence*. The single article, umbrella, ought to suffice to show that the art of needle-work would not have been utterly unkown, and that it must have been very considerably in demand for the "flowered robes" in all possibility. The latter-day *Pagri* or turban, which became all but universal after the establishment of the Muhammadan rule, — and which may therefore be taken to be a Muhammadan contribution to the dress of Indians, — is more likely to dispense with the tailor's skill altogether than such caps or head-dresses as may have been used in ancient times. The *Choli*, or the woman's bodice, covering the bust and shaped in accordance, must also have demanded considerable skill in cutting, shaping and finishing, though it is difficult to ascertain, with any degree of precision, as to the date when this garment came into vogue. Shakuntala does, indeed, speak of her tight-fitting bodice preventing her from breathing freely; but it is doubtful if the use was general in very early times.

As to the articles of personal adornment, there is the crown of hair, so surprisingly common in the paintings, in a bewildering variety of dressing and parting and adorning with flowers, or more costly jewels. The latter must, probably, have been a luxury possible only to the richer classes; but the sense of adornment must have been satisfied by the use of such household articles as the wild or garden flowers, that even such an exacting connoisseur as Babur admits there were in abundance in India. Bhavbhuti speaks again and again of the flower ornaments of Sita in her exile.

Ornaments were certainly used in profusion, at least among those who could afford them; and changes of fashion are reflected in the varying shapes, and, very rarely, in the changing places for putting them on. The ear-ring for example, is a very early ornament, noticeable in the very earliest poetry and painting; but the nose-ring is absent until the advent of the Muhammadans, suggesting thereby that it was another of their contributions. Anklets and bracelets and armlets vied with

ZENANA, THE FORT, AGRA
Gloria Photo, Indian State Railways

320

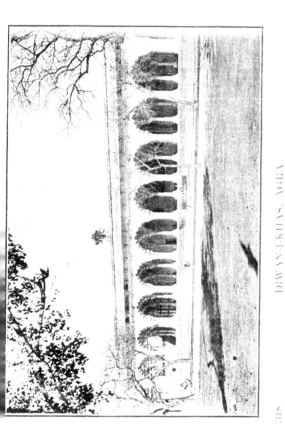

DIWAN-I-KHAS, AGRA

318

DIWAN-I-AM, AGRA

319

PLATE CIX

321   AKBAR RECEIVING MANSABDARS IN A
PALACE GARDEN
Painting by Manohar
(Victoria and Albert Museum, London)

322   THE THRONE, DELHI
(Photo: Indian State Railways)

323   SHAH JEHAN IN COURT COSTUME
(Victoria and Albert Museum, London)

collars, necklaces and girdles to add such ornamental splendour to manly vigour and womanly grace.

As for other means of personal adornment, or attempts to undo the effects of initial disadvantage resulting from inequality of natural endowment, we cannot say if such practices, as dyeing the teeth or the hands and feet by the *Mendi* or the Henna dye, were universal in ancient India. The double sensed description of Spring and her beauty in the Sanskrit Laureate's *Malavika-Agnimitra* suggests very clearly the lip-stick and the powder-puff; the *tilak* and the collyrium for the eye; while the special care and ornamentation of the feet amongst women is an ancient evidence of India's love for the sensuous. After the advent of the Muhammadans, such practices gradually developed, and became quite common with every one who could afford them. Similarly, the use of unguents for beautifying the body, of scents and essences in the bath and later in the clothes, of marks on the forehead for women,—these all date from time immemorial in this country.

Megasthenes and the other early Greek visitors have noted the use of the shoe to add to the height, besides protecting the foot. Certainly, to believe Kühnel and Goetz, the use of the high-heeled shoe is by no means a peculiarity of modern European civilisation, or, for the matter of that, a purely feminine weakness. The forerunners of Akbar were certainly accustomed to use the high-heeled shoe. The heelless slipper, which is noticeable in the classic Moghul portraiture, came into vogue under Jahangir and Shah Jahan; and it was under the latter that excesses in this regard became frequent in the high nobility, particularly with women. The wife of one of the grandees, Manucci alleges, used to wear shoes costing 30 lakhs of rupees, a story which all but angered the Emperor, but which was by no means unparalleled in his own Seraglio. Freaks of art in personal adornment, such as the diminutive foot of the Chinese *grande dame*, do not attract our notice in ancient or Mughal Indian, though the use of collyrium for improving the shade of the eye, for tracing the lines of the eye-brow with the clearest precision; or the setting off the bust and other limbs by close-fitting clothing, were as common as they are evident means of adding to the natural beauty of the female form.

Of extra-personal ornament, besides the profuse jewellery used from time immemorial by every one who could afford it, or the floral ornaments in substitution, we might mention the almost universal use of the *Cummerbund*, the waist-band, which both men and women affected throughout all the ages of Indian history. To the men, the waist-band served for a receptacle of the indispensable arms or implements of each individual's trade and profession; while to the women it was an additional means for the use of superabundant precious stones. For the rest it may suffice to say that every part of the body on which some ornament could possibly be hung or fixed was used with the utmost ingenuity to serve for the purpose, often perhaps at considerable pain to the wearer, who, however, was psychologically incapacitated from noticing such a pain.

As illustrations, let us take the dress and ornaments usually worn by Akbar, and as pictured by his biographer V. A. Smith. His outer garment was a surcoat or tunic of the kind called *cabaya*, reaching a little below the knees, but not coming down to the ankles like the long robes commonly worn by Muslims. It was made ordinarily of thin material, interwoven with gold-thread, decorated with embroidered patterns of flowers and foliage, and fastened by a large clasp. On his head Akbar wore a small tightly rolled turban, made so as to combine Hindu with Musalman modes. The head-dress was enriched by pearls and other gems of inestimable value. His trousers, made of the finest sarcenet, extended down to his heels, where they were tucked in and held by a knot of pearls. His shoes were in a peculiar style after a design of his own. He liked European clothes, and when in private often wore a Portuguese suit of black silk or velvet. He invariably kept a dagger in his girdle; and if at any moment he did not happen to be wearing a sword one always lay ready to his hand. Whenever he appeared in public a score of pages and guards were in attendance ready to place a variety of weapons at his disposal.

The main changes under the Muhammadan influence in the dress of Indians affected rather the material and fashioning of the garments than the garments themselves. Hailing from colder regions of the mountains in the North-West corner, the Muhammadan invaders were used to pay greater regard to the protective requirements in dress than the natives of the warmer regions. Wool in place of cotton thus found greater preference, and even silk was rather used in the form of velvets than the filmy gauze-like stuffs in fashion with the native aristocracy. Babur in his Memoirs notices the indigenous dress in contemptuous terms, because his observation embraced more the poorer peasants immediately falling under the conqueror's rule than the richer and nobler classes. By the time his grandson was firmly established on the Imperial throne, the Mughals themselves had been so completely naturalised in India, that to the courtiers of Jahangir and Shah Jahan the customs and manners of their own original kindred among the Chagatai Turks seemed subjects of unending mirth and ridicule. The articles of dress material, the number and style of garments actually in use among the courtiers of Akbar, as detailed with minute care in the Institutes of Akbar (The *A'in-i-Akbari* of Abul Fazl), show no doubt great changes. The wide trousers, for example, of the Babur and earlier epoch gives place to the *Pa'jamah*, more stylish and close fitting, of the Akbar style, which came to be called *Shurwal or Ijar*, the scarf or string by means of which they came to be tied at the waist, giving occasion for a lavish use of pearls and other precious stones, at least in the case of the tassels in the Begams' garments of that name. The high-heeled slipper also yielded to the heelless, but very highly ornamented, footwear of the Shah Jahan days. On the body proper, the *Jamah* became the usual court wear, with a waist cloth or band going round the centre of the wearer to serve for the hanging of the various waist weapons in the case of the male courtier. It was tied by ribbon instead of buttons noticeable in the portraits of Babur and Humayun, and the regulations of court dress seem to suggest that the line of difference between the Hindu and the Muslim courtier was marked by the *Jamah* being tied by the former on the left side and by the latter on the right, though the court paintings do not show even this to have been the case uniformly. The *Jhabha*, or a sort of sleeveless cloak, which is also noticeable in the portraits of the first two Mughals, seems to have been abandoned by their more fully acclimatised descendants, as also the Babur-and-Humayun turban. The court turban of the Akbar and post-Akbar days is relatively a light, low, well-sitting article, with the added ornamentation of a *Sarpech* that served to utilise some of the most brilliant jewellery in the possession of the Great Mughals. The use of ornaments on the arms and neck continued to be profuse as ever before, both with the males and the females, so that the spectacle of an Emperor like Shah Jahan, must have been literally dazzling.

In regard to personal ornamentation, the Moghul epoch is particularly remarkable for the vagaries of fashion,—and, at that, fashion set by the caprices of the great. Akbar, for instance, ordered beards to be abolished after 1584; and the ordinance remained in force at least throughout the reign of his successor. Aurangzeb is also reported to have warred against too lengthy beards, ordering that any beard longer than four inches should be summarily cut off, wherever the unlucky wearer be met with. Jahangir, again, ordered, after his recovery from a particularly severe illness about 1615, that every one about the court should wear ear-rings; and ear-rings for males also thenceforward came into fashion. The *Jamah* seems to be gradually lengthening, reaching almost upto the ankles in the later Mughal days, as against the knee-length favoured by Akbar's courtiers. The *Nadiri* dress invented by Jahangir, as a sort of a special honour to very highly favoured courtiers, did not affect a great revolution in fashions of dress; but its mention would serve to bring out the point that, if George IV or Edward VII were alleged by their carping contemporaries to be more expert in the design of a waist-coat than in the ordering of a regiment, the more lucky among the Mughals were no less unmindful of their Imperial functions to set the mode and prescribe the *ton* to their courtiers.

In the case of women, the minutia of dress becomes a little more difficult to determine at this stage, owing to the rigid and universal observance of the *Purdah*. The paintings of the great Court ladies of those days are either non-existent or highly apocryphal, so that we could scarcely say about their dress as much as we can about that of the men-folk. The women of the dancing classes were dressed in full, almost ample, skirts of the filmiest material, with a light gaugy Sari and a tight-fitting bodice with full length sleeves. The occupation of these,—dancing chiefly,—might have necessitated the use of that over-full skirt; but it may at least be questioned if the over-suggestive tightness in bodice of the professional performer would be equally acceptable to the high-born princesses. A reputed portrait of Nur Jahan Begum shows her in close fitting trousers and bodice reaching right upto the top of the *ijar* or trousers, and a small slight Sari to serve more for a setting than for clothing; but it may reasonably be questioned if the artist painting this portrait did not draw more largely on imagination than on an actual sight of this dazzling vision.

Of personal ornament, the use of the henna and of the *pan* to colour the hands and feet, and also the lips, as well as to sweeten the breath, became the rage during the Muhammadan ascendancy; while the plaiting and bejewelling of the hair must have certainly approximated to the finest of the fine arts. Of the head and face ornaments affected by the Muhammadan *grandes dames*, the centre mark in the fore head is conspicuous by its absence, and is explained by its being considered to be a Hindu superstition only. The Muhammadans contributed the nose-ring to the woman's face ornaments; while they made the ear-rings and hair bandeux much lighter, though far more brilliant and costly, than before. Thus we find throughout the centuries of our recorded history, the dress and ornaments of the noble and the princely in India displaying all the vagaries of the most inconstant of nymphs,— Fashion,—all the art and grace and splendour that ingenuity could devise and wealth could command.

AMUSEMENT

In amusement and recreation, too, the princes and nobles of ancient and medieval India maintained throughout the centuries those traditions of boundless magnificence, which, even in their present-day remains, astound the foreign visitor. The several sacrifices of the Vedic age assumed in Epic and Classic times a character of periodical *delaissement*, which must certainly have provided the poorer people with a most impressive and magnificent spectacle. The royal tournament, of the type mentioned in the *Mahabharata*, also lingered on all through the ages. The fairs and spectacles, which accompanied each great seasonal festival, particularly in Spring and Autumn, preferably on moonlight nights, seem to have been the most popular of their kind throughout ancient, medieval and Muhammadan India. The universal terrace in almost every Indian house of any pretensions was the unfailing scene of these seasonal rejoicings, in which men and women vied with each other in sport and dalliance of the most varied description. In ordinary times, and for the commonalty as much as the aristocracy, the game of chess, or *chausar*, seems to have been a universal and an eternal favourite. Akbar is said to have invented new games on the *chaupar* principle, as also with cards. But this was necessarily a quiet,— almost subdued recreation, unsuitable to the exuberant spirits of riotous youth, unmete for the days of general festivity. The pursuit or practice of the gentler arts,—music and dancing,—seems to have been common in every cultured home in India from time immemorial, and inevitable concomitant on such solemn occasions as marriage or investment with the sacred thread. For larger masses, the Sanskrit drama offered a most delightful entertainment, shading gradually off into more popular varieties down to the common tricks of legerdemain and rope dancers.

Of the more grandiose amusements, hunting was a royal prerogative and a noble, privilege. Secure in its exclusiveness, not only because of its exceeding costliness but also because of the innumerable regulations,—the Game Laws of modern parlance,—against the killing of certain sacred birds and beasts, it was no light matter for the ordinary citizen to go a hunting. Peacocks have in India been

PLATE CX

324   AURANGZEB RETURNING FROM HUNTING

325   RADHA'S TOILET   326 FULLY ARMED MOGUL WARRIOR

Prince of Wales Museum, Bombay

generally immune from the hunter's shot, as also monkeys. A native instinct of chivalry generally secured similar immunity to the female big game, while mere considerations of cost placed the larger beasts beyond the reach of the ordinary gentry. A veritable army of beaters was necessary for the great Royal Hunt, such as a Chandragupta or an Akbar delighted in; while another army of attendants of all sorts was needed to look after the dogs and horses, and *cheetahs* and elephants, necessary to complete the enjoyment of the game. Hawking, too, was a part of the same royal sport, though snaring birds was justly regarded as among the lowest of low occupations.

Racing, too, was familiar from the days of the Vedic Aryans. The passion for chariot-racing was, however, never carried in India to the lengths common under the first Cæsars in Rome; while horse-racing is, in its present-day popularity, a purely modern sport. Olympian games, contests of personal skill and swiftness, so dear to the heart of the Greeks, never became a regular institution in India; but gladiatorial combats, and, more still, fights of specially trained animals, were a common incident of every grand Durbar. Elephant-fights were, indeed, a most jealously guarded prerogative of Moghul royalty, none but the reigning Sovereign being allowed to maintain these lordly beasts for the purpose of bloody combats.

Recreation for the more sumptuous and voluptuous of the great Princes in India, in their vast parks and pleasances, must have taken a variety of forms to suit the peculiar fancies and disposition of each individual. Here, more than in any other sport, women joined their men-folk in the most perfect *abandon*. This need not be confined, in the case of princes and nobles, to the grand seasonal festivals already mentioned. A Jahangir or a Shah Jahan would rarely miss his exodus to Kashmir, or at least to the delicious retreats of his innumerable and carefully planted garden palaces. Pigeon-flying, so loved by Akbar and his son; training of parrots and other birds pleasing to the eye, alternated with the more quiet indoor games already named; while swimming seems to have been as popular with the princes and the nobles as it was with the poorest of their peasantry. Every palace had its park, and every park its delicious lake, with flocks of the dazzling swan and other aquatic birds and the ubiquitous lotus.

Drinking, so common among the descendants of Babur, can scarcely be classed as an amusement or a recreation, though Babur and Jahangir were accustomed to hold large parties of their intimate courtiers for the purpose. The use of drugs was, however, much too common, at least in Vedic and medieval India, to be quite so unmentionable as modern puritanism sometimes makes out. Even the poorest could have their glass of *bhang*, if opium was too strong or too expensive. The freedom from worldly care which it procured for a while could be really appreciated only by those who have hungered for a moment of self forgetfulness. Well might the Prince of Revellers cry with the poet:

> "Here with a Loaf of Bread beneath the Bough,
> A flask of Wine, a Book of Verse,
> And Thou Beside me singing in the Wilderness—
> And Wilderness is Paradise enow."

THE HOME AND ITS FURNITURE; FOOD AND DRINK

The splendour of the home in India is necessarily to be found in the Palaces of her Princes. We have already had a glimpse of these gorgeous buildings, where a Jahangir lived and loved, and noted their wealth of fountains and gardens, their splendid pillared-halls and jewelled arches. The furniture of the Palace was in fitting with its gorgeous setting,—the golden, jewelled throne, the gorgeous hangings, the softest carpets of the most exquisite workmanship. The floor was covered in every decent home with carpets of the highest degree of workmanship; and on these were placed *gadis*, with cushions along the wall, to permit the master of the home and his honoured guests to recline at their ease. In the halls of the nobles in the more liberal and luxurious days of the Mughals, there were large mirrors on the walls, and in rare cases pictures, though the latter were too often in miniature to be suitable for wall decorations. We know it as a fact, however, that the Imperial palaces of the ancient Indian rulers had painted halls. At night, the palace-halls were lit by lamps of gold and silver, burning perfumed oil; while the atmosphere was scented by the constant burning of incense, or blaziers smoking with fragrant herbs of the most varied character.

In food and drink, the excellence of early Indians is evident from the scattered allusions to royal kitchens and noteworthy gourmets of the age. Bhimsen, second of the Pandava brothers, becomes, in his year of concealment a royal *chef* indicating thereby that the art of cooking must have attained in his time to high dignity. Ashoka's Edicts bear further witness to the same factor. With the more authentic records of the *Institutes of Akbar*, or the memoirs of foreign travellers, we come upon detailed particulars of the innumerable dishes of meat and game and fish of sweets and savouries, of fruit and nuts and preserves, each in its appointed place in the *menu*, that only an accomplished gourmet can understand. The secretary to King James' ambassador at Jahangir's court is in raptures over Asaf Khan's banquet to the envoy; and rightly so, for ten times as many dishes were placed before the representative of the Britannic Majesty as those laid before his noble host, who in his turn had ten more than the secretary amazed at the wealth and variety before him. The appointments of the table, or the dining-hall, were of precious metals glass and china of the most exquisite workmanship and the most delicate colouring Flavoured *Sherbets* of a bewildering variety served to wash down the food and fragrant essences burnt or were sprinkled before the convives to perfume even the air they breathed; while the eternal *pan supari* and cardamom awaited them at the end of the dinner to assure a further lease of fragrant breath.

TRAVEL: CAMPING, VEHICLES

The splendour of the Imperial Guptas and the Sovereign Mughals was evident at its height in their vast paraphernalia of travel and encampment. In Muhammadan times, there is hardly a Prince of any importance, who is not in some way connected

PLATE CXI

SHAH JEHAN RECEIVING A EUROPEAN EMBASSY

with roadmaking. Great arterial high-ways, planted with a veritable arcade of trees all along their length, linked the principal centres of the Empire over hundreds and hundreds of miles. The comfort and convenience of the travelling public was duly secured by public hostels,—walled enclosures with ample lodging and stabling, water-tanks and provision shops, to supply all the needs of the travellers at convenient stages; while the distance travelled was indicated by mile-stones easily noticeable even at night. Where the nature of the country would not permit proper road-making, or where transport by water was more convenient, the rivers were utilised for popular as well as Imperial voyages, attended by all the pomp and ceremony of a most luxurious Court.

The people at large used the riding horse and the bullock-cart for all travelling purposes on land, while on water boats and ships of more pretentious dimensions were employed from time immemorial. The more wealthy classes employed horses and camels, and even the lordly elephant, in short as well as long journeys, for personal conveyance and baggage transportation. The housings and trappings of these animals gave occasion to a lavish display of the wealth and splendour of the travelling Mughals,—ropes of silk, saddles of cloth of gold, jewelled bits and bridles, gold and silver chains and bells and anklets, *howdahs* of precious metals studded with precious stones! Bernier and Mannucci in the seventeenth century, as much as Megasthenes in the 4th century before Christ, were awed into speechless wonder at the spectacle of an Indian Prince on travel with an army of elephants, horses and camels; chariots and palanquins; guards, bearers, beaters; traders and carpenters; tentmakers and water-sprinklers; cooks and scullions and camp-followers of every conceivable grade. The road was watered in advance, lest the dust should annoy His Majesty, if riding on horse-back or palanquin. For the greater ease and convenience of the Emperor and his grandees, the palanquin was modified into a *Takht-e-Rowan*; a travelling throne, to facilitate the transaction of urgent business on the road. For the safety and proper seclusion of the Purdah ladies, various forms of the mounted palanquin were also devised in Mughal times to suit the peculiarity of the particular motive force employed. Within these curtained conveyances, the ladies were waited upon by their *dames d'honneur* to serve and amuse them. Themselves unseen by the curious or the vulgar, these noble dames could gaze at their ease on the panorama spread at their feet as they travelled the country in such exalted and perfect security.

The marvellous regulations and innovations of Akbar governed the encampment of the Grand Mughal in peace and in war down to the most minute detail. The Imperial Camp was always pitched on a square piece of ground, properly levelled and cleared of all impediments by a whole host of campmakers, who marched always a day ahead of the Imperial Court. A double set of camp equipment was carried on all travels, so that while one set was in use the other was being carried to the next stage and set up there. The Emperor and his court need not wait a single moment in the open after their arrival at the camp at the end of the day's travel. Nor need any waste time in searching for their quarters, or fear any confusion or contest for precedence. Every detail had been carefully thought out in advance, and every tent was mapped out and assigned its correct place in a complete plan. Says Bernier, speaking of the travelling pomp of the Emperor:—

> "He is attended not only by the thirty-five thousand cavalry which at all times compose his body-guard, and by infantry exceeding ten thousand in number, but likewise by the heavy artillery and the light or stirrup-artillery, so called because it is inseparable from the King's person. The heavy artillery consists of seventy pieces, mostly of brass. Many of these cannon are so ponderous that twenty yoke of oxen are necessary to draw them along; and some, when the road is steep or rugged, require the aid of elephants, in addition to the oxen, to push the carriage-wheels with their heads and trunks. The stirrup-artillery is composed of fifty or sixty small field-pieces, all of brass; each mounted, as I have observed elsewhere, on a small carriage of neat construction and beautifully painted, decorated with a number of red streamers, and drawn by two handsome horses, driven by an artillery-man. There is always a third or relay horse which is led by an assistant gunner. These field-pieces travel at a quick rate, so that they may be ranged in front of the royal tent in sufficient time to fire a volley as a signal to the troops of the King's arrival."

For its transport alone, the Mughal Imperial camp required 100 elephants, 500 camels, 400 carts, 100 bearers, 500 pioneers, 1000 ferrashes, 100 water-carriers, 150 sweepers, 50 carpenters, and 30 leather workers.

With such a vast entourage to attend to, no wonder the *Mir Manzil*, or the Grand Quarter-Master, had no easy task. But much of his worry and labour was removed by the perfection of the regulations governing encampment. According to the *A'in-i-Akbari*, the military encampment was made as follows:—

> "On an open ground they pitch the imperial seraglio, the audience hall, and the Naqqarahkhanah, all occupying a space the length of which is 1530 yards. To the right and left, and behind, is an open space of 360 yards, which no one but the guards are allowed to enter. Within it, at a distance of 100 yards to the left centre, are the tents of Maryam Makani, Gulbadan Begum, and other chaste ladies, and the tents of Prince Danyal; to the right, those of Prince Sultan Salim; and to the left, those of Prince Shah Murad. Behind their tents, at some distance, the offices and workshops are placed, and at a further distance of 30 yards behind them, at the four corners of the camp, the bazaars. The nobles are encamped without on all sides, according to their rank.
>
> The guards for Thursday, Friday and Saturday, encamp in the centre; those for Sunday and Monday, on the right; and those for Tuesday and Wednesday, on the left."

Of the principal places within the Imperial quarters, the same authority says:—

> "The *Gulalbar*—red carnated court—is a grand enclosure, the invention of His Majesty, the doors of which are made very strong, and secured with locks and keys. It is never less than one hundred yards square. At its eastern end a pavilion of two entrances is erected, containing 54 divisions, 24 yards long, and 14 broad; and in the middle there stands a large *Chaubin raoti*, and round about it a *Sarpardah*. Adjoining to the Chaubin, they built up a two-storied pavilion, in which His Majesty performs divine worship, and from the top of which, in the morning, he receives the compliments of the nobility. No one connected with the seraglio enters this building without special leave. Outside of it, twenty-four chaubin raotis are erected, 10 yards long, and 6 yards

PLATE CXII

328 A MUGHAL EMPRESS
Daughter of Bihari Mal and wife of Emperor Akbar)

329 JODHBAI, WIFE OF EMPEROR JEHANGIR

30 MUGHAL NOBLE IN COURT DRESS
(Prince of Wales Museum, Bombay)

331 A RAJPUT CAVALIER
Kalian Rai Rahtore ready for battle

PLATE CXIII

332 PERSIAN NOBLEMAN DRINKING (AJANTA FRESCOES)
(Photo: Archaeological Dept., Hyderabad Dn.)

333 BANQUET OF THE MUGHAL DAYS

334 PORTRAIT OF A LADY WITH
SUNLIGHT EFFECT
By Govind Das

(333-35, From Smith's "History of Fine Art in India and Ceylon")

wide each separated by a canvas, where the favourite women reside. There are also other pavilions and tents for the servants, with Saibans of gold embroidery, brocade and velvet. Adjoining to this is a Sarapardah of carpet, 60 yards square, within which a few tents are erected, the place for the Urdubegis, and other female servants. Farther on, up to the private audience hall, there is a fine open space, 150 yards long and 100 yards broad, called the Mahtabi; and on both sides of it, a screen is set up as before described, which is supported by poles 6 yards long, fixed in the ground, and are ornamented with brass knobs on the top, and kept firm by two ropes, one passing inside, and the other outside of the enclosure. The guards watch here, as has been described.

In the midst of the plain is a raised platform, which is protected by an awning, or *Namgirah*, supported by four poles. This is the place, where His Majesty sits in the evening; and none but those who are particularly favoured are here admitted. Adjoining to the Gulalbar, there is a circular enclosure, consisting of twelve divisions, each of thirty yards, the door of the enclosure opening into the Mahtabi; and in the midst of it is a *Chaubin raoti*, ten yards long, and a tent containing forty divisions, over which twelve awnings are spread, each of twelve yards, and separated by canvases. This place, in every division of which a convenient closet is constructed, is called *Ibachki*, which is the (Chagatai) name used by His Majesty. Adjoining to this a Sarapardah is put up, 150 yards in length and breadth, containing sixteen divisions, or thity-six square yards, the Sarapardah being, as before, sustained by poles with knobs. In the midst of it the state-hall is erected, by means of a thousand carpets; it contains seventy-two rooms, and has an opening fifteen yards wide. A tent-like covering, or Qualandari, made of wax-cloth, or any other lighter material, is spread over it, which affords protection against the rain and the sun; and round about it, are fifty awnings, of twelve yards each. The pavillion. which serves as *Diwan-i-khas* or private audience hall, has proper doors and locks. Here the nobles and the officers of the army, after having obtained leave through the Bakhshis, pass before the Emperor, the list of officers eligible for admission being changed on the first of every month. The place is decorated, both inside and outside, with carpets of various colours, and resembles a beautiful flower-bed. Outside of it, to a distance of 350 yards, ropes are drawn, fastened to poles, which are set up at a distance of three yards from each other. Watchmen are stationed about them. This is the *Diwan-i-Am* or public audience hall, round which, as above described, the various guards are placed. At the end of this place, at a distance of twelve tanabs is the Naqqarah Khanah, and in the midst of the area the Akasdiah is lighted up. ''

This last was a mighty lantern, set up on a colossal staff, and visible at night for miles and miles to guide the stragglers to the Imperial Camp.

MANNERS AND CUSTOMS

Regarding the Indians' manners in the social intercourse *inter se*, the indications we now possess from their literary remains and pictorial representation, as well as from the written records of foreign contemporary observers, make it evident that, very early in their history, they had reached a degree of urbanity, a standard of polished amenities, which must have made their manners in social intercourse as pleasing as they were dignified. Taking the terms of address as an index, we find the employment of the second person singular,—though by no means unknown,—is so sweetened by its association of affection or reverence, that the idea of contempt finds no place at all in such modes of address. Even the King may be addressed in the second person singular; but the mode is usually adopted by the

Brahman, the Charioteer,—always a highly respected personage in the early Indian society,—and the Chamberlain, usually a right revered senior. Between husband and wife, or lover and mistress, *tutoyement* is common in classic Sanskrit as in modern French or German; though, somehow, with a subtle aroma of dignity that is impossible to describe in words. "I salute thee," says king Janaka to Arundhati, the wife of his friend Agastya, "as the whole world bows to the Goddess of Dawn."[1] What a wealth of affection! What a world of reverence! The modern theatre's nauseating exhibition of cheap endearments in conversation is unknown. *Aryaputra* was a sufficient term of address to the husband or the lover, and *Devi*, *Bhagwati* etc. more than etherealised the enthroned divinity of the lover's heart. More commonly they used that highly dignified third person singular, suggestive of "your Honour" "your Grace", "your Loveliness", which indicates by itself a very advanced standard of courtliness. Even a royal command is redeemed from becoming a brutal order by its being couched in the passive: "Let this be done."

In regard to salutations or greetings at the time of meeting or parting, the profound obeisance does not seem to have been very much in vogue amongst the classic Indians. They bowed, with hands folded in front, and head bending in a curve increasing with the lowliness of the person bowing and according to the dignity of the person bowed to. Complete prostration seems to have been reserved for the gods, or for the *gurus*, before whom even princes felt no loss of dignity thus to humble themselves. No kissing, however, or embracing, except by parents of their children; no hand-shakes, or other modes of personal greeting, were usual among the cultured and the refined; but the expression of blessing, of hopes for success or victory, for a long life and prosperity, were common and varied according to the occasion and the individual addressed or addressing, and so make a pleasing contrast with the somewhat monotonous "Hail" of the Romans.

Etiquette of a more elaborate—grandiose—kind must in all probability have been evolved for behaviour in the Royal presence, especially when the Imperial crown rested on such mighty brows as those of a Chandragupta or a Pulakeshin. Kautilya in the *Artha-Shastra* does lay down, no doubt, that:—

> "On the occasion (of the king's) going out of, and coming into (the capital), the king's road shall on both sides be well guarded by staff-bearers, and freed from the presence of armed persons, ascetics and the crippled." (I. 45.)

But this is far from that elaborate meticulous code of behaviour in royal presence, which made life in the Escurial or at Versailles a daily nightmare to the humbler members of the Court. In the Musalman courts, however; and particularly in the more regularised court of the Mughals, minutiæ of etiquette began to be appreciated and enforced with growing rigour. According to Abu Fazl in the *Ain-i-Akbari*.

> "Whenever His Majesty holds court, they beat a large drum, the sounds of which are accompanied by Divine praise. * * * * * * His Majesty's sons and grandchildren

जगद्वंद्यां देवीमुषसमिव वंदे भगवतीम्

the grandees of the Court, and all other men who have admittance, attend to make the *kornish*, and remain standing in their proper places.

When His Majesty seats himself on the throne, all that are present perform the *kornish*, and then remain standing at their places, according to their rank, with their arms crossed, partaking in the light of his impartial countenance, of the elixir of life, and enjoying everlasting happiness in standing ready for any service.

The eldest prince places himself, when standing, at a distance of one to four yards from the throne, or when sitting, at a distance from two to eight. The second prince stands from one and one-half to six yards from the throne and in sitting from three to twelve. So also the third; * * * * * *

Then come the Elect of the highest rank, who are worthy of the spiritual guidance of His Majesty, at a distance of three to fifteen yards, and in sitting from five to twenty. After this follow the senior grandees, from three and a half yards, and then the other grandees, from ten or twelve and a half yards from the throne."

Modes of salutation are likewise particularised by the same author as follows:—

"His Majesty has commanded the palm of the right hand to be placed upon the forehead, and the head to be bent downwards. This mode of salutation, in the language of the present age, is called *kornish*. * * * * * * *

The salutation, called *taslim*, consists in placing the back of the right hand on the ground, and then raising it gently till the person stands erect, when he puts the palm of his hand upon the crown of his head, which pleasing manner of saluting signifies that he is ready to give himself as an offering.

Upon taking leave, or presentation. or upon receiving a mansab, or jagir, or a dress of honour, or an elephant, or a horse, the rule is to make three *taslims*; but only one on all other occasions, when salaries are paid, or presents are made. * * * * * *
For the disciples of His Majesty, it was necessary to add something, viz., prostration (*sijdah*); and they look upon a prostration before His Majesty as a prostration performed before God; for royalty is an emblem of the power of God, and a light-shedding ray from this Sun of the Absolute."

EPILOGUE

Thus flits the pageant of a People—the panorama of a nation. The picture is brilliant, even dazzling at times; but the eye loves to dwell upon it, even though the inevitable contrast between what is and what has been makes for melancholy rather than exultation. The hurried survey of such a vast country, through so many centuries, must necessarily pass over those darker places and less familiar recesses, which, even if explored, will only heighten the general brilliance of the review. There has been no conscious effort at concealing these darker spots, though, of course, it is by no means the definite purpose of these outlines to lay bare the less agreeable aspects. Without denying, however, that the story of a people so old as ours must have its own blots or blemishes, we may yet glory,—and justly so,—in the achievements of our ancestors in every branch of culture and civilisation.

It has been the purpose of these pages to display these achievements. It is a brave show, take all in all, of glowing tints. But though its contemplation might touch a vein of despondency in the ardent, if somewhat impatient, patriotic heart, the present, too, is not altogether without its ray of hope. A reign of peace has succeeded a century or two of terror, disorder, anarchy. And peace hath its victories no less renowned than War, even in this prosaic age of wide-spread discontent. A modern poet of India has asked:

> Though Rome and Greece and Egypt are no more
> Why, still endures our race for evermore!

And the reply rises strident from a myriad throats: because our foundations are laid too deep and too firm for the entire fabric to topple over and vanish from the face of the earth. Already a keen observer of India's daily life can notice a new throb in the nation's pulse, rich with the promise of a new youth! Already the glories of a Buddha and a Chaitanya are being emulated from the regions of the rising sun by a Rama Mohan Roy or a Keshab Chandra Sen! New poets and philosophers are rising from the ashes of an undying past; new sages and savants are resuming the tale of India's contributions to the wisdom of the world, and the science of mankind. Prophets of a new age, they preach incessantly the gospel of new life, and evolve the formula of their new faith. And their message falleth not like a seed in a barren soil. New Universities, instinct with a mighty purpose, are rising on the banks of the sacred Ganges and the glorious Jamna, to take up the message of our time and train up the youth of the Nation, even as Nalanda or Taxila did before them, to follow in the paths hallowed and exalted by the tread of the great ones who have gone before us, and whose heritage we are beginning even now to recover. The ancient cult of the Mother takes on new habiliments; and the National Anthem, whether sung as a hymn in the key of *Bande Mataram*, or shouted as a challenge on the note of *Hindustan Hamara*, strikes a chord of hope resurgent which by itself infuses a new life among us. And if the glories of an Asoka or the triumphs of a Vikramaditya are not yet ours to repeat, we have even now resumed our march as a people, whose sense of solidarity and oneness owes not a little to the mingling of the wisdom of the East with that of the West.

The Splendour That Was 'Ind may seem to have vanished! Will it never return? There is no call to be tragic. The race of the Aryan and the Dravidian is not yet ended, nor its spirit gone! The sun shines forth even more brilliantly after an eclipse. However dark the night may have been, the Dawn glimmers already in the sky; and the Sun is sure to rise in the East.

INDEX

A

Abdur Razzak, Persian Traveller and Ambassador to Vijayanagar, 25; Quoted 187, 192.

Abhidhamma Pitaka, Buddhist Metaphysics, 77; See also under Buddhism.

Abhignana-Shakuntalam, Master-piece of Kalidasa, 85; See also under Shakuntala, and Kalidasa.

Abhimanyu, Son of Arjuna, Death of, 42.

Abhinaya-Darpana. Treatise on Gestures, 120.

Aboriginal, Tribes, 1.

Aborigines, most ancient, 14; Aryan Mixture with 23, 38.

Abu, Temples on, 99 (See Temples).

Abul Fazl, Friend of Akbar 54; conception of Art, 130; cited on Dress, 190.

   ,,   ,,   Camp, 217-18.

   ,,   ,,   Salutation, 218. See also *Ain-i-Akbari*, or the Institutes of Akbar.

Actors and Acting, Art of, 119 et seq.

Aditi, Lap of, 85.

Advaitism, Doctrine of, 102.

Afghans, Early Musalman Rulers, 29.

Afghanistan, land of 7, 8; Viceroy of; 49.

Africa, India connected with, 4; Trade with, 190.

Agastya, Author of Rig Veda Hymns 35; penetrates into the Deccan, 89.

Agni, Vedic God 30. See Marriage.

Agra, Capital of the Mughal Empire 10-11. Carpet manufacture, 191; See also under Architecture; Palace; Taj.

Agriculture, Wealth in, 15.

Ahimsa, Doctrine of, 98; See also under Buddhism and Jainism.

Ahmadabad, Buildings in, 168-169; Silk industry of 191.

                    Sugar   ,,   of 190.

Ahmadnagar, Siege of 53; 54. See also under Chand Bibi.

Ahmad Shahi Rulers of Gujarat 168.

Ain-i-Akbari, Institutes of Akbar, quoted; 69; 187; 210, 216; 217; 218.

Ajanta, meaning of, 125; Paintings, 124 et Seq. University of, 110-111; Dress in, 207. Cathedral Caves of, 150 et seq.

Ajit Sing, Infant Prince of Jodhpur 49.

Akbar, Emperor, 30. Foes of, 48-9; History of, 67; Literature culture under, 92; 95. Treasure of, 68; Character, 69-70. Encouragement of Painting, 132-133; Buildings of, 167 et seq. Abolishes Slavery in War, 182; Horses of; 189. Remission of Customs Duties, 193. Government of, 203-4. Dress of, 209-10. Camp Regulations of, 217. Modes of Salutation Prescribed, 218.

Alamgir, The Annexationist, 30; and music 134; See Aurangzeb.

Ala-ud-Din Bahman, Emperor of Deccan, (Hassan Gango) 66.

Ala-ud-Din Khilji, General of, 29; and Padmini, 46-7; Emperor, 52; History of, 64; mosque extension by 162.

Al Beruni, Quoted, 62, on Horse-trade, 189.

       ,,   Sankhya, 104.

Alexander of Macedon, Conquests of, 26-7; Enemy of 44; See also Chandragupta Maurya.

Algebra, Science of 108,

Ali Masjid, Fort of, 7.

Allahabad, Junction of the Ganges and Jamna, 11; Akbar's buildings in, 167.

Alluvial, Soil, 9; Plain, 11.

Altamsh, Second Slave Emperor. 51; History of, 65.

Altar, Placing of, and Geometry, 108.

Amalaka, In Temples,—Symbol of World-rule, 152 161.

Amateur, in Indian Art, 112.

Amar Singh, Mewar Hero, 49; Lexicographer, 106.

Amba, Princess of Benares, 40-41; See Bhishma and Shikhandini.

Amir Khushrau, Tughluq poet, 94.

Ambika, Princess of Benares, 39.

Amusements, In India—212-213.

Animals, Export of 179. See Trade.

Anjana, Son of, 43.

Apsaras, of Ajanta Frescoes 128.

Apastambiya, Dharma Sutra, Legal Treatise 106.

Arab, Love of Natural Science, 109; Traders, 4; 20; See Trade; inscription in mosque, 162. Pirates, 188.

Arabesque, carving, 160; 168.

Arabia, export market of India 178. See Trade.

Aranyakas, Forest Treatises, Philosophic works, 96-7.

Aravalli, Range of Mountains, 10, 15.

Arch, Foliated, 161.

Aristocracy, of Birth, 203.

Arjumand Bano Begum, tomb of 169.

Armour, Manufacture of, 180-181.

Army, Indian, 7; 15; of Akbar, 68.

Arrian, Greek writer, 207.

Art and crafts, 105; Remains of, 129; primary intention of, 30; See also under Painting, Sculpture, Architecture, Music, etc. of Writing, Introduction of 76; Traditional, 112.

Arthashastra, Treatise on Economics, 105. See also under Kautilya, Chanakya.

Aryabhatta, Arithmetic of, 108;

                Astronomy of, 109.

Aryan, Contribution of 194. Social System of, 106; 193-220.

N

V

Vachhagahtta, Questions Buddha. 101.

Vaidarbhi, Style in Sanskrit, 85.

Vaisali, Buddha born in, 98; seat of aecumenical council, 101 .

Vaisheshika System, Salient features of, 102; 105.

Vaishnavite Contribution, in Symbolism. 147.

Valabhi, King of Gujarat, 28.

Vallabhacharya, agnosticism of, 93.

Valmiki, Aryan, 20; Father of Sanskrit Poetry. 78.

Vamana and Jayaditya, Authors, 105.

Varaha Mihira, Famous Astronomer, 109.

Vararuchi, Prakrit grammarian, 108.

Varthema, on Indian Cotton Industry, 190.

Varuna, Displacement of, 21; Hymn to, 34. Vedic God, 33, 96.

Vashishta, Defeater of Ten Tribes, 35, Priest, 32; Author of Seventh Mandala of Rig-Veda, 34.

Vasumitra, the Pontiff, 98.

Vatsayana, Author of *Kama Sutra*, 107.

Vedas, Philosophy of 96-105; See Rig. Sama, Yajur. Atharva, Also Art.

Vedanta, Philosophy 102. See Shankaracharya.

Vedic, Age, 2; Aryans 24; Hymns 1, 19; 20; India 131; Function of King, 26; Kingship Elective 202; Origin of Language 74; Philosophy, 97; Poet 21; 102.

Vessels at sea, mentioned in Vedas, 174.

Vibhishana, ally of Rama, 26.

Viceroy, Court of. 10; Afghanistan. 49; 211.

Vidura, Epic Saint. 63.

Vignaneshwara, Author of *Mitakshara*, 106.

Vijayanagar, Empire of. 14; founded 65, Wealth of, 187-188. Industry in; 190. Gold in, 192.

Vikramaditya, Indian King, 106; 109.

Vikramorvashiyam, Kalidasa's play, 85.

Village, Gods. 102; Position of, 203.

Vimana, Name of Temple Shrine, 141, 153.

Vinaya Pitaka, Charvak in, 105; see *Pitaka*.

Vindhya, Range of; 1, 5, 11, 12, 15, 17; See Deccan.

Virata, King, 41.

Vritra, Demon, 34.

Vishnu, God (see Krishna, Rama) 38; Supreme Soul 102; and Narada, 114. Temples of, 151-153.

Vishnudharmottaram, Treatise on Painting, 125.

Vishwamitra, Sage and Warrior, 32; 34.

Vissudhimagga, of Buddhagosha, 78.

Vizagapatam, Harbour of, 13.

Vyakarna, Grammar, 105.

Vyasa, Epic Saint, 43-44; Poet, 78.

W

Wainganga, 14.

Wardha, tributaris of. 14.

Western, Coast Island in the Centre 4. Ghats, 2, 13, 15, 16.

Wheat, Prices of 6; see Trade.

Wheel of the Law, Carving of, 139. 142, 150.

Wiros, Aryan origin, 23.

Wizard, Name of Artist, 137.

Wood, Buildings of, 137.

Wood, fairies, Figures of, 144.

Wood-nymph, Carving of, 143.

Wool and Woollen, Trade in, 191; Dress made of. 210

Woolar lake, Waters of, 9.

Woman, and Ajunta masters 128 et seq. Ideal of Beauty, 127. Position of, 197-201; Dress of, 207-211.

World, Endless, 101.

World-soul, in Uttara-Mimamsa. 103.

Y

Yadava, Tribe, 38.

Yagnavalkya, Legist, 106.

Yajur Veda, School of 106; Surgery in. 110. Veda, 76

Yaksha, Hero of Meghaduta. 82; Cult of. 136. Figure of 138.

Yama, Abode of, 97.

Yashodhara, Wife of Buddha. 99.

Yavana, Greek, 83.

Yavanika, Name of Curtain. 83.

Yoga, Philosophy of. 104 et seq.

Yogin, Sanskrit name of Artist, 137; Buddha revered as, 151; Shiva 153-4; artist to be, 137.

Yudhishthira, sketch of, 34; 41.

Z

Zafar, History of, 66.

Zarokha-e-Darshana, 172.

Printed by FR. RAULEDER

Manager, Basel Mission Press and Book Depot Mangalore S. K.

and Published by Vicaji D. B. Taraporevala

of D. B. Taraporevala Sons & Co.,

190, Hornby Road, Bombay.

CPSIA information can be obtained at www.ICGtesting.com
Printed in the USA
BVOW060028050912

299609BV00003B/6/A

9 780766 157997